THE PROGRESSIVE MAHARAJA

Celebrating
30 Years of Publishing
in India

ABOUT THE AUTHOR

Rahul Sagar is Global Network Associate Professor of Political Science at New York University, Abu Dhabi. He previously taught at Princeton University and Yale-NUS College. His first book, *Secrets and Leaks: The Dilemma of State Secrecy*, was awarded the Myres S. McDougal Prize and the Louis Brownlow Book Award.

'*The Progressive Maharaja* introduces us to Raja Sir Madhava Rao's fascinating manifesto on statecraft, *Hints on the Art and Science of Government*. In rich detail, drawing on his extensive investigation of historical sources, Sagar delves into the story behind the man and the thoughtful text he produced, bringing us a fine, original and unjustly overlooked contribution to Indian political thought.'

—Shashi Tharoor, Indian MP and author of *Inglorious Empire: What the British Did to India*

'Sagar intervenes brilliantly in debates on good governance by bringing to light a hitherto unknown, but still immensely relevant, nineteenth-century treatise on statecraft. This beautifully written book would appeal to all those interested in the richness and plurality of Indian political thought.'

—Nandini Gooptu, associate professor of South Asian Studies, University of Oxford

'This book illustrates what historians do–masterful research identifying significant aspects of the past. Sagar's admirable talents recount the life of India's most successful political operator of the nineteenth century and reproduce his handbook on how to be a ruler. Machiavelli meets the British Empire!'

—Robin Jeffrey, professor, Institute of South Asian Studies, National University of Singapore

'A unique Indian contribution to the genre of Art of Government treatises that skilfully fuses liberal constitutionalism with raj dharma. Sagar's excellent introduction provides the context for this ambitious pedagogical experiment in producing an enlightened monarch proficient in statecraft.'

—Niraja Gopal Jayal, Avantha Chair professor, India Institute, King's College London

'Illuminating the interface between princely India and British officialdom, this is a valuable contribution to knowledge about princely states in late nineteenth and early twentieth-century India.'

—T.C.A. Raghavan, former Indian high commissioner to Pakistan and author of *History Men: Jadunath Sarkar, G.S. Sardesai, Raghubir Sinh and Their Quest for India's Past*

'This hitherto neglected but important nineteenth-century Indian political treatise on what makes a good ruler will fascinate anyone interested in Indian colonial history and political theory. Scrupulously researched, this is a clear, concise summary of the history of the princely states and their relationship with the British Raj.'

—John Zubryzcki, author of *The House of Jaipur*

THE PROGRESSIVE MAHARAJA

SIR MADHAVA RAO'S HINTS ON THE ART AND SCIENCE OF GOVERNMENT

EDITED AND INTRODUCED BY
RAHUL SAGAR

HarperCollins *Publishers* India

First published in the United Kingdom in 2022 by C. Hurst & Co. (Publishers) Ltd., New Wing, Somerset House, Strand, London, WC2R 1LA
www.hurstpublishers.com

First published in hardback in India by HarperCollins *Publishers* 2022
4th Floor, Tower A, Building No. 10, Phase II, DLF Cyber City, Gurugram, Haryana –122002
www.harpercollins.co.in

This edition published in India by HarperCollins *Publishers* 2023

2 4 6 8 10 9 7 5 3 1

P-ISBN: 978-93-5699-324-2
E-ISBN: 978-93-5489-600-2

Printed and bound at
Thomson Press (India) Ltd

For my parents, Prema and Jyoti

CONTENTS

PREFACE

In 2016, I was immersed in constructing an index of English-language periodicals published in colonial-era India. Trawling through the archives, I came across the quaint sounding *Feudatory and Zemindari India: An Illustrated Monthly Journal Published in the Interests of the Ruling Princes, Chiefs and Zemindars, etc*. Upon diving in, it became clear that far from being some amusing gallery of exaggerated pomp and pageantry, *Feudatory and Zemindari India* had in fact been a significant publication, serving as a platform for voices from the semi-autonomous Native States that comprised "Indian India". I was especially struck by a short article entitled "The Education of the Ruling Princes: A Note by the Late Raja Sir T. Madhava Rao", which called for Maharajas ruling these principalities to be given a "special education" that would enable them to live up to their "duties and responsibilities". Who was this highly decorated figure? And what had become of his plea?

I soon learnt how little I knew about "Indian India". The Raja Sir, it turned out, was one of the towering personalities of nineteenth-century India, and as Dewan of Baroda he had been responsible for its Maharaja's "special education". Rao's enterprise was fascinating, because it appeared to be a modern example of what is known as the "mirror of princes"—a genre of ethics in which writers directly address rulers on the tricky business of exercising power. Excited, I acquired a copy of *Minor Hints*, the book that apparently contained a facsimile of the lectures that Rao had delivered to Sayaji Rao Gaekwad, the ruler of Baroda. A swift inspection left me with mixed feelings. The content was certainly original and striking but the book itself was unpolished. It lacked an introduction, the lectures were obviously out of sequence, and there were no supporting materials. It left me with more questions than answers. What prompted the lectures? Why were they printed out of order? Did they have the intended effect?

I cast about for answers to little avail. There were a handful of marvelous works of the Native States, most notably by Robin Jeffrey, Barbara Ramusack, Ian Copland, Manu Bhagavan, Caroline Keen, and Manu Pillai, but none of these addressed *Minor Hints*.[1] There was a nice short essay by S. V. Puntambekar that summarized the lectures. However, as it was written in 1944, before British India's archives became available, the analysis was entirely abstract.[2] Widening the search, I came upon *Lessons on Raja Neeti*, a little-noticed book, published in 2011 by M. Rama Jois, the former Chief Justice of Punjab and Haryana. It reprinted Rao's lectures and sang its paeans, describing them as a "treasure of knowledge". Imagine my surprise when Jois revealed that *Minor Hints* had been recommended to him by the then-Chief Minister of Gujarat, Narendra Modi. Imagine my surprise when I discovered that the now-Prime Minister had even penned a Foreword to Jois' volume, in which he urged the "political class to spare a little thought and time" for the "teachings of the great administrator, Raja Sir T. Madhava Rao".[3]

Astonishing as this discovery was, it brought me no closer to figuring out the story behind *Minor Hints*. Seemingly at a dead end, I set the material aside. Then, a few months later, I came across yet another fascinating essay, "The Constitution of Native States: An Important Memorandum of the Late Rajah Sir T. Madhava Rao". Published posthumously in 1906 in *Indian Review*, one of the most influential periodicals of the era, it explained why Maharajas ought to establish a constitutional order that would give them a dignified but symbolic role while placing administration in the hands of experienced and impartial officials. Like the article in *Feudatory and Zemindari India*, this memorandum was elegantly constructed and carefully argued. Consequently, I began to suspect that the haphazard *Minor Hints* was printed without Rao's involvement. But, if so, then how had Rao's lectures actually unfolded? Where was the original manuscript? Compelled by growing admiration for Rao's intellect, I restarted the search for answers.

Since that time, I have systematically collected every available scrap of information on Madhava Rao. It has not been easy because the Native States were not always fastidious in their record-keeping, and many of the records they produced have perished due to neglect and folly. Still, with the aid of long hours in the archives, the increasing digitization of records, and a far-flung team of research assistants, I have been able to collect a very substantial number of records from libraries and archives around the world. All this has allowed me to assemble a comprehensive picture of Rao's life and times, and of the Native States in which he served as Dewan.

Luck—or fate—have contributed too. In October 2019, the index (www.ideasofindia.org) I had been constructing when I stumbled upon Rao, was about to launch. In search of some missing items, I double-checked the catalog of the Mythic Society in Bengaluru. I did not find the items I was looking for. Then, on a whim, I searched for items labelled "Baroda". All the results were familiar—except for one. The unusual entry was titled "Readministration of Baroda" and dated 1881. I guessed this was the widely distributed 1881 *Baroda Administration Report*. But, not wanting to leave a stone unturned, I asked my research assistant to call up the document. He replied a day later saying it was a lengthy "handwritten" document. This did not make sense because I knew the *Baroda Administration Report* was a printed document. Perhaps I had stumbled upon an early draft of the *Report*. If so, what was it doing in Bengaluru? "Could you send me photographs of the first few pages of the document", I asked. A day later, the sample arrived. I could not believe my eyes: there it was, Madhava Rao's original lecture manuscript! After my heart stopped pounding, I examined the document carefully. A stamp revealed that the manuscript had previously been housed in the private library of Sir T. Ananda Rao. This was none other than Madhava Rao's celebrated son, who had lived in Bengaluru during his long service in Mysore, which included serving as Dewan between 1909–1912. By that evening I was on a flight to Bengaluru, and the next day I was at the Mythic Society where the Honorary Secretary, Shri V. Nagaraj, kindly allowed me to make an archival quality copy of the original manuscript.

And so concluded, on an unexpectedly triumphant note, my quest to uncover the story behind the article in *Feudatory and Zemindari India*. The fortuitous discovery at the Mythic Society confirmed that the book popularly known as *Minor Hints* was a sort of pirated edition, likely published by the Gaekwad's aides long after Rao had departed Baroda. Having now painstakingly edited Rao's lectures, I place them before the public in the form and manner they deserve. I have titled them *Hints on the Art and Science of Government*. Based on Rao's correspondence, I believe this is the title he would have chosen for them. The laborious research undertaken over the past five years has also allowed me to definitively establish the fraught circumstances surrounding the lectures. I have summarized what I have learnt in *The Progressive Maharaja*, the introductory essay that opens this volume. I hope its merit is self-evident.

January 26, 2022

ACKNOWLEDGEMENTS

In the quest to recover and restore *Hints on the Art and Science of Government* I have incurred significant debts to a number of individuals and institutions.

It is no exaggeration to say that this volume would not exist without the research support provided by NYU Abu Dhabi. I am at a loss to express my gratitude to Hervé Crès, the Dean of Social Sciences, and Fabio Piano, the Provost. They believed in my research and did everything they could to help me across the finishing line. I am also much obliged to a number of colleagues and administrators for supporting or administering the grants this volume relied upon: Hannah Brückner, Kanchan Chandra, Janet Kelly, Julie McGuire, Diana Pangan, and Katherine Stevens in the Division of Social Sciences, Nada Messaikeh and Sana Ahmed in the Office of Research Administration, and Martin Klimke and the NYUAD Grants for Publication Program. I also want to take this chance to express my thanks to Dimitri Landa, Bernard Manin, Ryan Pevnick, Peter Rosendorff, Ron Rogowski, Shankar Satyanath, Melissa Schwartzberg, and David Stasavage for recruiting me to NYU Abu Dhabi and thereby making so much possible.

I would not have been able to complete this manuscript without the research assistance provided by Christian Fastenrath, Sanchi Rai, Khushi Singh Rathore, Tom Noble, James Elsey, Jonah Elsey, Nidhi Shukla, Sachin Tiwari, and M. Lakshmi Priya. Sanchi and Christian helped type up and format Madhava Rao's lectures, Sachin helped scan the original manuscript at the Mythic Society, and Khushi helped edit and arrange the resulting images. I am very grateful to Sanchi for helping navigate "the system" at the National Archives of India and the Gujarat State Archives, and to Lakshmi for doing the same at the Kerala State Archives. I am equally grateful to Tom, James, and Jonah for their steady, tireless, and always good-natured assistance at the British Library. I am much obliged to Khushi and Nidhi for organizing the sizable corpus of materials and tracking down missing items.

It is an honor to have this volume published by HarperCollins. I am deeply grateful to my editor, Prema Govindan, for her support and advice. My thanks also to Mei Jayne Yew and Daisy Leitch for editorial advice, to Sebastian Ballard for the elegant map, and to Gavin Morris for the regal cover. I am also very grateful to the two anonymous reviewers who, in spite of the pandemic, evaluated the manuscript promptly, and provided generous and constructive feedback. Thanks also to the Royal Collection Trust and the British Library for permitting use of the portraits in this volume. I want to express my deep gratitude to Nandini Gooptu, Niraja Gopal Jayal, Robin Jeffrey, Shashi Tharoor, T.C.A. Raghavan, and John Zubryzcki for their very kind endorsements.

A number of colleagues read the manuscript and provided valuable advice and encouragement. I am indebted to Robin Jeffrey and Manu Pillai for being so generous with their knowledge on "Indian India", to Rohan Mukherjee and Anit Mukherjee for patiently reading countless drafts about people and places far removed from their own pressing book projects, to Patrick French and Srinath Raghavan for their heartening reaction to an early version of the manuscript, and to Corey Brettschneider, Devesh Kapur, and Pratap Bhanu Mehta for urging me on.

Finally, I want to acknowledge friends and family. This volume was prepared over two summers in Singapore, where writing sessions were interspersed with joyful adventures with my beloved daughters Mia and Sophie, and my wife Una, and with laughter-filled evenings with cherished friends including Abhishek and Devika Rao, Shashi and Miranda Jayakumar, Rohan and Shailey Hingorani, Anit and Malobi Mukherjee, Kishore Mahbubani, Kanti Bajpai, Parag Khanna, Sinderpal Singh, Gaurav and Ankita Katyal, Syed Ali Abbas and Sehr

Rizvi, and John Donaldson and Qu Li, and the pioneers at Yale-NUS College, especially Andrew Bailey, Andrew Hui, Nomi Lazar, Steven Oliver, Ben Schupmann, Christina Tarnopolsky, and Matt Walker.

The highlight of those summers in Singapore was precious time with my parents, Jyoti Sagar and Prema Sagar. I have been fortunate to witness the choices they have made over the course of their lives: to work hard, to build institutions, to respect merit, and to embrace charity. It is to them that I dedicate this book, with undying love and gratitude for the life they have given me, and with utmost respect for the example they have set. I hope to be to my children what they have been to me.

PRINCIPAL EVENTS

1828	Born in Kumbakonam in Tanjore District of Madras Presidency
1841	Enters Madras High School (the precursor to Presidency College)
1846	Declared a "Proficient" of the First Class of Madras High School
1847	Employed as a "Junior Assistant" to the Accountant General in Madras
1849	Appointed tutor to Ayilyam Tirunal and Vishakham Tirunal in Travancore
1853	Appointed Deputy *Peishkar* (magistrate) in Travancore
1855	Promoted to Dewan *Peishkar* (divisional magistrate)
1857	Indian Mutiny or First War of Independence
1858	Appointed Dewan of Travancore
1860	Ayilyam Tirunal becomes Maharaja of Travancore
1866	Awarded Knight Commander of the Star of India
1870	Malhar Rao becomes Maharaja of Baroda
1872	Departs Travancore; declines a seat on the Viceregal Council
1873	Appointed Dewan of Indore by Tukoji Holkar; publishes *History of Travancore*
1874	Prepares "A Draft Constitution for Native States"
1875	Appointed Dewan of Baroda; Sayaji Rao becomes Maharaja of Baroda
1877	Receives honorary title of Raja at the Imperial Assemblage
1881	Delivers lectures to Sayaji Rao (unauthorized version published posthumously as *Minor Hints*)
1881	Sayaji Rao ascends to the throne

1883 Resigns the Dewanship of Baroda; begins writing columns under the pen name "Native Thinker"
1884 Publishes *Three Addresses* and *Reflections About Russia*
1885 First Indian National Congress held in Bombay
1887 Convocation Address at Madras University; publishes *Notes on Hindu Astrology*
1887 Presides over the First Indian National Social Conference
1887 President of the Reception Committee for the Third Indian National Congress
1888 Declines a seat on the Viceregal Council for the second time
1889 Publishes *Hints on the Training of Native Children*
1890 Resigns from the Congress; publishes *A Conversation on Female Education*
1891 Passes away in Madras

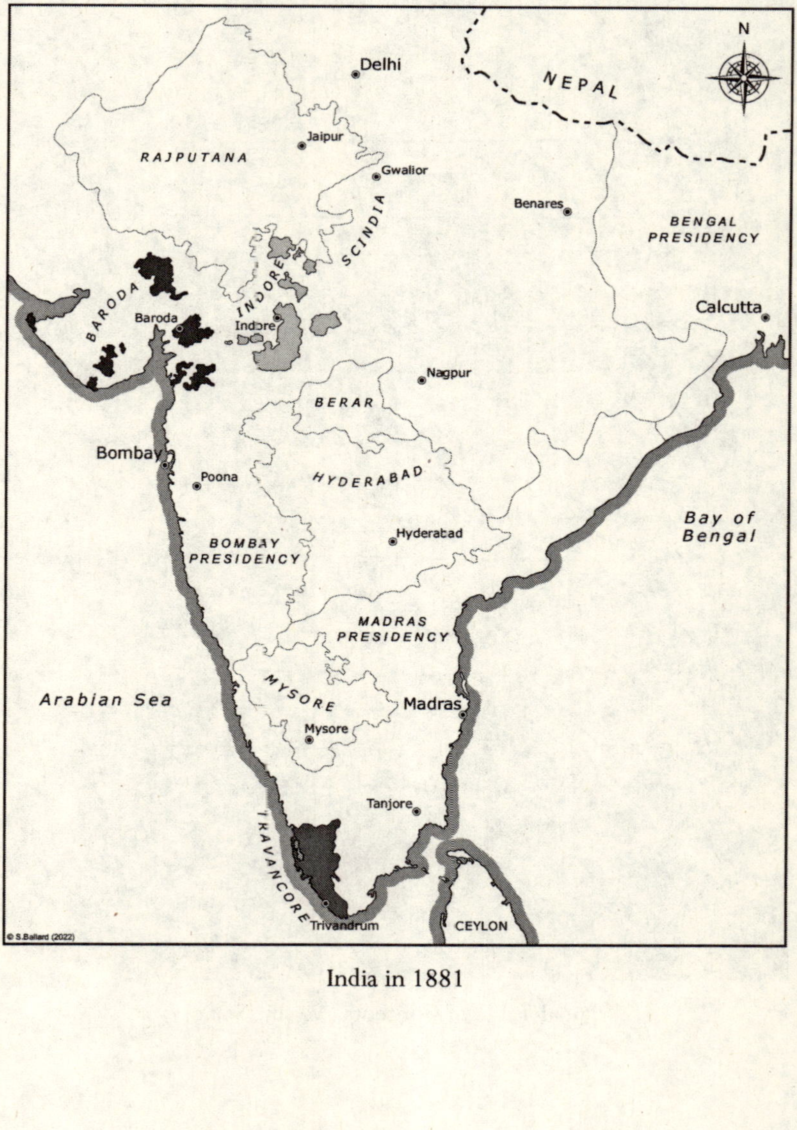

India in 1881

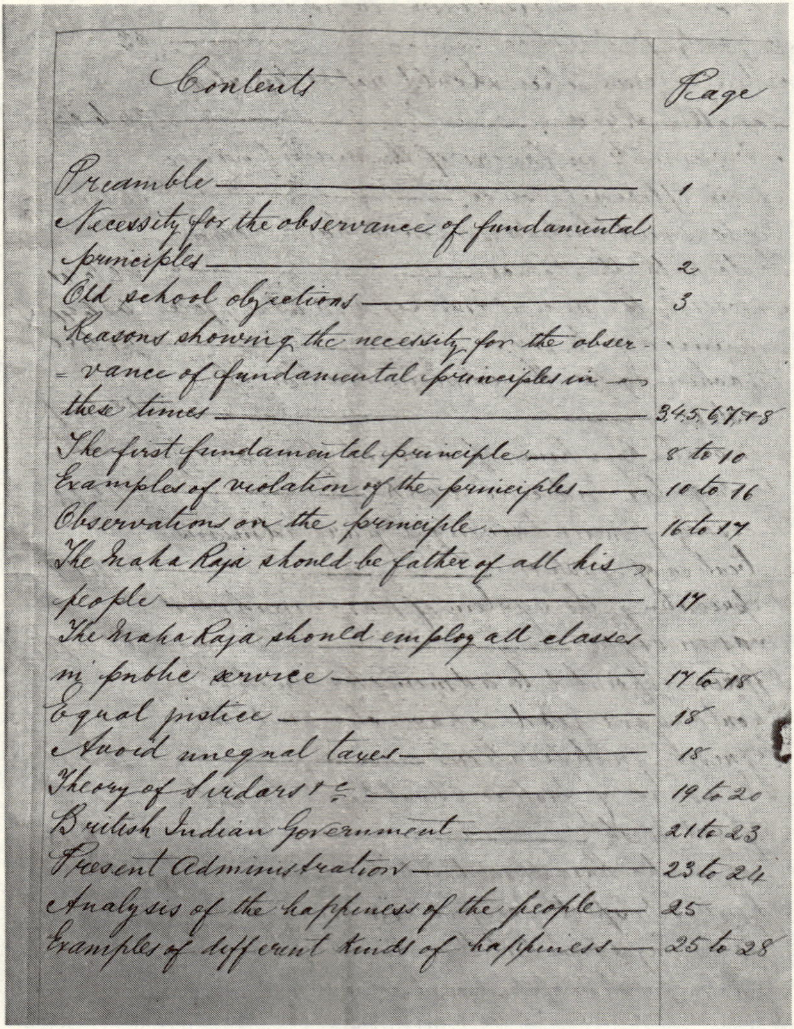

Contents | Page

Original Table of Contents (Mythic Society)

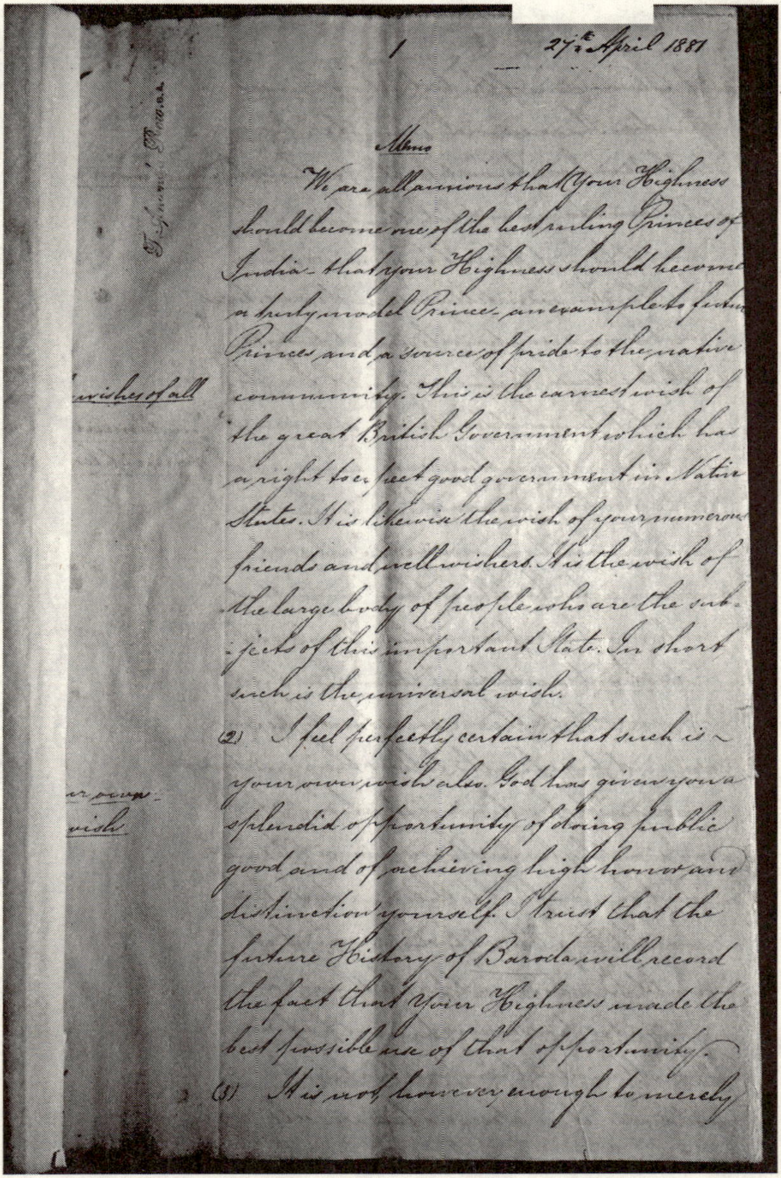

1

27th April 1881

Memo

We are all anxious that Your Highness should become one of the best ruling Princes of India — that your Highness should become a truly model Prince, an example to future Princes and a source of pride to the native community. This is the earnest wish of the great British Government which has a right to expect good government in Native States. It is likewise the wish of your numerous friends and well wishers. It is the wish of the large body of people who are the subjects of this important State. In short such is the universal wish.

wishes of all

(2) I feel perfectly certain that such is your own wish also. God has given you a splendid opportunity of doing public good and of achieving high honour and distinction yourself. I trust that the future History of Baroda will record the fact that Your Highness made the best possible use of that opportunity.

r own wish

(3) It is not however enough to merely

Opening Page of the Original Manuscript (Mythic Society)

Group Portrait of Sir Madhava Rao and the Ministers of Baroda, c. 1880 (British Library)

Sayaji Rao Gaekwad III, the Maharaja of Baroda, c. 1880 (Royal Collection Trust)

Tukoji Holkar, Maharajah of Indore, c. 1875 (Royal Collection Trust)

Visakham Thirunal, the Maharaja of Travancore c. 1887 (Royal Collection Trust)

Ayilyam Thirunal, Maharaja of Travancore, c. 1875 (Royal Collection Trust)

INTRODUCTION

THE PROGRESSIVE MAHARAJA

Raja Sir Tanjore Madhava Rao is virtually unknown today. This is a tragedy, for Rao was universally considered the foremost Indian statesman of the nineteenth century. His domain was what the British termed the Native States or what Indians pointedly described as Indian India. Between 1858 and 1883, Rao had the unique distinction of serving successively as Dewan (or Prime Minister) to the Maharajas of Travancore, Indore, and Baroda. In each instance, he was celebrated for displaying excellence in administration. On his watch, Travancore and Baroda in particular came to be seen as "model states", whose progress demonstrated that Indians were capable of governing themselves well.

Hints on the Art and Science of Government is the harvest of Rao's exceptional career. It came into being when Rao was tasked with preparing Sayaji Rao Gaekwad to become Maharaja of Baroda. Its contents are the lectures Rao delivered to the young prince. The lectures summarize the principles, gleaned from long experience, to which Rao credited his practical successes. These principles combine the classical Indian ideal of *raj dharma*, which enjoins rulers to govern dutifully, with the modern European ideal, familiar to readers of Charles de Montesquieu, that rulers must eschew arbitrariness. Put simply, Rao advised rulers to be tough on themselves but gentle toward citizens.

Hints commends itself to posterity for two reasons. First, because of what it is—the most important example there is of how the earliest generation of English-educated Indian elites tried to revise ancient ideals of statesmanship for the modern age. Second, because of what it teaches—it promises rulers who govern liberally and prudently, happiness for their people and fame for themselves. In this respect, *Hints* is not only timeless but also timely.

Who was Madhava Rao?

Madhava Rao was born in 1828 in Kumbakonam, a prominent town in Madras Presidency's Tanjore district, to a family long associated with public administration. His uncle, Venkat Rao, served as Dewan of Travancore from 1821–30, before being drafted to the Mysore Commission as Head *Sheristadar* (manager). His father, Ranga Rao, served as Deputy *Sheristadar* at the Madras Board of Revenue before also being recruited to Travancore, where he served as Acting Dewan between 1837–38 prior to his untimely death in 1839.

In 1841 Rao entered the newly-established Madras High School, the precursor to Presidency College. Under the tutelage of its legendary Principal, Eyre Burton Powell, Rao received a decidedly modern and liberal education: Isaac Newton, William Shakespeare, John Locke, Adam Smith, Alexander Pope, and Edward Gibbon were studied alongside calculus, trigonometry, algebra, astronomy, optics, and electricity. Powell prized Rao, deeming his abilities "far more extensive than those of most native young men", his proficiency in mathematics in particular being such as "would secure him an honorable position even in the University of Cambridge."[1] This was no minor compliment for Powell was a Wrangler—one of those demigods that had attained a First Class in Mathematics at Cambridge. Rao, in turn, revered his teacher. His successes, he would always insist, were "ultimately traceable to the influence of Mr. Powell's teaching", which had led "demonstrated truths" to take a "firm hold of our minds".[2]

After graduating in 1846 Rao entered the Madras Accountant General's office, earning 20 rupees every month. He was not to remain a "Junior Assistant" for long. Later that year Uttaram Tirunal ascended to the throne in Travancore. The Resident (the Government of India's local representative), William Cullen, persuaded the new ruler to provide his nephews and heirs—Ayilyam Tirunal and Vishakham Tirunal—with a "good English education".[3] When Cullen wrote to Madras for recommendations, the University Board promptly offered up Rao's name. After some anxious deliberation over moving to Travancore, where his father had been the target of nativist ire, Rao accepted Uttaram's invitation in July 1849, persuaded partly by the salary of 200 rupees per month and partly by John Norton, a prominent lawyer, who pointed out to Rao that he "might become the benefactor of millions of his countrymen" if he "excited in the breasts of those young princes a thirst for knowledge and a love of virtue".[4]

For the next four years Rao "threw himself heart and soul into the task" before him.[5] Accolades soon followed, the most notable being the compliments of the Court of Directors of the East India Company, who observed that "the proficiency of the young Princes in the English language and in general knowledge, under the tuition of Madava Row, is highly creditable both to the pupils and the teacher".[6] This record led Uttaram to appoint Rao Deputy *Peishkar* (magistrate) in April 1853 with responsibilities for *Chowkey* (customs) and *Devaswam* (religious institutions) as well as his English correspondence.[7]

At this time storm clouds began gathering over Travancore. Missionaries from the London-based Christian Missionary Society launched concerted attacks on Cullen and his protégé, the Dewan Krishna Rao, accusing the men of turning a blind eye to violence against their converts. Travancore's finances, meanwhile, nosedived as smugglers based in British Cochin undermined the State's profitable monopolies on the vending of tobacco and pepper. Urged by Madras to intervene, Governor-General James Broun-Ramsay, the Marquess of Dalhousie, pointedly replied that though the 1805 Treaty between Travancore and the East India Company did not permit him to intervene on behalf of the missionaries, annexation could follow if Travancore was unable to pay the tribute due annually to the East India Company.

This warning shook Travancore, especially after Dalhousie annexed Oudh in February 1856. In the midst of the turmoil, Rao seized his chance. Having been promoted to the position of Dewan *Peishkar* (divisional magistrate) in 1855, Rao now proposed to Uttaram that the *Peishkars* be entrusted with a certain number of *taluks* (administrative regions) each. The proposal was adopted, and Rao was given charge of Southern Travancore, "the very *taluks* from which complaints to the Madras Government had been most frequent and importunate".[8] Within mere months Southern Travancore was transformed. A crackdown on corruption trebled revenues. The missionaries, meanwhile, were won over by Rao's "integrity, energy, and impartiality".[9] As Rao's renown grew, his former student and now key ally, Vishakham, seeded a crucial idea. In a widely noticed essay, published in the *Madras Athenaeum* in October 1856, Vishakham warned that "the only way of saving the State" from the "all-grasping policy of the Paramount power" was to "place its management in the hands of a resolute and vigorous minister".[10] The hope was soon realized. In December 1857, the Dewan Krishna Rao expired and Uttaram promptly chose Rao as the successor. And so, with the Mutiny still smoldering up north, Rao became, at the age of thirty, the Dewan of Travancore on a salary of 2,000 rupees per month.

In 1860 Travancore underwent a generational shift when Cullen retired and Uttaram passed away. Cullen was replaced by Francis Maltby, a man of "high character and abilities", who forged a close bond with Rao, and Uttaram was succeeded by his nephew, Ayilyam, who agreed to free up the Dewan so that Travancore could enjoy "unimpeded progress".[11] Now came the reforms that would make Travancore a "model state".[12] In short order, most state monopolies were dismantled and more than a hundred minor local taxes were abolished. A trade agreement with British India helped double Travancore's exports from 35 lakhs in 1861 to 72 lakhs* in 1868. Land reforms were enacted on a vast scale: taxes were capped at a fourth of net produce, the cultivation of waste land was incentivized, and royal lands worth 1.5 crore† rupees that had previously been leased to tenants were converted to freehold.[13] Investment was stimulated as well, with coffee, tapioca, and tea plantations receiving special encouragement.[14] As a result of these measures, Travancore's revenues grew from 43 lakhs in 1861 to 51 lakhs in 1869.

---

* A lakh denotes a hundred thousand (100,000).

† A crore denotes ten million (10,000,000).

As surpluses replaced deficits, new possibilities arose. By 1863, Travancore's debts had been extinguished and a reserve of 13 lakhs ensured that it would be able to pay the tribute due to British India even in the event of a famine. Administrative reform followed thereafter. To enhance morale and probity Rao expanded the number of judges and police officers on the rolls and increased the compensation on offer. The desired results followed: heinous crimes decreased rapidly as did the time taken to process law suits. Alongside such reforms came waves of public investment. Before 1860, there was no public works department at all. By 1861, public works received 2.7 lakhs; a decade later, almost 10 lakhs. These funds were employed in constructing trunk roads, lighthouses, canals, bridges, schools, hospitals, dispensaries, and public buildings, and in lighting up lagoons, drilling tunnels, undertaking vaccination programs, and expanding the postal system. A simple statistic captures the scale of the change. Prior to 1860, Travancore's principal road was a poorly maintained 50-mile-long road connecting the capital to the south. By 1871, it had nearly a thousand miles of roadways. Or consider another statistic: public education, which was almost "non-existent" before 1860, had a budget of more than a lakh rupees by 1869.[15] Where previously Travancore had one English school and no vernacular schools at all, by the end of Rao's tenure, there were 16 English schools in the districts, 4 girls' schools in the major towns, and vernacular elementary schools in most of the 250 sub-divisions, supported by institutions to train teachers and to translate and supply textbooks.

Travancore's transformation was widely acclaimed. Madras lauded the Dewan for his "striking ability, firmness, and integrity" and his "enlightened" views.[16] The Anglo-Indian[‡] press followed suit. *The Friend of India*, for example, declared Rao "the highest development of the Hindoo intellect" and advised the hitherto more prominent states of Gwalior and Hyderabad to "follow the example" set by Travancore.[17] The Government of India at Calcutta and the Secretary of State in London were not far behind in signaling their approbation: in 1866, the Dewan received the great prize of the era, the Star of India, becoming Sir Tanjore Madhava Rao.

---

‡ In the nineteenth century, the term referred to British residents in India.

Beneath the surface, however, trouble was brewing. Rao's economic reforms earned him powerful enemies such as the Nambudiri Brahmin landlords who were now debarred from evicting their tenants at will. His social reforms incurred the wrath of conservatives when, for instance, he compelled Ayilyam to withdraw sanction for the "most shameful" restrictions placed on lower castes.[18] His administrative reforms, which included the importation of talented officials from British India, many of them educated Madras men like himself, angered Malayali[§] nativists.[19] His fiscal reforms, which saw the palace budget reduced to 4.5 lakhs per annum, nearly half of what it had been earlier in the century, prompted questions about who was really in charge in Travancore.

For more than a decade, Rao's achievements and Madras' paternal gaze protected him from reprisals. Then suddenly it was all over. In December 1870 Rao followed up a little too vigorously on a case of embezzlement in the Treasury. The inquiry exposed one of Ayilyam's favorites, leading the humiliated Maharaja to inform Madras that he intended to dismiss Rao. Taken aback, the Governor of Madras, Francis Napier, tried to mediate, but it quickly became apparent that the rupture was permanent. Ayilyam had come to feel intimidated by his much-feted Dewan, and disliked Rao's close relationship with his talented younger brother, Vishakham. Goaded by a nativist cabal that resented the Dewan for passing them over for high positions, Ayilyam dug in, leading Madras to give way to the inevitable. Consequently, in May 1872 Rao departed Travancore for Madras.

It did not take Rao long to find his feet. Appointed Acting Viceroy in the interim, Napier offered him a coveted seat on the Viceregal Council. To the amazement of his contemporaries, Rao declined the offer, uninterested in a largely symbolic appointment. He discreetly requested Napier to consider him instead for a position in Mysore where he might help prepare the State for its impending restoration to the Wadiyar dynasty. As he waited in Madras for a sign from Napier, Rao was unexpectedly approached by Tukoji Rao Holkar of

§ An umbrella term for various Malayalam-speaking ethnic groups located in modern-day Kerala.

Indore to become Dewan on the handsome salary of 3,000 rupees per month. Inferring from Napier's silence that there was no opening for him in Mysore, Rao eventually accepted Holkar's offer, arriving in Indore in November 1872.

Indore proved, as Rao fully expected, a challenging assignment. By the numbers Indore was thriving. Propelled by international demand for Malwa opium and cotton, its revenues had accelerated from 35 lakhs in 1865 to 55 lakhs in 1870. This had enabled the British to convince the notoriously tight-fisted Holkar to spend a little on sanitation and education. The Maharaja also had some notable ideas of his own, which included setting up the first-ever ironworks and cotton mill in a Native State, and lending British India 100 lakh rupees to build a railway line that would make Indore a transit point on the Greater Indian Peninsula Railway. But on the whole Indore was in a shambolic condition. Tukoji's "hard and exacting" revenue assessments left the *ryot* (tenant cultivators) "tottering and starving", while "vexatious cesses" and the near absence of transport and communication channels inhibited commerce.[20] Holkar's tragically high estimate of his own capabilities meant that he rarely delegated authority and never hesitated to overrule his officers and judges. His orders, it was well known, could be swayed by *nazaranas* (tributes). Indeed, so much did he love hoarding money that even the seat of his power, the town of Indore, was neglected, its notorious filthiness making it prone to cholera outbreaks and devastating fires.

Under the circumstances, Rao did what he could. He started with administrative reform: departments were created and staffed, correspondence was organized, business rules on topics ranging from accounting practices to leave policies were enacted. Judicial reform followed: courts appeared in the capital and provinces, an orderly circuit of appeals was established, and British-trained judges were appointed to raise the tone of the legal system. Law enforcement received attention in parallel, the centerpiece being an expensive new Central Jail to replace its infamous predecessor. Public works came into being under British-trained engineers, leading to the rapid expansion of roads and municipal improvements, including drainage, new tree-lined avenues, and piped water, which helped drive out filth and disease. Social expenditures grew as well, significantly increasing the availability of vaccines, medicines, and schooling. More complicated reforms were also drafted, for instance, working out how to expand trade and commerce by abolishing transit duties, improving postal and telegraphic systems, and framing new commercial laws.

These were not trivial achievements, but after a mere two years Rao was despondent. His reforms were constantly being checked by an array of vested interests that Holkar seemed least interested in combating. For instance, when Rao proposed restricting margin trading in the highly unstable opium *satta* (betting or futures) market in order to minimize the risk of bankruptcies, he was defeated by a cabal of powerful *darbaris* (courtiers) who had long used their privileged access to information to make handsome profits. Rao also had to battle the charge that his reforms were only for show or to please the British. Then there was the Maharaja's own temperament. Famous for being the "most jealous chief of Hindostan", Tukoji refused to give Rao independent control over Indore's finances, preventing structural reform.[21]

Why had Holkar hired Rao if not to reform Indore? The answer lay in an event that had brought Rao much fame. In 1868 John Liddell, Travancore's commercial agent at the port town of Alleppey, had been convicted for embezzling funds. Upon being sentenced to two years in prison, Liddell appealed to Madras, which canceled the sentence on the ground that Europeans were not subject to the laws of Native States. The official responsible for this decision was none other than the Dewan's old mentor, Norton, who had since become the Advocate General of Madras. Undeterred, Rao made a strong case, with help from John Mayne, a Madras legal luminary, that Travancore's residual sovereignty gave it jurisdiction over all who resided within its borders. Norton eventually had to reverse himself and Liddell remained in prison.

Enmeshed in complicated territorial disputes with the Government of India and having been swindled more than once by English charlatans who promised to raise his concerns with the Viceroy or Parliament, Tukoji had long been on the search for a capable Foreign Minister. The Liddell case was what had brought Rao to his attention. Not surprisingly then, at Tukoji's insistence Rao found much of his time devoted to appealing adverse decisions that the

Government of India had made prior to his arriving in Indore. It was an unpleasant business, especially since amateurishness had weakened the brief—in one instance Indore's *vakil* (representative) had relied on forged maps, in another he submitted evidence that proved the opposite of what Tukoji claimed. Being forced to constantly butt heads with the Resident, and to repeatedly appeal to the Viceroy, also hurt Rao's standing with the Foreign Department in Calcutta, making it harder for him to obtain their support in defeating vested interests within Indore.

As Rao was pondering his future, fate intervened. In April 1875 Malhar Rao, the ruler of Baroda, was deposed on grounds of gross misgovernment. To prove that the Government of India had no intention to annex Baroda, Viceroy Thomas Baring, the Earl of Northbrook, decided to appoint a Dewan of known ability and independence. Well aware that his Dewan was unhappy, Holkar assented to Northbrook's request for Rao's services. By the end of the month Rao was on his way to Baroda, where he would earn a salary of 5,000 rupees per month, making him one of the highest paid officials in the country. His colleagues in Indore did not let him leave without a rousing public goodbye. Chief Justice Dhande Garud's farewell speech, which was carried around the country by *The Times of India*, praised Rao's "singular tact" and "liberality of sentiment", and underscored that "every department of Government, public health, justice, public works, police, education and revenue, all have felt the influence of your master mind", adding tartly that "to those who may be skeptical on that point as was said of Pitt: *si monumentum requiris, circumspice* (if you seek his monument, look around)".[22]

Baroda demanded Rao's every waking moment. The immediate order of business was selecting Malhar Rao's successor. The local claimants being undesirable, Richard Meade, the Agent to the Governor-General (the Viceroy's representative) and Rao maneuvered into place Gopal Rao, a twelve-year old from a distant branch of the Gaekwad clan, who was subsequently adopted by a former queen, Jamna Bai, and retitled Sayaji Rao. The Gaekwad's youth was doubly advantageous: it permitted him to be groomed for office and gave the Dewan the opportunity to reform Baroda's *ancien regime*. Before long, Malhar Rao's mistresses and favorites had their lavish grants replaced with modest settlements contingent on good behavior. Baroda's hopelessly outdated military, which cost a staggering 31 lakhs per anum (more than a third of Baroda's revenue), was trimmed, its *Sardars* (nobles) and *Silledars* (military contractors) disallowed from filling vacancies and bequeathing their positions to their heirs. The jewelers and bankers that had been only too willing to give Malhar Rao jewelry on loan and overdrafts to fund his profligate ways had their bills paid, but only after suffering thorough audits.

Having cleaned the "Augean stable", Rao declared his intention to "prove the degree of excellence" to which native administration could rise.[23] Backed by Meade's successor, Philip Melvill, rightly described as "one of the very few official Englishmen in India who are not ashamed to call the dusky children of the soil their brethren", the Dewan now enacted his trademark reforms.[24] He reorganized and staffed the administration with talented officers, many on loan from British India, and set up a judicial system, whose well-paid officers made bribery a thing of the past. The *zamindari* (revenue farming) system was replaced with the *ryotwari* (direct taxation) system, land assessments were reduced and could no longer be collected by force, and waste lands were sold on favorable terms. Since Baroda lacked Travancore's abundant natural resources, Rao focused instead on stimulating manufacturing and trade by removing taxes on artisans, establishing institutions to teach industrial methods, creating prizes to stimulate workmanship, and organizing fairs to market Baroda's indigenous manufactures.

Over the next five years these initiatives led to "uncommon progress".[25] By 1881, Baroda's revenues had grown to 143 lakhs, a 50% increase since Malhar Rao's time. Its reserves, meanwhile, nearly tripled to 210 lakhs. The increased revenue permitted substantial capital and social expenditures. Between 1876 and 1881, Rao directed nearly 60 lakhs toward public works, resulting in significant growth in infrastructure, including roads, railway feeder lines, and wells; in public services, including schools, hospitals, and dispensaries; and in civil buildings, including district offices, courthouses, and well-designed jails. The Bombay journalist Behramji Malabari captured the change in his typically cheeky way, writing in his widely-noticed travelogue, *Gujarat and the Gujaratis*:

> Land of my birth! After twenty-four years of forced exile, I fly to thee... For a full fortnight I have tried, on the spot, to conjure up thy past glories. But where are they, Baroda? ... Where is thy bracing fever, thy benignant cholera, O land of my birth? Gone, gone are all thy glories, gone for evermore! And instead I see the jail and the court-house, parks and palaces, roads and tanks, schools and colleges; and that monster of a Municipal Commissioner![26]

Rao's "unceasing" efforts, "remarkable" abilities, and devotion to his "arduous duties" were praised throughout this time.[27] Melvill, in particular, never lost a chance to remind Calcutta that there was "nowhere to be found a more able, conscientious, and industrious administrator".[28] The Anglo-Indian press was equally enthusiastic in reporting Rao's success in "regenerating a State where misrule had attained the proportions of an art".[29] In 1877 Calcutta and London acknowledged the Dewan's services by granting him the honorific title of Raja.

By the end of the decade Rao was a national celebrity, feted as one of the "makers" of an emergent modern India. But within Baroda critical voices were growing louder. The tax farmers replaced by revenue officers, the customs agents swept away along with transit duties, the courtiers and mistresses compelled to return State property, and Brahmins who lost their exemption from capital punishment, howled at the new dispensation. Angrier still were the powerful banking families that lost the State's business when Rao created a modern Treasury, the jewelers who lost their primary customer when Rao refused to add to the Gaekwad's extravagant collection of jewels, and the hive of priests and retainers in the Palace whose illicit incomes were exposed by frequent audits. Angriest of all were the *Sardars* whose special privileges, such as their immunity from civil law and taxation, were steadily narrowed.

The resulting "popular disaffection" found an outlet in the vernacular press that portrayed the new regime as "destitute of all sympathy" and condemned Rao for being a "servile imitator" of Anglo-Indian statesmanship.[30] With Melvill entirely behind the Dewan, these complaints had little immediate effect. But there was worse to come. Calcutta had originally intended to make Sayaji's adoption conditional on his agreeing to root out opium and salt smuggling and reforming the antiquated Baroda Contingent, a military force that Baroda was bound by treaty to place at Bombay's disposal. However, the disquiet generated by Malhar Rao's removal stayed the Viceroy's hand. Five years later, the time was as ripe as it would ever be. It would be difficult to pressure the Gaekwad following his accession as this would weaken his standing in Baroda, where many still viewed him as a British imposition. By contrast, if Rao were compelled to satisfy Calcutta's demands, the resulting odium would attach to him rather than the Gaekwad, who could subsequently appease public sentiment by dismissing the Dewan.

And so it went. Bluntly warned that Bombay officials intended to enter Baroda territory and forcibly extradite individuals illicitly producing and trading salt, Rao agreed to outlaw salt that had not paid British duty. Similarly warned that Baroda would be debarred from the profitable opium trade unless it eliminated opium smuggling, Rao reluctantly agreed to introduce a State monopoly over production and sale of opium. Both these concessions, which raised prices for consumers, sent farmers and producers out of business, and hurt Baroda's balance of payments, aroused immense anger. Then, told in no uncertain terms that Baroda had to fork up the many lakhs required to modernize the Baroda Contingent or pay 3.75 lakhs annually in lieu of its obligation to maintain the Contingent, Rao chose the lesser evil. This decision injured the already aggrieved *Sardars* and *Silledars* who now faced the prospect of losing their ancestral employment.

Unable to see the extent to which Rao was working behind the scenes to contain British India's grasping hand, Baroda's denizens took these concessions as evidence of duplicity. Their fears were embodied in an anonymous 1881 pamphlet entitled *The Groans of Baroda*, which accused Rao of intending to relinquish the "cherished and valuable rights of the State" in order to please his British overlords.[31] The pamphlet was authored by a group of Maratha firebrands linked to Sayaji that reportedly included the young Bal Gangadhar Tilak.[32] Troubled by such intrigues, Rao was left to privately grumble that the Maharaja ought not to "form his own judgment upon matters which, at his age and with his inexperience, he should take upon trust".[33] It was the Dewan's dismay that prompted the lectures that have come down to us as *Hints on the Art and Science of Government*—

they constituted a last-ditch effort to open the Gaekwad's eyes to the responsibilities of power.

In December 1881 Sayaji ascended to the throne. In addition to their philosophical differences, personal relations between the Gaekwad and the Dewan had long been strained. Transformed overnight from a malnourished cowherd into the second richest man in India, Sayaji could not afford to doubt himself. His insecurity manifested itself in a keen sensitivity to slights, taking offence, for instance, when Rao scolded him for losing a valuable ring or bought him a cheaper American edition of the *Encyclopedia Britannica*. Rao, meanwhile, proud of all that he had accomplished, refused to defer to a lesser man. Nine months after the inauguration, an exasperated Rao departed Baroda, never to return.

Rao spent the last decade of his life in Madras. In 1883 he made another quiet bid for the long-cherished Dewanship of Mysore, which had been vacated by the death of his old schoolmate, C. V. Rungacharlu. It was not to be, however, as the Maharaja quickly settled on his long-serving aide, Seshadri Iyer. Rao thereafter devoted himself to social reform, a subject particularly close to his heart. In the face of bitter opposition from Madras' orthodox element, he campaigned to end child marriage and promoted female education and widow remarriage. He was never far from the public eye. Under the pen name "Native Thinker", he wrote many widely-read notes ranging from biting critiques of astrology and Theosophy to stern warnings about the threat that Russia posed to India and even advice on personal hygiene. His famed oratorical skills ever in demand, he accepted numerous invitations to inaugurate or preside over events, his Convocation Address at Madras University being one of the landmarks. In 1887 Rao was invited to the Madras Legislative Council as well as the Viceregal Council, which he declined once again, this time on account of his fading health. He continued, however, to meet privately with the Governor of Madras, Robert Bourke, the latter telling the Viceroy that "I do not know anyone with whom it is more agreeable to converse upon Indian politics" because "his remarks upon men, European and Native, are full of wisdom and humor".[34]

At the end of 1890 Rao's health gave way. A stroke left him paralyzed on the left side. For four months he persevered, his interest in public affairs still so keen that newspapers had to be read out to him daily. Then, on April 4, 1891, with his extended family by his bed, and his house filled to the brim with telegrams of concern from around the country, Rao breathed his last. The news of his death was reported throughout the British Empire with *The Pioneer*, the standard bearer of Anglo-India, describing him as exemplifying "the union of much that is best and most distinguished" in European and Indian civilization.[35] The obituary that Rao would have most appreciated came in the *Quarterly Journal of the Poona Sarvajanik Sabha*, the trumpet of educated Western India, which painstakingly outlined the ways in which, having discerned the "changed circumstances under which Native States had begun or were soon to live", Rao had enacted "what time would sooner or later have made imperative". Written by Mahadev Ranade, the brightest star of the next generation of Indian liberals, the obituary promised that when histories of the era were written, they would conclusively show that Rao had left "foot-prints deeper and more distinct than have been made by any other Indian statesman".[36]

What Was the Purpose of Hints?

Before we examine what *Hints on the Art and Science of Government* teaches, we ought to understand the context in which it was framed, specifically the political conditions prevailing in the Native States of British India.

Native States constituted a substantial portion of British India. Approximately 600 in number, they occupied 600,000 square miles out of 1,380,000 square miles of British Indian territory and contained a population of 55 million out of 250 million (the United Kingdom and Germany, by contrast, had populations of 35 million and 45 million respectively).[37] Native States thus constituted more than one-third of the total area of British India and one-fifth of its total population. Their revenues were considerable as well, amounting to £16 million (approximately one-fourth that of British India). Nearly 200 of these Native States were considered politically significant, with roughly a dozen, principally Hyderabad, Mysore, Gwalior, Baroda, Travancore, Indore, and Kashmir, dominating the pack. To provide a point of comparison: Baroda was equivalent in revenue (a little over £1 million) and population (approximately 2.2 million) to Greece.[38]

These Native States left British India confronting a knotty problem. Though the rulers of these States had ceded their external sovereignty to British India, and grudgingly permitted their internal sovereignty to be constrained in various ways as well, the rights and resources that remained with them were still far from trivial. For instance, they were entitled to make and enforce their own laws and to raise and spend revenue. This arrangement placed British India in a difficult position when a Native ruler behaved abysmally: if it remained silent, it was accused of complicity; if it intervened, was accused of violating what freedom remained to the Native States.

Anglo-Indians generally took the view that Native States were predisposed to behave badly because they were "despotic" regimes where "the prince is legislator, administrator, and too often supreme judge also".[39] This view peaked around the middle of the nineteenth century, perhaps best exemplified by Dalhousie who was, as one of his successors put it, "so firmly convinced of the superiority of British over Native rule that he felt when he extinguished a Native State that he was conferring an indisputable blessing upon its inhabitants".[40] Why this should be so was expressed most vividly by Samuel Laing, a former member of the Viceregal Council, during a parliamentary debate over whether Britain ought to return Mysore to the Wadiyars:

> He would mention one case for the purpose of showing what might be the nature of those evils. In the territory of that Prince it was a common practice to seize any unfortunate old woman suspected of witchcraft. A hook was passed through the muscles of the woman's back, and a cord being attached to it she was hung up and swung round with the view of seeing how long she could endure such torture. In the case to which he referred—which happened at Rajputana—the Prince complained very loudly to the Resident, on the ground that a British officer's interposition to prevent this cruelty was an interference with his Sovereign authority, and with the feelings or prejudices of his subjects. That was an instance of the scenes which we must expect to witness if we set up a Native Prince in India and then extended to him our protection.[41]

Occasionally, such anxiety was countered by pointing out that British India was not without its own grave flaws. This is precisely how the Secretary of State responded to Laing. If misgovernment was "to be quoted against Native government", Robert Cecil, the Marquess of Salisbury, told Parliament in 1867, then the forthcoming report on the 1866 Orissa Famine, which had claimed over a million lives, would "be found to be another and far more terrible instance to be quoted against English rule".[42] Such rebuttals had limited impact, however, as there was a meaningful distinction to be drawn between gross neglect on the one side and blatant criminality on the other. Laing's example may have been extreme, but there was no denying that most Native States were badly governed. In Baroda, for example, Sayaji's predecessor, Malhar Rao, had a well-deserved reputation for cruelty, having, among other things, abducted married women to make them *laundis* (slaves) in his palace, permitted his *Vahivatdars* (revenue collectors) to torture *ryot* to deliver up rents, and poisoned political opponents. Maladministration was rife as well, with the ramshackle bureaucracy, headed by his brother-in-law, Nana Khanvelkar, predicated on *nazaranas* (bribes) and arbitrary taxes that had more in common with extortion. As in other Native States, the Treasury was made to bear the Maharaja's ruinous expenditure on mistresses, astrologers, animal fights, jewelry, and even cannons cast in gold.[43]

Given such examples, British officials naturally refused to consider Native States as morally equivalent to British India. They did, however, come to see other reasons to tolerate them. Most pressing was the belief that Britain's ability to retain India depended on Native States' support because, lacking the men and money required to govern the entire subcontinent by force, it had to rely on the traditional authority of rulers. John Malcolm, the famed Agent to the Governor-General for Central India, was an authoritative early voice, warning Calcutta in 1824 that "the respect which the natives give to men of high birth, with claims upon their allegiance, contributes greatly to the preservation of the general peace".[44] This conclusion remained unchanged through the century, even as the locus of danger shifted from domestic insurrection to foreign invasion. As Russia made inroads into Central Asia, Viceroy Charles Canning declared in 1860 that Native States would prove one of British India's "best mainstays"—if they were convinced "that they have nothing to gain by helping to displace us in favor of any new rulers".[45]

Doubts also emerged as to whether Indians viewed Native States as disapprovingly as the British did. After sizeable numbers in Satara, Nagpur, and Oudh—Native States annexed by Dalhousie on grounds of misgovernment—sided with their former rulers in 1857, British officials came to the conclusion that imposing "Anglo-Saxon" tastes on India was counter-productive. Salisbury was once again a pivotal figure on this count, vigorously defending Native States as having "a fitness and congeniality" for local populations that compensated "to an enormous degree for the material evils which its rudeness in a great many cases produces".[46] George Robinson, the Marquess of Ripon, who stood on the opposite end of the political spectrum from Salisbury, pressed the same point, telling audiences in England that as Viceroy he had seen that "the body of the people" were "attached to the rule of their hereditary chief" whose despotic methods were "often more acceptable than the impartial and inexorable" ways of the British.[47]

Native States also came to be seen as outlets for "bold and ambitious men" who could not be accommodated in British India. As early as 1812, Thomas Munro, later the much-revered Governor of Madras, was complaining bitterly that "men who, under a Native government, might have held the first dignities of the state, who, but for us, might have been governors of provinces, are regarded as little better than menial servants".[48] Whereas Munro eagerly looked forward to "a time when Natives may be employed in almost every office", those who doubted that such a day was in the offing, because Europeans refused to serve under Indians, saw Native States as a "safety valve". This point was driven home during debates on Mysore. Since Calcutta could not see a way "to employing very largely the Natives of India", Salisbury told Parliament, it became necessary to preserve Native States like Mysore, because "they afford an outlet for statesman-like capacity", which was rapidly increasing due to the spread of English education.[49]

If Native States were to be maintained, then British officials had to find a way to prevent gross misbehavior. For decades the hope was that this difficulty could be obviated by tactful intervention on the part of Residents. In his influential 1821 *Notes of Instructions to Assistants and Officers* Malcolm directed that Native States "be courted and encouraged to good conduct". It ought to be British officials' "earnest endeavor" to give "rulers a pride in their administration", and so they ought to refrain from "minute checks and interference" as this would expose rulers to "mockery and degradation" and extinguish "all motive to good or great actions".[50] Occasionally, this approach worked well, Travancore being the most prominent example. But in most cases British officials found themselves confronted with capricious rulers who became only more self-centered after Queen Victoria promised in 1858 that British India would no longer annex Native States. Consequently, even sympathetic Anglo-Indians such as Henry Daly, who filled Malcolm's office in Central India half a century later, could not help but despair at the unwillingness of Native rulers to "come to a sense of the responsibility of Government, and not treat it as a mere milch cow".[51]

As the emergence of newspapers made instances of maladministration in Native States more widely known, and thereby deepened Anglo-Indian unease, a new idea came to the fore. Pressed in February 1867 to explain why Mysore, which had been under British supervision, would not be misgoverned when handed back to the Wadiyar dynasty, Salisbury stressed the importance of education, saying British India intended to give Chamarajendra "the advantages of a European education, and so prepare him, to the best of our ability, for the responsibilities which we hope it may one day be possible to commit to him".[52] Three months later his successor as Secretary of State, Stafford Northcote, reinforced the claim, telling Parliament that "Travancore forty years ago was in as bad a state as Mysore, yet its administration under British influence had so greatly improved that Travancore was now something like a model Native State".[53]

Northcote also touched on the idea, championed by Lewin Bowring, the Chief Commissioner of Mysore, that Britain ought to expend effort "not only in carefully educating the young Prince, but in devising such a system and regulations" that would "insure his administering it properly"[54]. Ideas have their time, however. In British India, officials were already coalescing around the notion that greater attention ought to be paid to the education of nobles. This topic had received some attention from the East India Company, which established Wards' Institutions in Calcutta in 1856 and in

Benares in 1857. But these institutions had only been able to educate the small number of princes placed under the guardianship of the Court of Wards, and that too in a very limited way, as they had no means to compel attendance.[55] Consequently, most princes' education remained at their families' discretion. The more progressive of these families allowed Residents (or their subordinates, Political Agents) to appoint a British-trained native tutor (Rao's appointment in Travancore being one of the earliest such cases). But British officials soon came to have doubts about the efficacy of native tutors who struggled to discipline their aristocratic wards and were prone to "make use of their position for political purposes".[56]

As the feeling grew that more needed to be done, Bombay, where more than half of the Native States were located, stepped up. At the prompting of Alexander Grant, the Director of Public Instruction, a circular was sent out in 1864 canvassing the views of local administrators on the "the best means of educating young Chiefs and fitting them for the discharge of their public duties".[57] Richard Keatinge, the spirited Political Agent for Kathiawar, was quick to respond. Expressing anxiety about the "degraded atmosphere" in which "lads" who were "destined to rule over several hundred villages" were being brought up, he proposed that Kathiawar have an equivalent of the Wards' Institute, but with one crucial amendment—the Principal ought to be a "European gentleman".[58]

As Bombay collected its thoughts, Bengal embarked on a trial of its own in 1866 when Lakshmeshwar Singh and Rameshwar Singh, the princes of Darbhanga, were withdrawn from the Wards' Institute in Benares and placed in the care of the Cambridge-educated Chester Macnaghten, whose father Elliot Macnaghten, a former Chairman of the East India Company, was on the Secretary of State's Council of India. Then, in March 1867, a month after Salisbury declared in Parliament that Calcutta would carefully attend to Chamarajendra's education, Bombay decided that it had "too long neglected the education of young Chiefs during minority", and permitted its officers to pressure families to place their heirs in suitable schools where they would be safe from "pernicious influences".[59] Keatinge, and his successor, William Anderson, wasted no time in raising funds from Kathiawar's nobles. In April 1868 the foundation stone was laid for the Rajkumar College at Rajkot, which opened in December 1870 with Macnaghten as the Principal and with one student, Takhtsinhji Bhavsinhji, the young Maharaja of Bhavnagar. With Kathiawar having shown the way, Viceroy Robert Bourke, the Earl of Mayo, invited the nobility of Rajputana to a Durbar in Ajmer in October 1870 to follow suit, setting in motion events that would lead to the establishment of Mayo College in 1872. Officials in other parts of British India swung into action as well. In a little over a decade, a half dozen institutions, later collectively termed Chiefs Colleges, would spring up in Indore, Nowgong, Raipur, Lahore, and Lucknow.

Ironically, precisely as British India was rolling out its plans to shape the character of the future rulers of Native States, Rao's experience with Ayilyam was making him painfully aware that education could do only so much. As Rao was licking his wounds in March 1871 following his rupture with Ayilyam, Bowring, having retired from Mysore, published his memoir *Eastern Experiences* in which he observed that those "who sympathize most with Native States, and who have seen how they are administered, are conscious of the great risk to which their stability is subjected by idle or headstrong rulers seeking to set aside all law, and to act on the impulse of the moment". Rao's ears pricked up when he read Bowring's proposed remedy, which Northcote had previously alluded to in Parliament. Though the Maharaja of Mysore must of course be "highly educated", Bowring advised, it was no less essential that he "should be guided by the law, and by a fixed system", the key feature being that "there shall be a written law, which judges and other functionaries shall not be at liberty to set aside, and that even the Raja shall be bound by it".[60]

When Rao subsequently wrote to Napier in March 1872 to decline the seat on the Viceregal Council and to propose that he be employed in Mysore instead, he appended the relevant sections from Bowring's *Eastern Experiences*, adding that nothing could be more interesting than participating in the development of "something like a constitution" wherein "a Native Administration" might be brought under "a system of fundamental principles, derived from the advanced political wisdom of Europe" albeit "carefully adapted to the conditions of the Native society". Such a constitution, Rao declared, would permit a Native State a "healthy existence" that "combined regard to the dignity of its Sovereign and the happiness of its numerous subjects". "Indeed, a model Native Government in every sense of the phrase could be founded", he enthused, which "might operate in the character of an example to all other Native States in India".[61]

Napier eventually forwarded Rao's letter to Northbrook, who took over as Viceroy in May 1872 with the comment that he could not see how Rao might be employed in the proposed manner. Unwilling to take such an intrusive step, especially when the transfer of power to Chamarajendra was at least a decade away, Northbrook quietly let the matter drop. That might have been the end of it—had it not been for Malhar Rao in Baroda.

Baroda had been unsettled since December 1870, when Khande Rao's death raised his brother Malhar Rao to the *gaddi* (throne). The new Maharaja immediately plunged into the "depraved voluptuousness" typical of Native States.[62] His fortunes took a turn for the worse in March 1873 when Robert Phayre took over as Resident in Baroda. Possessing "more zeal than discretion", Phayre began inundating his superiors with lengthy missives detailing Malhar Rao's "career of crime".[63] Not trusting Phayre's increasingly manic dispatches, Northbrook deputed Richard Meade, one of the most respected officers of the era, to examine what was wrong. Meade's February 1874 report declared that Baroda was indeed suffering from "general maladministration of a character urgently calling for reformation".[64] But he rejected Phayre's recommendation that Bombay ought to "resume the reins" in Baroda.[65] In his view, the introduction of "a few carefully selected men who have already received an adequate training in the British public services" would bring about "a more satisfactory state" without entailing "a minute and vexatious interference".[66] This recommendation did not sit well with the Bombay Legislative Council, which oversaw Baroda, three of whose members—Henry Tucker, Alexander Rogers, and James Gibbs—offered strong dissents.

Tucker argued that, since Malhar Rao had shown himself to be incorrigible, Meade's proposal would prove "inefficacious unless some limitation is placed on the arbitrary power of the Maharaja". Hence, Calcutta ought, he said, to "force the Maharaja to give to his subjects a written constitution". This might seem a "strange and inadmissible proposition", Tucker conceded, but on "broaching the subject to an eminent Native administrator, who has successively held office in two large Native States in different parts of India"—a description that left no doubt he was referring to Madhava Rao—he had learnt that his interlocutor had come to the same conclusion "long ago". To wit, Tucker shared with Calcutta a "scheme of constitution" drawn up by "this gentleman who does not wish his name to be made public at present". Though his interlocutor "had but little time" to outline his ideas, the draft was "so able and creditable", Tucker said, that it deserved Calcutta's careful attention.[67]

Rogers concurred with Tucker. Meade's proposal was, he argued, a "mere palliative" that would prove "practically useless". To "effect any permanent good" Native States had to be relieved from "despotic rule, dependent on the character and disposition of a single man" and instead made "in some measure constitutional". Such change was "feasible", he insisted, adding that "he had been shown the draft of a Constitution drawn up by an eminent Native Statesman of great experience", which he believed "with a few modifications" would work admirably.[68]

An elegant construction—and the earliest known example of its kind—Rao's draft constitution (reprinted in Appendix I) aimed at three ends. First, it sought responsible administration with decision-making to proceed in an orderly fashion under public servants led by a Dewan who could only be dismissed upon a showing of impropriety. Second, it sought the rule of law by requiring British India to concur in the appointment of well-qualified judges enjoying high pay and life terms, subject to checks against conflicts of interest. Third, it sought to impart a public character to the State, for instance by compelling the Maharaja to fund personal expenses from a privy purse and by eliminating opportunities for favoritism. Crucially, British India was to serve as guarantor or backstop for the constitution—with Calcutta's permission required before the Maharaja could amend its provisions.

This proposal was too much for Gibbs, however. He concurred with Tucker and Rogers that Baroda required a "more radical remedy", but he disparaged the "parrot-like imitations" put forward by the "eminent Native statesman". "I am not one of those", he declared, "who think good government in a Native State can only be obtained by introducing our own systems". The "system of government in existence" in Baroda was, he thought "perhaps the best for the people, if only it were honestly and purely worked".[69] This improvement could be secured by a traditional remedy, which was to appoint a Regent. His preferred candidate was Dinkar Rao, former Dewan of Gwalior and perennial favorite of Anglo-Indian conservatives who saw him as exemplifying an authentic India, untainted by the liberal education that had deracinated the English-speaking metropolitan elite.

Only too aware that his actions were being "jealously watched by all Native Rulers in India", Northbrook proceeded cautiously. Tucker's proposal was deemed to "go far beyond" what was "justifiable to adopt" and Gibbs' too "premature to take into consideration".[70] Instead, he gave Malhar Rao a chance to reform. The Viceroy had some reason for optimism: panicked by the turn of events, the Gaekwad had appointed the celebrated public intellectual Dadabhai Naoroji the Acting Dewan in December 1873. Northbrook's hopes were soon dashed, however. Opposed by Phayre and undercut by the *darbaris* surrounding Malhar Rao, Naoroji made little headway and resigned in disgust in December 1874. Later that month emerged evidence linking Malhar Rao to an attempt to poison Phayre, prompting Northbrook to suspend the Gaekwad while a Commission investigated. A hung verdict followed, but Malhar Rao was nonetheless deposed in April 1875 on grounds of gross misgovernment.

As a result of these extraordinary developments, in May 1875 Rao found himself Dewan of the Native State for which he had previously proposed a constitution. So why then did Rao end up lecturing Sayaji on good government rather than enacting a constitution?

For the first two years of Rao's term, there was no opportunity to do anything as novel as proposing a constitution. Irritated by the time and energy he had already had to expend on Baroda, Northbrook wanted no further trouble from it. He was annoyed that Lewis Pelly, the Special Commissioner he had appointed to govern Baroda following Malhar Rao's suspension, had "pushed on" the British Indian "system of administration rather too fast", provoking anxious petitions and violent protests from Baroda's denizens, who had begun sarcastically calling the British administrator "Pellyji Gaekwar". Hence,

Northbrook made it clear to the Dewan that he was to "apply remedies gradually".[71] The objective was to steady the ship by restoring law and order and reviving Baroda's revenues—and do nothing else.

So matters remained until Robert Bulwer-Lytton replaced Northbrook in April 1876. Lytton was convinced that it was a "fundamental political mistake" to believe that Britain could retain India by pursuing "good government". This might satisfy "Baboos", he wrote to Salisbury in May 1876, but this element, he sneered, represented "nothing but the social anomaly of their position". The great bulk of the country moved "in obedience not to its British benefactors, but to its native chiefs and princes, however tyrannical they may be". Consequently, figuring out how to "secure completely, and efficiently utilise, the Indian aristocracy" was "the most important problem now before us". Lytton hoped to rely on the credulity of Native States. "Fortunately for us", he told Salisbury, this "powerful aristocracy" was "easily affected by sentiment, and susceptible to the influence of symbols". A Maharaja, he was certain, "would do anything, or pay anything, to obtain an additional gun to his salute".[72] Hence, Lytton devoted much energy to seeing through the Imperial Assemblage, a grand spectacle intended to awe and inspire the Native States by tying them symbolically to the Queen who now became the "Empress of India". But even as the Imperial Assemblage got underway in January 1877, a showdown with Salar Jung, the Dewan and Regent in Hyderabad, was unfolding. Lytton, who disliked the slightest show of opposition, was affronted by Jung's vigorous efforts to press Hyderabad's claim to a contested territory called the Berars, the Dewan having gone so far as to visit England and appeal directly to the Queen. Seeking to cut Jung down to size, Lytton ordered him in June 1877 to accept a British-sponsored rival as co-administrator and co-Regent. After initially refusing to comply, Jung submitted in September under threat of deposition and exile.

Having learnt the hard way that the Native States were not placated by bunting and medals alone, Lytton's thinking began to change. The impending restoration in Mysore set the scene for a radically different approach. At the start of Lytton's term Salisbury had advised the Viceroy to think seriously about how to limit Chamarajendra's future powers, lest he endanger British interests. Lytton had baulked at the idea, fearing that imposing restrictions on Mysore would undermine his efforts to charm the Native States. Hence, he initially chose the more conventional approach, which was to overhaul Chamarajendra's upbringing, pushing on the notion that the Maharaja should have a "social and travelled rather than a cloistered education".[73] But now, chastened by events in Hyderabad, he wrote to Salisbury in February 1878 that "to prevent the future possibility of Mysorian Salar Jungs, I think that, before we restore the Province to native rule, it will be very necessary to make adequate arrangements for the independence of a good judiciary authority, the complete separation of the civil purse from the public revenue, and some sort of balance in the powers of the State".[74]

Preoccupied with the Second Afghan War, it took Lytton another eighteen months to work out with James Gordon, the Chief Commissioner in Mysore, and Alfred Lyall, the Foreign Secretary, the "constitutional principles" to be imposed when Chamarajendra turned 18 in March 1881. Gordon urged significant limitations, in particular that the full transfer of power be deferred until Chamarajendra turned 21. Caught between his desire to defang Mysore and to conciliate Native States, who had become even more important as the Second Afghan War exposed British India's military and financial weakness, Lytton demurred. A "nominal or partial transfer" of power "would be decidedly injurious to our own credit" with the Native States, he told Gordon in September 1879. Nor would Gathorne Hardy, the Earl of Cranbrook, who had replaced Salisbury as Secretary of State, approve "stringent" restrictions on Chamarajendra.[75] In the end Lytton and Lyall settled on a conglomeration of administrative and financial checks that would prevent the "concentration of executive authority" in the hands of "a single high official". These checks required the Maharaja to "permanently separate" his private account from the Treasury, and compelled the Dewan to conduct administration "under regularly constituted" rules and procedures, the most significant being that important decisions had to be made via a Council composed of leading officials.[76]

It did not take Lytton long to connect Hyderabad and Mysore to Baroda where Rao had been doggedly opposing Bombay's efforts to impose its preferred opium and salt policies. "Our first care", he wrote to Gordon in June 1878, "must be to provide against the possibility of all the powers of the new Native State falling eventually into the hands of any one man—be he the Prince himself, or a popular and powerful Minister—over whose use of them the Government of India could exercise no adequate control, without hostile, and possibly violent, intervention". "The trouble we have had in dealing with Sir Salar Jung is a significant warning", he underscored, adding, "I doubt if we are altogether free from danger of similar trouble, by-and-by, with Sir Madhava Rao".[77] Lytton expanded on this observation once Mysore's "simple constitution" had been settled, telling Lyall in 1879 that their labors ought to become a "point of departure" in how British India dealt with the Native States. In particular, what had been done in Mysore ought to be applied to Baroda where Sayaji was soon to come of age as well:

> The principles now being applied to the case of Mysore, therefore, have a two-fold object. Firstly, to guard against that financial or administrative breakdown of the government of the Native ruler, which might oblige us, however reluctantly, to take the management of the State once more into our own hands, and probably to depose the reigning Prince. Secondly, to guard against the possible eventual absorption into his hands of all the financial resources and executive powers of the State, by some capable, but possibly ambitious and unscrupulous Minister. Of this danger we have already an instance in Hyderabad; and between ourselves, I do not feel sure that we may not someday have another in Baroda. Madhava Rao is a masterful man and Melvill is his puppet, nor can I think that any Mahratta Brahmin is quite to be trusted.[78]

Lytton did not remain in India long after writing these words. In April 1880 the Conservatives were unexpectedly wiped out in the General Election, and Lytton, whose Afghan policy had long been the target of Liberal ire, was compelled to resign. His advice to Lyall did not go unheeded, however. In September 1880, three months after Lytton was succeeded by Ripon, Melvill proposed to Calcutta that the full transfer of power to Sayaji be deferred until he turned 21. It was easy for Lyall to persuade Ripon that, for the sake of consistency, Baroda ought to follow the precedent set by Mysore. Thus, in February 1881, Melvill was instructed that rather than defer Sayaji's accession, Rao and he should instead devise "some kind of regulative machinery, or some systematic methods of government, to assist an inexperienced ruler, and to maintain some checks over the exercise of his personal authority".[79] And so, by this long and winding road, in March 1881 Rao found himself, quite unexpectedly, made responsible for drafting a proto-constitution that Sayaji would be required to accept prior to his accession in December.

It took Melvill and Rao three months to prepare a draft for Calcutta's review. Their draft obliged the Gaekwad to seek the "advice" of the Resident prior to making any "radical change" to the "existing system of administration", and to give his "utmost attention" to the advice thus tendered. It also committed the Gaekwad to "ordinarily" conduct business through the "medium" of the Dewan and to consult with a Council comprising of principal department heads. Such rules, Melvill informed Calcutta in May 1881, "may be expected to relieve the Gaekwar of much of the actual weight of administration so long as they remain in force, while recognizing his position as head of the State and his responsibility for the general character of the Government".[80]

As Rao and Melvill fleshed out the initial draft, Sayaji began expressing his unease about what these rules implied, having "heard" that the proto-constitution imposed on Mysore had not left the Maharaja with much "liberty of action".[81] The two men reassured the Gaekwad that while he was required to give due weight to the opinion and advice of his Dewan and Council, he was still entitled to decide as he judged fit. This claim was not entirely believable, however, because subsequent versions of the draft contained provisions that would in practice limit the Gaekwad's freedom of maneuver. For instance, Rao proposed that the Dewan be required to bring important matters before the Council, whose proceedings were to be recorded and subject to a quorum, and whose members were entitled to "place on record" their opinion on "any question discussed".[82] Such provisions would make it difficult for the Gaekwad to quietly or abruptly alter laws or policies.

The final draft also contained outright restrictions that Rao surely knew the Gaekwad could not refuse without alarming the British. The Gaekwad was to commit that the "decisions and settlements made during the minority of His Highness will not be re-opened unless with the sanction of the Government of India", and that "no person shall be arrested or imprisoned or deprived of life, liberty or property unless in due course of law". A related constraint concerned the rule of law. The Gaekwad was to agree that the decisions of the *Varisht* Court (High Court) would "as a rule, be final", and that "in cases in which great interests are at stake", petitions would be "entertained by the Dewan", who would only involve the Maharaja upon reaching the conclusion that the court's decision was incorrect.[83] Publicity was also emphasized. In particular, the Dewan was required to continue publishing annually an Administration Report, which meant that expenditures, especially those on the Palace, would remain in public view.

As knowledge of these provisions spread, "intriguers" began working to "unsettle" the Gaekwad's mind.[84] The idea was seeded, by Holkar amongst others, that Sayaji was "about to be tied hand and foot by his Council" and would have "only the semblance of authority".[85] Fiery denunciations soon followed as the native press excoriated Rao for a plan that, unbeknownst to them, had originated in Lytton's anxieties. The *Amrita Bazaar Patrika* led the charge, howling that the Dewan was seeking to "take advantage of the minority of the Prince to force upon him a constitution". It was "well known", it proclaimed, that Rao wished to "reduce Princes to ciphers" whereas the people of Baroda "would prefer the sympathetic rule, though it might be despotic rule of the Prince, to the methodical but unsympathetic rule of a Dewan".[86] These newspapers only became more agitated when an equally unaware Anglo-Indian press came out swinging on Rao's behalf, *The Pioneer*, for instance, declaring itself relieved to hear that Sayaji would "not be allowed suddenly to free himself from all trammels", as "freedom of this kind" would be "a very cruel kindness on the part of the Supreme Government".[87]

The brouhaha had a predictable consequence. In July 1881 a riled-up Sayaji informed Calcutta that he would be "quite content" with the rules that Rao and Melvill had drawn up—if he "were allowed to introduce a saving clause" to the effect that the rules were "tentative and may be altered as found necessary".[88] Melvill tried to salvage the situation by assuring the Gaekwad that the rules were not intended to be permanent. Unconvinced, in September 1881 Sayaji expressed his "strong feeling that a time should be specified for the termination of these special arrangements".[89] Though his preferred time frame was one year he was willing, he told Melvill, to concede up to two years.

The stand-off was only resolved later in the month when Lyall visited Baroda. A meeting with Rao left Lyall with no doubt where the Dewan stood. "The Minister is himself at heart very favourable to the maintenance of some kind of constitutional machinery, whereby the influence of responsible advisers will be brought to bear on the ruler", Lyall subsequently memorialized, but Rao "could not openly take a side which might seem to lean toward curtailing his own Chief's power". An interview with Sayaji followed. The Gaekwad was blunt: unless the proposed rules "were clearly and publicly marked as provisional, the general impression among his people would be that he had allowed material encroachments to be made upon his prerogative as ruler, and that he had accepted checks and limitations of the Gaekwar's personal authority which would lower his status as an independent Chief". Impressed by Sayaji's forthrightness and persuaded of the "inexpediency of doing anything which might affect the Gaekwar's popularity or reputation with his own people", Lyall decided that it was preferable that the "compulsory maintenance" of the proposed rules be limited to "two years".[90] Thus ended, with nary a whimper, Lytton's hope of applying the Mysore model to Baroda.

This then was the context in which *Hints on the Art and Science of Government* came into being. The circumstances being entirely averse to the establishment of a constitution—with the Gaekwad staunchly opposed to limitations on his power and the British unwilling to compel him—Rao was left to defend the lonely ideal. He used his lectures, which were delivered in parallel to the negotiations over the draft constitution, to explain to the Gaekwad why curbing his power would secure happiness for Baroda and fame for himself. *Hints* should be read, in short, as a plea for constitutionalism.

Why is Hints *in the Form of Lectures?*

Having seen why British India chose education as a means of making Native States progress, let us now examine the training imparted to Sayaji, especially the thought and preparation that went into the lectures that constitute *Hints on the Art and Science of Government*.

Since Sayaji had been chosen precisely because he could be groomed to become a good ruler, his education naturally received great attention. It needed such attention because Sayaji had arrived in Baroda illiterate, his only education being a few hours of daily instruction in Marathi since his selection. With only six years remaining before he came of age, every month was precious. Meade thus submitted to Calcutta in August 1875 a detailed plan that envisioned a Tutor and Governor supervising daily instruction, with the Dewan providing the requisite funds and liaising with the Palace, and the Agent to the Governor-General exercising overall control of the scheme. Though Meade and Rao projected a united front, they did not agree on three fateful aspects of this scheme.

One was whether the Maharaja should be educated privately or in a school. Meade wanted Sayaji to be joined by a select number of boys from the "high classes", especially the sons of the *Sardars*, as this would closely associate the new Maharaja with leading elements of Baroda society and also produce a loyal elite capable of staffing Baroda's administration in the future. Rao, by contrast, thought the *Sardars*' sons "unfit companions" who would invariably press the Maharaja to revive their narrow privileges.[91] He went along with Meade, however, after being promised no child would be admitted without his express approval.

Thereupon followed the question as to the appropriate model for the school. Rajkumar College and Mayo College were deemed unsuitable. These schools were residential in nature because they were meant to educate the sons of minor chiefs who could not secure suitable facilities at home. This aspect of the Colleges had aroused immense anxiety amongst conservative elements in the Native States who worried that, away from their families, the princes would be deracinated and corrupted. They worried even more, as Jamna Bai certainly did, about being deprived of influence over the future ruler. At the same time, Meade and Rao, wanted Sayaji out of the Palace as much as possible, seeing as his only companions there were "females" and "menials", whose "private seductive influences" would "thwart" his "proper training".[92] Meade resolved the difficulty by drawing on his experience in Mysore, where he had been serving as Chief Commissioner before being temporarily assigned to Baroda. There he had been intimately involved in overseeing Chamarajendra's education under George Malleson at what would later come to be known as the Maharaja's College, a non-residential school near the Palace where the Wadiyar was joined daily in his studies by sons of nobles. Mysore being equal in rank and stature to Baroda, and the two Maharajas also being the same age, the Maharaja's College was accepted as a suitable model.

The second point on which Meade and Rao differed was about who should become tutor and governor. With his eye for talent, Rao zeroed in on Ambalal Desai, a prize-winning graduate from Elphinstone College who had served as Principal of Ahmadabad and Surat High Schools. But it was not to be. Influenced by Malleson and Macnaghten, who were deeply skeptical of the ability of native tutors to produce satisfactory results, Meade insisted that the Gaekwad's education be directed by an "European gentleman" who would not only educate but also be a "companion" to Sayaji such that "a feeling of personal attachment should spring up between them".[93] In a concession to Rao, Meade recommended that a "duly qualified native gentleman" serve as a deputy, with particular responsibility for overseeing Sayaji's life in the palace. This arrangement was opposed by Jamna Bai who saw it as a threat to her control over Sayaji. To her relief, Meade's strategy failed when Desai declined to serve in a subordinate position and was instead appointed by Rao to a judgeship.

Given the stakes, Meade was obliged to ask Northbrook to recommend a suitable tutor. This person, he wrote to the Viceroy in August 1875, would preferably be a young civil servant "whose erudition would qualify him for the scholastic duties of Principal of the school".[94] As Northbrook cast about for a suitable candidate there occurred one of those accidents that change the course of history. A fortnight after Meade's request, the Viceroy received a letter from Henry Butler, the renowned headmaster of his *alma mater*, Harrow, urging that his brother-in-law, Frederick Elliot, a Bombay officer, then temporarily serving as Director of Public Instruction in the Berars, be appointed to that position permanently. The following month Northbrook declined Butler's request on the grounds that Elliot was too junior for the position in the Berars. Upon learning of the disappointing outcome, Elliot's wife's brother-in-law, Herbert Birdwood, the respected district judge of Surat, proposed his name to Meade and Melvill, who promptly forwarded it to Northbrook. The Viceroy now connected the dots and sent the men Butler's note to review.

Elliot's pedigree was on the colorful side: he was the grandson of Hugh Elliot, the former Governor of Madras, infamous for eloping with his first wife and later dueling with her lover, and he was the son of Edward Elliot, the former Chief Magistrate of Madras whose adulterous relationship with, and subsequent marriage to Isabella Napier, Frederick's mother, had scandalized British India. But his credentials were more than suitable: he was a graduate of Harrow and Balliol and had performed well in the Berars. Then there was the promise of character: though "it is difficult to speak in praise of a near connection", Butler had written to Northbrook, "I cannot help saying that he is a man of extraordinary charm and beauty of character, and that he has the rare gift of elevating all who come in contact with him".[95] With the clock ticking, Meade and Melvill decided in October 1875 that Elliot was the "best man for the office" and within two months Elliot was in Baroda, having agreed to Melvill's stipulation that he stay in the post for six years and forego extended leaves until Sayaji reached 18.[96]

The setting and instructor having been chosen, the question of the curriculum remained. Here too Meade and Rao had very different ideas. Meade wanted Sayaji to obtain mastery over three languages of "practical use", namely, English, Marathi, and Gujarati, and be provided other elements "of a high-class education". What Meade, a rugged Bengal Army officer, well-known in Central India for capturing and hanging the famed Mutiny leader Tantia Tope in 1859, thought of these other elements was apparent. Sayaji's education, was "by no means to be confined to book-learning", but must include "athletic and military training, riding and games", which were, Meade stressed, "matters in which the head of the State should be expert".[97] The point was driven home by the site chosen for the Maharaja's School, a nineteen-acre lot affording ample space for a large playground and sporting activities including horse riding.

Rao did not show his hand until Meade had departed Baroda. The Dewan's first chance came in December 1875 when Elliot diplomatically asked Rao for "a few suggestions" about what Sayaji ought to be taught. Rao promptly responded with a "rough note" that was in fact quite detailed. The basics were easy to agree upon. Sayaji ought to be able to read and write Marathi "with ease and facility" and to follow basic arithmetic. Reading and writing in English was vital but being able to make polite conversation with correct pronunciation ought to be prioritized. But much more than this was desirable. An hour a day, Rao urged, ought to be set aside for Sayaji to be introduced to "useful information". For instance, he ought to read newspapers to keep abreast of important events, be shown maps and exposed to geography, and introduced to basic scientific instruments such as the telescope, microscope, compass, and thermometer. Of utmost importance was moral education, a subject to which Rao had paid much attention in Travancore. He strongly recommended that Sayaji read *Balmitra*, Sadasiv Chatre's Marathi translation of *The Children's Friend*, a popular nineteenth century text based on Arnaud Berquin's late eighteenth century *L'Ami des Enfans*. Above all, he insisted that Sayaji be "thoroughly taught" *Subodh Rajaniti*[*] (Essentials of Statecraft), which he described as a book that "explains well the duties of a modern ruler". Perhaps already discerning what would later become a much-discussed weakness in the Maharaja's character, Rao added in a postscript that it was important that Sayaji learn how to think clearly, especially to "weigh pros and cons" and to give "thorough and exclusive attention" to the subject before him.[98]

A little later Rao had a chance to indirectly express what he thought of Meade's curriculum. When Sayaji fell from his horse, Elliot proposed continuing with riding lessons, saying that he was sure Rao would agree that it was "absolutely necessary" that Sayaji "should learn to be a brave rider as befits a Mahratta Chief", a view supported by Sayaji's courtiers, who held that princes ought to practice "manly sports" in keeping with their "hereditary vocation".[99] To this, Rao politely replied that "while I am for useful accomplishments, I am not as much for hazardous ones" since it was "at least as important" that

---

* Narayana Bhikaji Nene, *Subodha Rajaniti: An Easy Code of Regal Jurisprudence, intended for the benefit of Royal youths and subjects*, Bombay: Induprakash Stream Press, 1872. This book is no longer in circulation. Elliot had not heard of it and had to request Rao for his copy.

the Maharaja "should be sound in limb as that he should be able to overleap hedges". It might "not matter much" to a private nobleman if he broke his arm, he observed, "whereas a ruler of a State disabled from writing would be a sad spectacle".[100]

With Melvill watching over his shoulder, Rao could only push so far though. Having earned at Haileybury a "boyish reputation for learning" after carrying off prizes "each term in Sanskrit and Persian", Melvill was sympathetic to the Dewan's point of view.[101] But he knew well that having approved Meade's educational scheme, Calcutta would not tolerate divergence. This was especially the case when Sayaji was so behind—when he started, he did not even know the four cardinal directions on the compass—that there was already too much to do and not enough time in which to do it. The Maharaja's proclivities further complicated matters: though he displayed "great industry", Sayaji preferred physical activity, especially wrestling and equestrian activities like tent-pegging and drills with English officers from the Bombay Army (the latter causing the Dewan such anxiety that Melvill and Elliot had to reassure him there was "no fear of a taste being given for military pursuits").[102] Distrustful of Jamna Bai and her intriguing relations, Melvill was only too happy to foster Sayaji's proclivities since "anything that gives an interest in life to a Native Prince outside the *zenana* is a benefit".[103] Consequently, the learned Dewan found his involvement limited to procuring items ranging from Arabian riding horses to boxing gloves, organizing the construction of tennis courts and shooting ranges, and recruiting instructors for billiards, gymnastics and fencing.

There were other distractions too. As Sayaji drifted away from her, Jamna Bai tried to limit his time with Elliot, her petty machinations leading to missed school days. Given Melvill's interest in languages and Rao's interest in science, classes in Hindustani as well as lectures on chemistry and electricity were introduced on the fly, further crowding the calendar. In the event, there was little chance to discuss public administration, save the odd instance such as when Rao sent Elliot a copy of the *Baroda Administration Report* for the Maharaja to "peruse".[104] Even slightly more ambitious plans, such as the Dewan's proposal that Sayaji visit the courts to understand judicial proceedings, were turned down by Melvill on the grounds that the Maharaja's general education ought not be interrupted prior to his turning eighteen.

Before long Rao was openly voicing concern that Sayaji was not being taught what was most important, namely, the principles and practices of good government. In November 1876 Rao had already sent Elliot a long note on the subject, warning that Sayaji's "future depends on this, than on anything else". "The ignorant and uneducated ruler is bad enough", he pointedly observed, but "he is worse by far, who is half-educated, has an overweening confidence in his wisdom, undertakes the onerous and delicate functions of administration himself personally, and pursues a headlong course despising aid and counsel". This was as accurate a description of Holkar as there might be, but Rao diplomatically avoided naming his former employer, saying only that he knew "from considerable personal experience that many Native Rulers are wanting in those respects and hence do themselves and their subjects not a little injury".

Rao's note went on to expand on the points he had pressed on Elliot in December 1875. The "chief objects to be aimed at in training a Native Ruler", he declared, were three-fold. In the first instance, the ruler should "realize the object of good government" and learn to "subordinate his wishes" to that object. Further, to attain the desired object, the Maharaja had to understand "the advantages of division of labor" and not attempt to perform "his high duties personally". Finally, since he would need the help of others, it was essential that he "know how to avail himself of proper agents", which in turn required knowing "the way to detect and despise" those of "selfish and sordid motives". Perhaps these "hasty" bits of advice had "little novelty in them", Rao said a little too humbly, but "reflection and experience" showed how important it was that Sayaji absorb them.[105]

Elliot more or less did the opposite of what Rao advised. Knowing that Calcutta would measure him by Meade's brief, he continued to focus on Sayaji's general education, and his literacy in particular. It also gradually became clear that Elliot disagreed with Rao philosophically, viewing the Dewan's notions of public administration as an alien imposition that would reduce the Maharaja to a ceremonial figurehead. His preference, in contrast, was to see the Gaekwad "strengthen his government".[106] As a consequence, Sayaji came increasingly under the sway of two—from Rao's perspective, disastrous—ideals. From traditionalists in the Palace came the suggestion, urged on by the meddlesome Holkar, that Sayaji ought to govern vigorously; from proto-nationalists in Poona came the idea that Baroda ought to manfully resist British paramountcy.

In August 1880, seven months before Sayaji was to come of age, Rao mounted a rearguard action. "I have a strong conviction", he wrote to Melvill, of the "necessity" of "a special education" covering "primary principles" that ought to be "carefully and earnestly" impressed "on the mind of the young Maharaja". Appending a list of some 65 principles, Rao calculated it would take about two days to "explain and instill" each, assuming Sayaji would spend two hours daily on the material. Combined with practical training "in the various details of departmental work", it was reasonable to estimate that the special education would take about one year. Cognizant that this meant Sayaji would continue to be under instruction even after reaching his majority, Rao reminded Melvill that "many a Native Prince" had, though "generally educated", more or less "failed to prove himself a good ruler". Rao added a heavy hint about who ought to instruct Sayaji. "It is only in Travancore that those fundamental principles have been planted and have taken root, and hence Travancore stands foremost among well-governed Native States", he noted, adding "I hope Baroda will follow the useful example".[107]

Having recently felt compelled to warn Sayaji "against the intrigues of unprincipled men in Baroda", an increasingly anxious Melvill now gave way.[108] At Melvill's request Rao converted his proposal into a memorandum (reprinted in Appendix II) that could be shared with Calcutta. Seeking to convey the gravity of the situation, Rao warned the Foreign Department that "some of the most illiterate and ignorant persons here cherish the wish and expectation of succeeding to the most important offices in the State when the Maharaja will have attained his age, and assumed the reins of government". This prospect would not be troubling in "civilized countries" where rulers were "restrained from incurring errors or perils, by some sort of checks". The "Native Prince", however, exercised "personal rule", which meant that the "character and complexion" of public administration depended entirely on "the personal intelligence of the prince". Though Sayaji had received a "general education", Rao underlined, the Maharaja had not been "specially instructed in his duties and responsibilities as a ruler". The "evils" of the past, in particular, had not been "made apparent to him"—for instance, the need to "guard against the too common system of having favorites", to avoid "the advice of irresponsible hangers-on", and to remember that "every post requires its own special qualifications". Given this defect, Rao concluded, the "only satisfactory and effective security for the reservation and promotion of good government in these territories hereafter is the proper education of His Highness". Specifically, it was essential to imprint on the Maharaja's mind the "large and enlightened principles" that "constitute the safeguards of public welfare". These principles ought to be condensed into a "series of notes" on which the Maharaja subsequently ought to be "interrogated", with a view to making sure "of his thorough comprehension and recognition of the same".[109]

The following month Melvill forwarded Rao's memorandum to the Foreign Secretary—with a significant amendment. Whereas Rao had sought to defer Sayaji's assumption of power by only a few months, Melvill recommended that the Gaekwad not be invested with power until he turned 21. This was because he felt that Sayaji needed time, sheltered from the intriguers that were waiting for him to assume office, to comprehend the "practical application" of the theoretical principles that would be imparted to him. To wit, Melvill appended a list of the experiences and skills, ranging from visiting jails to understanding accounting methods, that Sayaji ought to have or cultivate. Keen to limit Elliot's increasingly doubtful influence over his ward, Melvill underscored the Dewan's peculiar competence in undertaking the proposed scheme of instruction, saying "it would probably be found impossible to find in the whole of India a more thoroughly competent person than the present Minister of the Baroda State for inculcating right principles" in the Gaekwad.[110]

Unfortunately for Melvill and Rao, the Foreign Department that had appointed them to their positions in Baroda had since undergone a change in personnel—Lytton having filled senior posts with officers who shared his dim view of the effects of English education. The gauntlet included Lyall, who was appointed Foreign Secretary in April 1878, Henry Durand, who became Under Secretary in March 1880, and Joseph Ridgeway, who was promoted to Assistant

Secretary in November 1880. Melvill gambled that Ripon, a prominent liberal, who had replaced Lytton in June 1880, would be sympathetic to the view that the Government of India was obliged to secure good government in the Native States. But to reach Ripon, the memorandum had to pass through the Foreign Department, which promptly ripped it to shreds.

Ridgeway, a military officer recently back from the Afghan front line, went first. No one, he commented in November 1880, could peruse the "unnecessarily prolix" memoranda without feeling "compassion for the young Prince who is to be subjected to this terrible educational ordeal", which threatened to cram him with "dreary truisms" and not leave him "any time for manly exercises". A month later Durand, who loathed educated natives, and despised Rao in particular for taking up Holkar's appeals against the Foreign Department, weighed in. "It seems to me", he cuttingly observed, "that you might as well expect to teach a man swimming on dry land as expect to turn out a ready-made ruler in the way proposed". Far better, he argued, to entrust the Gaekwad "with some share of power and responsibility as soon as possible after attaining the age of eighteen". No doubt, Durand added, Rao "will prophesy innumerable evils if his own almost despotic rule is brought to an end" but "the transfer of power to somewhat less enlightened and talented persons may not be found an unmixed evil, even if the Administration Reports become a few hundred pages shorter, and we are deprived of the lectures upon international law which the Minister is wont to favor us".

When his turn came Lyall too complained about Rao having "inflicted upon us a somewhat tedious exposition of the general duties of a model prince, considered in the abstract". Still, he preferred not to interfere. He had a different concern: since Mysore's Chamarajendra was to be elevated to the throne when he turned 18 in March 1881, Calcutta would be compelled to "explain and defend the inconsistency" in prolonging Sayaji's minority to 21. In February 1881 the matter was put before the Viceregal Council, which concurred with Lyall on the need for consistency. As a result, Melvill was informed that while there was "no objection" to the proposed scheme of "special education", in Calcutta's view the "best method" to "qualify the Gaekwar for his future important duties" was to "place him as soon as possible in the actual exercise of responsible authority", subject to constitutional provisions that Rao was asked to draft simultaneously.[111]

Melvill responded to the outcome stoically. As Sayaji would ascend to the throne sooner than Melvill had hoped the practical component of the scheme, such as visits to public offices and law courts, was shelved. Instead, the Dewan and his team—Kazi Shahabuddin, the *Sar Subah* (Revenue Commissioner), Anna Tahmane, the Accountant General, Rustomji Cursetji and Janardhan Gadgil, the Chief Justice and Second Judge of the *Varisht* Court, Vinayak Kirtane, the *Naib* (Deputy) Dewan, and Pestanji Jehangir, the Settlement Officer—hurriedly set about preparing lectures on their respective areas of expertise.

The lectures began at the end of April 1881. Over the next nine months Sayaji received three lectures a week. The lectures were on alternating days so that Sayaji could review his notes in the intervals. The lecturers would then put questions to him to make sure he had "learnt the matter well".[112] Typically, of the three weekly lectures, two were by the department heads and one by the Dewan (usually on Wednesdays). Shahabuddin and Tahmane delivered 27 lectures on revenue and accounting, Cursetji and Gadgil delivered 25 lectures on law, Kirtane delivered 6 lectures on the police, and Jehangir delivered 9 lectures on land tenures and the military. Even a hostile observer like Elliot was impressed by the "immense amount of care" the officers devoted to the lectures in spite of their heavy workloads. Taken together, he wrote to Melvill, their lectures formed "a remarkable work, fit for the earnest study not only of the Gaekwar but of any Native Prince who may wish to fit himself in his youth for the due discharge of high duties".[113]

Grateful for the opportunity to say his piece, Rao shared some of his lecture manuscripts (or memos, as he termed them) with Melvill, assuring him that they were not simply read aloud but that he entered "into explanations, illustrations, and so on, so as to impress in detail what is noted in substance". Aside from the "regular lectures" on public administration, he added, he also gave the Maharaja lectures under the heading of "Minor Hints", which allowed him to place "before His Highness a lot of miscellaneous and personal matters which may be of no insignificant practical value to a young ruler".[114]

Melvill responded warmly to the samples, telling the Dewan that he would like to see all his memos "for they are very interesting".[115] Pleased, Rao thereafter sent Melvill every memo shortly after lecturing the Gaekwad on it. "I feel much encouraged by the favorable opinion you have generally expressed regarding these papers", he wrote back to Melvill, quietly adding, "I am taking some pains in the preparation of these papers in the hope and belief that they will have a beneficial influence on the future of Baroda State".[116]

Melvill tried to make Calcutta comprehend the significance of the lectures. He pressed the memos on Lyall when the outgoing Foreign Secretary visited Baroda in July 1881. When Lyall, notorious for his disinterest in official business, did no more than "take a mere glance at them", Melvill tried Lyall's replacement, Charles Grant. Unbeknownst to the Dewan, in September 1881 Melvill sent copies of two memos ('Subscriptions' and the first part of 'Relations with British Government') to Grant, telling the new Foreign Secretary that "these lectures of Sir Madava Rao are, in my opinion, very remarkable for the ability and insight into affairs which they display". Having gotten wind of the Foreign Department's concern that lectures might be "tedious", Melvill assured Grant that the lectures were "amply illustrated and enforced at the time of delivery from the stores of the Minister's fertile brain". As Melvill had requested, Grant forwarded the memos and Melvill's letter to Ripon, but not before Durand's protégé, the Under Secretary, Thomas Hope, was given the chance to add the covering remark that "fertile as is Sir Madava Rao's brain, he has a good deal of the snake in him" because the Dewan's "tone in lecturing the young Gaekwar is remarkably different from that in which he used to complain of the injustice of the British Government in appeals on behalf of Maharaja Holkar when he was Minister in Indore".[117] The implication was that Rao was using British India as a bogey to frighten the young Maharaja into submitting to his advice.

Constrained by his position Melvill could say no more. He knew that the Foreign Department viewed him as overly sympathetic to Rao, and when Ripon replied with nothing more than a curt acknowledgement, Melvill gave up. Ironically, it was left to Elliot—in a sense the cause of the lectures—to pen the official account. Tasked with preparing a closing report on the Maharaja's education,

Elliot recounted the Dewan's lectures with words too poignant to be mere affectation:

> It is not in my power to describe the manner in which these lectures were delivered. They themselves are excellent, as may be seen, but their delivery by the lecturer added a charm which no reprint of them can convey. Written at spare moments or during the quiet hours of the evening of a long day, the M.S.S. bore evidence of the care with which they were produced. The firm, delicate, clear running hand on the page was seldom defaced by an erasure betraying a second thought. Every sentence came out smooth and polished, and it was only subsequent reflection that enabled the listener to realize how logical was the sequence of thoughts, how full and varied was the treatment of the subject. I have, turn by turn, marveled at the exuberance of the ideas, the restraint of the method, the invariable sufficiency of the style. But the M.S.S., the writings themselves, cannot convey an impression of what a lecture by the Minister meant. Illustrations drawn from books which had perhaps not been read for twenty years, anecdotes, the results of the varied experience of a long life spent in Native Courts, the humorous laugh, the entrain of the whole man, the mingled wit and wisdom called out by the quick turn of thought, these were the riches prodigally set forth for a moment's enjoyment or instruction, which made of the lectures something to be prized and remembered for a life time.[118]

What Does Hints *Teach?*

Having comprehended the context in which *Hints on the Art and Science of Government* was framed, we are now in a position to examine what it conveys.

In keeping with the chronology of the lectures as delivered, let us begin with the discussion on public administration, which occupies Chapters 1–15. This section opens with an elucidation of fundamental principles, the foremost being that the ruler must promote the happiness of the people, regardless of class or creed. Before we study this "grand principle" and its derivates, it may be useful to highlight what *Hints* does *not* discuss.

Hints does not enquire into the origin of political power. In this respect, it is quite unlike Niccolò Machiavelli's *Prince*, which teaches how to secure and maintain power. This silence may disappoint those interested in the naughtier side of political life, but it is in keeping with the *raj dharma* tradition, which simply addresses itself to whoever is in power. Nor does *Hints* discuss the merits of the various possible forms of government. It simply assumes, as the *raj dharma* tradition does, that the sovereign will be a Maharaja, as had been the case for millennia. This distinguishes it from landmark texts in the modern West, such as John Locke's *Treatise on Government*, Jean Jacques Rousseau's *Social Contract*, and John Stuart Mill's *Considerations on Representative Government*, where the question of *who* ought to be sovereign is central, the objective being to justify popular sovereignty.

Hints is interested, almost exclusively then, in how power ought to be *exercised*. This is because, in line with the *raj dharma* tradition, it sees a regime's legitimacy and longevity as contingent upon *performance*, specifically the advancement of happiness. A ruler must make his subjects happy, says Rao, because on it depends his "safety, comfort, honour and prosperity". That people should and do value happiness is established by reference to empirics rather than abstract ideals or dense metaphysics. As Rao sees it, "history", that "great magazine of experience", reveals that those governments that promoted the happiness of the people "lived longest". By contrast, rulers that have neglected the happiness of their subjects, he contends, have invariably invited rebellion or invasion.

Having demarcated the terrain, a few observations may now be made about the fundamental principles outlined in Chapters 1–9. Consider three points.

Hints' normative claims are not bound by culture. It firmly declares that the duties it identifies and elaborates are "the very foundation of all good government", including that of England, whose "health and strength and durability" can be traced to its political institutions, which ensure that these duties will "never be neglected or set aside". This universalism leads *Hints* to break from the *raj dharma* tradition with respect to equality of persons. It departs, for instance, from the *Manu Smriti*, the ancient Hindu legal code, which demands that the ruler uphold the caste system, with its grossly differentiated rights and duties. It departs also from the *Ajnapatra*, the eighteenth-century Maratha text on the statecraft employed by Chhatrapati Shivaji, the revered founder of the

Maratha Empire, which had appeared in print in two parts in 1875 and 1876. Unlike the *Ajnapatra*, which urges the ruler to acquire "the favor of saintly persons", particularly via "special grants", *Hints* unambiguously instructs the Maharaja to treat "all his people impartially".[119] Specifically, the Maharaja is warned that justice and propriety as well as expediency demand that "some classes and creeds should not be made to suffer in order to show more favour to other classes and creeds".

The conception of happiness that *Hints* advances is entirely material. It rejects the notion that the State should cultivate morality (the *Ajnapatra*, by contrast, advises the ruler to firmly punish "heretic opinions").[120] To the extent that moral attainments are necessary for happiness, Rao counsels, these should be left to private initiative rather than public measures (except with respect to "general and universal morality", for example, the importance of honesty, which ought to be taught in public schools and bolstered by the Maharaja's own example). This distinction allows public policy to focus on relatively uncontroversial objectives. The *Sarkar*'s (government's) duty is to provide public goods and social services, principally an efficient police and military, a professional judicial system, public health and food security, and infrastructure and public education. Since these objects are easier to promise than to deliver, the bulk of the discussion in Chapters 2–9 concerns the principles (science) and practices (art) that must be mastered to secure them. A ruler who ignores these lessons, Rao warns, will be "just like a navigator in charge of a big ship who refuses the guidance of the compass and of the chart".

The ensuing focus on public administration may make *Hints* seem little more than a manual on how to apply liberal principles imported from Britain. Recall, however, that nineteenth-century Britons doubted that liberal values could take hold in their "backward" or "uncivilized" colonies. In India, these views were mirrored by Anglo-Indian conservatives who argued that traditional forms and modes of rule were better "fitted" to "the natives". *Hints* challenges both these narratives. It shows that liberal constitutionalism was not championed only by "benevolent" Britons or by articulate but powerless Indians in British India. On the contrary, liberal constitutionalism was also developed and defended by Indians in "Indian India", often in the face of opposition from Indian and Anglo-Indian conservatives alike. *Hints* therefore underscores that when we try to trace the story of how liberalism emerged and spread globally, we should resist the temptation to center the narrative on all-too-familiar metropolitan locations: Calcutta, Bombay, Madras, and Delhi. We ought to also appreciate those who, operating outside British India, championed and sometimes successfully enacted liberal ideals and constitutional practices long before their more "sophisticated" rulers and compatriots.[121]

Chapters 10–15 outline the norms that the Maharaja's administration ought to abide by. These lectures merit three observations.

Hints does not expect the ruler to be selfless or ascetic. This constitutes an important departure from the *raj dharma* tradition where the *Manu Smriti*, for instance, instructs the ruler to "apply himself to the conquest of his organs" because only "one whose organs are conquered is able to bring the people under control".[122] The *Ajnapatra*, similarly, warns the ruler to maintain "discipline" and forego "intoxication" and "entertainment".[123] By contrast, Rao concedes that a ruler will invariably seek "personal gratification", and therefore focuses instead on minimizing the conflict between the Maharaja's private interests and his public duties, instructing him in Chapter 10 to appropriate only a "fair portion"—preferably no more than ten per cent—of public revenues toward his private purse.

Having accepted that a Maharaja will have a sizeable appetite, *Hints* declines to rely on his self-control. Instead, Rao recommends that the ruler bind himself in a variety of ways. For instance, he counsels the ruler to publicly disclaim any role in judicial proceedings and to explicitly disallow public resources such as policemen from being utilized for private purposes. He especially stresses the need to subject finances to formal rules (e.g., the ruler should not guarantee private debts or accept gifts from individuals) and settled procedures (e.g., the ruler should regularize salaries, utilize written orders, routinize audits, and strictly cap budgets).

The most important piece of advice in this section concerns the *Huzur Cutcherry* (administration). The "essential condition of successful administration", Rao stresses in Chapter 13, is to make the *Huzur Cutcherry* "as strong as possible intellectually and morally". Though a ruler may be tempted to lead from the front, he must understand,

Rao warns, that given the need for experience and expertise, the "only way" a Maharaja can fulfil his "heavy responsibility" for good government, "is to have the best ministers for the conduct of the administration". Though this aspect of Rao's political philosophy was sometimes depicted by critics as self-serving and alien to local traditions, it was in fact in line with the *raj dharma* tradition, as exemplified by the *Ajnapatra*, which devotes the greatest part of its energies to praising ministers as "the pillars of the house whose name is kingdom".[124] Where Rao diverges from the *raj dharma* tradition is on the question of "organization and discipline" within the administration. Unlike the *Ajnapatra*, which advises the Maharaja to use advisors or spies to keep tabs on his ministers, *Hints* stresses that the *Huzur Cutcherry* ought to be judged by the fruits of its labors. With the example of an orderly British Indian civil service before him, Rao stresses that the *Huzur Cutcherry* cannot perform without the Maharaja's "confidence and support", as the Dewan needs this backing to maintain clear lines of responsibility, failing which "there is sure to be confusion".

The discussion in Chapters 14–15 on public servants is masterful. It bears witness to a life time spent handling people as well as matters. What is especially noteworthy about this discussion is its pragmatism, borne out nowhere more clearly than on the subject of salaries. The only way for a ruler to live up to his duties, *Hints* warns, is to have in his service educated, competent and upright officers. Since such individuals will always be hard to come by, a ruler must be prepared to attract and retain them by offering them "good and liberal salaries". As Rao puts it: "If we want a specially good article—not any article—we have to pay much higher for it".

Foreign relations are the subject of Chapters 16–21. These lectures merit three observations as well.

One striking feature of this discussion is its relative brevity. It is quite unlike the famously detailed and lengthy discussions in the *Manu Smriti* and the *Nitisara* as well as the *Ajnapatra* (Kautilya's *Arthashastra* had yet to be recovered at this time). There is a simple explanation for this divergence. Rao's lectures were delivered in full view of British India, which completely dominated the external relations of Native States. Native States were not permitted to communicate with each other, much less with foreign powers, unless through Residents. The Maharaja could not even travel without the Viceroy's permission. British India's military hegemony was even more fiercely guarded. Native States were encouraged to have their militaries headed by Britons and had to seek approval before reforming or altering their forces. The Government of India's permission was essential if a Native State wished to purchase weaponry, and such permission was only granted for weapons purchased from Britain and of an older vintage. Under such circumstances, it was neither advisable nor very meaningful for Rao to hold forth on foreign relations. It would certainly have brought the lecture series to a grinding halt.

Another striking feature of this discussion is its emphasis on conciliation and its adoption of a submissive tone. For instance, the ruler is instructed in Chapter 16 to refrain from accumulating "needless troops" and "needless arms" and not to show "the remotest disposition to combine with" Britain's enemies. These seemingly unmanly declarations may raise hackles today, as they did at the time, where contemporaries had before them the *Ajnapatra*'s frank advice that "the essence of the whole kingdom is forts".[125] But *Hints* is not the work of an effete individual. As Rao saw it, the terrible asymmetry between the Native States and British India rendered the latter "physically irresistible"—this was a "fact which daily stares us in the face", he quietly notes in Chapter 17. In the event, confrontation would not have been manly but rather imprudent, indeed reckless.* Hence, Rao restricted the discussion to what the ruler ought to do *under the circumstances*.

This brings us to a less obvious aspect of the discussion, *viz.*, the absence of any reference to British India's pressing strategic concerns: the so-called Eastern Question (which was about who would take over the declining Ottoman Empire's territories) and the Great Game

* Compare with Niccolò Machiavelli, *Discourses on The First Decade of Titus Livius*, trans. Ninian Hill Thomson, London: Kegan Paul, Trench & Co, 1883, II:26: "For abuse and menace take nothing from the strength of an adversary; the latter only making him more cautious, while the former inflames his hatred against you, and leads him to consider more diligently how he may cause you hurt".

(which was about countering Russia's steady expansion into Central Asia). British India's anxieties on these fronts were heightened by intelligence reports that the Ottomans and the Russians were seeking the support of Indian Muslims and Native States respectively. The latter threat in particular prompted the Government of India to behave in a more conciliatory fashion toward the Native States, especially after the Second Afghan War revealed how constrained British India was with respect to finances and troops. The more nervous the Government of India became about Russia's advances, the more important it became for the Native States to maintain a diplomatic silence on the topic.

Let us finally consider the fascinating and varied lectures on personal conduct, which span Chapters 23–46. These lectures can be divided into two types: those that deal with public protocol and those that address personal disposition.

The lectures on public protocol explain why the manner in which the Maharaja interacts with subjects, servants, and visitors has grave implications for the dignity of his office. For example, *Hints* advises the ruler to avoid familiarity with "menials", to refrain from corresponding with "tradesmen", to decline visits from "strangers", and to disallow *vakils* (pleaders) from soliciting his intervention in cases. Because such interactions foster excessive "familiarity", they serve to undermine the Maharaja's "exalted" position. This advice shows that Rao comprehended the value of the European tradition of *arcana imperii* (mysteries of rule), which teaches rulers that mystique is desirable because it generates awe. No less importantly, *Hints* also shows how unguarded private access to the ruler undermines settled routines and procedures. For instance, allowing palace servants to informally transmit petitions to the Maharaja, Rao warns, encourages corruption and also makes it harder for his ministers to efficiently carry out their duties.

The lengthy discussion on "intriguers" in Chapter 24 is one of the most important lectures in the series. "All palaces", says Rao, "are more or less, infested by intriguers". The question is whether Maharajas can avoid "falling into their snares". To wit, *Hints* offers a detailed side-by-side comparison of the qualities that distinguish an intriguer from a "real well-wisher". Though the entire list is marvelous, especially striking is Rao's observation that a well-wisher speaks "more against measures than men" whereas an intriguer usually does the opposite. To ascertain whether a given individual is an intriguer or a well-wisher requires great labor, he concedes, but "repeated practice" of the "sifting process" will, he promises, eventually enable a Maharaja "to judge almost with the rapidity of natural instinct".

In reading Rao's advice on personal conduct it is important to bear in mind that the lecture notes he shared with Sayaji exclude the examples and anecdotes that he chose, for obvious diplomatic reasons, to discuss in person only. Having previously examined the fraught context in which Rao was operating, we are now better placed to make sense of some of his very abbreviated remarks. Thus, for instance, the observation that "an intriguer is base metal only coated with gold" whereas "a real well-wisher is a solid mass of gold" may appear a "dreary truism" (as Ridgeway in the Foreign Department put it) until we recall that the chapter on "Menials and Intriguers" was written when Rao was battling the Maratha radicals behind *The Groans of Baroda*, whose seductive vision of Baroda leading the charge against British India he considered implausible and dangerous.[126] Hence his elliptical warning to Sayaji that—to use another truism—all that glitters is not gold.

The lectures on personal disposition are notable for treating the Maharaja as prone to ordinary human errors and weaknesses; they eschew the "criminal flattery" that typically led Maharajas to consider themselves infallible. As with the discussion on protocol, Rao is ever at pains to show how far the Maharaja's ostensibly private behavior will affect public administration. Thus, for example, *Hints* advises the Maharaja not to "overburden himself with work" so as to preserve his capacity to work in the long run, to "avoid worry" by refusing to entertain favor seekers, and to "refrain from speaking or acting" when possessed by anger lest he needlessly make enemies among those in his immediate vicinity. Of particular significance under this heading is the advice in Chapter 45 that the Maharaja should engage in private study for a few hours every day so as to remain "conversant with the thoughts of the most enlightened of mankind" and thereby escape the "narrow and fossilized" company ordinarily found in the palace. The contrast with Machiavelli's *Prince* is telling: the Maharaja is advised to study not the classics of war and the lives of those who beat a path to empire, but Parliamentary Blue Books and William Gladstone's speeches.[127]

These lectures contain two pieces of advice that may seem insincere or naïve. The first concerns fame, which Chapter 31 readily accepts as "a legitimate and laudable object of a ruler's ambition". Unlike Machiavelli's *Prince*, which advises the ruler to undertake spectacular projects with a view to enrapture the public, *Hints* advises the Maharaja to earn fame by doing good "steadily, constantly and unostentatiously". This advice may appear sanctimonious, but it is in fact prudential. Rao lived in an era when newspapers seemed an unrelenting force, so much so that even the Government of India, with all the weapons at its disposal, including the recently passed Vernacular Press Act and a secret fund to bribe the Anglo-Indian press, could not tamp down criticism. This being the case, Rao felt, not unreasonably, that there could be "no shortcut" to lasting fame. A ruler who was "impatient to get fame" could employ "mercenary advocates" to engage in "puffing", but a "discerning public" would soon expose "false or exaggerated claims".

It should also be borne in mind that *Hints* addresses a ruler whose authority is unchallenged. This is quite unlike Machiavelli's "new prince" who must rally the people against real or imagined enemies in order to cement his uncertain authority and bolster his doubtful legitimacy.[128] Since Rao is addressing a ruler whose right to power is not in doubt, and whose objective is to improve subjects' lives, it is not surprising that he thinks that a ruler would do poorly to "inconsiderately meddle with many resettled things" merely for "the sake of notoriety".

The other piece of advice that may seem questionable is *Hints*' unambiguous declaration in Chapter 40 that "good faith is absolutely necessary in the conduct of public affairs". This recommendation appears directly opposed to that famously offered in Machiavelli's *Prince*.[129] Bear in mind, however, that *Hints* is silent, perhaps deliberately so, on the precise question that the *Prince* addresses, namely, is a ruler obliged to keep faith with those who might harm him? *Hints* addresses a different question, which is—should a Maharaja behave faithfully *in general*? Rao answers this question in the same way that Montesquieu does in *The Spirit of the Laws*—by underscoring how important credibility is to the modern economy.[130] The difficulty that a Native State would face in raising a public loan reveals, he cautions, that "security and confidence, and public progress and prosperity require that the Maharaja should scrupulously fulfil the promises he may make".

A closing thought in relation to the lectures on personal conduct: Rao is at pains to note that *Hints* can do little on its own to make a ruler behave appropriately. This is because virtuous conduct ultimately depends on habit. The parallel with Aristotle is striking. In the *Nicomachean Ethics*, Aristotle describes *phronesis* (or prudence) as the ability to discern *and* do what is right. The closing illustration Rao gives in Chapter 46 would not at all be out of place in the *Ethics*:

> His Highness knows well how to write with his right hand. So far as the theory of writing is concerned, the left hand is quite equal to the right hand. And yet, let His Highness try to write with his left hand and he will see that he can do it very imperfectly or perhaps not at all. Why? The theory is all right with respect to both hands, but the right hand has had the benefit of practice, which the left hand has not had. Mark the immense difference thus observable as arising from want of practice, and let it restrain overconfidence resulting from theoretical knowledge alone.

Let us close this overview of *Hints* by highlighting three distinctive features of the statecraft it commends.

One laudable feature is its commitment to moderation. Rao urges rulers to "avoid extremes" and to understand that "there is nothing disgraceful or derogatory in exercising a judicious spirit of compromise". The declaration that "statesmanship is a series of compromises" is especially memorable. Importantly, Rao's advice is not only about give and take in the sense of striking bargains. *Hints* invites circumspection with respect to moral claims and personal conduct as well, for instance, warning the ruler to refrain from interfering with religion and to employ temperate language when censuring officials. The advice, then, is to adopt a "mild and considerate" approach *in toto*.

Another distinctive feature is the conscious effort to combine ancient Indian and modern European principles of statecraft. From the *raj dharma* tradition comes a definitive account of the purpose of government, which is to ensure "security of the life, liberty, person and property of the people". From modern Europe comes an appreciation of institutions, as summarized by the lengthy quotation from

François Fénelon's *The Adventures of Telemachus*. Thus we find the Maharaja with his *Khangi* and *Cutcherry* being advised to adopt modern systems of budgeting and taxation, contracting and auditing, education and medicine, and tribunals and policing. This outcome—the marriage of the time-tested with the modern—was very much Rao's signature. A parallel can be witnessed in the famed palace—Laxmi Vilas—that Rao constructed for Sayaji. The palaces that Sayaji inherited were notorious for being cramped and lacking in light and ventilation. To symbolize the change that Sayaji represented, Rao commissioned a design that embodied "harmonious combinations" of "indigenous elements" fitted for "modern purposes". Thus, on the outside, Laxmi Vilas looks like palaces in other wealthy Native States, but on the inside, it is unusually airy and well-lit, permitting the inhabitants ease and health as well as suitably grand spaces to host dinners and give speeches in the English way. Like Laxmi Vilas, *Hints* signifies how "sincere sympathy" for an "ancient civilization" can be unified with "a mind liberalized by study".[131]

Finally, note *Hints*' ambiguity about what produces enlightened rule. At times it seems that knowledge is sufficient, as when Rao assures Sayaji in Chapter 22 that the "principles with which Your Highness has become acquainted will largely enable you to discharge these responsibilities satisfactorily". Yet a few lines later Rao concedes that even an educated ruler will need to be shepherded, telling Sayaji that maintaining high ideals "requires that you surround yourself with advisers who have such an ideal of duty". And at yet other moments Rao falls back on the age-old tactic of frightening the ruler into behaving well. Given the ability of the "enlightened public" to call upon British India for help, he warns the Gaekwad in Chapter 20, the "soundest way for the Maharaja to avoid or to minimize the interference of the British Government" is to "govern his country in the best manner possible". Rao's statements are not conflicting—knowledge, good counsel, and fear may all be necessary to produce enlightened rule. Even so, they indicate that knowledge and counsel alone may not always convince rulers to display "great self-denial". Indeed, it is worth pondering whether a person with Rao's views would have been allowed to lecture the Gaekwad were Baroda not subject to British India's stern gaze.

Did Hints *Have the Desired Effect?*

In his report on Sayaji's "special education" Elliot declared the lecture series a resounding success, writing:

> His Highness devoted to these lectures all the powers of mind he possessed. It is not exaggeration to say that he left no point in them unnoticed, and that, as far as in him lay, he tasked his memory to retain the information they conveyed. That they have borne fruit and will bear fruit is undoubted.[132]

Rao made a similar claim in the 1881 *Baroda Administration Report*, writing there that the Maharaja gave the lectures "his most earnest and sustained attention" and that he "studied the notes again in a thorough manner". As a result, Rao promised, the Maharaja had become "very fairly conversant with the great principles and the general practice of good government", which meant there was "every reasonable prospect of his striving to promote the welfare of his subjects and to respect their rights and liberties".[133]

The reality was more complicated. Following Sayaji's investiture, Melvill retired from the Indian Civil Service. His closing letter to Ripon outlined the challenge ahead: surrounded "by an excellent body of advisors", there was "every reason to hope" that Sayaji's reign would prove successful—if only he would "trust them".[134] Elliot, he stressed, ought not to be allowed to stay on in Baroda, as this "would be opposed to the best interests of the Baroda State".[135] The Foreign Department had other ideas, however. Hoping to win over the Gaekwad, it agreed to Sayaji's fervent pleas to extend Elliot's stay in Baroda. Predictably, within weeks the vernacular press began reporting "serious differences" between the Maharaja and his Dewan and speculating on "probable successors" including Elliot.[136] Soon it was all over. After "eight months of constant mortification"—his advice disregarded, his opinions not consulted, and orders given over his head—Rao quit Baroda in September 1882.[137]

Barely had the dust settled than the Gaekwad was in Calcutta seeking Ripon's approval for a restructuring of the administration. The Foreign Department could not stomach the inexperienced Elliot being appointed Dewan, but it did agree to his becoming Superintendent of Revenue and Settlement—a powerful new position that made him a rival power center to Rao's former deputy, Shahabuddin who limped on as Dewan for three years before also retiring in exasperation. Meanwhile, Vasudev Samarth, Vasudev Athalye, and Wasudeo Bapat, the prime movers behind *The Groans of Baroda*, the anonymous pamphlet attacking Madhava Rao, were appointed to high positions. This coup, advertised locally as the revival of Maratha rule, indicated what was to come. Sayaji would govern not cautiously and constitutionally, as Rao had counseled, but in the old way—boldly from the front and surrounded by loyalists. Of the ill-effects that followed, two stand out: a provocative foreign policy that nearly led to Sayaji's deposition, and the continued personalization of rule, which gravely damaged the Gaekwads' legitimacy. Let us consider these developments in turn.

Sayaji had reasonable demands of British India. He wanted Calcutta to refrain from interfering while he resumed the rent-free lands hitherto enjoyed by his *Sardars*, to quit guaranteeing the independence of his tributaries, and to stop imposing policies that damaged Baroda's economy and restricted its military capabilities. Rao, a lifelong champion of Native States, had wanted nothing less. The issue was *how* to attain the desired outcome. The firebrands gathered around Sayaji viewed Rao's methods as typical of an unmanly, overeducated office worker beholden to the British. Rao's lectures had sought to show the Gaekwad that British India's overwhelming power made compromise and tact necessary. When Sayaji nonetheless chose confrontation the outcome that Rao had predicted followed.

The downward drift in relations with British India started almost immediately as Sayaji attempted to revise agreements that Rao had been compelled to sign, particularly with respect to the Baroda Contingent. Though he was eventually allowed to retain the Contingent, Sayaji was not allowed to modernize or expand it. Frustrated, he subsequently refused to contribute to the Imperial Service (troops raised from the Native States in order to counter British India's vulnerability to a Russian or Afghan invasion) unless he was allowed to reform the Contingent. Calcutta predictably interpreted this move as extortion to which they could not submit without inviting other Native States to try their luck as well. It was not long then before Durand, who had looked forward to Rao's dismissal, was cursing Baroda as "one of the least trustworthy of our Native States" due to the Gaekwad being "ambitious" and surrounded by "bad advisors".[138]

This breach, which deepened when the Gaekwad donated money to the Congress and to Dadabhai Naoroji's electoral campaign in London, was laid bare in 1895 in a scathing memorandum by the bad-tempered Resident, John Biddulph. Having been taught by Elliot to believe that Baroda was "politically equal" to British India, Biddulph wrote, Sayaji suffered from "a feeling of perpetual grievance". These "wrong notions" had been compounded by the "most powerful party in the State", namely, Maratha Brahmins, who enjoyed Elliot's "special protection and patronage". There is a "constant danger", he warned, "that they may push the Gaekwar on to some serious act". What this might involve, Biddulph darkly added, could be inferred from the fact that when given Machiavelli's *Prince* to read, the Gaekwad "at once adopted the work as his political guide" and then commissioned a Marathi translation to which he appended a preface in which he declared the condition of India akin to that of Italy as described by Machiavelli in the "last portions of the book" (which, Biddulph helpfully reminded Calcutta, was entitled "An Exhortation to Liberate Italy from the Barbarians").[139]

Relations steadily worsened over the next two decades. Initially, the causes of friction were personal in nature, revolving around the Maharaja's prolonged absences from Baroda, which had an adverse impact on governance, with Sayaji demanding that all important matters be referred to him via telegram or letter. Compelled to establish a Council to govern in his absence and then forced to request "permission" to travel, the Gaekwad became increasingly sullen at being treated like a "common servant".[140] A new phase began after the turn of the century when Baroda began giving refuge to increasingly bold Indian nationalists. For some years the Gaekwad was able to fend off Calcutta's complaints with "lukewarm" policing. Then matters came to a head, following a series of assassination attempts in Calcutta, Bombay, and London between 1905 and 1910. With upwards of a dozen militant nationalists, including Aurobindo Ghosh and Ganesh Savarkar, having spent time there, Baroda was declared a "plague spot of extremism and anti-British sedition".[141] Sayaji's relations and officials were placed under watch, many of whom, including Sampat Rao (his brother) and Shivaji Rao (his son) were found wanting. The Gaekwad himself was tailed during his foreign travels, where his "amazing indiscretion" in meeting Indian nationalists in Paris and Vancouver sent Calcutta into paroxysms.[142] Then came Sayaji's "deliberate rudeness" at the 1911 Coronation Durbar where he declined to follow the prescribed protocol for greeting the Emperor. This proved the final straw. Delhi now let the Gaekwad know how much it really knew about his doings and warned that it was prepared to use "forcible measures".[143]

Brought into painful contact with reality, Sayaji promptly changed course. He abjectly apologized in private and public, issued statements decrying sedition, shut down institutions and confiscated publications that criticized British India, expelled individuals and demoted officials the British deemed disloyal, adopted British laws prohibiting the possession of weapons, and even permitted the British to establish a detective force in Baroda.[144] Consequently, by 1919, less than a decade after Sayaji had been depicted as a figurehead in nationalist pamphlets, Delhi could confidently inform the Secretary of State that relations with Baroda were "consistently friendly" and the Maharaja was "anxious to cooperate" in the maintenance of the Empire.[145] The irony was profound. Having set out to enhance his dignity and sovereignty, Sayaji ended up humiliating himself. Worse still, this very public retreat suggested that he cared most about preserving his position. This impression only deepened when events *within* Baroda, described below, revealed how unwilling the Gaekwad was to loosen his grip on power.

From the start of his reign, the Gaekwad based his legitimacy on performance. He projected Baroda as superior to British India because he was sincerely committed to uplifting its people. To his great and lasting credit, Sayaji lived up to this claim in many respects. Though successive Residents criticized his decision-making style, asserting that he was reluctant to delegate, was amenable to flattery, and prone to vacillation, Baroda generally retained its reputation for sound management. The Maharaja recruited honorable men to serve in Baroda, and there were, even the British admitted, "phenomenal" advances with respect to the provision of public infrastructure and public services, especially education.[146] His economic initiatives, especially in the industrial sphere, and his social reforms, particularly those relating to gender and caste, were rightly celebrated as well. As a consequence, Sayaji Rao would come to be cited as a leading example of a "progressive Maharaja".[147]

Invaluable though these achievements were, they ignored what Rao had counseled as the true essence of progress—namely, replacing arbitrary personal rule with an impartial constitutional order. In this regard an early sign of what was to come was Sayaji Rao's decision in 1884 to send his relations and associates—Sampat Rao, Ganpat Rao and Khashirao Jadhav—to study at Oxford, with Rao's successor, Shahabuddin, instructed to debit the sizable costs to the public treasury.[148] Then, long fascinated with everything European, it was Sayaji's turn. After a mere four years in the harness, he declared himself broken from the stress of work. Thereupon began travels on health grounds that would see him away from Baroda for the bulk of his reign, spending many months at a time either abroad (principally in Europe but with extensive visits to other continents as well) or at hill stations in India (Ooty and Mussoorie being particular favorites). Purportedly unwell, the Gaekwad had no trouble sightseeing and socializing or even allegedly, per reports from British officials, having romantic affairs with European women.[149]

These doings fostered resentment in Baroda where—as Rao warned the Gaekwad (see Chapter 30)—subjects expected their ruler to live "in their midst" and look "after their welfare" rather than to leave the country "in search of personal pleasure". To make matters worse, the immense cost of these sojourns, which included an entourage of aides, relations, and servants, was once again debited to the public treasury rather than the *Khangi* (private pursue), which at 18 lakhs per annum was the second largest in India. Partly as a consequence of such creative accounting, by 1901 the Gaekwad was able to put aside nearly 100 lakhs as his "private fortune".[150] For a while the British fretted that Sayaji might transfer these funds overseas from where he could covertly fund Indian nationalists (now *that* would have been a spectacular example of patriotism). Fortunately for them, the Gaekwad proved to have only prosaic interests such as purchasing securities and estates in Europe and India.[151]

Another scandal that highlighted the arbitrary nature of Sayaji Rao's rule concerned Elliot. Upon assuming office in 1883 Elliot initiated an examination of Baroda lands that had been hitherto been rent-free. The task was important seeing as nearly a tenth of Baroda lands had previously been gifted away as rent-free. Rao had shied away from such an enquiry because it would generate the kind of political conflict that Northbrook did not want to see. When his turn came, Elliot boldly forged ahead. The problem was that aside from entirely lacking experience in revenue management, Elliot was frequently away with Sayaji, leaving his protege, Bapat, in charge. Bapat and his subordinates used their discretion to engage in "wholesale plunder", demanding bribes in return for favorable assessments. When stories of extortion made their way into the vernacular press, Biddulph and the well-regarded Dewan, Manibhai Jasbhai, took advantage of Sayaji's absence in Europe to institute a Commission of Inquiry in 1895. The Commission promptly convicted Bapat of "systematic corruption". Prodded by an embarrassed Elliot, Sayaji hurried back to Baroda, dismissed Manibhai and reversed the Commission's decision, which had in the meantime earned the support of Baroda's much-praised Chief Justice (none other than Ambalal Desai whom Rao had once hoped to make Sayaji's tutor). The ensuing uproar over the Gaekwad's decision ("a blot that can never be obliterated", as one observer put it) prompted Calcutta to recall Elliot and prohibit his future employment in Baroda.[152]

Given this background, it should come as no surprise that by the turn of the century demands for representative government that had begun to gather steam in British India appeared in Baroda as well. Sayaji tried to stay ahead by establishing a *Dhara Sabha* (Legislative Council) in 1904. But with two dozen, mostly nominated, members and a purely advisory function, the Sabha did not pacify critics. In October 1909, a month prior to the advent of the Minto-Morley Reforms, which introduced partial self-government at the local level in British India, the Poona Sarvajanik Sabha, the leading political association in Western India, urged Sayaji to expand the franchise and give the people of Baroda "a decisive voice in Legislation and Taxation". To this proposal the Gaekwad coolly replied that Baroda had no need for representative government because, unlike in British India, in Native States "the rulers were of the people, they could perceive with no great difficulty the real wants and difficulties of the people, and their interests hardly conflicted with those of their subjects".[153] A month later, in a speech before Minto during the latter's visit to Baroda, Sayaji elaborated further on why Baroda would chart its own course when it came to representative government. Without any sense of embarrassment, the Gaekwad declared that only "he who can subordinate his private interests to the commonweal is he who is fitted for a voice in affairs of State", and he warned those "confound liberty with license and seek to undermine authority" that they would be "repressed with a firm hand".[154]

This defense of the Gaekwad regime, which already sounded implausible at the time, became galling as time passed. A significant factor was Sayaji's inability to groom a credible heir, which raised troubling questions about how Baroda would be governed in the future. His first son, Fateh Singh, had to be withdrawn from Oxford and Cambridge after earning a reputation for "disgraceful proceedings with drink and women".[155] He died in 1908 after a long battle with alcoholism. His second son, Jai Singh, graduated from Harvard with a reputation for leading "a fast and riotous life associating much with women of low character".[156] He had to be removed to Germany in 1919 to be treated for insanity and alcoholism, eventually passing away in 1923. His third son, Shivaji Rao, being only "too fond of games and pastimes", was expelled from Oxford for indiscipline. Seeing work as "beneath him", he turned to drink and intrigue prior to his premature death in 1919.[157] Consequently, in 1919 Sayaji's eleven-year-old grandson, Pratap Singh, became the heir apparent, but the boy appeared (and eventually more than proved) morally deficient.[158] In the background was Sayaji's fourth son Dhairyashil who, having taken to drink at an early age, was "a very serious nuisance", picking fights and racking up "enormous debts" (and would eventually have to be removed to England for treatment for derangement).[159]

Even as the Gaekwad clan was showing itself to have none of the virtues that its patriarch sought in his subjects, Delhi enacted the Montagu-Chelmsford Reforms in 1919 that expanded representative government in British India. Baroda was instantly rendered out of touch with the times. With discontent growing, the Baroda chapter of the Praja Mandal, a Congress-linked movement demanding responsible government in the Native States, rapidly gained adherents. Sayaji's response was to blame the British for introducing changes that had "upset" India's long-standing "balance of functions" and he expressed the view that "the only hope for the future" was a "restoration of the equilibrium in accordance with Indian tradition".[160] Rao had shown him how such an equilibrium could be attempted under modern conditions, namely by establishing a constitutional monarchy. But unwilling to do what this required—to curtail his absolute power—Sayaji chose instead to repress his critics, setting Baroda on a collision course with the nationalist movement, and the Congress in particular. Thus was lost the chance to develop a British-style, modern liberal alternative to the agrarian, traditionalist worldview associated with Mohandas Gandhi or the state-centered, socialist approach associated with Jawaharlal Nehru (both of which were far removed from the liberalism that the Indian National Congress espoused when it was launched in 1885).

Why Was Hints *Forgotten*?

Rao was one of the personalities that toward the close of the nineteenth century began to consciously knit a modern polity out of the strands of the past. In an era when the means of travel and communicate widely were limited, Rao's career allowed him to patronize persons and associations—ranging from Keshub Chunder Sen and Dayanand Saraswati to the Poona Sarvajanik Sabha and the Indian National Social Conference—that sought to make Indians aware of broader identities and common concerns. Why, then, in spite of his unprecedented career and celebrated contributions, that led him to be acclaimed as one of India's "Representative Men" and among the first "Nation Builders", was *Hints on the Art and Science of Government* entirely forgotten?

We have to start with the fact that Rao refrained from publicly discussing, much less publishing, his lectures to the Gaekwad. We know he did not lose interest or faith in these ideas, which he continued to espouse to the very last. Rather, it appears that the lectures were not Rao's to publish or discuss—they were considered the Gaekwad's property. Unfortunately, the Gaekwad was ill-disposed to advertise *Hints*. He certainly appears to have valued them. He directed either Elliot or Shahabuddin to have the lectures printed for private circulation under the misleading heading *Minor Hints* (or so two of his biographers subsequently claimed, with one even suggesting that he "enjoined" all State officials "to go through them").[161] He was known to show guests his copy of the book, seeking to impress them with the unique training he had received. He even had Jadhav deliver a similar set of lectures to Pratap Singh, his grandson and eventual heir (albeit in this case the lectures were intended to help Pratap Singh pass the "Administration" paper of Bombay University's matriculation examination).[162] At the same time, it is clear that Sayaji never overcame his ill-feeling toward his former Dewan, angrily rejecting in 1906 a proposal from the Government of India to place a commemorative medallion on the wall of Mastu Bag, the villa formerly occupied by Rao. He gave speeches honoring various figures associated with Baroda, including Dadabhai Naoroji, Aurobindo Ghosh, and Romesh Dutt, but scarcely recalled Rao.

As a consequence of the Gaekwad's coldness, subsequent generations had no opportunity to read *Hints*, save for two appearances in heavily abridged form. In 1913 the celebrated Benares institution, Kashi Nagari Pracharini Sabha (Society for the Promotion of the Nagari Script and Language), published a Hindi-language edition entitled *Rajya Prabandh Shiksha* (or *Instruction on Public Administration*), translated by the renowned literary critic Ramachandra Shukla. This development owed entirely to the famous conservative intellectual, Uday Singh, the Raja of Bhinga who, having retired to Benares, decided in his closing days to share his rare copy of *Minor Hints* with his fellow *talukdars* (great landlords) of Oudh. Unfortunately, *Rajya Prabandh Shiksha* was a modest version of the original, being heavily abridged and cast in a language that had limited appeal at the time. It was also poorly timed, appearing on the eve of World War I, a cataclysm that brought radical ideals, specifically Gandhianism and socialism, to the forefront. A decade later extracts from "Minor Hints" were published in Kesari Pancholi's *Selections for Young Princes on Efficiency as a Ruler*. Presented by Pancholi to his student, Gulab Singh, the Maharaja of Rewa, upon his investiture in 1922, this book was little noticed. The extracts were so heavily abridged in any case that they were rendered a series of exhortations rather than a coherent argument.

During the inter-war period, authorized biographies of the Gaekwad finally made *Hints*' existence more widely known. But by this time almost no one—aside from a publication like *Feudatory and Zemindari India*—had any interest in tracking down the old Dewan's lectures. Rao was not only a distant figure, he was an awkward one to praise or admire. To understand why, we need only briefly consider Rao's troubled relationship with the Congress.

Rao was initially reluctant to associate with the Congress because he worried that it would unduly deprecate Britain's contribution to India. "The truth must be frankly and gratefully admitted", he urged, that British rule "is incomparably the best Government we have ever had".[163] Those who thought that life was better before the British ought to live under the Nizam in Hyderabad for twelve months, he wrote. The experience would make them "infinitely wiser and more lively" in their gratitude for the government under which they lived.[164] Rao was also unmoved by the Congress' complaint that Britain profited from its imperial venture in India (as Naoroji's famous "drain theory" contended).[165] "It would be contrary to human nature", he replied, "to expect that the British nation should undertake the heavy duty of governing and defending India without any advantage to itself"[166]. And without Britain's "powerful patronage and protection", he warned, a "weak and fascinating" India would quickly become the prey of "imperial dacoits" like Afghanistan and Russia. Since the path to self-discovery and self-reliance was a long and difficult one, India could not, he concluded, "for a long time to come, be a self-governed and independent country".[167]

Rao also bluntly pointed out to "Congress-wallahs" their deficiencies, foremost of which was that few of them had had "the benefit of sobering experience in the management of affairs". As a consequence, they tended to be "more familiar with abstract things than concrete ones" and knew "little or nothing of the country and the people out in the *mofussil*".[168] A particular target of his ire were the moving spirits behind the Congress—retired British civil service officers such as Allan Hume and William Wedderburn and British radicals like William Digby and Charles Bradlaugh. These "deluded strangers", he warned his countrymen, had their own motives in stirring up Indians, which included settling scores with the Government of India and burnishing their radical credentials in England.[169]

These concerns notwithstanding, Rao eventually agreed to serve as the President of the Reception Committee for the 1887 meeting in Madras. His widely reported welcome address was cautiously optimistic. The diversity of faces in the audience showed, said Rao, that a turning point had been reached. It was now clear that a half-century of material and intellectual developments were dissolving "local differences" and revealing "a powerful bond of union, which makes our hearts vibrate with sympathy and mutual love and a common affection for our mother-country".[170] This statement was "universally acknowledged to be an event of the greatest possible importance", newspapers in India and England declared, because, coming from a statesman of the "soundest judgment and highest integrity" it "spoke much for the reality and weight of the movement".[171]

The bonhomie was short-lived. Rao's objective in joining the Congress had been to introduce caution into an association he saw as being characterized by "youthful impetuosity".[172] A collision occurred sooner than he perhaps expected. Early in its career the Congress began demanding that the Legislative Councils, which advised the Viceroy and the various Governors, ought to include Indians as executive members. Rao agreed that such reform was needed because "human nature is so constituted" that "political virtues have an inherent tendency to deteriorate" unless subject to "watchfulness and criticism".[173] In the case of British India, the particular vices to be guarded against included partiality toward British interests and high-handedness when questioned by Indians. What Rao vehemently and publicly disagreed with others in the Congress about was over *how* representatives ought to be chosen. In his view, these representatives ought to be nominated rather than popularly elected. He held this view for two reasons.

One related to the context. In an "immensely heterogenous" country like India, decades would have to pass, he felt, before ordinary people would readily place national interests above provincial attachments.[174] Hence, popular elections, he fretted, would be productive of "vast evils" in the form of communal and regional conflict.[175] Rao had experienced this reality first-hand, having been viciously attacked in the local press in Travancore, Indore, and Baroda as a "Madrasi interloper".[176] He was not alone—his classmates from Madras High School had encountered similar hostility when serving in Mysore and Cochin.

The other reason was foundational. In line with the *raj dharma* tradition, Rao held the view that counselling was "a high order of work" that required "special qualifications", the most essential being "possession of a sound judgment".[177] This disposition—being able to identify and balance competing interests—was not to be found among the masses who were "seldom educated and qualified enough to judge correctly". It was also not to be found in the rapidly swelling ranks of the university educated, the great bulk of whom, having spent their youth cramming, were "too theoretical" and unable to appreciate the need for compromise. The requisite disposition could only be gained through experience, and so the masses, he urged, "should respect and trust, and be guided by, the educated, experienced, and qualified part of their community".[178]

The disagreement quickly grew into a breach. At the 1889 meeting in Bombay, radicals led by Eardley Norton, the son of Rao's mentor, John Norton, declared that the Congress would prove "worse than useless" unless it championed popular representation.[179] Rao answered by pouring scorn on "mischief makers" who preached "that all men are equal" in every respect.[180] The fact that all triangles were equal did not mean, he argued, that every triangle was equally useful to the mechanic or the architect. Ever intemperate, Norton responded savagely, writing in *The Hindu* that whatever Rao "may once have been, he is no longer a factor of any power...politically, economically, numerically, physically, geometrically or even algebraically".[181] Rao's friends, he added, ought to "give rest in time to that old horse for fear at last he founder amid the general jeer".[182] His health rapidly declining, and having foreseen that it was "the character of renovated youth to be carried away by excessive zeal", Rao resigned from the Madras Congress' Standing Committee on April 1, 1890.[183] The Congress did him the honor of a curt reply, saying that it regretted the resignation "was not tendered earlier".[184]

With popular representation now the Congress' "cardinal doctrine", Rao's long cherished vision—that Native States could provide the terrain on which a distinctively Indian form of liberalism might be fashioned—suddenly seemed archaic and backward. His relevance receded almost overnight. For Rao, liberalism had meant "fair and safe progress", which could be realized, he thought, by means of constitutional monarchy, wherein the Maharaja would provide stability or permanence, the Dewan would enact progressive reform, and the British would provide oversight until a sufficiently mature public opinion could take over this function.[185] But by 1890 the "wild and mischievous theories of Europe" had begun to transform metropolitan India. To the rising generation, liberalism was now associated with individual freedom—that is, each person was entitled to decide what course to follow in private and public life. The Native State with its hereditary Maharaja and unelected Dewan was incompatible with this worldview. "Nearly all the native aristocracy and the older and more influential members of the Hindu community are in entire accord with Sir Madhava Rao", the *Times* mourned upon his resignation from the Congress, but "few of them had the courage of their opinions" because they feared becoming the targets of the "violent section of the native Press".[186] When Rao passed away a few months later, these angry young men relished the change of guard, the cruelest declaring that the Dewan "had long outlived his period of practical usefulness" and that his later contributions to public discussion had "scarcely led the younger generation to endorse the high opinion in which their fathers had held this erstwhile eminently capable man".[187]

This contemptuous attitude goes a long way toward explaining why *Hints on the Art and Science of Government* was ignored even after its existence became public knowledge. In retrospect, it is not difficult to see that the generation that founded and subsequently championed the Congress were more confident than they should have been. Had they paid heed to Rao's warnings about the fragility of order and the challenges of governance, India might have been better prepared for what would follow when popular passions were unleashed in 1947—the bloody sectarianism, impoverishing populism, rampant corruption, and gross dynastism that disfigured the early decades of Indian democracy.

One can only hope that, chastened by bitter experience, Indians will come to better appreciate the need to build public institutions and reward merit in public life. Perhaps *Hints* can play a small part in this endeavor. Because it teaches whoever governs—be it Maharajas or ministers—to advance happiness, *Hints* is timeless. Because it shows how much sound judgment depends on experience, *Hints* will always be timely. May its rediscovery prompt reflection on how to advance good government.

A NOTE ON THE TEXT

Hints on the Art and Science of Government is based on the original handwritten memos traced to the Mythic Society in Bengaluru (the *Mythic* Mss.) and a British India Press edition of the text (the *Desai* edition) printed toward the end of the nineteenth century. For detailed information on prior editions please see 'A Note on Previous Editions'.

All prior editions display three enigmatic features. First, they do not present the lectures in chronological order. As actually delivered, Madhava Rao's lectures alternated between public administration (which he termed his "major" hints) and personal conduct (which he termed his "minor" hints). Rao proceeded this way deliberately, breaking up the drier lectures on principles with livelier lectures on personal conduct. However, prior editions reorganize the lectures into two distinct sections: personal conduct (Chapters 1–24) and public administration (Chapters 25–46).

Second, prior editions place the lectures on personal conduct ahead of those on public administration and misleadingly title the entire work as *Minor Hints*. This rearrangement runs contrary to Rao's declared plan (as outlined in his memorandum to the Foreign Department, which is reprinted in Appendix II). As the dates on the original memos indicate, Rao intentionally began with the lectures on public administration (or "major" hints) and only introduced the lectures on personal conduct (or "minor" hints) a month later.

Third, prior editions mangle the original text. They open with the lecture on 'Subscriptions'. But the title and date of the lecture entitled 'Hints on Personal Conduct', which was delivered in June 1881, make clear that *this* was the inaugural lecture in the series that Rao terms "minor" hints. The lecture on 'Subscriptions', by contrast, was delivered in September 1881. By placing the lecture on 'Subscriptions' ahead of the lecture on 'Hints on Personal Conduct', prior editions undermine the coherence and readability of Rao's lectures.

Unfortunately, as some of the memos are undated, it is not possible to reorganize them in precisely the order that Madhava Rao delivered them to Sayaji Rao. This does not rule out improvement, however. In keeping with Rao's declared plan, I have reorganized the material in three ways. First, I have moved the lectures on public administration (the "major" hints) ahead of the lectures on personal conduct (the "minor" hints). Second, I have moved the lecture entitled 'Hints on Personal Conduct' to the front of the section on personal conduct and I have moved the lecture on 'Subscriptions' to its correct chronological place. Third, using Rao's own terminology, the collection has been given a more fitting and representative title—*Hints on the Art and Science of Government*.

I have also rectified a number of textual anomalies in prior editions. Typographical errors (such as "effected" instead of "affected") have been corrected. Redundant dashes, commas, and periods have been removed. Missing words have been introduced to render sentences intelligible. All such insertions have been placed within square brackets [ ]. The sources of quotations have now been identified and footnoted. Typographical errors in these quotations (e.g. where "of" has been printed as "if") have been corrected without comment. But where Rao's quotation actually differs from the original source, the variance has been noted in the corresponding footnote. Spelling errors have also been corrected (e.g. Vathel has been changed to Vattel). Such corrections have been footnoted. Nonstandard terms (such as "patriotical" and "nativial") have been retained to keep the flavor of the original text. British spellings have been adopted. Spellings have also been made consistent. For example, Oudh and Cutcherry are used throughout (and not Oude and Kutcherry). Spellings have been modernized as well. Thus, "every-day" and "worth-while" are now rendered as "every day" and "worthwhile" respectively. Similarly, a place name like "Race-course" has been rendered as the more recognizable "Race Course". The above also holds true for transliterations: *Sirkar* has been rendered as *Sarkar*, *Guddee* as *Gaddi* and so on. Transliterations have been italicized except in cases where their usage is common (thus, for example, Maharaja and Dewan have not been italicized). The transliterated terms are defined in the Glossary. In a number of instances the printed text features inconsistent use of capitalization (for instance, "judge" and "Judge" are used interchangeably in the same paragraph). Consistency has now been introduced where necessary to prevent confusion. Lastly, to improve readability, a few lengthy sentences featuring multiple semi-colons have been split into two, or else the semi-colons have been replaced by dashes. In no case has the meaning of the original text been affected.

GLOSSARY

abkari	excise on the manufacture and sale of liquor and drugs
abru	honor
assamies	stipends; pensions
Bai	lady
bhag-batai	land revenue collected in kind as a proportion of produce
bhangi	sweeper
Bhil	tribal community in Western India
Brahmin	the priestly caste
chhatri	distinction granted to the military class (literally, an umbrella)
chobdar	carrier of the *chobe* or scepter
chopdas	account books
coolies	porters
Cutcherry	building or place where public business is transacted
dakhala	certificate substantiating a bond
dans	donations
Darakdar	hereditary office bearer
Darbar	royal court

darbaris	courtiers
Dassera	Hindu festival celebrating the victory of good over evil
Deccani	person from the Deccan or southern part of the Indian peninsula
Dewan	prime minister
dharmshala	rest house (literally, a religious sanctuary)
Dharma Shastras	treatises (shastras) on righteousness (dharma)
doomala	land or villages held on inam tenure (rent-free and transferable), where the title remains with the State
dukan	banking house; shop
Fadnis	record-keeper; auditor; accountant
Fadnavis daftars	the records (daftars) of the record-keeper (fadnavis or fadnis)
gaddi	throne (literally, the cushion on which the ruler would be seated)
gaddi nazarana	tribute due when a new ruler ascends to the throne
Gaekwar	the dynastic title of the rulers of Baroda; the corrected modern spelling is Gaekwad (literally, protector of cows)
ghasdana	tribute to a military chief in the form of fodder
ghat	a landing-place or path of descent to a river
giras	cash allowances from the public treasury, which originated as protection money paid to raiders
Girasia	holder of a wanta or inheritable grant of rent-free land
gau-dan	charitable gift to a Brahmin of a cow
howdah	cabin positioned on the back of an elephant
Huzur	majesty; royal authority
Huzur Cutcherry	office of the administration
Imarat Karkhana	public works office (literally, buildings workshop)

izardar	revenue farmer
jhab	fly whisk or fan, granted as a mark of stature or rank
jahirnama	notification; proclamation
jamabandi	annual settlement of revenue due from a cultivator
jamindar	landlord; revenue farmer
janghur	goods deposited with buyer for trial prior to sale
jasood	messenger; courier
Kamdar	administrator
karkhana	establishment; office; workshop
karkoon	agent who manages financial and legal matters
khana	store room
Khangi	department for the palace or royal household; the ruler's private purse
khatpat	bribing officials to secure or fix a favorable outcome
kharita	official letter (literally, the ornamental covering or envelope)
Kothi	bank or chest or room in which valuables are stored
lakh	hundred thousand
Maharaja	king or monarch
mahout	the person who drives and tends to an elephant
Mankari	class of nobles descending from courtiers that waited on the Peshwa (the chief of the Mahratta Empire)
masal	torch
meherbani	favour; kindness to a supplicant
Mughlai	pertaining to the era of Mughal rule in India
mukhtiar	attorney or agent
mamul	custom; usage

munsif	local judge; native civil judicial officer of the lowest rank
Naib	deputy
nakah	customs station; toll booth
Nawab	historically, the governor of a Mughal territory; later, an honorific title
nazarana	tribute or gift from a dependent or supplicant
nemnuk	stipend or fixed allowance
pagah	unit in the irregular cavalry belonging to a *Silledar* (military contractor)
palki	palanquin
pan supari	betel-nut and leaf offered as a ceremonial parting gift
Peishkar	magistrate
poshak	ceremonial gift of dress
pankha-puller	a servant operating a rope-drawn pankha (fan)
Raj	kingdom; state
raj dharma	a ruler's duty
ryot	tenant cultivator
ryotwari	revenue system wherein land tax is assessed and collected directly by the State, and not by landlords or revenue farmers
sanad	a document under the seal of the ruling authority granting privileges
Sardar	Maratha noblemen or minor chieftains
Sarkar	government
Sarkari	belonging or relating to the government
Sar Subah	revenue commissioner (literally, head of the divisions or districts)
sidha	provisions; rations
Silledar	military contractor who supplies irregular cavalry units

sowar	mounted soldier employed by the *Silledar* (military contractor)
sowkar	banker; money-lender
Sheristadar	manager
Shravana dakshina	offering to Brahmins in *Shravana* (fifth month of the Hindu calendar)
Subah	civil and revenue administrator at the divisional or district level
tabut	replica of the tomb of Hussain carried in Muharram processions
talab	pond; lake
taluk	sub-division of a *zilla* (revenue district or administrative region)
talukdars	major landlords
Thakur	petty native chief; landed proprietor
Thuggee	police department that pursued Thugs (gangs that preyed on travelers)
vakil	lawyer; pleader; negotiator
Varisht	high court
Waghirs	tribe from the Okhamandal region
wanta	inheritable grant of rent-free land
warshasan	annual allowance; pension
zenana	household quarters in which women were secluded
zilla	administrative region; revenue district
zulm	injustice; wrongdoing

HINTS ON THE ART AND SCIENCE OF GOVERNMENT

CONTENTS

Chapters

1

FUNDAMENTAL PRINCIPLES*

29th April 1881

The Maharaja should become a model ruler.

We are all anxious that Your Highness should become one of the best Ruling Princes of India, that Your Highness should become a truly model prince, an example to future princes and a source of pride to the Native community. This is the earnest wish of the great British Government, which has a right to expect good government in Native States. It is likewise the wish of your numerous friends and well-wishers. It is the wish of the large body of people who are the subjects of this important State. In short, such is the universal wish.

A splendid opportunity of doing good.

(2) I feel perfectly certain that such is your own wish also. God has given you a splendid opportunity of doing public good and of achieving high honour and distinction yourself. I trust

* On 3 May 1881 Madhava Rao shared a "pencil note" version of his "first lecture" with William Waterfield, who filled in as Agent to the Governor-General when Philip Melvill went on leave between May and July 1881. The lecture outline was, he bashfully declared, "rather rough and badly written". The actual lecture extended over two and half hours because "each point" was "dwelt upon" and "further explained" to the Gaekwad.

that the future history of Baroda will record the fact that Your Highness made the best possible use of that opportunity.

The Maharaja must work.

(3) It is not, however, enough to merely wish to become one of the best Ruling Princes of India. The mere wish cannot realise itself. You have to work for it—you have to take pains to accomplish that wish. It cannot be a difficult task to one of Your Highness' intelligence and earnestness.

A few principles recognised by all good governments.

(4) It is now my privilege and duty to lay before Your Highness a series of fundamental principles, the due observance of which will enable you to become one of the best Ruling Princes of India. These are great principles recognised by all good Governments. It will not be enough that you learn those principles. You must understand and digest them. Further, you must keep them constantly before you, and practically follow their guidance in every act of administration. If you simply learn those principles, but neglect to give effect to them in daily life, it would be quite as foolish as, and it would be more culpable than, a navigator possessing himself of a good mariner's compass, but not looking at it in steering his vessel.

Old-school objections.

(5) Some persons of the old school might possibly say: "Why should the present Gaekwar learn and follow those principles? The preceding Gaekwars did not do so, and yet they managed to govern this State. The present Gaekwar may do just as they did."

The old days and the new.

(6) But let me frankly tell Your Highness that the preceding Gaekwars were hardly among the best Ruling Princes. They governed in the old arbitrary Asiatic fashion. They did not pay much regard to the happiness of the people, and, even

if they did pay some regard, they did not know the best way of promoting that happiness. Sometimes they made great errors. Occasionally they got involved in serious difficulties. Some narrowly escaped dethronement. And Your Highness well knows of the sad fate which overwhelmed Malhar Rao. All this could have been avoided if those Gaekwars had learnt and observed right principles. The former Gaekwars, however, were not so fortunate as to have the opportunity of learning those principles as Your Highness now has. This is not all. Times and circumstances have undergone a great change. Formerly bad government in Baroda did not attract much attention, as Baroda was then an out-of-the-way place. But nowadays Baroda has rapid railway communication with Bombay and with other important centres, both north and south. Everything that takes place in Baroda territories becomes widely and quickly known.

How misgovernment might affect outsiders.

(7) Again, in consequence of railway communication, the outside people come into Baroda territories oftener and in larger numbers. And misgovernment in these territories would therefore affect such people more than before and would be a matter of louder outcry.

The natural desire of the people to compare.

(8) Again, our own people have close and more frequent intercourse with Bombay and other centres. They thus have far better opportunities to compare the Government under which they live with that under which their neighbours live.

A higher ideal of government.

(9) Again, in consequence of the progress of intelligence and education, our own people have now a higher ideal of good government

than before. What bad government they tolerated in past times, they would not tolerate now. What little (good) government satisfied them in past times would not satisfy them now.

Progress with the times.

(10) Again, formerly almost all Native States were misgoverned more or less; and even British territories were in a backward condition. But now there is good progress all round, though in different degrees. The consequence is that, if we do not also fairly advance, the fact would become marked and would cause dissatisfaction.

The British Government more sensitive to misgovernment in States.

(11) And lastly, it should be noted that the British Government, as the paramount power in India, is nowadays more sensitive to misgovernment in Native States than before. The British Government holds itself responsible to prevent gross misgovernment in Native States. In effect, the British Government says to each Native Prince: "Formerly, if you grossly maladministered your territories, a nativial remedy came into operation, namely, your subjects rose in rebellion and put an end to the tyranny. The fear of such a contingency acted as a check upon misgovernment. But now we do not and we should not permit the violent remedy of rebellion on the part of your people. We have undertaken to put down any such rebellion by employing our military force whenever necessary. We have thus deprived the people of the power of correcting tyranny. But tyranny must be corrected. Who is to correct it? We, the paramount power in India, have undertaken this duty on behalf of the people. When, therefore, the people complain of gross misgovernment in a Native State, we, the British Government, will enquire into the matter, and set it right. If found necessary, we, the British Government,

will even depose the misgoverning prince and place another on the *gaddi* of the State."

Illustration from history.

(12) Such is the reasoning of the paramount power. It has much force and justice in it. Every Native Prince must bear in mind the fact that such is the reasoning of the great paramount power which completely holds India from Cape Comorin to the Himalayas. The deposition of Maharaja Malhar Rao here in Baroda itself is a recent illustration of such reasoning. History furnishes other illustrations.

Govern well.

(13) It follows, then, that the paramount power has become an important judge as to good government and bad government in the Native States. We, in Native States, must not overlook this great fact. We must constantly take care that the British Government is fairly satisfied that we are governing well—that, at least, we are not misgoverning.

Study what is good and what is bad government.

(14) Hence, it further follows that we should study what the British Government would consider good and what bad government. We should study the fundamental principles recognised by the British Government itself.

We must be more careful in these days.

(15) Your Highness will thus see how times, conditions, and circumstances have changed—how we, in our days, have to be much more careful in the work of government than former Gaekwars were. Hence the absolute necessity of this preliminary special preparation, on the part of Your Highness, for the great and responsible duties which will devolve on you before long.

The first duty of the ruler is to promote the happiness of the people.

(16) I will now proceed to lay before you some of those great fundamental principles which are essential to good government. I beg your most earnest attention to them, because I feel sure that by your being guided by those

principles, you will secure for yourself the most honourable and prosperous career. The most important principle is that it is the first duty of the ruler to promote the happiness of his people. What the happiness of the people consists of, and how that happiness should be promoted, are matters which we shall consider hereafter. They are matters of extensive detail and may admit of some difference of opinion. But there can be no doubt—there can be no divergence of opinion whatever—as to the principle itself that it is the first duty of the ruler to promote the happiness of his people.

Apply the principle constantly.

(17) Repeat this grand principle again and again. Give it the very best place in your memory. Apply it constantly to your public acts. Insist on your servants through all their gradations, from the Dewan downwards, paying the utmost respect to that principle at all times and places.

Be true to it.

(18) Be always true to that grand principle as the very foundation of your safety, comfort, honour and prosperity. The Hindu *Dharma Shastras* strongly prescribe that principle. It has the strongest approval of your people. It has the strongest recommendation of your best friends and well-wishers, among whom Mr. Elliot* and myself claim a place. Many a prince, while he readily enough accepts that grand principle when generally enunciated, fails to act up to it in the actual work of administration. We are all sanguine that Your Highness will not be one of such princes.

Examples contrary to this principle.

(19) The grand principle I am earnestly endeavouring to impress is that it is the first duty of the ruler to promote the happiness of

* Frederick Elliot, a Bombay Civil Service officer who served as Sayaji Rao's tutor between 1875–1882.

his people. A few examples of acts which would be contrary to this principle will probably strengthen the impression desired. I proceed to give a few simple examples.

(a) Diverting public funds to a selfish purpose.

(*a*) A Maharaja wishes to lay out excessive sums of money in purchasing personal jewellery and for this purpose makes large demands on the public treasury beyond the fair and reasonable proportion of the revenue which he may have for Palace or personal expenditure. He then acts contrary to the grand fundamental principle I am trying to impress, because he diverts public funds to a selfish purpose—public funds which would otherwise have gone to promote the happiness of the people in one way or another. Let no one hastily conclude that I forbid the purchase of all jewellery by the Maharaja. The Maharaja may, of course, make purchases whenever necessary or desirable, but it must be within reasonable limits. This will be evident from a careful consideration of the words I have used in the preceding paragraph.

(b) Building palaces.

(*b*) To proceed to another example. A Maharaja goes on building palace after palace beyond reasonable requirements and for this purpose makes large demands on the public treasury beyond the fair and reasonable proportion of the revenue which he may have for Palace or personal expenditure. He then acts contrary to the grand principle under reference. It is quite desirable that the Maharaja should have sufficient [accommodations]. [But] there is a limit in this direction. The Sultan of Turkey and the Khedive of Egypt have ruined their finances and brought themselves into serious difficulties by building an endless succession of new palaces. It would be folly of a culpable character to build costly palaces only to be whimsically abandoned for other new palaces.

(c) Cannons of gold and silver.

(*c*) I come now to another example. A Maharaja wishes to make cannons of gold and silver. This would be another instance of the violation of the grand principle of public happiness I am trying to impress; similarly, when a Maharaja increases his army beyond the requirements of his country and merely for the personal pleasure of reviewing a large force.

(d) Grants to relations and favourites.

(*d*) Another example of this sort will be when the Maharaja wishes to make extravagant grants to relations, favourites, etc., and to feed his extravagance, he draws from the public treasury excessive funds which would otherwise have been devoted to promote the happiness of the people. Here, too, are reasonable limits which must be respected.

(e) Religious grants.

(*e*) Even religious, charitable, and benevolent grants on the part of the Maharaja have their due limits under the principle I am advocating. Such grants must be moderate in order that the means of promoting the happiness of the people should not be crippled.

Give up the proposed expenditure if opposed to the principle.

(20) In short, whenever the Maharaja wishes to incur any considerable expenditure, he should call to mind the principle under advertence, and ask himself, "Would this proposed expenditure promote the happiness of my people?" If he cannot conscientiously answer the question in the affirmative, then he must give up the proposed expenditure as opposed to the principle under advertence.

Private expenses to be borne by the *Khangi*.

(21) There may, however, be items of expenditure which have no bearing on the happiness of the people and which the Maharaja still wishes to incur for his personal gratification. He

may indulge the wish provided he incurs such expenditure from that fair portion of the public revenues which is appropriated for his personal expenses, *i.e.*, for the *Khangi* department.

The Raj is a public trust.

(22) No Maharaja who respects the principle under advertence will consider that he is at liberty to spend the public revenues just as he likes. The Raj is not the Maharaja's private estate but it is a public trust. He is entrusted with the public revenues under obligation to spend them for the public advantage. This must be constantly borne in mind.

Use discretion.

(23) This obligation, however, need not deprive the Maharaja of the liberty to spend as he likes within certain reasonable limits. As I have already said, the Maharaja may exercise this liberty with that fair portion of the public revenues which is appropriated for his personal expenses, *i.e.*, for the *Khangi* Department.

Make yourself and the people happy.

(24) It will thus be seen that the Maharaja's private interests are quite reconcilable with the grand principle under advertence. The Maharaja may make his people happy and at the same time may make himself also happy.

Do not sacrifice public happiness.

(25) What is to be always avoided is the Maharaja seeking his personal gratification at the cost of the happiness of his people.

A few more examples contrary to the principle.

I may here give a few more examples of the infraction of the grand principle under advertence.

(a) Want of an efficient police.

(*a*) A Maharaja spends the public revenues in personal gratifications and cares not to maintain an adequate and efficient Police for the protection of the people. The people become unhappy from the prevalence and increase of crimes, such as murder, dacoities, robbery, etc.

(b) Want of judicial courts.

(*b*) Again, the Maharaja has no proper machinery for the administration of justice between man and man, then disputes increase and lead to crimes and violence in the country. The people become seriously unhappy.

(c) The ruler and the officers acting arbitrarily.

(*c*) Again, the Maharaja himself acts arbitrarily and allows his officers to act arbitrarily. They arbitrarily throw men into prison, they arbitrarily confiscate men's property, they arbitrarily put men to death. The people feel great uncertainty and alarm. They become very unhappy.

A few observations.

(26) The grand principle under advertence is a warning against such courses. I proceed to offer a few further observations on the grand principle under advertence, namely that it is the first duty of the ruler to promote the happiness of his people.

No partiality to a particular class or creed.

(27) By the words "his people" I mean all his people, generally all classes and all creeds. So far as it may be possible in practice, the Maharaja should treat all classes and creeds with favour and consideration. Some classes and creeds should not be made to suffer in order to show more favour to other classes and creeds. The Maharaja should promote the happiness of all his people, whether Hindus or Mahomedans or others, whether rich or poor, whether *Sardars, Darakdars* or the common people. In short, the Maharaja should be the father—not only of any section of his people—but of all his people.

Maharaja should be the father of all his people.

(28) This is not only just and proper in itself but it is very desirable as a matter of good policy. The Maharaja who treats all his people with favour and consideration is sure to obtain the support of all his people. On the other hand, the Maharaja who treats only a section of his people with favour will be weakened by the

antagonism of the other sections. This is a very important consideration, which deserves to be remembered in the work of administration.

Employ all classes in public service.

(29) One consequence of what I have just stated is that persons of requisite qualifications should be eligible for public employment, from all classes and creeds of the subject population in due proportion. It would be wrong to employ Deccanis only, or Gujaratis only, or Mahomedans only, or Parsis only. As already stated, all these should be employed in due proportion.

Unequal taxes to be avoided.

(30) Another consequence of what I have stated is that no one section of the people should be burdened with taxes beyond or in excess of other sections.

Equal justice to be dispensed to all.

(31) Another consequence of what I have stated is that equal justice should be dispensed to all people, irrespective of class and creed. Suppose there is a suit between a Brahmin and a Mahomedan, it would be highly wrong in a Hindu ruler to show partiality to the Brahmin simply because he is a Brahmin.

No partiality to friends.

(32) It would be equally wrong in a Mahomedan ruler to show partiality to the Mahomedan simply because he is a Mahomedan. Similarly, no partiality should be shown to friends, favourites, dependents, etc. One great mark of a good government is that impartial justice is rendered to all.

What a few *Sardars* think.

(33) Certain persons of the *Sardar* and *Darakdars* class have said to me (I am not sure with what degree of seriousness) that they regard the State as made for the Maharaja and for themselves; that it is the duty of the ministers to collect the largest revenues possible and to make them available for the happiness of the Maharaja and of themselves. As for the people

in general, little or no importance is attached by those persons to their (people's) happiness. Now I need not say that that is an absurdly wrong theory. It is quite opposed to all I have been saying today. I have no doubt that those persons will speak to Your Highness in the same way or to the same effect. Your Highness will not, of course, give any countenance to such foolish ideas. And I trust that the progress of intelligence will speedily drive out such ideas from all heads in Baroda altogether.

Their happiness not to be secured at public cost.

(34) The *Sardars* and *Darakdars* are, of course, entitled to protection and consideration as forming a component—perhaps an important component—part of the people. But it cannot be allowed that the happiness of the *Sardars* and *Darakdars* is to be secured at the sacrifice of that of the great body of the people.

Summary.

(35) To sum up then: The first duty of the Maharaja is to promote the happiness of his people—of all his people impartially. The Maharaja who fulfils this fundamental duty to the utmost extent in his power secures the greatest attachment of his people and is, therefore, most firmly seated on his *gaddi*. He will have the least troubles and anxieties in the government of his country. He will secure his own personal happiness to the utmost. He will be maintained, supported and honoured most by the paramount power.

People will be happy in the ruler.

(36) The people must always have reason to say to themselves: "We are governed by a Maharaja who feels most anxious for our happiness and who does his best with this view. Such a Maharaja is sure to teach his children to follow his own good example. We must therefore always pray for the continuance of his dynasty."

Governments that have lived longest.

(37) History is a great magazine of experience. It will be found from this experience that, as a rule, those governments which most promoted the happiness of the people—which most respected the grand principle under advertence—lived longest, and *vice versa*.

Success of the British Indian Government.

(38) At this moment we have before our eyes a great and conspicuous example. Look at the British Government of India. With all the unavoidable disadvantages of being a foreign government, it is really far more powerful and far more durable than any that had preceded it. Why? Mainly because its first principle is to promote the happiness of the people as a whole. Here and there the British Government may have made errors—may have failed in this respect—may have exposed itself to adverse criticism. Yet, on the whole, I feel, and every thoughtful man must feel, that India cannot have any other better or even an equally or nearly equally good government. Such a feeling is one of the strongest securities for the durability of the British Government in India. So long as such feeling lasts, the British Government in India may be expected to last, as it is most desirable it should. Indeed, it is not possible to assign any limit to the durability of the British Empire in India, because British principles and institutions are such that the grand principle which is our subject today will never be neglected or set aside. On the contrary, it will be more and more effectually carried out, under an elevated sense of national duty and of national interest on the one hand, and under the pressure of popular wishes and aspirations on the other.

The value of the principle which is

(39) If, then, a vast alien empire derives so much health and strength and durability from the grand principle under advertence, Your

the foundation of good government.

Highness will appreciate the value of this principle in its bearing on the State of which you are the head. The grand principle we have been dwelling upon today is at the very foundation of all good government. I trust, therefore, that Your Highness will thoroughly accept and assimilate it. This done, we shall derive from that principle a series of other principles of the utmost value in the work of administration.

The policy of the present administration of the State.

(40) I need not inform Your Highness that the present administration of the State has been actuated by a sincere anxiety to give effect to the principle I have been this day explaining—that is to say, as far as practicable in the circumstances. Under that principle we have attempted the gradual rectification of many things. For instance, we have provided for the security of life and property by establishing a good Police. We have organised a system of judicial tribunal for deciding disputes and for punishing offenders. We have established schools and hospitals. We are going on with public works. We have abolished several bad taxes, which had been found to be excessive. We have generally abstained from putting on new or increasing old taxes, with one or two exceptions which I will explain at the proper time. We have reduced such expenditure as had little or no bearing on the happiness of the people; and we have incurred new or increased old expenditure wherever it would promote the happiness of the people. I wish Your Highness will peruse our Administration Reports in the light of the fundamental principle which I have begun to explain to Your Highness. Though there must invariably be some shortcomings, Your Highness

will, I trust, find that on the whole, and as far as circumstances allow, we have acted up to those principles.

2

THE POLICE

4th May 1881

The first duty of the Maharaja.

When we met here last Wednesday, we dwelt upon the fundamental principle that it is the first duty of the Maharaja to promote the happiness of his people. From this great primary principle there flow a series of other principles of great value in the work of good government. We shall notice these one after another.

Happiness of the people is of two kinds.

(2) It is easy to perceive that the happiness of the people may be divided into two parts or kinds, *viz.*, first, that which each individual of the community may obtain for himself by means of his own exertions, and secondly, that which the individual cannot obtain for himself by means of his own exertions, but which must be secured to him by the action of the *Sarkar* as representing the whole community.

A few examples.

(3) I will now give a few examples of each of these kinds of happiness. The following are examples of that kind of happiness which an individual may obtain for himself by means of his own exertions, namely:

Happiness which can be obtained by one's own exertions.

The happiness which arises from having sufficient food, clothes, etc.;

That arising from having a comfortable house;

That arising from having vessels, furniture, carriages, jewels, etc., etc.;

That arising from attention to personal health;

That arising from the reading of books;

That arising from the practice of virtues;

That arising from the exercise of religion;

And so on. In fact, a large, a very large part, of the happiness I am speaking of depends on the individual himself—depends on his own industry, intelligence, economy, forethought, etc.

That which cannot be so obtained.

(4) The following, on the other hand, are examples of that kind of happiness which the individual cannot obtain for himself by means of his own exertions but which must be secured for him by the action of the *Sarkar* as representing the whole community, namely:

The happiness arising from the feeling that he will not be robbed or otherwise forcibly dispossessed of his property—or fraudulently dispossessed of the same;

That arising from the feeling that he will not be murdered or wounded, or otherwise injured in his person;

That arising from the feeling that his disputes with others will be fairly investigated and justly decided;

That arising from the feeling that he is free to labour for his own benefit without being molested or interfered with by others;

That arising from the feeling that there are good roads and other communications available in the country for the purpose of commercial and other intercourse;

That arising from the feeling that good sanitary arrangements are enforced in cities, towns and hamlets, so that diseases and other evils are prevented as far as possible;

That arising from the feeling that good medical assistance is within reach for the cure or mitigation of diseases;

That arising from the feeling that good schools are available for the instruction of children;

And so on.

The first sort to be left to the people but the *Sarkar* to look to the other.

(5) The happiness of the people thus falls into two classes. First, that which each person can obtain for himself, and secondly, that which each person cannot himself obtain but which must be provided by the *Sarkar*. Bearing this division in mind, I proceed to say that the first mentioned class of happiness may generally be left to the people themselves, that is to say, the *Sarkar* need not generally trouble itself about it; and the second mentioned class of happiness must be provided by the *Sarkar* as a matter of fundamental duty. Let us dwell further on this topic as it is of great practical importance. Be it especially noted that the *Sarkar* must perform the fundamental duty just mentioned, not only because it provides much happiness in itself to the people, but also because it is essential to enable the people to obtain for themselves that happiness which generally lies in their own power. In other words, if the *Sarkar* fail to perform that duty, it puts it largely out of the power of the people to make themselves happy by their own exertions. In other words, again, if the *Sarkar* fail to perform that duty, it results in the general unhappiness of the people.

Maintain a good police.

(6) We must then recognise and remember that the most imperative duty of the *Sarkar* is to do that for the happiness of the people which they cannot individually do for themselves. I proceed to give the main particulars of that great duty. The *Sarkar* should establish and maintain a good Police for the country in general. The object of doing so is, of course, to prevent offences as far as possible, and when, notwithstanding preventive measures, offences are committed, to find out the offenders, and bring them to punishment.

The police to be efficient.

(7) The Police force should be efficient to fulfil that object. In other words, it should have a sufficient number of men and officers, in proportion to the area of the country and to the population of the same. It should be well paid as an important inducement for good behaviour. It should be selected so as to secure men and officers of intelligence, activity and integrity. It should be carefully distributed throughout the country so as to benefit every part of the same.

Rules to be laid down for their guidance.

(8) Moreover, good rules should be laid down for the guidance of the Police. What it should do and what it should not do should be clearly defined. Any misconduct on the part of the Police should be brought to light and duly punished. Otherwise the Police would in itself become a source of oppression to the people.

The stupid idea that the police costs much but yields no revenue.

(9) Bad and avaricious Native rulers fail more or less in establishing and maintaining a good Police force. Their reason is that the Police costs a large sum of money, while it yields no revenue to the Maharaja. Such Maharajas are certainly very stupid indeed. The Police is as necessary for the people as the Palace guards are necessary for the Maharaja himself. The Police

as much protects the lives, persons and property of the Maharaja and family. How stupid would it be for the ruler to say, "I will have no Palace guards because they eat up money while they do not yield any money"! It will be equally stupid for any Maharaja to say, "I will have no Police for the country because they eat up money while they do not yield any revenue."

The police are kept to prevent multiplicity of crimes.

(10) Without proper Police, the people suffer in their lives, persons and property. Crimes are committed often and everywhere, such as murders, wounding, robberies, thefts, and so forth. The people greatly suffer from such crimes. They suffer also from constant fear—anxiety—and alarm. The feeling of insecurity thus caused, while painful in itself, deters or diminishes the exertions of individuals to promote their own happiness. For instance, they become afraid to accumulate riches lest they should be robbed. They fear to travel lest they should be murdered, or wounded and robbed, and so on.

The present efficient police ought to be maintained.

(11) In fulfilment of the fundamental duty we have been speaking of, the present administration has established a fairly good Police. This Police has worked well and secured its objects. It costs about 7 lakhs of rupees per annum. If the Palace guards cost 50,000 rupees per annum, 7 lakhs per annum are certainly not too much to protect the lives, persons and property of all your subjects throughout the country. Your Highness will thus perceive that it will be your imperative duty to fully maintain the existing Police. You may further improve it. But I trust Your Highness will never think of doing away with it, or of even reducing it.

Its efficiency not to be impaired.

(12) As the happiness of the people so very largely depends upon the maintenance of a good

Police, Your Highness should at all times be very particular to prevent its efficiency being in any way impaired. (The Police force should be mainly set apart for only police work and should not be diverted to any other).

The tendency to misappropriate the police.

(13) In Native States, there is a perpetual tendency to misappropriate the Police—to divert the men and officers from the service of the people to the service of private individuals. I beg Your Highness will be perpetually on your guard against this abuse. The abuse generally begins by some influential lady of the Palace calling for and obtaining the services of some policemen for her private or personal use. The men soon lose all discipline. They make interest* and it becomes impossible to get them back. In short, the men are really lost to the service of the people, though borne on the list of the Police.

Its bad effects.

(14) One bad example leads to another. The example of the ladies comes to be followed by the gentlemen of the Palace. The example of the Palace leads to imitation by the public servants. The abuse multiplies. What is the consequence? While there is a large police force on paper, a considerable portion is really doing private personal service. In connection with this subject, it should be remembered that every policeman withdrawn from the public service diminishes the protection of the people. I have given one example of abuse, others may also arise, but I need not dwell longer on this part of the subject. I will only repeat to Your Highness

* Policemen lent to the Palace were adept at cultivating patrons who would then intervene to have their deputations extended.

that it will be most essential to good government that you maintain an adequate and efficient Police at all times.

They are a source of political strength.

(15) I will now adduce another weighty consideration in favour of your maintaining an adequate and efficient Police. It is this: that such Police will be a source of political strength to yourself. There are some turbulent tribes and classes of people in these territories, easily excited or misled. They are apt to join in any movement against the *Sarkar*. There are past instances of their having repeatedly done so. And more intelligent intriguers are not wanting, who would make any use of those troublesome elements if there be good chance of success. Now an adequate and well-distributed police force will watch all those fellows, who will be deterred from mischief from the very knowledge that they are being watched. Much mischief will thus be absolutely prevented. Again, if notwithstanding any mischief does take place, it will be observed at its very outset, and will be checked easily before it gathers force. This is of the utmost importance, for remember this—that every day a mischievous movement is left unnoticed and unchecked, it grows stronger and more extensive. The confidence of the mischief-makers increases. They compel or persuade others to join them. By [looting],* they acquire money to support the movement. They get their followers to commit serious offences and then tell these followers, "The *Sarkar* will never excuse you for these offences. On the contrary, if you yield, the *Sarkar* will

* British India Press edition: looking

punish you most severely. Your only hope of escaping punishment is to defy the *Sarkar* as long as you possibly can. At worst, better to die fighting against the *Sarkar* than to yield and be ignominiously hanged." In this way, a small beginning might swell to great proportions. What an efficient Police could have easily put down at its incipient stage might require an Army to suppress. It may be compared to the progress of a conflagration. If the fire be noticed at the very commencement, it can be easily quenched. But the longer it is left unchecked, the more formidable it grows.

Even the British subjects may suffer for want of an efficient police.

(16) I have not exhausted the arguments in favour of the maintenance of an efficient Police. Without an efficient Police, not only Your Highness' subjects but the subjects of the British Government will suffer. With abundant facilities for communication, British subjects come into these territories constantly and in large numbers. If British subjects are often murdered, wounded or looted in our territories in consequence of our not having an efficient Police, the British Government may take notice of the fact as evidence of maladministration. Your Highness well knows how much it is our interest to keep the British Government fairly satisfied.

We should help the British police.

(17) Again, it is generally our interest and duty to prevent any bodies of our people going into British territories and committing serious offences. We should prevent such things reasonably, and if our people do commit offences in British territories and come back into ours, we should by all means, apprehend them and make them over to the British authorities for trial and punishment. But how is all this to be done without an efficient Police?

And expect help from them in return.

(18) Again, we always want the cordial assistance of the British police in apprehending and delivering over to us those who commit serious offences in our territories and take shelter in British territories. Unless we bring such culprits to punishment, our territories will suffer terribly. But how can we expect cordial assistance from the British police without ourselves having an efficient Police to reciprocate such assistance?

Our territories to stand honourable comparison with other territories.

(19) What I have said in regard to British territories more or less applies also to other neighbouring territories. I think I have said enough to strongly impress on Your Highness the vital importance of maintaining an adequate and efficient Police for the protection of the people. Such Police has been already established. It is now working so well that our territories can stand honourable comparison with neighbouring British territories in respect to public peace, order and security; whereas a few years ago, the Baroda territory was very badly off in these respects. What you have then to do is to maintain the Police we thus already have. Let nothing whatever induce you to impair that Police. You can, of course, further improve it.

Worthless opinions of certain persons.

(20) Certain persons here (and I am glad they are very few) will probably tell you that the present administration has done wrong in establishing this police force and thereby adding to the public expenditure. When any person tells you so, my advice is quietly take out Your Highness' notebook and mark him as a person whose opinion is worthless in public affairs. As bearing on the subject under consideration, let us read paras. 82, 83, 84 of our *Administration Report for the Year 1878–79*, page 52. (Here read

and explain the same).* There are also other paras. of the same *Administration Report* which may be read and explained with interest in connection with the subject under treatment. Let us turn to paras. 98 to 106, inclusive [of] page 55. (Here read and explain the same).†

The *Sardars* to have nothing to do with the police.

(21) It follows that, as a rule, the *Sardars* and *Silledars* should have nothing to do with the Police so long as the difficulties just explained continue. I assure Your Highness that it is much better that the *Sardars* and *Silledars* should go on as they have been going on, than that they should be forced into the Police so as to impair its discipline and efficiency and to bring themselves into trouble. In short, no desire for economy, no wish to utilise the *Sardars* and *Silledars*, no anxiety to meet their wishes, should be allowed for a moment to interfere with the satisfactory performance of the fundamental duty of the *Sarkar*—to protect the life, person and property of the people by the maintenance of an adequate and efficient Police.

The primary duty emphasised.

(22) The Hindu *Dharma Shastras* repeatedly and most strongly enjoin this primary duty on kings. I must conclude this day's lecture by declaring that he who fails to discharge this great duty is not worthy of the position or even the name of a ruler.

* Rao's instruction to himself. For the Report, see Appendix III.

† Rao's instruction to himself. For the Report, see Appendix III.

3

THE MILITARY FORCE

11th May 1881

The obligation of all governments.

We began by laying down the great and fundamental principle that it is the first duty of the ruler to promote the happiness of the people. We derived from that principle the foremost obligation of all governments to take measures with the view of protecting the life, person and property of the people.

An efficient police.

(2) We have seen that the first of these measures is to establish and maintain an adequate and efficient Police for the whole country.

The twofold functions of the police.

(3) Now, the Police acts in two ways. First, it prevents offences as far as may be possible. Secondly, when offences are committed in spite of preventive efforts, the great duty of the Police is to catch the offenders and to bring them to punishment.

The police represents the ordinary physical force of the ruler.

(4) In both these respects the Police has, or may have, to use force—mainly physical force. It has to use force to overcome the force with which it may be opposed. Offenders cannot be expected to quietly obey orders or to surrender

themselves without resistance. The Police should be strong enough to overcome the ordinary resistance which it may encounter. It is evident, then, that the Police represents the ordinary physical force of the ruler. A ruler without a Police is like a man without muscular power. He may talk, write, issue orders ever so wisely, but he will not be able to act—he will not be able to compel obedience.

But a superior force is necessary.

(5) I have said that the Police represents the ordinary physical or muscular power of the ruler—that is of the State. But this is not sufficient for all contingencies. Sometimes, though not ordinarily, it may appear that many offenders combine and offer such a degree of resistance that the Police is not strong enough to put down such resistance. For example, the Police proceed to catch a Bhil murderer, hundreds of Bhils turn out to aid the offender, and to prevent the police catching him. Suppose the assembled Bhils are so strong in numbers and deadly weapons that the Police on the spot is unable to put them down even with the assistance of the neighbouring Police. Take another example. Some excitement or quarrel arises between a body of Hindus and a body of Mahomedans, and they proceed to attack each other in numbers. Take a third example. Some time ago, a dispute arose between the Parsis and the Mahomedans of our town of Nowsari in regard to the route which the *tabut* procession should take. I investigated the matter and decided that the Mahomedans should be allowed to take the route which has been customary for many years. The Parsis did not like my decision, but they had to submit to it, and I am glad to say that they did submit to it with that good sense which distinguishes that class of people. But suppose that the

Parsis had been so foolish as to refuse to submit to the *Sarkar*'s order—so foolish as to oppose the carrying out of the *Sarkar*'s order. Suppose that large numbers of the Parsis assembled and, with arms in their hands resolved to resist the progress of the *tabut* procession passing as directed by the *Sarkar*. When such contingencies arise, when the Police is not strong enough to overcome the extraordinary resistance offered—the *Sarkar* must not stand still. Once allow such unlawful resistance to prevail—once allow the *Sarkar*'s authority to be set aside or defied—such resistance will be repeated and will be repeated until the *Sarkar*'s authority is destroyed and anarchy ensues.

The military force and its necessity.

(6) It being so necessary to enforce the authority of the *Sarkar*—so necessary to compel the resisting people to submit to the just orders of the *Sarkar*—we must supply some physical force far superior to that of the ordinary Police. I allude to the Military force. Hence the necessity of a sufficient Military force for the use of the State on such occasions. The State, then, must maintain a Military force. It is a duty which should be fully attended to in the interest of peace, order and security.

The police and the military form the whole muscular force.

(7) The Police represents the ordinary muscular power of the *Sarkar*. The Police and the Military together constitute the whole muscular power of the *Sarkar*. With this whole muscular power in good condition, the *Sarkar* is able to obtain obedience to its orders, which it has to execute for the good of the people, for promoting the happiness of the people.

The degree of efficiency of the military force.

(8) Let me now lay before you some of the more important points in relation to the Military force of the State. It is self-evident that

the Military force should be efficient to the requisite degree. Let us now consider what this degree of efficiency is. The degree of this efficiency must be determined by references to the purposes which the Military force is required to accomplish.

It should be more efficient than the police.

(9) I have already stated that the Military force is to be called into play when the Police is not strong enough to put down resistance. It follows then as a matter of course, that the Military force should be more efficient than the Police. In another words, a Military department of 100 men should be more efficient than an equal Police department. We thus have the inferior or lower limit of efficiency. The limit to start from is quite clear.

It need not be as efficient as the British force.

(10) On the other hand, it should be remembered that our Military force has no occasion to fight with Afghans, Russians, etc., as British regiments have or may have to do. It follows, then, as a matter of course, our Military force need not be as efficient as the British forces. We thus have the superior or higher limit of efficiency. The degree of efficiency of our Military force must then be somewhere above the efficiency of our Police and below the efficiency of British regiments. Provided we keep fairly within these broad and clear lines, any little error in the fixation of the exact degree may not be of much consequence.

The present efficiency is sufficient.

(11) I may here inform Your Highness that I consider that the present efficiency in which our regular force is maintained is generally sufficient for our purposes. Your Highness will, therefore, have to maintain that degree of efficiency.

The irregulars are of no use.

(12) From what I have above explained, Your Highness will readily perceive that our

irregular forces (by which I mean the old *Silledari* horse and foot) are of little or no use for the purposes in view because they do not fulfil the important condition already noted as regards efficiency. They are even much less efficient than the present ordinary Police. In short, the *Silledari* is an old, rusty and almost useless weapon.

Do not raise the efficiency of the regular force.

(13) Another conclusion following from what I have said is that Your Highness will do well to firmly resist the temptation to raise the efficiency of our regular force to the British standard. Such temptation may arise from a mere personal love of display or from hasty and thoughtless recommendations made by our own or even by British officers. Military officers have a natural and excusable wish to raise the quality of their forces to the highest possible standard without much regard for the necessities of the case, or for the expenditure involved.

But the present efficiency to be maintained.

(14) On the other hand, it will be necessary to take care that the present efficiency does not fall off. In Native States, laxity is very apt to creep in in consequence of neglect or indifference. There is need to be vigilant against such a tendency.

The usefulness of this physical power.

(15) I think it will be useful here to peruse the observations made in the *Administration Report for 1878–79* under the head of Military Department.[1] The sum and substance of what I have been urging is that the present regular Military force should be maintained in its existing Police, both representing the physical power of the *Sarkar*, a power absolutely necessary for the proper performance of the *Sarkar*'s fundamental duty of protecting the life, person and property of the subjects. With this physical power at the com-

mand of the *Sarkar*, the *Sarkar* will be able to enforce obedience to its orders, whether these orders are in the shape of laws or those [decrees] which are issued from time to time.

Another requisite is a proper machinery for the administration of justice.

(16) To proceed. The protection of the life, person and property of the people requires something more than a Police force plus a Military force. An equally essential requisite is a proper machinery for the administration of justice. By a proper machinery for the administration of justice, I mean courts—such as that of the magistrate, that of the *munsif*, that of the *zilla* judge, and that of the *Varisht* judge—a series of courts with graduated powers, for administering civil and criminal justice, the duty of these courts being to decide justly all the numerous disputes which constantly arise among the people themselves.

To settle the innumerable differences and disputes.

(17) The people are, of course, a body of individuals. Differences and disputes constantly arise between individual and individual. If these differences and disputes are not justly investigated and decided as they arise, see what grave evils will ensue. Individual will fight with individual, family with family, bodies of persons with other bodies. Small matters will grow into large matters. Strong passions will be excited. Breaches of the peace will constantly occur. Killing, wounding, plundering will become very common. The motives for peaceful, steady industry will be greatly weakened—perhaps extinguished. The motives for the accumulation of wealth will similarly suffer. In short, great confusion will prevail and the happiness of the people will be destroyed.

Courts of justice to be established.

(18) But we started with the fundamental principle that it is the first duty of the ruler to

promote the happiness of the people. Of what use that ruler be, who allows the happiness of the people to be destroyed in the manner I have just stated? It will thus be seen how essential it is for good government to establish courts of justice. Maintaining good courts of justice, the *Sarkar* says to the people, "Don't you quarrel and fight among yourselves. Whenever any individual feels he has been injured by another in respect of person, or property, or otherwise, let the complainant represent the matter to the judicial tribunals, and these tribunals will carefully enquire into the matter and decide the dispute justly. The wrongdoer will be found out, he will be compelled to make reparation for the wrong he has done, and when such is necessary, he will be also punished for the wrong he did."

Wrongdoers are restrained by the fear of courts.

(19) The great body of the people like such an arrangement. The very existence of the arrangement largely prevents many wrongs and many disputes. Each individual says to himself, "I must not do any wrong to my neighbour or take from him what is justly his, for as soon as I do so, I will be deprived of my gain, and I may also be punished." Many people will reason in this way and abstain from wrongdoing. This, Your Highness, is an immense and incalculable benefit to society. To realise this benefit adequately, you must think over the matter. Meanwhile let me assure you—and on reflection you will thoroughly understand it—that the great body of the people who do not actually use the judicial machinery (*i.e.*, the courts) really benefit by that machinery much more than those comparatively few people who do use that machinery. Why is it that the great

body of the people do not resort to the courts? Because they have not been wronged. But why have they not been wronged? Because wrong-doers have been restrained by the fear of the courts. To make the matter clearer, let us take some figures merely by way of example. Our subjects are, say, 20 lakhs. Out of this, suppose half a lakh have recourse to the courts. Then I wish to explain to Your Highness that this half a lakh derive much benefit because they obtain redress for their grievances, but the rest of the people—19½ lakhs—benefit still more because they have been successfully protected against injuries—protected in consequence of the very existence of the courts.

The whole population is benefitted.

(20) Your Highness will thus see that the courts are of great benefit to the whole population—that the courts constitute one of the most effective instruments for the protection of life, person and property—a protection which we have recognised to be the fundamental duty of the ruler.

Peace and order prevail, and the people's happiness promoted.

(21) It is owing to the operation of the judicial tribunals that the weak are protected against the strong—the good are protected against the bad. It is owing to the operation of the judicial tribunal that peace and order prevail, and that men are enabled to enjoy as much liberty as possible, and are enabled to exert themselves for their happiness without being molested by others. It is owing to the operation of the judicial tribunals that society is kept well together; that the forces which tend to promote the happiness of society have free action; and that those forces are prevented from acting against each other and consequently neutralising or weakening each other. All the forces tending to pro-

mote the happiness of society being thus directed in one channel, the greatest and best results are secured. Take any two States equal in all other respects, but the one having a good judicial machinery and the other having a bad judicial machinery or none. It is quite certain that that State which has a good judicial machinery will prosper beyond the other in a very decided manner. We thus see how essential and valuable the administration of justice is to accomplish the great object of government, namely, the happiness of the people.

The existing judicial machinery must be maintained.

(22) Now we have succeeded in establishing in these territories a series of judicial tribunals, such as the country requires. These judicial tribunals have been working well and are fulfilling their objects. If all that I have been this day saying has made a sufficient impression on Your Highness (and I need not doubt it), I feel sure that Your Highness will earnestly maintain and support the existing judicial machinery. A contrary course would be ruinous alike to the people and to the ruler. I feel quite certain of this; and pray remember one additional circumstance, that when a community has already known and felt the advantage of a good administration of justice, the mischief and the peril of depriving that community of a good administration of justice would be all the greater.

The Maharaja cannot do judicial work personally.

(23) In connection with the administration of justice, I wish Your Highness to realise the fact that, in any large State, it would be utterly impossible for the Maharaja to himself personally do regular judicial work. It would be too burdensome to the Maharaja, and it is not possible for every Maharaja to qualify himself with the necessary amount of legal knowledge and

experience, to acquire which years of study are required—perhaps a good portion of a lifetime. It follows that there should be a regularly constituted judicial machinery, such as at present exists—a machinery which will work steadily from day to day without necessitating the Maharaja personally taking trouble. It would be wrong—it would be contrary to the interests of the people—to delay justice because the Maharaja is engaged in ceremonies, or festivities, or tired of work, or feels indisposed in point of health or for such other reasons.

If he undertakes it, he must fail.

(24) Let me inform Your Highness of the clear result of my study and experience, namely, that any Maharaja who undertakes to administer public justice personally must inevitably fail.

Trained judges should dispense public justice.

(25) There are yet other strong reasons in support of the maintenance of the existing judicial machinery. I must lay them before Your Highness. Judges who have made law and justice their special study, who hold office on the express condition of dispensing justice—who are constantly alive to their responsibility—who are under fear of discredit and disgrace consequent on misdecision—I say that judges will generally deserve and command far greater confidence as dispensers of public justice than even the Maharaja himself. This will be quite evident on reflection. It being so, it is for the best interests of the people that trained and constituted judges should dispense public justice, and not that the Maharaja should undertake the task personally. I must frankly tell Your Highness that if I had a suit of any importance, I would consider it better and safer that the judges should decide the case than that the

Maharaja should do so, even though the Maharaja is a well-educated ruler. It is just like this, namely that, in case of serious illness, I would decidedly prefer to be treated by a trained doctor to being treated by the Maharaja. Again, I would decidedly prefer that the railway train in which I am to travel, be driven by the trained driver, to its being driven by an amateur Maharaja. Your Highness will find that those few who would prefer the Maharaja as a judge are very few indeed—a mere drop in the ocean. And the preference shown by those few persons clearly arises not from a wish to obtain pure justice, but from the wish to obtain decisions in their favour under the very objectionable system of *meherbani*.

Why the Maharaja should not dispense justice personally.

(26) Again. If the Maharaja were to dispense justice personally, he would be sure, in a few years, to incur the enmity or ill will of great numbers of the people, for he must inevitably displease all those against whom he ever decides. It is difficult to set limits to the possible consequences of that enmity or ill will. I need not be more explicit. Why should the Maharaja expose himself to such enmity or ill will? It is quite needless. It would certainly be very unwise in any Maharaja to place himself in such a position.

The parties are sure to appeal.

(27) Again. The dissatisfied parties are sure to appeal to the Agent to the Governor-General. They may appeal to the Viceroy. They may appeal to the public through the newspapers. Now, if the Maharaja were to personally administer justice, all those appeals would be directed against the Maharaja personally. All the appeals would go to question the Maharaja's legal knowledge, to question his impartiality, to

question his care and diligence. Harsh words would be applied to the Maharaja, such as ignorance, partiality, carelessness and many other worse things. Would this be pleasant to the Maharaja? Would it be consistent with his dignity? Would it be consistent with that high respect and veneration in which it is desirable the Maharaja should be held? When the Maharaja's name is roughly handled as just indicated, the Maharaja might be tempted to resent the same. The resentment might take very unjustifiable forms and might bring the Maharaja into more or less serious difficulties. Why incur all this risk?

It would look bad to have his decision reversed.

(28) Let us pursue the subject a little further. Suppose some of the appeals result in the conclusion that the Maharaja's decision appealed against was wrong, and must therefore be reversed. What would be the consequence? Why, the Maharaja would surely feel a degree of humiliation, which would be painful to him, which would probably deprive him of his sleep and digestion for some time. This would be the case especially when the Maharaja is compelled to cancel his own decision with his own hand and to pass a fresh order in favour of the party against whom he has decided—the very party who had probably abused the Maharaja in the appeal. In such a situation, how would the Maharaja look in the eyes of his people?

Bribery is sure to creep in.

(29) Again, if the Maharaja administers justice personally, he would be more or less assisted in the work by certain *karkoons* or other officials around him. As the parties themselves cannot have free access to the Maharaja, those officials would be likely to be openly or secretly engaged by the parties to make representations or expla-

nations in their behalf to the Maharaja. Bribery is pretty sure to creep in and take root. Defeated parties will attribute their defeat, not to the weakness of their cause, but to bribes paid by the opposite party. Charges of corruption, true or false, will be prepared. Investigation of such charges cannot be refused, as a rule. Prosecutions will have to be ordered. Such prosecutions may involve not only the officials about the Maharaja but even higher persons—perhaps friends, relations, *Mankaries*, etc. All this would be unpleasant in the highest degree, especially when convictions and punishments follow.

The British Government watches the kind of justice imparted.

(30) The administration of justice has, in these days, become a matter of far greater difficulty than ever before. The concerns of the people have become more complicated. The demand for justice on the part of the people is more exacting. And, in consequence of railways, etc., many British and other outside people come under our justice. It is to be always remembered that the British Government watches to see what kind of justice its subjects get in Native States. This is another important reason why the Maharaja should not burden himself with judicial work.

The high reputation of the administration.

(31) Your Highness will thus see what weighty reasons there are for maintaining the existing judicial machinery and for giving it your hearty support. We now enjoy a high reputation in respect of the administration of justice. It is a source of immense strength to us. May Your Highness always enjoy this strength.

In other States the administration of justice not properly looked after.

(32) In Native States, I am ashamed to say, the administration of justice is not much looked after, because it does not bring in revenue largely; and what revenue it may bring in, is hardly sufficient to pay the judicial machinery. I

do not say this of all Native States, for there are exceptional instances of some States maintaining a very fair system of judicial administration. But a Maharaja who knows what his great and fundamental duties are, will never fail to maintain a good judicial administration essential for the happiness and prosperity of his people.

The courts pay a portion of their cost by fees and fines.

(33) I cannot too strongly impress on Your Highness the prime necessity of maintaining a pure administration of justice. Without it, human beings, with their various feelings and passions, cannot long live together and prosper in their concerns. Cost what they may, the existing courts of justice must be maintained. But they pay a good portion of their cost by means of fees and fines.

The special court for suits against *Sardars*.

(34) Among the existing courts, Your Highness knows that there is a special court for suits against *Sardars*. This special court has been designed to conciliate the feelings and sentiments of this class of people, who do not wish to be subject to the ordinary courts. As long as these feelings and sentiments prevail, this special and distinct court of justice must be maintained. The great principle to be remembered in this respect is that the *Sardars* cannot for a moment be allowed to claim to be beyond the reach of public justice. They cannot be allowed—no human being can be allowed—not even the Maharaja himself—to say, "We shall do any unjust things we like." This is so self-evident that no arguments are necessary. Do anything and everything that may be reasonable to gratify the *Sardars* in respect of their peculiar feelings of dignity, etc., but it must be all consistent with the great principle that they must be substantially subject to public justice, like other members of the community.

Maintain a proper and self-working judicial machinery.

(35) The particulars as to the Constitution, the powers, and the functions of the various tribunals of justice fall within the province of Mr. Cursetji* to explain to Your Highness. But in expounding fundamental principles of good government, my duty is to impress on Your Highness the absolute necessity of maintaining a proper and permanent and self-working judicial machinery. As your sincere well-wisher, as a faithful and experienced public servant, I assure you that the maintenance of an efficient judicial machinery is quite essential to the stability of your power as a ruler.

The abominable system of *nazaranas* to get favourable decisions.

(36) In connection with the administration of justice, I must here allude to the abominable system of *nazaranas* which prevailed here. In fact, the parties to a suit freely offered money to the Maharaja to get decisions in their favour. That party who made the largest gift of money generally got the decision in his favour. This was really selling justice to the highest bidder. This is the worst kind of avarice that any ruler can be guilty of. A ruler making money by selling justice is worse than that despicable man who makes money by selling his own children. I earnestly hope that the *nazarana* system I am speaking of has received its death blow, and it will never more raise its horrid head again.

Bribery should receive its death blow.

(37) It will not, however, be enough for the ruler himself to abstain from taking *nazarana* or bribes in connection with the administration of justice. He must be always vigilant to prevent his friends, relations, dependents, etc. from doing the same directly or indirectly—openly

---

* Cursetji Rustomji Thanawalla, the Chief Justice of the *Varisht* Court.

or secretly. There are lots of hungry wolves infesting palaces, though they appear like lambs; and the Baroda Palace is not an exception. I know that even among those who are well off, and who are outwardly respectable and gentlemanly, there are some quite ready to take bribes without caring anything for the good name of the Maharaja, and for the welfare of the people. Against such rogues, Your Highness should be perpetually on your guard. When, therefore, Your Highness assumes power, you must unmistakably make it known to all around you that, if anyone takes bribes, he will have no mercy, but that he will be turned out of the Palace by you; that he will lose his *nemnuks* and privileges; and that he may be prosecuted in due course of justice and adequately punished. If, notwithstanding such previous and particular warning, anyone misbehaves, let him certainly feel Your Highness' displeasure, more or less, in the manner above stated; and one or two practical examples will surely stop the evil. The exposure and punishment of a possible friend, relation or dependent may be very unpleasant, but it is an imperative duty which you owe as a ruler to your subjects. If the fellow did not care about your reputation, you need not care about his. In relation to this subject, let us always remember that it was bribery and corruption which mainly brought about the downfall of Malhar Rao.

The officers to be of good character.

(38) I have stated and repeated that a pure administration of justice is essential to the well-being of the people. To make sure of such an administration of justice, other conditions are also required and let us notice the chief of them. It is very important that the officers appointed

to administer justice should be men of good character and possessing the requisite knowledge of judicial work. In fact, there can be no good government without men of honesty and qualification to work in all the main departments of government. How such men should be sought out and availed of, is in itself a very important subject, which I shall treat of separately hereafter. I will here only say that magistrates, *munsifs* and judges should be very carefully selected persons. Above all, the judges of the *Varisht*, or your highest court, should be the very best men possible. This advantage secured, all the rest will follow easily enough.

They must be well paid.

(39) The judicial officers—indeed all officers—must be well paid. Of this subject, also, I will speak hereafter in a distinct lecture.

And promoted according to merit.

(40) The judicial officers—indeed all officers—must be generally promoted according to merit and good public service.

Should not be removed arbitrarily.

(41) The judicial officers especially should have confidence in the tenure of their offices, so long as they behave well, and have health and strength for work. They must not be afraid of being removed arbitrarily. Above all, they should have no reason to fear that they might be injured because of the displeasure that they might incur by doing impartial justice.

The administration should be impartial.

(42) The Maharaja should scrupulously abstain from asking the judicial officers to decide this way or that way in particular cases. The Maharaja should not even show that he would be pleased if any particular party be favoured. He should show no special interest on either side. His attitude should clearly indicate that he cares only for the impartial administration of justice, and that he will strongly

support every judicial officer who distributes justice without fear or favour. To maintain this attitude, the Maharaja will have to resist importunities of friends, relations and dependents, with great firmness. These should be once for all ordered not to trouble Your Highness in that manner. If, notwithstanding, anyone does trouble Your Highness, Your Highness' reply should be—"I cannot influence the judicial officers in any way. I have appointed good judges and they will do justice. If you are not satisfied with the decision, you may appeal to the higher court. In this way, you can obtain what justice you may be entitled to." Some such reply, firmly repeated, will effectually check importunity. Otherwise, that is to say, if you yield to importunity in a few instances—importunity will increase and multiply; you would be perpetually worried every moment of your life, and the administration of justice will go wrong—your reputation as a good ruler will suffer.

No special relaxation in favour of Palace servants.

(43) Again. The Maharaja will do well to show his respect for justice by supporting the courts when they require the attendance of Palace servants and officials. All requisitions which are right and proper should be readily complied with. Those servants and officials should be made to feel that they are not above justice—that they are responsible to justice—that they must respect others' rights—just like other subjects. They should feel that no special relaxation of justice will take place in their favour, though they will be well protected as long as they behave well. They are all generally shrewd people, who will be anxious to study the disposition of the Maharaja and to submit to the same.

Refer all civil and criminal matters to the courts.

(44) The Maharaja should personally set a good example to all by his own habitual and cordial respect for justice. For instance, the Maharaja should abstain from using or causing any personal violence to—from inflicting any personal ill-treatment on—any of his servants. His Highness should abstain from himself ordering arbitrary imprisonment, attachment, or confiscation of property, etc., etc. His Highness should refer all offences and civil disputes to his courts, who will do the needful in the proper way. Again, His Highness should readily pay all the monies due by him to others. He must satisfy all just claims just like any private individual. He should satisfy such claims, as far as possible, without compelling the claimants to abandon their claims or to resort to the courts of justice. Such a course on the part of His Highness will save him much personal enmity and will promote his popularity while strengthening the cause of justice generally.

But see that the courts fulfil their duties.

(45) From what I have said it is not to be supposed that His Highness has nothing whatever to do with the courts of justice—that His Highness is simply to look on as an indifferent or unconcerned spectator—that His Highness is simply to let the courts do what they like. No. It is the great and imperative right and duty of His Highness not only to maintain the judicial machinery, but to see that this machinery properly fulfils its purposes. I shall take another opportunity of explaining how this is to be done. In fact, I propose to explain how this is to be done in the instance of each department of the administration, so that Your Highness may have a complete and comprehensive view of this important subject.

The Maharaja should perform sovereign duties.

(46) The great thing is that the Maharaja should be able to distinguish his own high and superintending duties from less important and mere ministerial duties. The Maharaja's ambition should be to perform sovereign duties and not the subordinate duties of officers and *karkoons*. It is only that Maharaja who is ignorant of sovereign duties or who is incompetent to perform sovereign duties, it is only such a Maharaja, I say, that abandons sovereign duties and wastes his time and energies in doing lower duties, which officers and *karkoons* would do much better, more steadily and more accurately.

Lessons from the writings of Fénelon.

(47) I will conclude this day's lecture by inviting Your Highness' best attention and study to two eloquent passages in which a great Frenchman of the name of Fénelon* conveyed to his Royal pupil lessons similar to those which I have been endeavouring to convey to yourself. I will leave Mr. Elliott to tell Your Highness all about that great Frenchman, but I am here chiefly concerned with the leading ideas which he inculcated—ideas which strongly confirm what I have already said, whether particularly as regards the whole administration of justice, or generally as regards the whole administration of the *Raj*. The following are the two passages I allude to:

Decide new questions of right but not of private property.

> Idomenes** then complained of the perplexity he suffered from the great number of causes between private persons, which he was pressed, with great importunity, to decide. "Decide" said Mentor, "all new questions of

* François de Salignac de la Mothe-Fénelon, famous seventeenth-century French cleric and writer, and tutor to Louis *duc de* Bourgogne.

** Per the original: Idomeneus.

right, by which some general maximum of jurisprudence will be established or some precedents given for the explanation of law already in force, but do not take upon you to determine all questions of private property; they would overwhelm you and embarrass you by their variety and number. Justice would necessarily be delayed for your single decision, and all subordinate magistrates would become useless. You would be overwhelmed and confounded, the regulation of petty affairs would leave you neither time nor thought for business of importance; and, after all, petty affairs would not be regulated. Avoid, therefore, a state of such disadvantage and perplexity; refer private disputes to subordinate judges, and do nothing yourself but what others cannot do for you. You then, and then only, fulfil the duties of a king…

To do everything yourself is a poor ambition. To form great designs, all must be freedom and tranquillity. Government requires a certain harmony like music and just proportions like architecture.

…The proof of abilities in a king as the supreme governor of others, does not consist in doing everything himself; to attempt it is a poor ambition, and to suppose that others will believe it can be done, an idle hope. In government the king should not be the body, but the soul; by his influence and under his direction the hands should operate and the feet should walk; he should conceive what is to be done, but he should appoint others to do it. His abilities will appear in the conception of his designs and the choice of his instruments. He should never stoop to their functions, nor suffer them to aspire to his; neither should he trust them implicitly; he ought to examine their proceedings and be equally able to detect a want of judgement or integrity. He governs well who discerns the various characters and abilities of men, and employs them to administer government under him in departments that are exactly suited to their talents. The perfection of supreme government consists in the governing of those that govern; he that presides, should try, restrain and correct them; he should encourage, raise, change and displace them; he should keep them for ever in his eye and in his hand; but to make the minute particulars of their subordinate departments objects of personal application, indicates meanness and suspicion, and fills the mind with petty anxieties that leave it neither time nor liberty for designs that are worthy of royal attention. To form great designs, all must be freedom and tranquillity. No intricacies of business must embarrass or perplex, no subordinate objects must divide the attention. A mind that is enchanted* upon minute particulars, resembles the lees of wine that have neither flavour nor strength; and a king who busies himself in doing the duties† of his servants, is always deterred†† by present appearances and never extends his view to futurity; he is always absorbed by the business of the day that is passing over him and, this being his only object, acquires an undue importance, which, if compared with others, it would lose. The mind that admits but one object at a time, must naturally contract; and it is impossible to judge well of any affair without considering many, comparing them with each other, and ranging them in a certain order by which the relative importance will appear. He that neglects this rule in government resembles a musician who should content himself with the discovery of melodious tones, one by one, and never think of combining or harmonising them into music which would not only gratify the ear, but affect the heart; or he may be compared to an architect, who should fancy the powers of his art exhausted by heaping together large columns and great quantities of stone curiously carved,

* Per the original: exhausted.

† Per the original: duty.

†† Per the original: determined.

without considering the proportion of his building, or the arrangement of his ornaments; such an artist, when he was building a saloon, would not reflect that a suitable staircase should be added, and when he was busy upon the body of the building, he would forget the courtyard and the portal; his work would be nothing more than a confused assemblage of parts, not suited to each other, nor concurring to form a whole; such a work would be so far from doing him honour, that it would be a perpetual monument of disgrace; it would show that his range of thought was not sufficient to include all the parts of his design at once; that his mind was contracted and his genius subordinate; for he that sees only from part to part, is fit only to execute the designs of another. Be assured, my dear Telemachus that the government of a kingdom requires a certain harmony like music and just proportions like architecture. If you will give me leave to carry on the parallel between these arts and government, I can easily make you comprehend the inferiority of those who administer government by parts and not as a whole. He that sings particular parts in a concert, however great his skill or excellent his voice, is still but a singer; he who regulates all the parts and conducts the whole is the master of music; so he that fashions the columns and carries up the side of a building, is no more than a mason; but he who has designed the whole and whose mind sees all the relations of part to part, is the architect. Those, therefore, who are most busy, who despatch the greatest number of affairs, can least be said to govern; they are inferior workmen; the presiding mind, the genius that governs the State, is he who, doing nothing, causes all to be done; who meditates and contrives, who looks forward to the future, and back to the past, who sees relative proportions, arranges all things in order, and provides for remote contingencies."[2]

4

LAWS AND CUSTOMS

1st June 1881

Summary of the previous chapter.

We began by stating that it is the first duty of the ruler to promote the happiness of his people. In order to promote the happiness of the people, the first thing which the ruler has to do is to take measures for the security of the life, liberty, person and property of the people. The first of these measures is to establish and maintain an adequate an efficient Police backed by a Military force of sufficient strength and discipline, the Police and the Military bodies representing the physical or the muscular force of the *Sarkar*—the force by which the *Sarkar* is to compel obedience to law. The next immediate measure is to establish and maintain proper judicial tribunals for dispensing justice to the people—for deciding their various disputes as they arise, granting redress to injured parties, and punishing offenders whenever it is desirable to do so.

The judicial tribunals to have

(2) We have dwelt on the importance of the proper administration of justice, but for this purpose it is obviously essential that the judicial

proper instructions from the State.

tribunals should have proper instructions from the State. It is evident that the several judges and magistrates cannot be left to dispense justice just as they like. They ought to have principles and rules given them by the State for their guidance. These principles and rules are known as the laws of the country.

Good laws to be laid down for their guidance.

(3) The State, then, must lay down laws for the guidance of the judges. These laws are, in fact, the well-considered orders of the State, once for all issued for the information and guidance of the judges, and also of the people in general. These standing or permanent orders of the State, known as laws, must be good, that is to say, the laws must be calculated to promote the happiness of the people. The happiness of the people ought to be the chief and ultimate aim of the laws.

Good laws are a product of long experience.

(4) It is certainly one of the most difficult of human labours to frame a complete body of good laws for any community. Transactions between man and man are extremely numerous and sometimes very complex. Again, it requires very long experience and careful observation to determine the effect of any particular transaction or of any set of transactions on the general happiness of the community. Good laws must, therefore, be the product of long experience, careful observation and intellectual labours of the highest order.

In preparing laws, note the common principles of justice known to the civilised world.

(5) We, here in Baroda, cannot pretend to evolve from our own brains all the laws which are required for the regulation of the affairs of our people. To do so would be impossible, undesirable and, after all, unnecessary. No community ever does so. One example may be adduced here to make more clear what I have

just said. Suppose we wish to cure sickness among our people; there are thousands of forms of sickness and some of the most complex character. Surely, we are not to set aside the accumulated knowledge and experience of the world in general, and of similar countries in particular. We are not to set aside all that and to study all those forms of sickness ourselves and to devise our own medicines—so with respect to civil and criminal laws. What should we then do with respect to laws? I will briefly answer. We should note what few laws we already have. We should carefully note the great and universal principles of justice known to the civilised world as axioms or common principles. We should also note the laws which govern similar neighbouring communities. We should further note the good customs which have prevailed in these territories. On a combined consideration of all these, we must frame our instructions to our judicial tribunals.

It is the course followed by the present administration.

(6) This is exactly the course which has been actually followed by the present administration. Indeed, any better course is not to be practically found at the beginning. It was not possible to start with a complete code of laws of our own. A work of many years cannot be done in such a comparatively short time.

The guidance of our higher judges is necessary.

(7) Our higher judges are all men who have more or less studied law as a science. They are conversant with the great and universal principles of justice. These principles enable them to keep within the broad path of justice and to avoid any gross deviations. These principles are great safeguards in this way, and their guidance is all the more necessary at a time when we have no complete and specific code of laws of our

own, when so much has therefore to be left to the discretion of the courts.

Apply the laws framed by the British Government.

(8) Again, our community is not different from the neighbouring community under British rule. If there be any difference, it is not considerable. It may therefore be presumed that the laws framed by the British Government for the neighbouring community, and which have been found to work well, are generally applicable to our community also. And it is to be remembered in this connection that the laws of the British Government are framed by eminently able and experienced men. Our judges know these laws or have access to them. They may well follow the spirit of these laws in the absence of anything better to guide them.

Local customs to be respected.

(9) Again, there are long-established local customs—customs recognised and acted upon by our own people. Our judges respect such customs as a most important condition of the administration of justice.

The Hindu and Mahomedan Laws, and other customs.

(10) Again, we have got authoritative works on Hindu and Mahomedan Law regulating marriage, adoption, succession to property, partition of property, etc., etc. These works are guides to our judges as much as to British Indian judges. Customs which are not mentioned in these works, but which may still be found to exist in particular places or in particular classes of people, are also the guides of our judges, who specially ascertain such customs from time to time. Under such combined guidance, our judges are enabled to render substantial justice to our people in a manner far more satisfactory than at any time before in the history of the Baroda State. And it is to be added that our judges render substantial justice without that,

without those technicalities and elaborate forms which are a matter of complaint elsewhere.

But there is ample room for improvement.

(11) In this way we have done the best that has been possible in the circumstances of the situation for the administration of justice. So far, the people feel satisfied in this respect, and we are not, of course, to mind any dissatisfaction expressed by those who wish to evade justice but who are now compelled to submit to justice. This state of things must necessarily go on for some time, but there is ample scope for progressive improvement. We must gradually make laws of our own to some extent. In this respect, I will here indicate my views briefly and generally.

Adoption of the Indian Penal Code strongly recommended.

(12) I would strongly recommend our early adoption of the British Indian Penal Code. With a few modifications and omissions, I may assure Your Highness that it is a splendid code of the Penal Law. It is one of the most national codes of the sort in existence in the whole world. It is a better Penal Code than what is in use in England itself. It is a code which is the result of the experience and reflection of the most eminent Jurists of Asia, Europe and America. General crimes are universal, that is to say, they are taken as crimes not only in this or in that State but in all civilised States. The Indian Penal Code treats of such crimes or offences. It is therefore applicable to India and to any part of India. Indeed, it was framed for India itself. It has been applied to the wide regions of the British Indian Empire and has generally worked well. I am decidedly of opinion that we cannot do better than adopt it here, with, as I have already said, the requisite modifications and adaptations. These will be very few indeed.

Also of the Criminal Procedure Code.

(13) A similar course seems desirable in relation to Criminal Procedure with considerable simplification, and so on. In short, the broad lines I would recommend are to go on with the administration of justice as at present, and to begin making laws gradually and from time to time, as it may be found necessary to do.

Regular laws must be made gradually.

(14) Law and Justice generally and practically are subjects which Mr. Cursetji will deal with better than I can. I must not trench upon his field. But the few very general observations I am offering fall within the category of the fundamental principles of good government I am to communicate to Your Highness. I have said that we must begin to make regular laws gradually and from time to time as may be found necessary hereafter. In this important connection, I would suggest some points to be kept in view. They are as follows.

No good custom to be set aside.

(15) No existing custom which is fairly good and has long been recognised and acted upon by the people should be set aside or altered; strong sound reason must be shown for such action. The evil which is sought to be corrected must be clearly shown; what is the evil exactly; what is its magnitude; how many persons does it affect; do the people themselves complain of the evil; does the evil really diminish the happiness of the people, which is the great object of good government? In short, unless the evil is so material that the people themselves or an intelligent portion of them would wish it to be remedied, leave the long established customary law as it is.

Remedy an evil custom.

(16) On the other hand, if the evil is clearly substantiated, so that there is no doubt about it, proceed to its remedy. Without this, there would be no progress—no improvement. What

I have said about setting aside or altering existing customary law equally applies to setting aside or altering existing written law.

No new law to be hastily passed.

(17) No new law should be passed in any haste. The utmost deliberation should precede the passing of any new law. See that the proposed law is not opposed to any fundamental principle recognised by civilised communities. If the proposed law be unique—be utterly without analogy in civilised communities of modern times—suspect its soundness.

The proposed law to be discussed with the ministers and judges.

(18) Discuss the proposed law with the principal ministers and the principal judges, and some of the principal intelligent members of the general community, and take their opinions. Consult also intelligent members of that part of the community which may be affected by the proposed law. Freely elicit objections in order that they may be known and may be duly weighed.

Agree with the majority.

(19) As a rule, do not pass any law which is opposed by the greater portion of those with whom you have fully discussed it. Indeed, it would be quite unsafe—it might be even dangerous for any Maharaja to pass any law or any part of a law, without at least some of his ministers and some of his judges assenting to the same, and being prepared to defend the same if assailed, and to be fully responsible for its soundness.

Adopt the analogy of the British law. Copy the good of another.

(20) Adopt the analogy of the British Indian law except where there are strong reasons to the contrary. Do not let any law differ from the corresponding British Indian law merely for the unreasonable sake of showing independence or originality. This spirit would be petty and irrational. Never mind if certain people say that we

are merely copying. Provided the law itself is good and is applicable to our people, there can be nothing blameable in copying. One country may well adopt the good things of another. The most advanced—the proudest and the most independent—nations follow that course, otherwise the knowledge and experience of one country would become useless to another.

"Conflict of laws" not desirable.

(21) There is another strong reason to recommend that our laws should differ as little as possible from those of our neighbours, and it is this. If the important laws governing similar and adjacent communities materially differ, there ensues what is called "conflict of laws", which brings great difficulties and perplexities in the administration of justice. The difficulties and perplexities are so numerous and so serious that they have been the subject of bulky volumes by some of the ablest jurists.

Law not to interfere with religion.

(22) Again, see that the proposed law does not trench upon the domain of religion. Every law should abstain from interference with the religious community concerned. The State should be neutral and impartial in its policy. The policy of the State should be to let every individual practise any religion he likes, provided he does not thereby injure others, that is to say, violate the rights of others.

It should do more good than evil.

(23) Again, every proposed law must, more or less, affect the liberty or property of the people—must curtail liberty or diminish property. This is an evil in itself. Make sure, before passing the law, that the good of it will be clearly in excess of the evil attended to, if not, the proposed law cannot be a good one.

It should be simple and impartial.

(24) Make each law as simple and as intelligible to the people as may be possible consistently with the object to be accomplished. See

that the proposed law does not unduly favour any particular section of the people at the expense of another section. The laws should be impartial to all sections.

It should not curtail personal liberty.

(25) See that the proposed law does not curtail, or curtails as little as possible, the liberty of anyone to make himself as happy as he likes and in any manner he judges best—provided he does not injure others. As a rule, every member of society is the most interested in his own welfare. He will not neglect himself. His self-interest will powerfully prompt him to promote his own happiness. The State need not burden itself with any serious anxieties in this respect. The best policy for the State to pursue is to leave each individual to make himself happy in the manner he judges best—provided he does not injure another—provided he leaves other individuals similar liberty. The more this principle is kept in view and acted upon, the greater will be the quantity of happiness earned by each individual, and hence the greater will be the total quantity of happiness earned by the whole community.

Avoid passing bad laws.

(26) I have thus given Your Highness a few hints—a few rough hints—which will generally enable you to avoid passing bad or objectionable laws. All those hints you may not be able to carry in your memory. But, as you are getting these notes copied in your book, you may refer to them when you have occasion to consider any proposed law.

The subject of regular law.

(27) I have still a few further observations to offer. Heretofore, many things have been done by the several departments by means of circular orders, *jahirnamas* or notifications. It was necessary to do so at this stage, the main object

being to do away speedily with the darkness and confusion which had prevailed and to arrange things in a rough and ready manner, leaving nicer adjustments to follow at greater leisure. But hereafter, say from the time Your Highness will assume the powers of Maharaja, every measure which affects or materially affects the person, property or liberty of the people should be the subject of regular law framed and passed in Your Highness' name in due form. This will ensure greater precision and uniformity. It will carry greater weight. It will better enable the people to know what laws they are to obey and what the consequences of disobedience are. It will be a greater convenience to those officers themselves who have to give effect to the laws.

Do not give any order opposed to the laws.

(28) I beg Your Highness will always remember that the laws are the well-considered and permanent orders of the State. The Maharaja must not himself counteract them publicly or privately. The Maharaja must not give any orders opposed to the laws. He must not privately ask or hint to any judge or magistrate to favour or to disfavour anyone by setting aside the law. I mention this particularly and emphatically because Maharajas are under great temptation to do what they must not do. It would be false and treacherous conduct for any Raja or Maharaja to pass a deliberate order in public in the shape of a law and to ask judges and magistrates privately to break that very order.

The more the laws are respected, the better.

(29) The more the laws are respected, the better it is for the happiness of the people, which is the first duty of the ruler. And the ruler himself must most respect the laws as an example to the people.

Do not be influenced by foolish persons.

(30) Foolish, ignorant or selfish persons will constantly ask you—urge you—to do something yourself, or to get others to do something against the laws. They will even venture to say, "Is not the great Gaekwar able to do what he likes? Is there any power to restrain the Maharaja himself? If there is, then the Maharaja is not supreme in his country. He is a timid or weak Maharaja", and so on. Such things will be told you constantly in one form or another. Your Highness must not allow yourself to be influenced or excited thereby in the least. Take it all coolly and calmly. With a gentle royal smile, answer them by saying, "My education and my reflection have convinced me that that Maharaja is truly great who constantly respects the laws which have been designed for the good of the people. I am determined to act under that conviction." By pursuing such a course you will become truly great. You will be the greatest benefactor of your people. You will have a high place in the history of your country.

(31) It remains for me to say that the Hindu *Shastras* also repeatedly and most powerfully inculcate the same thing. One of their happiest maxims is that "Law is the king of kings." It is a precious maxim which must be engraved on the memory of rulers.

5

DUTIES OF KINGS

8th June 1881

The Maharaja is the depository of the greatest wealth and power and should devote himself to public good.

The great and fundamental truths which I have had the honour of offering for Your Highness' acceptance are the results of my sincere and thorough conviction. Those truths have been my guidance in the conduct of public affairs while filling the office of Chief Minister in three Native States successively for a series of more than twenty years. In following the guidance of those grand truths, in doing my best to assist in promoting the welfare of the people concerned, I have felt an inward satisfaction which words cannot adequately describe but the like of which, I trust, Your Highness will yourself enjoy in all its plenitude. It is probably the purest and noblest of human pleasures. It is a pleasure that lasts to the end of life. It is a sublime maxim of the Vedas that he alone lives who lives to do good to others. Who can do more good to others than the ruler of a community—than a Maharaja who is the depository of the greatest power and wealth in his country? I have alluded to myself personally not in a spirit of self-praise, but with the view of strengthening your impressions. If a humble private individual like myself has been liberally rewarded with honour and distinction in consequence of faithful endeavours to promote the happiness of the people, you may easily conceive what brilliant and lasting fame will be your reward as a Maharaja devoting himself to public good. But there is a far brighter reward to be looked for than worldly praise and fame. I refer to that great source which ordained your exaltation to your present position and opportunities.

The ideas of Vattel.

(2) In advising Your Highness in the interests of good government, let me call to my aid an eminent teacher of mankind in general, and of princes in particular. I refer to Vattel,* a famous European author, who lived in the last century. The following are some of his ideas bearing on the topics I have already submitted to Your Highness:

A good prince will not seek his own satisfaction.

> A good Prince, a wise conductor of society, ought to have his mind impressed with this great truth that the Sovereign power is solely entrusted† to him for the safety of the State and the happiness of all the people; that he is not permitted to consider himself as the principal object in the administration of affairs, to seek his own satisfaction, or his private advantage, but that he ought to direct all his views, all his steps, to the greatest advantage of the State and people who have submitted to him.[1]

Criminal flattery and posts given by

> But in most kingdoms a criminal flattery has long since caused these maxims to be forgotten.

* Emmerich de Vattel, Swiss jurist and scholar of international law.

† Per the original: intrusted

favour, to the neglect of merit.

A crowd of servile courtiers easily persuade a proud monarch that the nation was made for him and not he for the nation. He soon considers the kingdom as a patrimony that is his own property and his people as a herd of cattle from which he is to derive his wealth and which he may dispose of to answer his own views and gratify his passions. Hence those fatal wars undertaken by ambition, restlessness, hatred and pride. Hence those oppressive taxes, whose produce is dissipated by ruinous luxury, or squandered upon mistresses and favourites; hence, *in fine*, are important posts given by favour, while public merit is neglected, and everything that does not immediately interest the Prince is abandoned to Ministers and subalterns. Who can, in this unhappy government, discover an authority established for the public welfare? A great Prince will be on his guard even against his virtues. Let us not say, with some writers, that private virtues are not the virtues of kings—a maxim of superficial politicians, or of those who are very inaccurate in their expressions[.] [G]oodness, friendship, gratitude are still virtues on the throne; and would to God they were always to be found there! But a wise king does not yield an undeserving* obedience to their impulse. He cherishes them, he cultivates them in his private life, but in State affairs he listens only to justice and sound policy. And why? Because he knows that the government was entrusted† to him only for the happiness of society, and that, therefore, he ought not to consult his own pleasure in the use he makes of his power. He tempers his goodness with wisdom, he gives to friendship his domestic and private favours; he distributes posts and employments according to merit, public rewards to services done to the State. In

* Per the original: undiscerning

† Per the original: intrusted

a word, he uses the public power only with a view to the public welfare.[2]

He is the guardian of the laws.

He is, by virtue of that power, the guardian and defender of the laws; and while it is his duty to restrain each daring violator of them, ought he himself to trample them under foot?[3]

He should submit to the laws himself.

But while these laws exist, the sovereign ought religiously to maintain and observe them. They are the foundation of the public tranquillity and the firmest support of the sovereign authority. Everything is uncertain, violent, and subject to revolutions in those unhappy States where arbitrary power has placed her throne. It is, therefore, the true interest of the Prince, as well as his duty, to maintain and respect the laws; he ought to submit to them himself. We find this truth established in a piece published by order of Louis XIV,* one of the most absolute Princes that ever reigned in Europe. "Let it not be said that the sovereign is not subject to the laws of his State, since the contrary proposition is one of the truths of the law of nations, which flattery has sometimes attacked and which good princes have always defended as a tutelar divinity of their States."[4]

Manu on the duties of the king.

(3) I will now proceed to quote a passage or two of similar effect from Manu, the great Hindu Law-giver:

He says:

> Let the king act [...] as a father to his people.[5]

Again:

> Let the king prepare a just compensation for the good, and a just punishment for the bad. The rule of strict justice let him never transgress.[6]

* Per the original: Lewis

Again:

> A king is pronounced equally unjust in releasing the man who deserves punishment, and in punishing the man who deserves it not. He is just who always inflicts the punishment ordained by law.[7]

Kings have high duties and responsibilities.

(4) All this eminently shows that kings have high duties and responsibilities—that they are not to act wildly and arbitrarily like wild animals—that they have great principles and rules to respect. Their great duty is to promote the happiness of the people over whom the Almighty has placed them.

Good government is a science and an art.

(5) To promote the happiness of the people is an object easily enough understood in the gross, but it requires much study and it costs much self-denial to effectuate that object in these times when the interests of the people have become very numerous and very complex and when good government has become a regular science and also an art which needs to be regularly learnt. Principles and rules of good government have to be carefully learnt. They have to be constantly respected and observed. In other words, it is not enough for a Maharaja to say, "I know that it is my duty to be a father to my people", and to proceed to act under the capricious impulses of an untutored common sense. The fact is, the Maharaja has to learn his high profession and to practise it in conformity with its great laws and rules. The Maharaja who does not accept and observe such laws and rules will be just like a navigator in charge of a big ship who refuses the guidance of the compass and of the chart.

Why Oudh was annexed.

(6) I have already submitted to you some important quotations from authority in order to

strengthen the impressions I desire to make on your mind. I will here invite Your Highness' attention to a few more quotations, and these are taken from papers relating to the recent annexation of the large and important country of Oudh. I have laid great stress on the ruler's duty of maintaining the security of life, person, liberty and property and have pointed out the means to be employed to effect that object. The rulers of Oudh greatly failed in that object, and this was one of the strongest grounds for the annexation of that territory, as seen from the following extracts from the Oudh papers:

(a) The officers incompetent and the ruler's disregard to his duties.

(*a*) The Resident of Oudh reports:

> In spite of all that I have urged upon His Majesty (the King of Oudh), he continues to confide the conduct of his affairs to the same worthless and incompetent characters; to devote all his time to personal gratifications and frivolous amusements; and to manifest the same utter disregard to* his duties and high responsibilities. The same insecurity of † life and property in all parts of his dominions is felt, the same maladministration and malversations prevail in all departments.[8]

(b) The Nawab with low associates and no education.

(*b*) In another part, the Resident says:

> It was not to be wondered at that the young Nawab on his accession to power, with low people about him, and with only that degree of education which Native Princes receive, considered himself as having arrived at the highest of earthly felicity, and wondering what bonds and laws were to curb the will of a king, etc.[9]

* Per the original: of

† Per the original: to

(c) Absence of judicial courts.

(*c*) Again, the Resident reported to the Governor-General,

> of judicial courts there are none, except* at the Capital, and those which are there maintained are of no value.[10]

(d) The administration miserable.

(*d*) The consequence of this was that the administration of justice in Oudh was miserable. It is instructive to observe how the Government of India took notice of a case in which a person was, through influence, allowed to go unpunished, though there was clear evidence to prove that he had committed murder. The Government of India wrote, on the occasion, to the Resident at Lucknow in the following words:

> You will demand an audience of the King. You will represent to His Majesty the indignation with which the Governor-General views the scandalous denial of justice, which has just been exhibited at Lucknow, in the acquittal of this murderer, in the face of the clearest proofs of his guilt. And you will add that such acts are rapidly filling up the measures of the King's misgovernment—misgovernment which, His Majesty has been already warned, must end in the entire subversion of his kingly power.[11]

(e) Even the British subjects suffered.

(*e*) The Resident also complained that in consequence of want of administration of justice in Oudh, the subjects of the British Government, who were in that territory, also suffered. The British Government could not remain indifferent when their own subjects thus suffered from the maladministration of justice in Oudh.

(f) No efficient police.

(*f*) The Resident also complained that there was no efficient Police in Oudh territories. To quote again from the Oudh papers:

* Per the original: save

> Under the present regime, I do not think there is a shadow of security for life or property in Oudh In this part of the country, it is almost impossible for people to travel unless escorted by a large body of armed men.[12]

A Raj without any security of life, person and property must fall.

(7) I hope that I have now said enough and quoted enough to produce an unshakeable conviction, in Your Highness' mind, of the vital importance of an efficient Police supported by a Military force, and of the vital importance of an efficient administration of justice. Without these there can be no security of life, person, liberty, or property. And I say emphatically that, without such security, a Raj must inevitably fall, the fall being only a question of time. Fall it must, sooner or later.

Let these convictions be handed down to posterity.

(8) As one of the warmest well-wishers of Native States—as one who most earnestly desires that the existing Native States should ever continue to live—I will not be satisfied with Your Highness' entertaining and cherishing the convictions abovementioned, but I entreat Your Highness to take the utmost pains to communicate your conviction to your children with injunctions to them to communicate those convictions to their children again, so that, there may never arise any break in the continuity of those convictions in the Gaekwar House. Let every ruler of Baroda—good or bad or indifferent—maintain fair security of life, person, liberty and property in these territories and I guarantee the perpetuity of the Baroda Raj.

If such security is not maintained, rulers will lose their sovereign power.

(9) On the other hand, if the Native States fail to maintain such security, I predict that their rulers will, sooner or later, one after another, lose sovereign power and subside into the states of mere wealthy *jamindars*. It is a contingency, most

painful to contemplate, but it must be foreseen in order that it may be averted. (The proverb says: "To be forewarned is to be forearmed.")*

A most important piece of public service.

(10) It is on these grounds that the administration during Your Highness' minority has taken decided and vigorous action by way of organising an efficient police and an efficient system of administering justice—calculated to establish fair security of life, person, liberty and property. We consider this a most important and most essential piece of public service performed. We are proud of the action taken.

Those who ruin Native States.

(11) If, therefore, anyone, under the influence of ignorance or of a factious spirit, tells Your Highness that we have done wrong in this respect—that we have done wrong in incurring the cost of establishing the police and the judicial machinery—and advise you to do away with these and to revert to the old state of things, Your Highness should regard him as unfit to take part in your counsels. Such persons are just those who have already unconsciously ruined some Native States, and they are just those who will yet similarly ruin others.

The mistakes of former times.

(12) In connexion with the subject in hand, I must draw Your Highness' attention to one of the grave conclusions which Sir R. Meade's† Commission has recorded against Malhar Rao Gaekwar, the then ruler of Baroda, namely,

> That the Judicial Department and Administration require entire reform, the existing abuses

---

* Refers to the Latin proverb: *Praemonitus, praemunitus*.

† Richard J. Meade, renowned Anglo-Indian administrator. Chaired the 1873 Baroda Commission, which investigated Malhar Rao's maladministration of Baroda.

> being abolished, so as to remove the present uncertain and irregular application of the law and want of confidence in the proceedings of the courts and magistrates.[13]

How the Judicial Department is established on a firm basis.

(13) The entire reform pointed out by the Commission has been happily effected in its main features—one proof of this is to be found in the following passage extracted from a recent report of the Agent to the Governor-General to the Government of India, namely:

> The Judicial Department of the State is now established on a firm basis. It is sufficient for the work, is well paid, is officered, except in some of the posts in the lower grades, by thoroughly qualified men, and the work is done generally in a highly satisfactory manner. The judges of the *Varisht* Court and of the Session Courts would do credit to any service. There is, of course, still room for improvement in regard to despatch and precision. There is certainly no branch of the administration which gives greater satisfaction to the people than the Judicial.[14]

Its progress to be maintained.

(14) It will thus be seen, beyond all doubt, that it will be Your Highness' most important duty to maintain the progress so far made, and to make further possible improvements. I beg Your Highness to thoroughly digest and assimilate the general and special points I have been endeavouring to impress upon you.

6

PUBLIC HEALTH

22nd June 1881

The first object of good government.

I have dwelt somewhat longer on the subject of the security of life, person, liberty and property, because it is the condition of pre-eminent importance to the wellbeing of the people—the wellbeing of the people being the first object of good government. Unless a government has established and will steadily maintain such security, it cannot claim to be good—the ruler cannot say he has done his duty to the people.

The next duty is to maintain the people in good health—public health.

(2) The next important duty of government is to do what may be possible to maintain the people in good health. The health of each individual in a community depends, in a great measure, on himself—on his food, clothing, exercise, medical treatment, etc. As everyone has naturally a very strong desire to enjoy the blessing of health, he may be expected himself to take care of his health. But there are some important matters connected with public health which individuals cannot insure. They

are matters which the governments alone can properly arrange. If the government do not take up such matters, they will not be attended to at all. I will now proceed to state the chief of such matters.

Sanitation.

(3) Where people live in numbers and close to each other as in cities and towns, cleanliness has to be maintained as an important condition of public health. Dirt and refuse have to be removed from the streets. The drains have to be kept in good order. Abundance of fresh air has to be let in—and so forth. All this is called sanitation. With this may be combined several arrangements for public convenience, comfort, and safety. For example, good carriage roads may be made. The roads may be watered and lighted. Appliances may be kept ready to put down fires.

A sufficient and pure water supply.

(4) Another measure of great importance to public health is to give the people a sufficient and pure supply of water for daily use. In tropical climates, this is one of the most valued of blessings. The Maharaja who confers this blessing is sure to live in the memory of a grateful people.

Airy places for recreation.

(5) Another measure conducive to public health is to give to the crowded inhabitants of the city some pleasant and airy places to which they can drive, ride or walk; and where they can spend some portion of their leisure during the morning or evening with great benefit to their health. The Race Course and the Public Park in the city of Baroda are examples of such places of resort.

Vaccination.

(6) Another measure conducive to public health is to arrange for the vaccination of the people and the consequent prevention of the dreadful attacks of smallpox.

Hospitals.

(7) Another measure conducive to public health is to establish, at the various centres of population, hospitals and dispensaries, where sick persons may easily obtain medical advice, medical treatment, and the requisite medicines themselves.

The health of the people, a subject of primary importance.

(8) Any Government which cares for the happiness of the people will earnestly attend to all these measures and, perhaps, to others also of the kind which I need not stop here to specify. Money spent on such measures is always well spent. The people have an undoubted right to be thus protected in their health. The Maharaja, who acts as the father of his people, will always cheerfully arrange for the health of his people.

Action already taken.

(9) During Your Highness' minority, therefore, the administration has taken some action in this important direction. The city of Baroda, your capital, is now cleaner than before. It has better roads, it is better watered and better lighted. It is more efficiently protected against fires. The people have the Race Course and the new Public Park to take fresh air in. Vaccination is better attended to, and good medical institutions have been established and are well maintained. Towns in the *taluks* have also had some attention paid to them in these respects. For more detailed information as to what has been heretofore done, I beg to refer Your Highness to the Administration Reports.

There is scope for further action.

(10) But it is certain that we are yet far from the complete fulfilment of our duty in this branch. There is much scope for further action, to which, I trust, Your Highness will turn your attention among other important things. Much yet remains to be done, and all this will be

brought to your notice in detail hereafter. But I will here mention one or two salient points.

A water supply scheme for Baroda.

(11) It is most unfortunate that we have not been able to provide a good water supply for this city of Baroda though most anxious to do so. Large and costly undertakings require to be carefully investigated before proceeding to execution. This is the only way of avoiding blunders and losses. A thorough investigation was therefore instituted in order to ascertain what alternative projects were available. It was made by employing exclusively for the purpose Mr. Crosthwaite,* a Bengal engineer specially versed in the water supply of towns and cities. The result may be briefly stated. Water cannot be brought to this city from the Narmada River, nor from the Orsang tributary of the Narmada, nor from the Mahi River, nor from Pavagadh, nor from the Muval *talab* near Savli. The only project open was declared to be that of sinking two or three gigantic wells near the railway station, drawing water from them by means of powerful steam machinery, storing up the water to a certain extent, and distributing the same through the city in the usual manner. Here the matter has rested for some time. This project involves certain risk and uncertainty which will be explained to Your Highness when the subject is seriously taken up for consideration. I will, therefore, only say that if Your Highness succeeds in giving the city a good water supply, Your Highness will, on this account alone, be remembered as a great benefactor.

---

* Thomas Crosthwaite, employed as a Special Engineer in the Public Works Department between 1876–79.

The drainage.

(12) The improvement of the drainage of the city is another very important question. It is really one of the most difficult and puzzling questions.

Improvements in other towns.

(13) In other towns, those in the *taluks*—we have as yet confined ourselves to the maintenance of cleanliness and even this has been, I am afraid, very superficial. In the town of Nowsari, however, much has been done in comparison. Some lakhs of rupees have been sanctioned for securing good drinking water wells for the various villages throughout these territories, and the work is, I believe, already commenced. It has to be urged on to completion. Hospitals and Dispensaries and Vaccinating Agencies have been fairly spread over the country. In connection with this subject, I beg to say that whatever is done to promote the health of the people, to prevent disease, and to cure or mitigate suffering cannot fail to be appreciated as one of the most direct and practical benefits of good government. A benevolent ruler will give a large share of his attention to the promotion of public health, which is a very important component element of public happiness, the main object of government.

Individual liberty not to be interfered with, to promote public health.

(14) In our anxiety to promote public health, we have, however, to be careful not to interfere unnecessarily with the liberty of the individual—a liberty which is one of the most valuable blessings. The individual must not be forced to take particular diet, to take particular medicines, to take particular exercise, etc. Of these the individual himself is the best judge. The government will do well to limit its action to matters which affect the community in the gross—such as general cleanliness, good drain-

age, good water supply, good hospitals and dispensaries, efficient vaccine operations, etc., etc. In these matters, the government acts as representing the community itself and for the benefit of the community.

The public good and popular resistance are both points to be considered.

(15) Even while thus acting, the Government has to be careful that it is not carried too far by its benevolent zeal—that it does not go too much in advance of the views and wishes of the people in the present state of their intelligence and education. How far the government may go and when it should stop, in a given case, are practical questions which will have to be decided from time to time after a careful comparison of the public good proposed to be effected on the one hand, with the popular resistance which might be expected on the other hand.

Government may give useful advice.

(16) I have said above that in the matter of health, the liberty of the individual should not be unnecessarily interfered with. But, without interfering with that liberty, Government may give [useful]* advice. For instance, Government in the Medical Department may notify to the people that such and such precautions are instrumental in averting attacks of cholera—that, when an attack actually occurs, such and such a remedy has been found to be good—that such and such precautions are useful to prevent the spread of the disease—and so forth.

Special preventive and curative measures.

(17) Whenever any general diseases break out, such as cholera, fever, smallpox, etc., the Government should take special preventive and curative measures. For instance, additional

* British India Press edition: usual.

medical men should be sent off for acting in the locality concerned. Medicines should be made available to the people concerned. The Medical Department will propose the necessary measures, and these must be promptly sanctioned.

The Medical Department the best adviser.

(18) In matters relating to public health generally, the Medical Department is the best adviser of the government.

Maintain the medical institutions.

(19) After all that I have said about public health, I am sure Your Highness will readily recognise the great duty of maintaining and in no way curtailing the various Medical Institutions which have been brought into existence during your minority and which are largely saving life, promoting health and mitigating suffering. The father of the people must never say, "Never mind how the people get sick, suffer, and die—I want to save money by abolishing or reducing these Medical Institutions." I do hope that the great Gaekwar House will never produce so avaricious and cruel a father of the people.

A summary to show the great duties of the government.

(20) I will close this day's lecture here by a very brief retrospect:

(*i*) We began by saying that the first duty of the government is to promote the happiness of the people.

(*ii*) We recognised the fact that the security of life, person, liberty and property is indispensably necessary to the happiness of the people.

(*iii*) We saw how necessary it is for this important object to maintain a sufficient and efficient Police, to maintain a moderate and effective military force, to maintain a well-organised and efficient judicial machinery and to uphold and enforce the laws with firmness and impartiality.

(*iv*) And today, we have seen how important it is for public happiness to maintain and improve sanitation in towns and cities and to maintain and improve the various medical agencies which are at work—in a word, to maintain and improve the health of the population.

We do well, occasionally, to thus briefly review the leading principles we have already dwelt upon, because it strengthens the impressions made, it shows in a small compass what the great duties of the government are, it shows them in the order of their importance, and it shows their mutual relations.

7

FOOD SUPPLY

30th June 1881

Another important duty—the supply of food.

The last time we met here, we dwelt on the duty of the government to promote the health of the people and briefly noticed the principal methods in which this may be done. We will now proceed to another very important duty of government, namely, the duty of doing all that may be possible to enable the people to obtain sufficient and even abundant food. Without sufficient food, the people, it is obvious, cannot be happy.

Individual exertion.

(2) I may observe at the outset that, in this respect, the government cannot do much. Much must be left to the exertions of the people themselves. Each member of the community has to work for himself and family, and to thereby earn the means of living. Nature has made food so absolutely necessary to everyone, that everyone may be expected to do his utmost to acquire food without being urged to do so from the outside. In short, natural motives act with great force in this direction.

Government to see that the natural motives act freely.

(3) Natural motives prompt individuals to acquire not only food but many other things which are the means of happiness. The main duty of the government is to let those motives act with all legitimate freedom, to see that those natural motives are not needlessly impeded or weakened by artificial causes. This duty of the government should be clearly realised and steadily fulfilled.

The security of life etc. necessary for the acquisition of wealth.

(4) Let us here consider what the government should do and what it should not do, in order to let those natural motives operate fully and bear all good fruit. As I have already stated, every member of a community is prompted by natural motives to acquire the means of his own happiness. Prompted by such motives he will employ his best exertions to acquire wealth. Now, government should, by maintaining security of life, person, liberty and property, maintain those natural motives in all their strength, allow free scope for those exertions, and secure that wealth fully to the acquirer. Just see what would take place if there were little or no security of life, person, liberty and property. Many a man would say to himself, "Why should I acquire wealth, or to acquire it why should I save anything while I am liable to be murdered at any time, or wounded or thrown into prison, or despoiled of my wealth." It follows, then, the security of life, person, liberty and property is necessary for the acquisition and growth of wealth in the community. The people should have no fears of the sort indicated above. I will state the matter somewhat more in detail. No one should have reason to fear that he might be plundered of his property, whether in town, or in country, or on the highway. The *sowkar* must

be secured in the possession of his money. The *ryot* must be secured in the possession of his stock of grain; even the poor woman who carries a basket of vegetables to the market must feel secure as regards those vegetables. In short, everyone, rich and poor, must feel that he is pretty sure of keeping and enjoying his property, great or small. He must feel secure against violence, against fraud, against unjust litigation and arbitrary action by the *Sarkar*.

How these conditions will be secured.

(5) All these conditions will be secured by the means I have already explained, namely, by maintaining a good Police in villages and towns, by maintaining an efficient judicial machinery, and by maintaining good laws. The government should do many other things in order to promote the growth of wealth, and I will proceed to state some of them.

Let the people enjoy their wealth freely.

(6) The government should allow the people to enjoy their wealth freely, that is to say, without needless restrictions or fears. For example, I say, no one should be prevented from driving a carriage and pair. Again, no one should be prevented from building the firmest houses by the sides of the high roads. Again, no one should be prevented from wearing rich clothes or costly ornaments. In short, the people should be quite free to enjoy or display their wealth as they may like. Indeed, the happier the Maharaja sees his people, the happier should he himself be.

Importance of the administration with respect to the *ryots* and to land.

(7) To proceed to another matter of importance. A large portion of our people derive their subsistence from the cultivation of soil. The land is a great source of wealth. The *ryot* labours on the land and the land gives him a return. It follows that the administration with respect to the *ryot* and with respect to the land

has a very important bearing on the happiness of our subjects. It should be remembered that the *ryots*—those who pursue agriculture as their profession—form the great body of our subjects who reside permanently in the country, who are the fixed population. As the land they cultivate is immovable, they, the cultivators, are also in a great measure immovable. As a body, the *ryots* would not think of abandoning their lands and of leaving the country unless great and continuous *zulm* was practised. The *ryots*, then, constitute a very important portion of our settled population, and the produce they raise every year from the land constitutes a very important portion of the wealth of the country. Hence the great importance of the administration with respect to the *ryots* and with respect to the land.

Taxes to be moderate.

(8) To make the *ryots* happy and to promote the growth of wealth from land, the *Sarkar*'s tax on the land should be moderate, so moderate as to leave to the *ryots* enough to maintain themselves and their families in fair comfort. In many Native States, the principle practically followed is unfortunately more or less different. Some of these States wring as large a revenue as possible from the *ryots*—and this, of course, impoverishes this very useful class of subjects. It is quite contrary to the fundamental maxim with which we started, namely, it is the first object of government to promote the happiness of the people.

The *ryots* should have a good tenure.

(9) Another important thing necessary to make the *ryots* happy and to promote the growth of wealth from land is that the *ryots* should have a good tenure for holding the land. The *ryots* should feel every confidence that they will not be deprived of their land so long as they regu-

larly pay the *Sarkar* tax due thereon. The *ryots* should feel that, provided they pay the tax regularly, they can hold the land for generations. It has been proved by reasoning, and it has been found by experience, that nothing is more prejudicial to agricultural prosperity than insecurity of possession.

Taxation not to be increased.

(10) Another important thing necessary to make the *ryots* happy and to promote the growth of wealth from land is that, when the land is made to yield more in consequence of the application to the land of the *ryots*' labour and capital, the *Sarkar* should not increase its tax on that account and thereby deprive the *ryots* of the fair return due to their labour and capital. If the *Sarkar* pursues a contrary policy, the *ryots* will feel no inducement to lay out their labour and capital for the improvement of the land; the yield of the land will not increase and may even decrease.

Do not employ farmers of revenue between the *ryots* and the *Sarkar*.

(11) Another important thing necessary to make the *ryots* happy and to promote the growth of wealth from land is that *izardars*, or farmers of revenue, should not be employed between the *ryots* and the *Sarkar*. Such agents used to be extensively employed in former times, and they used to oppress and impoverish the *ryots* terribly. The best system is that known as the *ryotwari*, that is to say, that system under which the *Sarkar* deals with each *ryot* directly. This system is really most favourable to the *ryot*; it secures him the best justice and the best consideration, and promotes his self-respect and independence. The only thing is that such a system will require the employment of an extensive agency and an agency most carefully selected with reference to knowledge, experience, judgment and probity.

The cost of such agency will be more than repaid by the saving of what the *izardar* would otherwise have pocketed, while an immense advantage is that the *ryots* will be protected against heavy and arbitrarily exactions.

Bhag-batai system not desirable.

(12) I must take this opportunity to impress another truth on Your Highness' mind. Kazi Sahib* has, no doubt, explained to you what the *bhag-batai* system is. Its main feature is that the *Sarkar* takes actually a portion of the produce of the land as the *Sarkar*'s revenue, instead of taking the revenue in cash. The result of my consideration of this system is that, though it may answer for [minor] States, it would not at all answer for a large State like Baroda. It has happily been mostly got rid of in these territories. The credit of this belongs to the late Maharaja Khande Rao.† I hope that the great and beneficial change which that Maharaja introduced will be fully maintained. In the Amreli Mahals, however, the *bhag-batai* system still continues. Some steps have been taken to apply a corrective in this respect.

A regular survey and reassessment necessary.

(13) I have already brought to Your Highness' notice the great importance of the land tax being moderate. To fix the land tax moderately and equitably, a regular survey and reassessment are indispensably necessary. It is an operation of great magnitude and great cost, but, I repeat, it is quite necessary. The present administration has had no leisure to undertake that operation. But I hope that so necessary a measure will not be long delayed, for on it the

* Kazi Shahabuddin, head of the Revenue Department, and former Dewan of Cutch.

† Khande Rao Gaekwad, the Maharaja of Baroda between 1856–1870.

welfare of the great body of the *ryots* largely depends.

Arbitrary taxes not to be imposed.

(14) When the land tax has been moderately and equitably fixed by means of the operation just alluded to, the Maharaja should most resolutely abstain from superadding arbitrary and unjust taxes like the *gaddi nazarana*, Palace *nazarana*, marriage *nazarana*, and so forth.

Grant of special privileges objectionable.

(15) I would also warn Your Highness against another abuse. It has happened that some individual of religious or other influences came to the Maharaja and applied for an annual subsidy. Instead of disposing of the matter in some ordinary way, it has sometimes happened [that] the Maharaja issued a *sanad* authorizing the said individual to levy a tax on each *ryot* or on each plough of a *ryot* in a certain village or in a certain group of villages. The grant of such a right or privilege is most objectionable, because [it is] injurious to the *ryots* concerned. I hope that such grants will never be made hereafter. By giving effect to the leading principles I have mentioned, the *ryots* will be made happy and the land will yield wealth steadily and to the greatest possible extent. I have, however, to draw Your Highness' attention to one or two more matters in the same connection.

Agricultural produce not to be taxed when exported.

(16) I think it is essential to agricultural prosperity that agricultural produce should not be burdened with any heavy duties when the same is exported. If the produce could be altogether freed from export duty, this would be the best thing. But if circumstances make this difficult, the export duty must be very moderate. I should say, generally, that the duty should be as much as possible below 5 per cent on the value of the commodity exported. Special articles

such as opium, etc., are, of course, exceptions to the general principle.

Food grains to be free from duty.

(17) It being desirable that food should be cheap to all, and especially to the poorer classes, I think that all food grains should be free from duty altogether.

Encourage the multiplication of production.

(18) Again. Any measures which tend to increase the produce of the land, or to make the produce more valuable, are most beneficial. Produce is increased, for instance, by better ploughing, better manuring, better weeding, etc. More valuable crops may be raised by providing or improving the means of irrigation. By such means, land which has been yielding some poor crop may, for example, be made to yield sugarcane. Instead of yielding 20 rupees worth of crop per acre, it may be made to yield 200 rupees worth—an immense gain to the *ryot* individually and to the people generally. Hence, the *Sarkar* should do everything possible to encourage the multiplication of wells and other means of irrigation.

Reduce the cost of carriage.

(19) Again. The great bulk of agricultural produce has to be carried to the market for sale. The charge for such carriage may seem small in individual cases, but, on the whole, it is a serious item. It follows that any measure which will reduce the cost of carriage will be a great benefit to the *ryot* and to the community. Therefore, the *Sarkar* should make roads of different classes, according to local requirements and resources, and should even make railroads where ever suitable. It should be remembered that when produce has to be carried on the heads of *coolies*, the cost of carriage is highest; when pack bullocks carry the produce, the cost of carriage is lowered; when carts carry the

produce, especially on metalled roads, the cost of carriage is still further lowered. And carriage of produce by railway is the cheapest of the whole.

Give the *ryots* waste land on easy terms.

(20) Another means of increasing the production of land in a country is to have rules by which the *ryots* of the country are enabled to obtain waste land on easy terms and on a secure tenure.

Encourage manufactures.

(21) But, besides land, there are other sources of wealth. Manufactures form the most important of these; manufactures supply the means of living to a portion of the population. As such, manufactures must be encouraged in every legitimate manner. This is all the more imperative because the population is increasing and there is not land enough to occupy all the population. That part of the population which cannot get land to cultivate must have recourse to manufactures. It follows that the *Sarkar* should not tax the manufactures of the country. If the *Sarkar* must tax to some extent, the tax must be very moderate indeed—it must be so moderate as not to repress or restrict the manufactures to an appreciable degree.

Do not tax raw materials or the machinery used.

(22) Again. To promote the manufactures of the country, the *Sarkar* should refrain from taxing the raw materials used in such manufactures, for taxing the raw materials would be, indirectly but in effect, taxing the manufactures themselves. Similarly, to promote the same object, all machinery used for local manufactures should be free from *Sarkari* taxes. So also coal, which may be necessary to make the machinery go. I say this particularly in reference to any spinning and weaving mills which may be introduced in these territories.

Government not to come in the way of the people undertaking any profitable work.

(23) Bearing on the general subject of the *Sarkar* affording every facility to the people in view to their finding employment—to their getting the means of livelihood—to their acquiring wealth—I may here allude to another principle. It is that the *Sarkar* should generally abstain from undertaking any work which would otherwise be done by the people themselves. To the extent the *Sarkar* undertakes such work, the people are deprived of the same and deprived of the profits thereby arising. It is, in fact, taking so much livelihood from the people. To elucidate this, I will give only one example. Suppose the *Sarkar* undertakes a system of lending money at interest to the people—in other words, that the *Sarkar* undertakes the business of the *sowkar*. It is evident that by so doing, the *Sarkar* deprives a certain number of *sowkars* of the means of their livelihood.

Do not undertake private trade.

(24) For the same reasons it would be wrong for the *Sarkar* to undertake private trade. Some Native princes have been so grasping, or so ignorant, that they have, contrary to the general principle under advertency, undertaken a great deal of employment which ought to be left to the people themselves. Such princes, no doubt, obtain more money thereby, but it is at the expense of their people.

Summary of the above.

(25) To sum up—

To promote the acquisition of livelihood by the people—to promote the production of wealth in the country—the following are the chief conditions to be observed:

(*a*) Security of life, person, liberty and property should be maintained.

(*b*) The people should be allowed to enjoy wealth freely.

(*c*) Land being the chief source of wealth, the *Sarkari* tax on land should be moderate.

(*d*) The tenure of land should be secured.

(*e*) The improvements made in land at the cost of the labour and capital of the *ryots* should not be taxed by the *Sarkar*—at least for a long time.

(*f*) The *ryotwari* system of land administration is the best; the farming system—that of employing *izardars* as formerly—is very pernicious.

(*g*) The *bhag-batai* system is bad for a large Native State like Baroda.

(*h*) A regular survey and reassessment of lands should be made.

(*i*) There should be no arbitrary tax like the *gaddi nazarana*, etc.

(*j*) There should be no grants to priests, etc., of the privilege of levying imposts on ploughs, etc.

(*k*) Produce should not be charged with export duties. At least such duties should be very moderate.

(*l*) All food grains required for the sustenance of our people should be free from duties altogether.

(*m*) All facilities should be afforded for the better ploughing, better manuring, better weeding, etc., of the land.

(*n*) Wells and other means of irrigation should be encouraged.

(*o*) Roads and railways should be made to reduce the cost of carriage.

(*p*) The *ryots* of the country should be enabled to get waste land for cultivation on easy terms and on good tenure.

(*q*) Manufactures should be encouraged.

(*r*) The manufactures of the country should not be taxed. If taxed, the tax should be very moderate indeed.

(*s*) The raw materials required for those manufactures should not be taxed.

(*t*) Machinery, coal, etc., required for the manufactures should not be taxed.

(*u*) The *Sarkar* should not undertake the work or trade which belongs to private individuals. In a few exceptional cases, however, where individuals would not come forward unless the *Sarkar* takes the initiative, the *Sarkar* might for a time do this.

The work of the present administration.

(26) The foregoing is not an exhaustive list, but it will indicate the general policy to be pursued and the reasons for pursuing the same. The matter being studied so far, other measures may suggest themselves hereafter. The broad principles being understood, it will be easy to discuss the merits of any new measure that may be brought forward for consideration. The present administration has kept these general principles in view and endeavoured to give effect to several of them, more or less. But much yet remains to be accomplished in the same direction.

8

PUBLIC WORKS DEPARTMENT

13th July 1881

Observations on the Public Works Department.

Today I will submit to Your Highness some observations on the Public Works Department, which has an important bearing on the public welfare.

A professional engineer to be at the head.

(2) This department constructs and repairs all important public works, such as palaces, jails, schools, hospitals, dispensaries, military buildings, roads and so forth. As such, it is necessary that a professional engineer should be at the head of this department.

Important department that gives us useful public works.

(3) It is an important spending department. It spends several lakhs of rupees every year and gives us in return useful public works such as those above enumerated. What it spends in any year depends on the requirements of the State and also on what funds the State can spare from the surplus revenue—that is to say, the savings of the State. No State like Baroda can get on without the Public Works Department, because there are always valuable public works to be

maintained in repair, without which those works would go to ruin more or less rapidly, and because there are also some new bridges to be constructed, and so on.

Want of public works at the commencement of the administration.

(4) When the present administration began, we found that many public works of the most necessary character were wanting. There was not even a *Cutcherry* for the Dewan and for the heads of the various departments of the States. There were no courthouses. There was nothing like proper jails, schoolhouses, hospitals, or dispensaries; they were either very deficient or totally wanting. There was almost an entire absence of roads. The requirements of civilised government in these respects had been neglected by the State, for how many years I do not know. We experienced grave and numerous difficulties. We therefore organised the Public Works Department and set it going. Many public works have been already finished, many are in progress, and some are in contemplation. The particulars may be learnt from the Administration Reports.

A few general principles.

(5) I proceed to lay before Your Highness some general principles which deserve to be kept in view in connection with this important department:

(a) A trained head.

(*a*) This important department always requires a professionally trained and qualified head, as indeed every important department requires. Men like Gulam Ali* of the old *Imarat Karkhana* would never do hereafter.

(b) A good Account and Audit Department.

(*b*) There should be a good account and audit establishment in connection with the Public Works Department to duly register and check

* Gulam Ali Lukmanji Vohra, head of the *Imarat Karkhana* under Malhar Rao, dismissed and penalized in 1875 for mismanagement and corruption.

every rupee of the expenditure. This department should be readily supplied with the requisite funds. Failure in this respect would keep the department more or less idle, which would be bad economy.

(c) Employ the best architect for a costly building.

(*c*) Where a large, costly, and conspicuous building has to be erected, especially at the Capital, employ the best architect available to make proper designs and plans for the same. This is of the highest importance. Without such precaution, lakhs of rupees would be wasted—perhaps worse than wasted—because crude and clumsy edifices would be raised as monuments of the sad want of judgment of those who raised them.

(d) Do not blindly adopt European styles.

(*d*) Do not blindly adopt European styles for such buildings. European styles are best for Europe. We, in India, should follow the best styles which are suited to India, and which have been for ages adopted in India. In this respect, the course we have already taken in the instances of the new Palace, the new College, and the new Jamnabai Dispensary, is the only proper one, and ought to serve as an example for the future.

(e) Plans and estimates to be previously prepared.

(*e*) As a rule, no public work should be begun without a plan and estimate previously prepared and submitted and sanctioned by the *Sarkar*. Whatever public work is undertaken, let it be done in the best manner. The work should be sound and durable and should reflect credit on the period in eyes of future generations. No trouble and expense should be spared to secure this great object.

(f) Get work done by contract.

(*f*) Get works executed by contract as far as may be possible. The contract system has many advantages over the departmental system.

(g) Prefer our labourers to outsiders.

(*g*) As far as may be possible, make our public works conducive to the livelihood of our labourers and artisans. Employ them in preference to outsiders. Employ local material in preference to foreign material.

(h) Do necessary repairs.

(*h*) Do not grudge the cost of necessary repairs to buildings, roads, bridges, etc., etc. If the Maharaja does not add to the public works, he should at least properly preserve what he has inherited from the past. Public works out of order, owing to want of repairs from time to time, always reflect disgrace on the *Sarkar*.

(i) Give permanent sanctions for annual repairs.

(*i*) Where the annual cost of repair is not likely to vary much, give permanent or standing sanctions for the repairs so that time and trouble may be saved and the necessary repairs may be executed in due season. For instance, such sanction may be given for the repair of the road from the City to the Camp and of the road from the City to Makkarpura.

(j) Do not spoil the original design.

(*j*) In repairing large and costly buildings, which have been built upon proper designs or after appropriate styles, or in making any additions or alterations to such buildings, be careful not to act arbitrarily, be careful not to violate the original design or style. This is a mistake constantly committed in Native States.

Public works deserve special attention.

(6) Public works such as *cutcherries*, court-houses, jails, schools, etc., etc., are indeed necessary to a civilised government. But they are not what are called reproductive works—they are not works which directly increase the wealth of the people, but they are the most important and deserve special attention.

Promote all reproductive public works.

(7) A *Cutcherry* is not a reproductive work, because it does not add to the production of the country or diminish and save the expenditure of

the country. An irrigation well is a reproductive work, because it increases the crop of the land watered thereby. A road I consider to be a reproductive work, because it reduces and saves the cost of carrying goods. Earnestly, then, promote all reproductive public works. The more this is done, the better will it be for the country. The Gaekwar cannot conquer new territories, but it is in his power to increase the value of the territories already in his possession—to increase their value by means of reproductive public works.

Multiply wells and roads.

(8) The main thing in these territories is to arrange for the multiplication of irrigating wells and of useful roads.

Fair weather roads to be made.

(9) Fair weather roads should be made in abundance at a moderate cost per mile, so that ordinary country carts may move about easily in fair weather.

Metalled roads to be sparingly made.

(10) Metalled roads are very costly in the soil of Gujarat in consequence of the cost of procuring metal from a distance. Their annual maintenance is also very costly. Such roads have, therefore, to be very sparingly made—they should be made only where such high cost would be justifiable.

The best road is the railroad.

(11) The best road for Gujarat is the little railroad, such as already connects our town of Dabhoi with the city of Baroda, with Bahadurpur, with Chandod and with Miyagam. In the long run, it is really much cheaper than a metalled road, while it is infinitely more convenient. The advantages of a railroad of the sort over a metalled road may be briefly stated as follows:

(*i*) The cost of construction and repair is lower.

(*ii*) The charges for moving goods and passengers are clear.

(*iii*) The journey is performed much more comfortably and much more safely.

(*iv*) The journey may be performed in all seasons, irrespective of the state of the weather.

(*v*) The railroad pays some return on the capital spent on the same, whereas a metalled road does not.

Multiply railways in Baroda.

(12) Therefore, the government of Baroda ought to multiply such sorts of railway in its own territories wherever there is need for the same.

Repair tanks.

(13) In India generally, and in Gujarat specially, tanks and *talabs* are of great use to the people. The Public Works Department ought to keep such reservoirs in good repair.

Reclaim marshy tracts.

(14) The same department should undertake the reclamation of large marshy tracts for purposes of cultivation wherever this can be done at reasonable cost.

Give attention to temples.

(15) Temples, *dharmshalas* and such other public buildings should also have due attention in those instances in which their repair is the duty of the *Sarkar*.

Utilise surplus revenue on public works.

(16) In conclusion, let me see what perhaps it is needless to say: that it will undoubtedly be much better—infinitely better—for the State to spend the surplus revenue on useful public works than adding to the already large stock of Palace jewellery. We have enough of personal ornaments. Let the country have its ornaments in the shape of useful public works. It is these that will raise the name and fame of the Maharaja.

Burke on irrigation works.

(17) As bearing on what I have just said, I feel tempted to read to Your Highness an eloquent passage from Edmund Burke, who was a great orator of the period of George III. I read this

passage when I was a young man about to enter the world, but I vividly remember it to this day. Speaking on the irrigation works of a part of the Madras Presidency, Burke said:

> These are the monuments of real kings, who were the fathers of their people; testators to a posterity which they embraced as their own. These are the grand sepulchres built by ambition, but by the ambition of an insatiable* benevolence which, not contented with reigning in the dispensation of happiness during the contracted term of human life, had strained, with all the reachings and graspings of a vivacious mind, to extend the dominion of their bounty beyond the limits of nature, and to perpetuate themselves through generations of generations, the guardians, the protectors, the nourishers of mankind.[1]

* Per the original: unsatiable.

9

EDUCATION

20th July 1881

It is the duty of Government to look after the intellectual and moral advancement of the people.

We set out by declaring that the first duty of the Government is to promote the happiness of the people. We have been considering various means by which the happiness of the people should be promoted. We have been chiefly considering the physical happiness of the people. It is now time to state that it is also the duty of the government to look after the intellectual and moral advancement of the people. The origin of this duty is self-evident. The Maharaja is the father of his people, and the father wishes to make his children not only healthy and happy but wise also.

The State to take an active part.

(2) In India at least, it is evident that the State should take an active and leading part in the education of the people. If the State did nothing, the people themselves would do very little in the cause of public education.

The Maharaja to improve existing conditions.

(3) What measures have been taken in the performance of this great duty of the government, during these six years of the administra-

tion during Your Highness' minority, may be gathered in detail from the Annual Reports which have been printed and published. Your Highness will have not only to maintain the advance which has already been thus made, but to make further advances.

Some general principles.

(4) I will now place before Your Highness some general principles which have to be followed in the Educational Department of the State.

(a) English education to be placed within the reach of those disposed to acquire it.

(*a*) High Education through the medium of the English language, should be placed within the reach of those who are disposed to acquire the same. Those who have acquired high education through the medium of the English language will probably be the most enlightened members of the community. They will probably be the most effectual promoters of progress: they will probably be the foremost to correct the gross errors of ignorance and superstition. Indeed, my belief—my strong conviction—is that any Indian community in the present age would be stagnant without some such elements as just mentioned.

(b) The highest English school to be at the Capital.

(*b*) The highest and the best English school should be at the Capital of the State, as it is. I hope it will, before long, become one of the regular Colleges of India. We are providing it with a building which will do honour to Baroda.

(c) The Central School to have English professors.

(*c*) English literature, science and philosophy are best taught by Englishmen. Therefore our Central School at the Capital should always have English gentlemen as professors. The temptation to appoint Natives for patriotical or economical motives should be firmly resisted. Natives, however, may answer well as Assistants to the English professors, especially in mathematics and natural sciences.

(d) The number of Anglo-Vernacular schools to be increased.

(*d*) It is not enough to have one central school at the Capital as described above. Several feeders to the same should be established both at the Capital and in the Districts, in the shape of Anglo-Vernacular schools. The number we already have must be gradually increased.

(e) The scheme of studies to be the same as in English schools.

(*e*) The scheme of studies in all the above mentioned schools should be the same as in corresponding British schools. The reason is this: if our scheme of studies were different, our youths would not be able to pass the Bombay University examinations; our youths would not be able to get employment outside our territories. But it is highly desirable that we should so educate our youths as to enable them to find employment, whether in our own territories or in the much larger field of British India.

(f) Let education make useful citizens.

(*f*) Though the scheme of studies is to be the same as in British India, I would urge our Professors to pay greater attention to the object of making our youths orderly and useful citizens. Cramming should be discouraged. The valuable faculty of thought and judgment should be better developed.

(g) No special religious instruction to be given.

(*g*) The education given should be elemental* in regard to religion; that is to say, no special religious instruction should be given.

(h) General morality to be taught.

(*h*) I would, however, strongly recommend that general and universal morality be taught in all our schools by means of a small and well-chosen tract. Similarly, let that morality be taught which the State enforces by pain and penalties—that morality which is embodied in

* British India Press edition: mental. The implication is that instructors should teach religion in a basic, conceptual, non-doctrinal sense only.

the Penal Code. It seems to me quite essential that our youths should be taught early what motives, intentions, and acts are wrong and which of these are punishable by the State. Such teaching will not occupy more than a short time, but it will save many a youth from committing acts which are morally wrong or acts which are criminally punishable.

(i) The masses to be educated through the vernacular schools.

(*i*) The great mass of the people must be educated through the vernacular schools established at all centres of population including the Capital.

(j) State schools in towns and grant-in-aid ones in the villages.

(*j*) The schools in the towns may well be entirely State schools. Those in the villages may be grant-in-aid schools. A judicious system of grants-in-aid will enable the State, at a comparatively small expense, to extensively control the education of the people.

(k) Schools for girls.

(*k*) The vernacular schools above-mentioned include schools for girls wherever there is a demand for these.

(l) One central vernacular school to impart high education.

(*l*) There may be one central vernacular school at the Capital to impart high education. We already have one here known as the Vernacular College of Science. It has been tried as an experiment on the strong recommendation of such men as Rao Bahadur Vinayak Rao,* Rao Bahadur Janardhan Gadgil,† Dr. Bhalchandra‡ and others. The experiment has, I am glad to say, proved a good success in several important respects. Further experience may suggest some modifica-

---

* Vinayak Rao Janardhan Kirtane, *Naib* Dewan, and Minister for Education, Police, and the *Khangi*.

† Janardhan Gadgil, Pusine Judge of the *Varisht* Court.

‡ Bhalchandra Krishna Bhatawadekar, the Darbar Physician, and Principal of the Vernacular College of Science.

tions in its details, and may perhaps enable us to reduce its cost.

(m) Special school for Eurasians.

(*m*) A special school for Eurasian children we already have at the Capital, and this must be kept up, of course.

(n) Study of Sanskrit not to be neglected.

(*n*) There are a few Sanskrit schools also; and in a Native State, these are popular. Sanskrit learning must not be allowed to perish from neglect. But too many must not be tempted to become devotees to make a living by its means. I would prefer that Sanskrit schools should be in connection with and at the cost of well-endowed Hindu temples.

(o) The school fees to be low.

(*o*) At first at least, the school fees should be fixed low, so that education may be availed of to the largest extent. As education comes to be more valued—as the demand for it increases—the scale of fees may be raised gradually.

Induce *Sardars* and others to send their children to school.

(5) The Maharaja should use his great influence to induce the *Sardars, Silledars, Darakdars, sowkars*, etc., etc., to send their children to school. As an example to these classes, the Maharaja should send to school the children of his own relations and friends.

Prefer educated men in service.

(6) It should be remembered that education is much stimulated by giving educated men a decided preference in the exercise of patronage. In filling up vacancies in the various departments of the public service, the heads of departments should be directed to accord such preference consistently with the efficiency of the service.

Encourage higher study by scholarships.

(7) Scholarships may be given to enable some of those who may have finished their course in our schools to prosecute their studies to a higher standard at Bombay or Poona, the scholarships being given to the deserving and on certain judicious conditions.

Preside at educational functions.

(8) His Highness the Maharaja should show his interest in education by personally presiding at the principal examinations or distribution of prizes, and by making encouraging addresses. This is one of His Highness' public duties.

Encourage libraries.

(9) Public libraries, reading rooms, lectures and all other similar educational agencies should be assisted and encouraged.

Improve the moral tone by personal example.

(10) By steadily acting on the main lines above suggested, the intellectual and moral welfare of the people will be gradually but effectually promoted and one of the most important duties of the State will be fulfilled. His Highness the Maharaja, being the highest and most powerful personage in the country, may do much to improve the moral tone of the people. The Maharaja's example must operate daily and hourly. His Highness' very conversation will be pregnant with results.

Encourage virtue and check vice.

(11) It is, therefore, most desirable that His Highness the Maharaja should avail himself of the numerous occasions, which will often occur, to make known his love of virtue and his aversion to vice. He may easily do this by throwing out remarks as each occasion may suggest. For instance, His Highness may say, "I do not at all like those who speak untruths", or "I hate public servants who take bribes", or "I have a great contempt for talebearers", or "Let no one suppose that he will prosper by intrigues", or "If a man breaks the law he must suffer for it", and so forth. The same remarks may be varied thus, "I esteem those who are truthful", "I am much pleased with honest public servants", and so on. Be sure that numbers of people will closely watch such remarks falling from the Maharaja and will disseminate them far and wide.

Every such remark will produce a most salutary effect. It will encourage good people, and it will reform bad people. It will warn all. Indeed I think that the Maharaja may thus become a powerful teacher. He may, in a few years, acquire the glory of improving the general moral tone. And let it be remembered that the more the general tone is improved, the easier and the better will government become and the greater will be the happiness of the people. In short, it is one great duty of the Maharaja to employ his authority and influence to encourage virtue, and to check vice. His words, his deeds, the distribution of his favours, the bestowal of appointments and honours must all be directed to that great and beneficial end.

10

THE PALACE DEPARTMENT

27th July 1881

An important department.

I wish to speak today about the Palace. This is a very important department because it is the personal establishment of His Highness the Maharaja, the ruler of the State. The main objects, with reference to which Palace affairs are to be arranged and managed, are to make the Maharaja and his family perfectly comfortable and happy and to enable them to maintain the requisite degree of state in the eyes of the people.

The high expenditure necessary to maintain the pomp.

(2) Whatever expenditure is necessary for these purposes must, of course, be incurred and is quite justifiable. This expenditure must be higher in an Asiatic State than in a European State, because of the difference of circumstances, and of the difference of habits, customs and feelings. [Our]* Indian community has been for ages accustomed to associate a great deal of pomp and show with the possession of power.

* British India Press edition: An.

In fact, the people estimate power by the display of wealth that accompanies it.

But it should be reasonable.

(3) At the same time, it is clear that the Palace expenditure should bear a reasonable proportion to the income of the State. If it exceeds the reasonable proportion, what follows? The sources of the State for promoting the happiness of the people get diminished. In other words, a certain part of the happiness of the people is sacrificed. It has to be remembered that the first duty of the ruler is to make his people as happy as possible.

It should not exceed one tenth of the revenue.

(4) What the reasonable proportion which the Palace expenditure should bear to the income of a State like Baroda is, cannot be so precisely determined as to command the assent of everybody, still it cannot be left altogether an indeterminate quantity. My own common sense, assisted by my experience, leads me to think that in the existing circumstances the annual Palace expenditure should not ordinarily exceed 10 (ten) per cent of the income of the State, that is to say, one-tenth of the income.

Fix the reasonable proportion.

(5) It is exceedingly desirable for the Maharaja to fix for himself the reasonable proportion and to command the Palace authorities concerned to keep the expenditure within that proportion. Those authorities must be made with a strong will to obey the Maharaja's commands in this important respect. If His Highness is really earnest in the matter, he will find no difficulty in adhering to the limit.

Fix a budget for each sub-department.

(6) Each sub-department of the Palace should have a budget or scale of expenditure prescribed, and the Maharaja should insist on this being addressed. The great principle is to leave as few items as possible undefined; for, leave any item undefined, and it will be found that

that item has a great tendency to grow from year to year.

Reserve the power of giving special sanctions.

(7) But there must be some few items which, from their nature, cannot admit of being defined. Such items should be kept under control by the Maharaja, preserving for himself the power of giving special sanctions from time to time.

There should be a distinct Treasury for the Palace.

(8) There should always be a distinct Treasury for the Palace. It should draw the appointed funds from time to time from the Public Central Treasury. There should be no confusion of these two Treasuries. Every item of Palace income and of Palace expenditure should be credited and debited respectively to the Palace Treasury, so that the accounts of this Treasury may afford a complete view of the Palace receipts and expenditure.

Orders to be given in writing.

(9) In money matters let the orders be given as much as possible in writing. Oral orders are very slippery and unsafe, and after the lapse of time cause all sorts of doubts and difficulties. Written orders are especially necessary where unusual or special or large expenditure is concerned.

Salaries to be regularly disbursed.

(10) See that salaries and other payments are regularly and promptly disbursed. This will be a great boon to a large number of servants, small and great, and also to tradesmen, etc.

Loans from the Treasury to be avoided.

(11) Loans of money from the Palace Treasury should be totally avoided. The Palace Treasury is not to be a bank. Great firmness is required in maintaining this principle; otherwise, a most pernicious and wasteful system would spring up.

Salary of six months may be advanced.

(12) The utmost assistance which may be given to a deserving Palace servant is to accommodate him with an advance of salary or allow-

ance for a period not exceeding 6 months or at most one year. His Highness' special sanction should be made necessary for giving any such advance, and such advances should be strictly recovered at the appointed time.

A reliable Head Accountant to be in charge of accounts.

(13) A thoroughly competent and reliable Head Accountant should be made responsible to keep the Palace Accounts regularly and systematically. All tendency to laxity and delay should be firmly checked. Every expenditure should be immediately brought to account. To the utmost extent possible, the year's account should include every expenditure incurred in the year. In other words, avoid the expenditure of a given year being charged to some future year. It is thus alone that the expenditure of one year can be fairly and usefully compared with the expenditure of another year.

Audit of accounts.

(14) The regular audit of the Palace Accounts by the *Huzur* Auditor must be well maintained; otherwise, there would be little or no practical check, and all would slide into confusion.

No private expenditure from the Public Treasury.

(15) No private expenditure of the Maharaja, that is to say, no expenditure which properly belongs to the Palace, should be ordered from or transferred to the Public Treasury. This used to be done largely before, for the purpose of showing less expenditure at the Palace. It was a fraudulent system which should never be revived.

Do not increase expenditure arbitrarily.

(16) As a general rule, the expenditure in any particular item should not be increased unless there are funds available from savings elsewhere. Let increase here be balanced by decrease there. This simple principle being steadily kept in view and acted on, the aggregate Palace expenditure will be generally maintained at its usual level.

Example: A *chobdar* begs for some increase of pay. Let it not be granted blindly. There are lots of *chobdars*. When a vacancy occurs, either abolish the post or reduce the pay of the post, and thus find funds for increasing the pay of the *chobdar* concerned. In short, when any increase is to be given, inquire what disengaged funds are available for it and give the increase out of such funds. For this purpose, the Palace Head Accountant should be consulted on such occasions, and he should be directed to keep His Highness informed of the progress of the expenditure.

Examination of the Treasury balances every month by officials.

(17) A monthly examination of the balances in the Palace Treasury is most necessary. Two or three of the principal officials of the Palace should make such examination personally and certify to His Highness in a memo, under their signature, that the balances stood at such a figure and tallied with the accounts. These memoranda should be regularly entered in a book, and the book itself should be preserved as a record.

Consider past *dakhalas*.

(18) Priests, astrologers and other persons of such class are ever desirous of increasing the expenditure and need to be kept under close control. They should be considerately treated, but must not be allowed to transgress their limits. The best method of effecting this object is to lay hold of past moderate *dakhalas* (precedents) and to insist upon these not being exceeded.

Tendency of the ladies to increase expenditure.

(19) The ladies of the Palace care nothing about public finances, and have a great tendency to propose increased expenditure constantly in one way or another. Here, too, past moderate *dakhalas* must be availed of to restrain the tendency. *Dakhalas* are much respected in Native

States, and an appeal to *dakhalas* is generally conclusive. By appealing to *dakhalas* a great deal of personal unpleasantness is avoided.

Banks in the name of ladies.

(20) The former practice of opening *dukans* or banks in the name and on behalf of these ladies, and of other relations and friends, was an exceedingly pernicious one. It has been totally discontinued and must, on no account, be revived.

The Palace not to assist the ladies in their private debts.

(21) These ladies and indeed all others concerned should be made to understand clearly that the Palace will not assist them in regard to any private debts they may incur. Indeed, they must not incur such debts, and if they do, they must themselves pay the debts off from their allowances.

The evil of accumulating hoards.

(22) The Maharaja should never and need never think of accumulating hoards in the Palace as personal funds. Any desire on the part of His Highness to make private hoards must lead him much astray. There are many sad instances showing that such desire has led to the greatest public evils.

Reduce wasteful expenditure.

(23) There is much needless, useless, or wasteful expenditure in the Palace, which the Maharaja may well reduce. It contributes neither to His Highness' comfort and happiness nor to His Highness' dignity and state. The funds thus disengaged would more than suffice for making needed improvements and for supplying existing deficiencies. Reductions and retrenchments, however, should be so made as not to cause any sudden or serious hardships to individuals.

The *Kothi* to be properly managed.

(24) The *Kothi* branch of the Palace should be conquered and subjugated by the firmness of the Maharaja. It has been a stronghold of irregularities and abuses. Its existing condition and working should be carefully examined. Some things

may be immediately rectified and others gradually according to opportunities afforded by changes and vacancies.

New *sidhas* to be ordered by the Maharaja in writing.

(25) No one except the Maharaja himself should have the power of ordering the issue of new *sidhas*; and when His Highness himself orders any such, it is essential that the order should be in writing, and also that the orders should distinctly specify the time for which the *sidhas* are to run. This precaution is so necessary because the most temporary issues of *sidhas* have often run on for years and have become ever hereditary!

Don't add to the religious expenditure.

(26) Religious and charitable expenditure is already very large. Every care has to be exercised to prevent fresh additions to it. Readjustments may be made if necessary or desirable.

The practice of granting *warshasans* not to be revived.

(27) The reckless practice of granting *warshasans* should not be revived. If rarely granted in special cases, the amount should be moderate; it should come out of some saving caused by a vacancy. It should not go beyond the life of the grantee.

Dakshina and *Dans*.

(28) The *Shravana dakshina, Bidaji Ramnath*, and such other items have a very great tendency to break loose from control. Certain limits have nowadays been fixed for these, and the Maharaja's firmness may well be shown in compelling adherence to these salutary limits. There are many *dans*—such as *gau-dans*, etc.,—which are repeatedly given by the Maharaja and other members of the Gaekwar family. I apprehend that many abuses have crept in this direction. It is desirable for His Highness to give some attention to these matters and make these many and costly *dans* subservient to really useful ends—such as the encouragement of learning or the relief of penury and distress.

11

THE PALACE DEPARTMENT—(CONTD.)

3rd August 1881

Guard against misappropriation.

There is probably some theft, misappropriation, abuse, and waste going on still in different branches of the Palace, though much, no doubt, has been reduced under the eye of Her Highness the Maharani Jamnabai Saheb. The Maharaja may, under proper arrangement, be able to minimise those things.

The jewellery requires special attention.

(2) There is a very large and costly stock of jewellery in the Palace, which will require the special and early attention of the Maharaja—there is much of gold and silver things also to be looked after. Lists of the foregoing have been made, and copies are available in the Palace and *Fadnavis Daftars*. It is very desirable that the Maharaja should go over the whole stock and become personally acquainted with what there is. His Highness' personal inspection will have its moral effects.

Its periodical examination by a Committee.

(3) The whole stock being once clearly gone over by the Maharaja himself personally, arrangements should be made for a regular periodical

examination of the stock by a trustworthy committee, who should certify to His Highness in writing that it is all right. The committee should see also to the identity of the precious stones, pearls, etc., which are liable to be changed.

Jewellery to be in the custody of responsible persons.

(4) The whole should be in custody of trustworthy and responsible persons. One official would hardly suffice, for he might fall sick, or have to go on leave, or even die. I would suggest a sort of committee composed of persons who have sufficient allowances, property, etc., etc. In short, there should be sufficient security against loss.

Iron room for jewellery.

(5) Formerly the jewellery, etc., used to be placed in miserable little dark rooms and scattered about. Everything was very loosely managed. Now, however, the main stock is placed in a strong iron room which contains separate boxes, but which is under one lock. This is a safe and convenient arrangement in many respects, and ought, I think, to be by all means continued.

Excessive presents from the stock to be avoided.

(6) This being an inherited stock of very valuable property, the Maharaja may well be proud of maintaining it. Therefore, needless or large or excessive presents from the same should be avoided. When, however, some presents become necessary, the minor items may be used.

Jewellery to be arranged under different heads.

(7) It suggests itself as a good plan to divide the things into those which are for the personal use of the Maharaja, those for Maharani, and so on. The rest will go under the head of "Miscellaneous", and may be available for presents, etc., when presents become necessary.

Accounts to be kept with care.

(8) It is of the utmost importance that the accounts of the jewel *khana* should be kept

with the greatest regularity, punctuality, and strictness. The chief Palace authorities should be held fully responsible for this. I mean accounts of stocks, of presents, of loans for use, of changes made by breaking up one ornament and making another, and so forth. The accounts should be written in regular bound books, not in loose pages, not even in loosely bound *chopdas*. The accounts should bear the signatures of the writing *karkoon* and of the immediately responsible officials, and should be countersigned or initialled by one of the chief officers of the Palace.

Loans from jewellery to be very sparing.

(9) Formerly there used to be a bad system of lending the jewellery, etc., for the use of various persons. It led to many and grave abuses and loss. I have had many instances before me, in which jewellery merely given on loan has been retained or claimed as gifts. Loans should, therefore, be as sparing as possible. When made, they must be made under the sanction of the Maharaja. Every loan should be entered unmistakably as a loan. Receipts should be taken from those to whom the loan is made. The loan should be expressly stated to be for a certain period, at the end of which the things should be replaced. Responsibility in all these respects should be clearly defined and strictly enforced. Unless these and other careful and strict arrangements are made, laxity and loss are pretty sure to ensue. Property has its trouble in taking care of it!

Further investments in jewellery not desirable.

(10) I would strongly advise His Highness against any further investments in jewellery and plate. What there is already in hand is really much more than sufficient for the largest and the most ambitious Royal family. If any new

ornaments are ever required, they may well be made out of the materials available in the jewel room. If there are rough ornaments, they may easily be converted into elegant ones. It would be unwise to leave unused a lot of costly ornaments and to make new purchases, and thereby needlessly swell the Palace expenditure.

Resist the temptations offered by jewellers.

(11) I would warn the Maharaja against the many temptations which jewellers are sure to offer to make new purchases. They will show their ornaments in fine new cases to the ladies and induce them by various arts to press His Highness to purchase them. They will not hesitate even to bribe those who may have influence with the ladies. Such temptations will have to be firmly resisted. It is a matter which furnishes abundant scope for the exercise of the virtue of firmness. The ladies may often be assured that similar ornaments are already in the Palace stock, or that similar ornaments may be made out of the stock in a very short time.

Janghur not to be revived.

(12) What is known as *janghur* has been discontinued and should by no means be revived. By *janghur* is meant a number of ornaments brought by jewellers and left at the Palace for purchase by His Highness as opportunities occur. It has been a source of the most troublesome disputes. The jeweller contends that his ornaments are actually purchased, whereas they were kept only on inspection. Then disputes arise about prices and payments—matters in themselves complicated by crafty men at the Palace inducing the ladies to use ornaments not yet purchased! Such troubles and complications are best avoided by making it a rule not to take any ornaments from a jeweller until after the price has been settled and the purchase has been made. This is a simple rule.

Carriages, etc., to be the best, and personal attendants to be well dressed.

(13) To proceed to other matters. The carriages, horses and other equipment of the Palace have not been in the best order. The Maharaja may greatly improve these without material increase of expenditure. The general rule should be that whatever His Highness personally uses should be of the best description. For it is better to have ten good carriages than twenty bad ones. This principle applies to a great number of matters connected with the Palace. I will here give just one more instance. The personal attendants of the Maharaja should be well-chosen and well-dressed men, which they hardly are at present.

Improve the Palace gardens.

(14) The Palace gardens cost annually very large sums of money and yet scarcely any garden is what it ought to be in beauty or production. There is room for considerable improvement in this direction.

Improve sanitation.

(15) The sanitary condition of the Palace, though somewhat improved of late, is yet far from what it might be. Too many servants live in the Palace, and they are allowed to live in the most dirty manner.

Arrange rare or curious things.

(16) A great number of rare or curious things have been, from time to time, purchased by the Gaekwar, but they are lying scattered about the Palace. It is desirable to collect and arrange them at one convenient place, so that the Maharaja may know what things exist, and put them to use.

Punctuality in *Darbars*.

(17) Greater punctuality may be observed in regard to Palace *Darbars*, ceremonies, etc. All concerned, being once or twice duly warned, will attend at the appointed hour, and time will thus be saved and convenience promoted.

Order of precedence in *Darbars*

(18) A certain order of precedence is now observed at these *Darbars* and in State proces-

not to be disturbed.

sions. For the sake of peace, this order should be strictly maintained, and no change should be made unless found to be clearly necessary. There is great ambition and great rivalry in these matters. Several *darbaris* will come and entreat and press His Highness to give them higher seats, etc., and will adduce the most abundant arguments. But His Highness will find it the best course to meet all such solicitations by saying, "I must adhere to the existing order and arrangements, and can make no change unless I am convinced that a change is absolutely necessary." If changes were lightly or incautiously made, much disturbance of feeling, much heartburning, and many troubles and embarrassments would be sure to arise and continue a long time. If, however, any change must be considered, the Maharaja would do well to appoint a committee and to direct it to enquire into the matter and submit their opinion to His Highness. Such a committee should include the representatives of the various sections of the *Darbar*, such as a *Sardar*, a *Darakdar*, a *Mankari*, etc., etc. The head of the Military Department of the *Huzur Cutcherry* may also be associated in the inquiry. On the committee reporting on the matter, His Highness may consider and dispose of the same. The Dewan may well be consulted also with advantage. The great principles to be kept in view in dealing with such matters are, first, to make as few changes as possible in the existing arrangements and, secondly, to make no such change as would disturb the feelings of many *darbaris*.

A diary for recording daily events.

(19) It is very desirable to arrange that a regular diary be kept in the Palace, fully recording the particulars of daily occurrences. Everything

worth remembering should be entered therein. Such a record will be exceedingly useful for various purposes, and especially for preserving precedents for future guidance.

Proper organisation of the Palace is wanted.

(20) The foregoing enumeration of important points will be of use to His Highness when he assumes the management of the Palace and its appurtenances. His Highness will also have some idea of how much requires attention and arrangement. The work to be done is immense, and it is clear that His Highness alone cannot do it. What is required is proper organisation in the Palace. The work and responsibility should be appropriately distributed. The servants should be grouped and placed under superior officials. These superior officials should have certain powers, and the subordinates must be made to obey their superiors. Otherwise, business would not go on properly. The Maharaja cannot himself see that every servant duly attends and does his allotted work. He cannot himself grant leave of absence to every servant from the *bhangi* to the *Kamdar*. He cannot himself appoint and dismiss *pankha-pullers*, gardeners, *mahouts*, etc., etc.

The *Kamdar*, with sufficient powers, to be at the head.

(21) At the head of the whole, and immediately under the orders of His Highness, should be the Palace *Kamdar*. He should be a high officer of capacity and integrity, not much inferior in these respects to the head of any department in the *Huzur Cutcherry*. He should be given sufficient powers* for the conduct of ordinary business—I mean certain limited powers for appointing, dis-

* *Footnote in original*: The Palace authorities, however, exercise no civil or criminal jurisdiction. Cases falling under such jurisdiction shall be transferred by them to the constituted authorities of the State.

missing, fining, granting leave, etc., and for incurring ordinary expenditure. He should be well supported by His Highness in the exercise of his legitimate powers and influences.

Annual Administration Report to be prepared.

(22) At the end of each official year, the Palace *Kamdar* should be directed to prepare and submit to His Highness a full report of the Palace administration, together with statistics and explanations. This report will be of great use to His Highness in controlling Palace affairs.

12

HUZUR CUTCHERRY

10th August 1881

What constitutes the government.

The Maharaja as the ruler represents the power of the State, and the *Huzur Cutcherry* is the machinery kept in motion by that power. The whole, in effect, constitutes the Government of the country responsible to promote the welfare of the people.

The essential condition of administration.

(2) The *Huzur Cutcherry* should, therefore, be intellectually and morally strong. This is a most essential condition of successful administration by the Maharaja. The more that *Cutcherry* is strong intellectually and morally, the more will it be a credit and comfort to the Maharaja, and the more will it command the respect of the people.

The ideal of a Dewan.

(3) The Dewan being at the head of the *Huzur Cutcherry*, he ought to be, as near as possible, the ideal of a Dewan. In point of capacity and probity, he should deserve and possess the confidence of the Maharaja. He (the Dewan) should also deserve and possess the respect of the British Government. He should be a person

who has had experience in the work of administration. Better if this experience has, partly at least, been in administering a Native State. Still better, if the experience has been gained in the service of the Baroda State itself.

Choose your Dewan from the *Cutcherry*.

(4) These are very important considerations which must be kept fully in view by the Maharaja in selecting his Dewan. They point clearly to the desirableness of so arranging that there may always be some men of the requisite capacity and character in the *Huzur Cutcherry* itself and trained in the work of administration. It will be best to choose the Dewan from such men.

That is, from the heads of departments.

(5) It is the special interest of the Maharaja to have such men for the heads of the department of the *Huzur Cutcherry* as may, in time, be fit to be promoted to Dewanship. In looking after the interests of the Maharaja during His Highness' minority, I am glad that this important principle has by no means been overlooked. At this moment, there are such men in the *Huzur Cutcherry*.

Importing an outsider not very desirable.

(6) If the policy above indicated were not adopted and followed, the Maharaja would be in great embarrassment whenever the Dewan's post becomes vacant. Not finding suitable men in His Highness' own service, His Highness would have to import some outsider—a course certainly attended with much risk and with many disadvantages.

Reasons.

(7) It can seldom be comfortable to the Maharaja to have a perfect stranger as Dewan—one with whom he has had no previous intercourse—one whose temper and ways are unknown to him—one who does not know the country and people—one who is unacquainted with the principles and details of the local

administration—one who perhaps may depend for support on external powers or influences more than on His Highness himself. More might be said on this part of the subject, but probably it would be needless, for the Maharaja can easily realise the disadvantages of bringing in a stranger as his Dewan.

Qualifications of a Dewan.

(8) To pursue the qualities necessary in a Dewan of His Highness, he should, of course, be well versed in the English language. Without this, no Dewan of such a large State as Baroda would get on at all usefully even for a short time. He should be a warm friend and well-wisher of Native States. As such he should always be ready to do his best to protect and preserve the Native State and all its legitimate rights and privileges. He should be firm yet conciliatory, just yet mild and merciful, energetic yet patient and considerate, zealous yet discreet and circumspect, sensitive to honour yet by no means quarrelsome, agreeable to the Maharaja yet free and frank in giving sound advice. He should be a friend of progressive improvement in all branches of the administration, yet he should possess discrimination enough to conserve what is old, natural, and useful.

The Maharaja to cordially support the Dewan.

(9) Having most carefully selected the right person as his Dewan, the Maharaja should give him his cordial support and encouragement.

Bad policy of changing the Dewan at short intervals.

(10) It would be very bad policy for the Maharaja to change his Dewan at short intervals, without strong reasons. A Dewan should have the fair prospect of holding his office at least for five years. It is only a sign of weakness in a Maharaja to change his Chief Minister frequently, and thus to interrupt useful service.

Heads of departments to be carefully selected.

(11) We may pass on to the heads of departments under the Dewan. These also need to be very carefully selected. They should be quite qualified to perform well the important duties entrusted to them, and they should afford a fair promise of being trained, so as to undertake the duties of Chief Minister, if at any time required. It follows that the heads of departments should be selected for qualifications similar to those which the Dewan himself should possess.

They should know English.

(12) As a rule, the heads of departments should be conversant with English. The only exception to this that may be tolerated is the *Fadnis*.

Diversity of castes desirable.

(13) Some diversity of castes and creeds in these heads of departments is desirable. Indeed, it is desirable throughout the public service.

The heads to co-operate with the Dewan.

(14) The heads of departments should cordially co-operate with the Dewan in the work of good government. All being men of high character and principles, there should be nothing like intriguing or factious oppositions. The Maharaja and the Dewan should have every reason to feel that these departmental heads render loyal assistance at all times. The expectations of the Maharaja in this respect should be clearly and decidedly made known.

Important matters to be discussed by all the ministers.

(15) These departmental heads are, in fact, the several departmental ministers of the Maharaja, and the Dewan is the Chief or Prime Minister. The whole is the cabinet of the Maharaja. The ordinary business of each department may be conducted by its head under the orders or supervision of the Dewan. But, if any business of considerable importance or difficulty is to be done, all or most of the ministers should meet, discuss, and decide. Should any

serious differences of opinion arise, His Highness the Maharaja will do well to patiently hear the opinion and arguments of each of his ministers. How His Highness himself should decide in such a situation, I have indicated under the head of "Minor Hints".

Ministers to be treated with confidence.

(16) All the ministers should be treated with consideration and confidence. Credit should be fully and even liberally given to each for the good administration of his particular department. An occasional expression of deserved praise by the Maharaja is sure to have an encouraging effect beyond any amount of money rewards, for honourable men are ambitious of honour and fame. In short, each minister should be made to feel it to be his interest, pleasure and pride to have his department in the best order, and thereby to contribute to the high reputation of the whole administration of His Highness the Maharaja.

Their trivial errors may be passed over.

(17) It should be remembered that even the best of men are liable to err. Men who are continually acting must make errors to a certain extent. Trivial errors, such as are the common lot of humanity, should not be made too much of in these ministers. Such trivial errors may be altogether passed over by the Maharaja, or, if they must be noticed, let them be lightly noticed.

Censure to be in moderate terms.

(18) A serious error, however, may be sometimes committed, and may require a regular censure. Even then, the censure should be in carefully measured and moderate terms. It should be reluctantly dealt out. It should not cause more pain than absolutely necessary in the public interests. Therefore, the sensitiveness and self-respect of the person to be censured

should be fully taken into account. And the justice of the censure may be enhanced by a judicious mixture of deserved praise. The right dispensation of censure is a little science and art in itself.

Let the minister explain.

(19) In this connection, it should be remembered that it would not be just or judicious to pass any censure on any minister before hearing what he has to say in defence or explanation of that part of his conduct which appears questionable.

Avoid the tone of peremptory command.

(20) All the ministers are, of course, the servants of the Maharaja, yet a wise Maharaja will avoid the use of the terms and tone of peremptory command. It is avoided by noble natures even in dealing with common menial servants. It is not necessary because the wishes of His Highness will carry weight of their own.

Organisation and discipline extremely necessary for successful administration.

(21) The *Huzur Cutcherry* is a large establishment. In it, therefore, and indeed in the public service generally, organisation and discipline are extremely necessary for successful administration. In Native States, however, there is too great and constant a tendency to relax, and even to destroy organisation and discipline—a tendency which the Maharaja has, therefore, to be all the more careful to resist. Organisation, roughly speaking, means the proper division and distribution of work—making certain officials do the work assigned and holding them responsible for the proper performance of the aforesaid work, and placing under their orders the necessary hands for doing that work. The work is thus divided from top to bottom. Every portion of the work is entrusted to some responsible official, and every officer from the lowest *karkoon* to the minister is placed imme-

diately under the orders of some superior officer. Such organisation, then, embraces the whole establishment and makes the whole establishment one organised body or one machine, each part of which works in subordination to some other part. And discipline, roughly speaking, means the enforcing of such subordination in all its gradations. It is thus and thus alone, that large bodies of men can be made to direct all their consistent energies to the accomplishment of great and complex ends. Without organisation and discipline there is sure to be confusion. There will be little or nothing to compel each man to act in constant reference to the common end. Men will not only not act in concert but they may act so as to counteract each other. Much power will thus be actually wasted. Organisation and discipline make a very great difference in the effectiveness of a body of men. This is most prominently exemplified by an army with the advantage of organisation and discipline as compared with an equal army not possessing that advantage. The former will most easily beat the latter. Indian history shows repeated instances of immense numbers of unorganised and undisciplined forces being put to flight by a very small but efficiently organised and disciplined force.

Illustrations to show the importance of discipline.

(22) The Maharaja, I repeat, should fully maintain organisation and discipline in his service. Official A, who is placed under the orders of official B, will come and say to His Highness, "I do not like to be under the orders of official B, I prefer to be directly under the orders of Your Highness, or at least under the orders of the Dewan." This should by no means be permitted. Again, a *Subah*, instead of obtaining

leave of absence from his immediate superior, makes a direct application to the Maharaja. The Maharaja should return such application and tell the applicant that he has acted irregularly and direct that he should apply to his immediate superior. He pleads that he did so because the *Bai Saheb* wanted him in connection with some business. The Maharaja should not allow this, but have the conduct of the officer duly noticed. Again, a *karkoon* rushes up to His Highness and complains that the *Subah* has unjustly fined him. The *karkoon* should be directed to represent the matter to the *Huzur Cutcherry*. Again, a *Sardar* calls upon His Highness and complains that the *zilla* judge has made a decree which is quite unjust, and that the *Sardar* requests that His Highness himself, or at least the Dewan, may call for the decree and revise it. The *Sardar* should be directed to appeal to the *Varisht* Court. Again, a jeweller comes up to His Highness and says,

> "Mr. Vinayek Rao has decided my case very unjustly. Let Kazi Saheb examine my case and decide again." Similarly, a *ryot* comes up to His Highness and says, "Kazi Saheb has assessed my lands very high. Let Raoji Vithal call for and examine my papers, and I am sure justice will be done to me." Similarly, a public works contractor comes up to His Highness and represents: "The Engineer unjustly refuses to give me a certain work on contract. I pray that Mr. Pestonji may be directed to look into the matter and to do me justice."

And so forth. Such applications are very common in Native States, because of the lack or deficiency of organisation and discipline. Now, if such applications were complied with by an easy-going and thoughtless Maharaja, what would be the inevitable consequence? Surely, the greatest confusion of work and responsibility. There would be an end of all organisation and discipline. Misgovernment could not but follow.

Each minister to have powers.

(23) To enable each minister of His Highness to administer his allotted department efficiently, he should have powers to punish or reward within certain limits as respects his own subordinates. So long as he exercises these powers fairly, he should be strongly supported.

Petitions against ministers how to be dealt with.

(24) In Native States, the most false or reckless imputations are often made in petitions against the ministers. The ministers, being honourable men, such petitions require to be dealt with, with the utmost caution and discrimination.

Anonymous and vague petitions.

(25) As a general rule, anonymous petitions, or petitions bearing fictitious names, should be left unnoticed. Similarly, petitions which make vague and general imputations should also be left unnoticed.

Specific charges may be examined.

(26) When a petition comes from a known person and contains clear and specific charges affecting the minister's public conduct, the matter may possibly require some consideration. The writer may have to be sent for and questioned as to the sources of his information, as to what evidence he is in a position to offer, as to the particular motives he may be actuated by, and so forth. What may be elicited from him will have to be judged as to probability or improbability in reference to the high character of the public officer concerned. After all this, some correct decision may be taken as to the course to be adopted. I would recommend to the Maharaja that he should refer such petitions to the Dewan who will, after due consideration

and consultation, submit his best advice for His Highness' consideration.

The public to know that the ministers enjoy the ruler's confidence.

(27) The Dewan and the departmental ministers being chosen as suggested, not only should they actually enjoy the confidence and support of the Maharaja, but it should be made known to the public that they enjoy His Highness' confidence and support, for any supposition or suspicion to the contrary on the part of the public would be sure to lead to innumerable intrigues and would weaken the whole administration and injure the interests of the country.

How it can be made known to the public.

(28) The question here arises as to how that fact is to be made known to the public. The Maharaja may effect this end in many ways. For instance, by His Highness generally accepting the opinions and the statements of his ministers, by treating these with consideration and friendly feelings, by occasionally speaking of them in favourable terms, by checking those who recklessly blame them, by refusing to join in the expression of pleasure by petty or thoughtless men at violent and groundless attacks on the ministry, and so on.

The minister's influence not to be weakened in the eyes of the public.

(29) Even when a minister has done something which needs to be cancelled or reversed, the necessary action should generally be so taken as not to shake or weaken the authority and influence of that minister in the eyes of the public. For example—suppose a minister has dismissed a *karkoon* or other official without sufficient reason, and that it is desired to restore that *karkoon*. In such a case, it would not be necessary to make any fuss about it. It would not be necessary to record a formal order that the said dismissal was wrong and that the *kar-*

koon should be reinstalled. It would generally be sufficient to speak quietly to the minister and ask him to restore the *karkoon* quietly. It is in this spirit, as far as possible, that such business should be done.

Differences to be adjusted privately.

(30) In short, the Maharaja and his chosen ministers should be, and should also appear, as one and not as divided among themselves. Any differences which might arise among them should be adjusted confidentially and should not be exposed to the public view.

Bad policy to make the ministers fight against each other.

(31) After what I have said, it would be quite needless for me to point out the bad policy—the very bad policy—of making the ministers fight among themselves as a check against each other. It would be a very clumsy check indeed, and applicable only if the ministers were a set of bad, unprincipled persons. But by hypothesis, the Maharaja has chosen good ministers. By all means, let thieves quarrel among themselves, but not good men.

Rather, prevent quarrels.

(32) On the contrary, I say it is one of the most important duties of the Maharaja to prevent quarrels among his ministers. His Highness should occasionally express pleasure when his ministers work harmoniously together, and express or indicate displeasure when discord makes its appearance among them. Again, whenever the Maharaja sees that any intriguers or others try to break the harmony prevailing among His Highness' ministers and try to bring about quarrels among them, His Highness should firmly check such attempts.

How to promote harmony among the ministers.

(33) One great means of promoting harmony among the ministers and of making them collectively responsible for good administration is to arrange that each minister should discuss

with his colleagues every matter of great public importance or difficulty which he has to deal with, and come to a common agreement about the course to be pursued. In this way, every matter of importance will have the benefit of discussion, and all the ministers will be responsible for the action of each. No minister will have it in his power to say that another minister has done wrong. Indeed, the chances of wrong action will be reduced to a minimum, and this is exactly what good administration requires.

The continuity of useful practical knowledge.

(34) Another advantage of great value accruing from the principle I have just stated is this: As each minister discusses important departmental matters with the other ministers, every minister becomes acquainted, not simply with the business of his own department, but with the important business of all departments. Such being the case, should any minister happen to go away, there would be no gap of knowledge in the ministry on that account. The successor of the last minister will soon be trained to his work by the other ministers. Thus the continuity of useful practical knowledge will be provided for.

13

HEADS OF DEPARTMENTS

24th August 1881

A few observations on the heads of departments.

I have pointed out the great importance of the *Huzur Cutcherry* being made as strong as possible intellectually and morally as the essential condition of His Highness' successful administration. And I have indicated in general terms what sort of men the Dewan and the heads of departments should be. I will now offer some further observations regarding these heads of departments.

Qualifications of the head of the Revenue Department.

(2) The head of the Revenue Department should be specially conversant with the principles and details of his work. He must know all about the *ryotwari* system of land revenue. He must know all about opium, *abkari*, customs, and other sources of revenue. In respect of all these matters, he must know (1) the past history of each, (2) its present condition, (3) its condition in British India, and (4) its theory or science as enumerated by the best authorities. He must be versed in finance generally. He must be familiar with Political Economy. It is only then that he will be able to do justice to the

important department of Revenue, on which the happiness of the people largely depends.

Why the heads under the former regime were not successful.

(3) Those who were at the head of this department under the former regime mostly fell short of this standard. Not knowing the English language, they had no access to valuable and necessary information. Their chief idea was that the largest possible revenue should be extracted from the people with the least trouble to themselves. What was the consequence? The interest of the people suffered more or less materially. Here there was excessive and crushing taxation. There the taxation was unequal. Here taxation was accompanied by oppression and vexation. There it was attended with the greatest vagueness and uncertainty. Every *izardar* imposed or increased taxes at his own pleasure. The extent to which trade suffered from unprincipled duties and from the most extensively mischievous network of *nakahs* cannot be adequately imagined by the superficial observer. Many other instances of mismanagement might be mentioned here if he had time to do so. The fact is, those who were at the heads of departments in former times did not even know that great evils existed. How could they then think of improvement?

The Revenue Department to be properly managed.

(4) It may be remembered in this connection that this department constantly comes in contact with hundreds of thousands of people. These will be in a reasonable state of contentment if the department is properly managed. If not properly managed, great will be the outcry.

The head of the Judicial Department to be a lawyer.

(5) To proceed to other departments of the *Huzur Cutcherry*. The head of the Judicial, Police and Extradition Department must be a clear-headed lawyer. He must be familiar with the

leading principles of jurisprudence as well as the practical details of judicial administration. To fulfil this qualification, he must, of course, be an English scholar. He must be conversant with those principles of International Law which have a bearing on our relations with our neighbours. It has to be remembered that it is this officer who has mainly to advise the Dewan in all judicial matters generally, in disposing of appeals from the *Varisht* Court, in settling legal doubts or difficulties coming from all departments, in making laws and rules, and in conducting that portion of the correspondence with the Residency which relates to the extradition of criminals and to other matters involving judicial principles.

A properly qualified head guarantees good government.

(6) If the Maharaja fails to secure a proper head for the department under advertence, many difficulties and embarrassments are sure to be the consequence. Many things would, more or less, slide back into their old condition. Under the old regime, extradition was involved in the greatest imaginable confusion. Extradition was exacted from Baroda by all around, but it was very imperfectly reciprocated to Baroda. The consequence was that our territories were the scene of numerous offences, the perpetrators of which could not be brought to punishment at all. Violent crimes were of everyday occurrence. Life, person, and property were very insecure everywhere. Again, there was little that deserved the name of police, the consequences of which might be better imagined than described. Again, there were no courts of justice deserving the name, the consequences of which also might be better imagined than described. In short, the *Sarkar*

failed to fulfil the most elementary duties of a civilised government. Bearing all this in view, it will be seen that if the Maharaja has a proper head for the department under advertence, as is the case at present, it will be a great guarantee for good government.

The impression that no special qualifications are necessary for the post of the head of the Military Department is not correct.

(7) Military, Settlement and *Giras* matters may well go, as they at present do, under one department. The efficiency and good reputation of the administration largely depend upon the careful choice of the officer to be at the head of this department also. It is a department which deals with many matters of importance, of complexity, of difficulty, and of delicacy. It also deals with many persons of consequence, or of a troublesome or turbulent character. The wisdom and experience and the judgment and tact of its present head have been of great service during these six years. Many practically useful principles and methods of transacting business and of settling disputes have now been attained in this department which deserve to be adhered to as the results of anxious reflection and laborious progress. The Maharaja has to be all the more careful in having a fully qualified officer at the head of the department under advertence because an impression prevails among certain classes in the city that no special qualifications whatever are required for the post, that even the most ordinary person would be able to get through its duties. That impression arises from a misconception. The post of Civil Minister is mistaken for that of Commander-in-Chief of the Irregular Forces.

Grave abuses under the former regime.

(8) Under the former regime there was a lamentable want of system in the management of affairs connected with the Military, Settlement

and *Giras* branches of business. It was, indeed, much worse than a want of system, for grave and manifold abuses prevailed. These have been mentioned in the Administration Reports, which, I hope, His Highness will go through. Many of these have been corrected and others are in course of correction. The tendency of these abuses is to spring up again and again, and such tendency should be checked with firmness and vigilance, and the process of correction should be steadily continued. For this purpose, the head of the department should be, as already stated, a well-qualified officer.

The head of the Public Works Department.

(9) The Public Works Department is also one of the most important departments of the *Huzur Cutcherry*, and as such requires a duly qualified officer at its head. This officer, too, must be conversant with the English language, as he has to correspond with the Chief Engineer in English and to study English books bearing on public works. The present head fulfils the requirements completely.*

Duties of the several departmental heads.

(10) The principal departments of the *Huzur Cutcherry*, I have above noticed, stand as follows:

(1) Revenue Department,
(2) Military, Settlement, and *Giras* Departments,
(3) Judicial, Police, and Extradition Departments,
(4) Public Works Department.

All these departments require for their heads first-rate officers, who will not only do their

* The Public Works Department was placed under Kuvarji Cowasji in June 1875. The *Naib* Dewan, Vinayak Kirtane, took over in 1877. The State Engineer was G. F. Hill.

respective duties in a scientific, systematic, and satisfactory manner but will, in conjunction with the Dewan, form the Cabinet of the Maharaja—that is to say, that body of His Highness' ministers who will, under His Highness, be collectively responsible for the good government of the country.

Have the best ministers for the conduct of the administration.

(11) The primary responsibility for the good government of the country rests, of course, with the Maharaja himself. It is a weighty responsibility. It is a responsibility increasing with the general progress of India. It is a responsibility which must cause serious anxiety to the best of rulers. The only way in which His Highness can fulfil that heavy responsibility is to have the best ministers for the conduct of the administration. These ministers should possess abundant intelligence, knowledge, experience and high character to command respect and to withstand hostile criticism from whatever quarter the same may come, either from British authorities or from the general public. The very best Maharaja, with incompetent ministers, is pretty sure to be a failure.

Demand for the best ministers imperative in Baroda.

(12) The demand for the best ministers is especially imperative in Baroda because of its situation and circumstances. There is probably no other Native State in all India which has to deal with interests more involved, more intricate and more trying to the intellect. And there is probably no other Native State which is more exposed to public observation and criticism.

A few observations on the other departments.

(13) I have mentioned above four principal departments of the *Huzur Cutcherry*. These, however, do not comprise all the branches of business done there. There are numerous other branches besides, such as Accounts and

Audits, *Khangi*, Education, Medicine, Municipalities, Boundary Settlements, General or Miscellaneous, and last, not least, the English Correspondence. On these I beg to offer a few observations.

(a) Accounts to be entrusted to a qualified head.

(*a*) Accounts and Audits are absolutely necessary for the proper conduct of the administration. They are necessary even in a private family, and they are much more necessary in a State. They should be entrusted, as they at present are, to a distinct and specially qualified head.* He must be versed in the old system of accounts and audit and also in the more improved modern system. He will largely assist the administration in keeping the finances in order.

(b) The *Khangi* to be entrusted to one of the Heads.

(*b*) The *Khangi* work may be given to some one of the heads of the principal departments. That work requires much watchfulness, judgment and tact. Extravagant and wasteful expenditure has to be kept within the limits fixed by His Highness. And yet, needless offence and annoyance have to be carefully avoided in the performance of this important and necessary duty.

(c) Education and Medicine.

(*c*) "Education" may also be given to some one of the heads of the principal departments. That head may be chosen for the purpose who is most familiar with the modern system of education. "Medicine" may go with education very well.

(d) Other minor branches.

(*d*) "Municipalities" may go with Public Works, "Boundary Settlement" had better generally go under the Revenue Department. "General

* Anna Bhivrao Tahmane, who was appointed Accountant General in September 1878, succeeding Appaji Ramchandra.

or Miscellaneous" may be with some one of the heads of the principal departments.

A fifth minister may be required.

(14) In process of time, as work increases, as it is sure to do, it may become desirable to put some of these branches of business under an additional or fifth minister. Indeed, I think that four ministers, as above stated, would hardly suffice for the work of the administration, inasmuch as one of them might go away on leave, or might fall sick at any time.

Necessity of having a qualified secretary in the English Correspondence Department.

(15) The English Correspondence Department of the *Huzur Cutcherry* is one of the most important departments. The credit of the whole administration largely depends upon the efficiency of this department. It is to be remembered that the Dewan has to carry on extensive correspondence in English and the correspondence with the Residency includes matters of great moment, difficulty, delicacy, or confidence. It is to be further remembered that the annual Administration Report is prepared and compiled in the English Office of the *Huzur Cutcherry*. It is, therefore, essential that at the head of this office there should always be a thoroughly qualified secretary or manager like the present incumbent.* He should be quite trustworthy, intelligent, well-versed in English, able to write with ease and facility, active, energetic and industrious, possessing a good memory, and of a conciliatory disposition in order that he may communicate with the heads of the various other departments without friction.

* This was N. Padmanabha Pillay. Tragically, Pillay passed away in October 1881 while the lecture series was still underway.

The *Fadnis* and his duties.

(16) It remains that I shall say a few words about the *Fadnis* Department of the *Huzur Cutcherry*. The *Fadnis* is the head of this department.* The *Fadnis* is a hereditary officer of the State, and it is desirable that it should be so. It is desirable to have a permanent element amidst so many shifting elements in the *Huzur Cutcherry*.

(a) Custodian of documents.

(*a*) The *Fadnis* is already the depository of the most valuable records of the past. He should continue to be so, and in this respect his usefulness should be extended. In fact, he should be the custodian of all valuable documents and decisions and of all important records of all departments. He will thus be a most useful referee.

(b) Examining cash balances.

(*b*) Another important function assigned to the *Fadnis* is to examine the cash balances in the Central Treasury and certify to their correctness. This should, by all means, be continued.

(c) Writing all the orders to the Treasury involving payment.

(*c*) Another important duty which the *Fadnis* has been doing is to write all or most of the orders to the Central Treasury involving money payments. In other words, he is the main channel of communication between the *Huzur Cutcherry* and the Central Treasury. This very judicious arrangement should also be continued.

(d) Preparing communications to the Residency.

(*d*) He also prepares all routine communications to be addressed to the Residency in the vernacular. This may well be continued also.

The *Fadnis* may have two *Darakdars* under him.

(17) I may here suggest the desirableness of giving some assistance to the *Fadnis* in all these respects by placing under him two or three *Darakdars*, such as are doing no work but are drawing considerable allowances.

---

* The *Fadnis* was Madhava Rao Ramchunder.

14

SALARIES

31st August 1881

Observations on the subject of salaries.

In connection with the *Huzur Cutcherry* and as applicable to all public establishments in general, I may here submit some observations on the subject of salaries. This is an important subject, regarding which His Highness should have clear ideas.

The idea that any man could fill any post.

(2) Formerly, almost any person, it was thought, could fill any post and perform any duty. In such circumstances, there was no difficulty in getting persons for the public service. Shoals of candidates offered themselves when any vacancy occurred, and they would accept any salary, however low.

Why men could be got on low pay.

(3) Again, public servants in those days made plenty of money over and above their salaries. These were acquisitions which we, in these days, very properly deem unlawful and most discreditable. In short, and to speak plainly, they took bribes. They took employment not so much for the salary given as for the opportunity to plunder. There may have been exceptions,

but I am speaking of the general state of things. This is another reason why men could be got on low pay.

The State must pay higher salaries.

(4) The state of things nowadays is very different. Happily, the requirements of good administration are far better understood and appreciated. For the public service we now want educated men—men possessing the requisite qualifications—and men thoroughly upright and honourable who would not stoop to any unlawful gain. If we want a specially good article—not any article—we have to pay much higher for it. In other words, the State has to pay higher salaries.

The salary not to be less than what the British offer.

(5) In regulating our salaries, we have to attend also to other considerations. There is a large demand in British India for educated and upright men. The remuneration which we offer to such men cannot be less than what the British Government offers. The Imperial service absorbs a great number of such men.

A retiring pension.

(6) Again, in the British service, there is provision made for a retiring pension. As this is wanting here, the actual salary has to be made proportionately higher.

The tenure of office to be more secure.

(7) Again, in the British service, the tenure of office is far more secure. The higher public servants hold office during good behaviour. In other words, they are not liable to be turned out arbitrarily. On the other hand, in Native States generally, the case has, I am sorry to say, been considerably different. The best behaved public servant is not sure of retaining his appointment for any length of time. Indeed, it has not unfrequently occurred that the best-behaved servants have been the least liked by the Maharaja, because their good principles

would not allow them to do any dirty work which might be assigned to them. In consequence of this uncertainty as to tenure of office, good men look for much higher salary in the service of the Native State than in the British service. The higher salary has to cover the greater risk of losing the appointment itself.

The remarks about Native States in general not applicable to Baroda.

(8) Earnestly do I hope that what I have just said about Native States in general will not apply to Baroda under the rule of the carefully educated prince who is about to assume power. Yet, obviously, public confidence cannot be gained in a day. It will take years of good government before public confidence becomes fairly established. Meanwhile, the difference between the British service and that of the Native States in respect of security of tenure of office must be operating in [inducing]* good men to demand higher pay in the latter than in the former service.

The earnings of educated men have increased.

(9) Again, the earnings of educated and able men in the independent professions have much increased. A successful doctor or a successful pleader or merchant earns quite as much as he would have earned had he entered the public service. The public service, too, has its influence in rendering it necessary to offer higher salaries in the service of the State.

There is a demand for educated men.

(10) Again, some of the Native States themselves are improving and therefore are adding to the demand for educated and upright men. The price of such men has increased on this account. No doubt, the supply of such men has also increased owing to the many educational

* British India Press edition: reducing.

agencies at work in different parts of India. Yet, the balance of effect is in favour of giving increased salaries to such men.

The present scale not excessive.

(11) Considering the reasons above stated, it will be found that the scale of salaries adopted by the present administration is not excessive. This will be all the more evident when it is noted that the heads of departments in the *Huzur Cutcherry* here are doing work really more difficult and responsible than that done by officers in the British service drawing equal pay. The matter may be regarded from another point of view. The existing salaries are not in truth so much higher than those of the past as may seem to a cursory observer. The former salaries were, it should be recollected, largely supplemented by means of extra allowances in diverse shapes and from diverse sources. For instance, there were granted *chhatri, masal, jhab, palki*, horses, *pagah, warshasans, assamies* and villages. Moreover, there were shares in *nazranas* sometimes. As to unrecognised or secret gains, these made a considerable addition. If all these things be included in the calculation, my belief is that the present rates are really lower, at any rate not higher.

Sardars need not envy the salaries of officers.

(12) The *Sardars* and *Darakdars* need not envy the existing salaries of the State officers because some of those *Sardars* and *Darakdars* are themselves getting very large emoluments without any work to speak off.

Liberal salaries cut off corrupt acquisitions.

(13) It is undoubtedly some economy on the part of the State to give good, even liberal salaries to the higher functionaries of the State and thereby cut off corrupt acquisitions. It should be borne in mind that formerly for every corrupt acquisition of one thousand

rupees made by an officer, he put the State probably to a loss of three or four or more thousand rupees. What the State may now be paying by way of salaries in excess of the past is, it must be remembered, [repaid] manifold by the cessation of corruption.

The political advantages.

(14) What I have just mentioned is only the pecuniary advantage accruing from good and liberal salaries. But the political advantages of having a set of able and upright men to conduct the administration are beyond estimate. Without such men, the administration would become despicable. The State would lead a sickly and weakly life which could not last very long. These various considerations forcibly point to the justice and expediency of maintaining the existing scale of salaries undiminished. In the lower grades of the service, some salaries will probably have to be yet increased.

The propriety of obtaining the loan of British Government servants.

(15) I proceed now to another subject, which this seems to be an appropriate place to notice in. We have in the *Huzur Cutcherry* and other establishments several officers whose services have been borrowed from the British Government. A question here arises: Is this right and proper, and is the State to continue to obtain the loan of British Government servants? On this topic, I beg to offer some remarks. The State has been most fortunate in having been able to obtain the services of the British Government servants we at present have in our establishments. On the deposition of Malhar Rao, the work of reform which had to be done was one of great magnitude and seriousness, and its successful prosecution necessitated the assistance of some trained and experienced hands. As these were not available at Baroda,

they had to be got from outside, whether from the British Government service or elsewhere. They have done excellent service and have become even more valuable than ever before, because of the additional knowledge and experience they have gained in Baroda territories.

They diffuse their knowledge.

(16) These officers should, of course, continue to serve the State not only because their services are in themselves so valuable but also because they are instrumental in diffusing their own knowledge and experience around them.

The necessity of engaging them may ultimately disappear.

(17) As our own people learn business and get trained, the necessity for borrowing outsiders may be expected to diminish and to ultimately disappear. This is a result much to be desired. It must be steadily kept in prospect and pressed forward, too, in earnest.

Advantages and disadvantages attaching to Native British servants lent to the State.

(18) It is here desirable to take a view of the advantages and disadvantages attaching to Native British servants taken on loan by the State.

(a) Higher salaries.

(*a*) In the first place, the State has to pay them much higher salaries than they draw in the British service, to induce them to come and work in our service. We have to pay at least 50 percent more, not [in]frequently even 100 percent, [or] more.

(b) Pension contribution.

(*b*) Then we have to pay their pension contribution to the British Government, and this is a further additional charge.

(c) Possibility of leaving service.

(*c*) Then there is the possibility of their leaving our service at any time and reverting to that of the British Government.

(d) Misbehaviour.

(*d*) Again, if any of them misbehaves and has to be dismissed, the State has to take care that the dismissal is upon such strong grounds as to satisfy the British Government also of their validity.

(e) They are too technical.

(*e*) They are, generally speaking, a little too regular and technical, at least at the beginning of their service in the Native States. I mean that they are guided more by rules than by principles. In other words, they are somewhat defective in that elasticity which the circumstances of the Native States require.

(f) They lack the qualities of statesmanship.

(*f*) Also, generally speaking, they are imperfect in the qualities of statesmanship for the simple reason that, in the British service, they fill very subordinate posts—that they do not rise to those higher positions which necessitate the acquisition and exercise of those qualities. In the vast and complex machine of the Imperial Government they turn some distance with almost mechanical regularity without learning—without having to learn—all about the machine as a whole and as composed of parts all dependent on one another and each contributing its share to the fulfilment of the common purpose.

(g) A large field of selection.

(*g*) On the other hand, the facilities afforded by the British Government for our obtaining the loan of their servants enable the Native State to have the advantage of a very large field of selection—to choose from so large a field men of tried and trained ability and probity—to pick out men just suited to given requirements.

(h) A public servant independent of local connections.

(*h*) It is also a great advantage that the Native State is thus enabled to occasionally introduce into its service a public servant independent of local connections, of local combinations and of local prejudices.

(i) Increase of efficiency.

(*i*) Another considerable advantage of such introduction is that the British servant, thoroughly trained as he is in his particular work, is instrumental in having many under him in the

Native service and thereby raising the standard of efficiency. And I will only add that a carefully selected British servant introduced into the service of the Native State becomes very valuable after some years experience in Native administration. Of this, there are bright examples at this moment in our *Huzur Cutcherry*.

One or two warnings.

(19) It is not out of place here to suggest one or two warnings. The high character of the administration being a matter of vital importance, the Native State should scrupulously avoid introducing into its service any persons who have been dismissed from the service of the British Government for gross misconduct importing moral depravity. Such persons will offer themselves for employment on cheap terms. They will press themselves on the Maharaja's attention in various ways. But they must be firmly rejected; they would say that they do not want any salary, but they simply desire to be in attendance upon His Highness and to make themselves useful in miscellaneous ways, as for instance, in giving private information, in discussing matters and offering counsels in writing to the newspapers, etc., etc. But my opinion is that the Maharaja should summarily reject all such overtures.

The practice of engaging British retired servants indiscriminately is not desirable.

(20) Nor should the Native State indiscriminately take into its service such British servants as have retired on pension. As a general rule, those who have been deemed unfit to render further service under the British Government, must be equally unfit to render further service under the Native Government. Instances, however, sometimes occur in which a pensioned British servant still retains the capacity to work. There is no objection to employ such person for

a time in the service of the Native State, if he possesses more than ordinary merit.

Salary to be one lump sum.

(21) Formerly, the remuneration of our public servants was a conglomerate of salaries, *assamies*, *warshasans*, lands, fees, *palki* allowances, etc., etc. It was altogether a most confused and complex matter. It was a system of concealment, deception and fraud. It made it difficult for the Maharaja to know what the total remuneration of any servant was. And it often happened—it happened too frequently—that though the service was dispensed with, some and even several items of the remuneration continued to be paid! This has now been happily done away with, and every care has to be taken against its resuscitation. A public servant should have a defined salary in the lump and in cash, and this should cease the moment the man ceases to be a public servant.

15

PUBLIC SERVICE

14th September 1881

An extensive organisation.

The public service constitutes an extensive organisation which is felt in every part of the country and which comes in contact with the people in all their relations with the government of the country. Every part of this organisation should be made sound and further means should be devised to provide for the continuity of the soundness.

Heads of departments to have powers.

(2) The heads of the various departments being proper men, they should have powers liberally given them for making appointments, promotions, etc. They should have powers also to fine, suspend, dismiss, etc. Without such powers, they would not be able to maintain discipline and efficiency. The very essence of an efficient organisation is that subordinates should be grouped together under superior officers and that the latter should have the means of influencing the hopes of the former.

Right principles to guide them in the

(3) The heads of departments should exercise their powers above mentioned not arbitrarily or

exercise of their power.

just as they like but under the guidance of right principles. What these principles are may be observed from a circular order sent in 1875 by the existing administration.*

The ruler to supervise and control.

(4) His Highness the Maharaja, in the exercise of supervision and control, has to see that the provisions of the circular order are generally attended to. The result will be that the public service will be required, from time to time, [to be inspected],† so as not only to maintain but to improve its efficiency.

The opinion of the head in matters of patronage to carry much weight.

(5) It is the head of the department who can most correctly know what qualifications are required for any given post under him and whether a given candidate possesses these qualifications. He best knows also which of his subordinates has earned promotion, etc. Therefore, as a rule, his opinion in matters of patronage should carry much weight.

Advice of selfish persons.

(6) Ignorant or selfish persons will advise the Maharaja to concentrate all the patronage in his own hands and to make appointments without reference and even contrary to the views of the heads of departments. The sagacity of His Highness will summarily reject such advice as prejudicial to organisation and efficiency.

Promote efficiency.

(7) The primary object being to appoint and promote the most efficient persons, recommendations conflicting with that object should be rejected, from whatever quarter they may come. For instance, such recommendations may come from friends and relations. They may come from British officers, they may come from the newspapers. The Maharaja's firmness may

* This document is republished as Appendix IV.

† The note-taker appears to have missed a clause.

be abundantly exercised in steadily pursuing the primary object aforesaid.

Favours to be sparingly shown.

(8) Cases may sometime occur, in which His Highness wishes to show favour to a particular person irrespective of his merits and qualifications. Such cases, of course, must be few and far between. Better, then, to appoint such person to some quiet sinecure post in which he would do no harm than to place him in charge of duties which he could not perform satisfactorily.

Transfers not to be made indiscriminately.

(9) Another point to be kept in view by His Highness is this. The public service has various branches. Each branch requires its own special qualifications. It follows that a person who answers well in one branch would not necessarily answer well in another branch. Therefore, transfers from one branch to another should not be made indiscriminately. The caution herein given applies particularly to the Revenue and Judicial Departments of the State.

Nazaranas and bribes for appointments are a poison to government.

(10) The Maharaja should never take any *nazarana* for any appointment or promotion in the public service. His Highness should not allow anyone to receive any bribe for any appointment or promotion. It is a poison which is fatal to all good government and must be shunned as such. Whoever acts contrary to this principle should be expelled from the service, whether private or public, and should be liable to an unsparing criminal prosecution.

How unscrupulous men may tempt a ruler.

(11) There is another way in which bad and unscrupulous men tempt a Maharaja to appoint them to considerable and responsible posts. For instance, one of them says to His Highness, "Give me such an appointment, and I will increase the revenue by such an amount." The money-loving Maharaja swallows the bait. And

what is the consequence? Simply the misery of the subject population. That certainly is not the way to increase revenue. That increase of revenue alone is creditable which results from steady good government, from the increased wealth and prosperity of the people and not from increased exactions.

Bad government due to an ignorant exercise of the rights of patronage.

(12) The several suggestions I have offered in this paper deserve attentive consideration on the part of the Maharaja; indeed, they need to be carefully studied, because I know from actual experience that many evils and troubles arise in Native States from want of a clear comprehension of principles on which patronage should be exercised. Much of the bad government of Native States, and much of the dangers to which Native Princes become exposed, is due to an ignorant exercise of the rights of patronage.

16

RELATIONS WITH BRITISH GOVERNMENT

21st September 1881

Relations with the British Government to be carefully studied.

Nothing is more important than that the Maharaja should study carefully and thoroughly the relations of his State with the British Government. They involve many momentous, difficult and delicate matters, of which the Maharaja should have an accurate and complete knowledge. Upon such knowledge depends in a very large measure His Highness' safety, honour, strength and happiness. I have no doubt, therefore, that the observations I am going to offer will receive the utmost attention.

The British Government exercises supreme sway.

(2) There are some broad facts which must, at the outset, be fully and clearly realised, and I proceed to state them. The first and foremost fact is that the British Government exercises supreme sway over India from Cape Comorin to the Himalayas and from Calcutta to Peshawar. The area of this imperial sway comprises both the British territories and the territories ruled by the Native Princes. It is the

British Government which maintains the general peace of this vast tract.

Their power is a combination of physical with intellectual and moral power.

(3) The British Government fulfils this great function with a power which is irresistible. It is a power which could crush resistance singly or combined and from whatever quarter in India it might arise. The power of the British Government is all the more irresistible because it is derived from a combination of physical with intellectual and moral power. Owing to this happy combination the British Empire in India is far more powerful and far more durable than any empire which had preceded the same.

Every Native Ruler to conciliate the British Government.

(4) It follows that every Native Prince should conciliate the British Government, which possesses such irresistible power. It would be the greatest folly for any Native Prince to provoke it seriously against him. This must be unmistakably understood. Conciliation is an absolute and unavoidable necessity of the situation and circumstances. This necessity must be accepted, and if accepted cheerfully, so much the better in the interests of the Native Princes.

Conciliation not difficult.

(5) Happily, however, the character and qualities of the British Government are such that conciliation is not difficult or costly.

The noble quality of the British Government.

(6) Moreover, while the British Government is physically irresistible, it wisely permits itself beyond all example to be irresistible in the peaceful field of reason, justice and morality. It is anxious to abstain from everything unreasonable, unjust or immoral. The consequence of this anxiety is that, if it ever be unconsciously led into any unreasonable, unjust or immoral action, you have only to prove to it that the action is such and it may generally be expected to withdraw from such action. This is a great

and distinguishing characteristic of the British Government. It is this noble quality of the British Government which greatly restrains the abuse of its irresistible physical power. It is this quality which protects the Native States from becoming the victims of the lawless exerçise of that power. It is this quality from which the Native States derive the hope of living securely, honourably, happily and long.

Conclusions on which the Native Ruler should build his policy.

(7) The conclusions we have reached may be thus very briefly stated, namely:

(*a*) The Native Prince should recognise the power of the British Government as irresistible.
(*b*) He may depend upon it that the British Government, though possessing [ir]resistible power, is amenable to reason, justice, etc., and morality, and is therefore open to argument.
(*c*) The British Government may be conciliated without much difficulty or cost.

Upon these simple axioms should the Native Prince build his whole policy.

Never think of coercing the British by physical force.

(8) I will now briefly state what his whole policy should accordingly be. He should never think of coercing the British Government by means of physical force. The British Government should have no reason given it to suspect any such thought on the part of the Native Prince. He should avoid the maintenance or increase of needless troops. He should not store up needless arms and ammunition. He should not set up the secret manufactories of military stores. He should not show the remotest disposition to combine with those who may be hostile or even unfriendly to the British Government, whether they be individuals or nations. He

should not join or support any political agitation directed against, or embarrassing to, the British Government. These broad hints suffice for the purpose in view and may be suggestive of many minor hints in the same direction.

Appreciate the benefits of British rule.

(9) Further, the Native Prince should show a cordial appreciation of the great benefits which India in general, and the Native States in particular, undoubtedly enjoy under British supremacy.

Argue on grounds of reason, justice and morality.

(10) The Native Prince may, when any differences arise with the British Government, respectfully argue with that Government, on the grounds of reason, justice and morality. It is in this peaceful manner and in this manner only, that the Native Prince can defend his rights, honour and privileges and interests of his subjects. He must appeal to those principles of reason, justice and morality by which the British Government has repeatedly declared itself bound.

Govern your State well.

(11) He should conciliate the British Government, which, as already stated, it is not difficult or costly to do. The best means of conciliating the British Government in these days is for the Native Prince to govern his own State well, and also to see that his arrangements are not in such conflict with those of the British Government as to be a source of constant irritation or annoyance to the British Government. Any Native Prince who steadily pursues the policy thus indicated is sure to get on smoothly and well. His security, his happiness and his durability are insured so long as the British Government endures in India and is true to its own declared principles. This will be very long. Indeed, human foresight cannot assign any limit of time in this respect.

Contrast the present with the past.

(12) Just mark here, please, the contrast—the very great contrast—which this state of things presents to that which existed before the establishment of British supremacy in India. In the *Mughlai* and even in the Maratha period, no Native Prince enjoyed any sense of security. Uncertainty, strife, confusion and anarchy prevailed in their most intensified forms. Just note how the Gaekwar suffered even at the hands of the Maratha Government at Poona. The sufferings of the people in general were even greater than those of the prince. History bears abundant evidence.

What these principles of reason, justice and morality are.

(13) As I have already said, the Native Prince may when any differences arise with the British Government, respectfully argue with that Government on the grounds of reason, justice, and morality. In defence of his rights, honour and privileges and the interests of his subjects, he may respectfully appeal to those principles of reason, justice and morality, by which the British Government has repeatedly declared itself bound. It becomes, therefore, very important that the Maharaja and his ministers should be acquainted with the chief of those principles. Let us go over some of these, drawing them from such sources as are at this moment within our reach.

(a) The Proclamation of 1858. The British Government will not take territory from any Native State.

(*a*) I must begin by referring to that great document—Her Majesty's Proclamation of A. D. 1858. One paragraph of it runs thus:

> We desire no extension of our present territorial possessions, and while we will permit no aggression upon our dominions or our rights to be attempted with impunity, we shall sanction no encroachment on those of others.[1]

One great principle which we derive from the above is that the British Government has solemnly bound itself not to take any territory from any Native State. Upon no grounds or pretexts whatever will the British Government take any territory from any Native State. The British Government will thus resist one great temptation; the Native States are thus freed from one great danger. The whole constitutes a solemn and permanent guarantee for the continued existence of the Native States in their territorial integrity. The Native States must be profoundly grateful for this great security.

(b) Though a ruler may be deposed, the State will be preserved.

(*b*) The foregoing assurance, however, does not mean that the British Government will never deprive a Native Prince of his territories—that it will never depose a Native Prince. The British Government does retain this power. If a Native Prince is guilty of gross misgovernment, the British Government has the power to depose him. Similarly, if a Native Prince is grossly disloyal to the British Government and becomes its enemy or joins its enemies, the British Government may depose such a prince. But even in that case the British Government will not annex to itself the territories of the deposed prince. Though the prince may be deposed, the Native State will be preserved in its integrity. Some other person—probably some heir or relative of the deposed prince—will be put in possession of the Native State. Though the ruler may be changed for some sufficient reason, the Native State itself will remain in its territorial integrity.

Example of the above.

The principle was fully exemplified in the instance of Baroda itself. Malhar Rao Gaekwar was deposed and a distant relative of his was substituted. But Her Majesty's word was fully kept, inasmuch as not one inch of the Baroda territories was taken away by the British Government.

(c) Where lineal descendants fail.

(*c*) Even where lineal descendants fail in the case of a Native Prince, the British Government will not take the Raj but will give it to the nearest or one of the nearest of the surviving relatives.

(d) Adoption of sons by Native Princes.

(*d*) The British Government also recognises the adoption of sons by the Native Princes, which is a course equally of justice and good policy. It may be stated here merely for information that the right of Native Princes to adopt heirs has been recognised by the British Government mainly from the period Her Majesty the Queen assumed the direct government of India.

(e) Exchange of territory by mutual consent.

(*e*) The part of the Queen's Proclamation under remark does not, however, prevent exchanges of territory by mutual consent.

(f) Aggression on the British dominions not allowed.

(*f*) Her Majesty will punish any aggression on her dominions or on her right. Nothing need be said on this point because Baroda has never attempted any such aggression and never will attempt the same.

(g) No encroachments on the rights of others.

(*g*) Her Majesty will sanction no encroachment on the dominions or rights of others. This refers principally to the Native Princes and secures their protection.

The continuance of the Native States is the desire of the British.

(14) All these things being considered, the British Government has bound itself to protect the Native States to an extent and in a manner unknown to the preceding history of India. This is undoubtedly a matter of the highest satisfaction to all India, because all India most earnestly desires the continuance of the Native States.

17

RELATIONS WITH BRITISH GOVERNMENT

28th September 1881

Social advancement can be secured by peace and good government.

Another very important paragraph of Her Majesty's Proclamation is now to be noticed. It runs as follows:

> We shall respect the rights, dignity and honour of Native Princes as our own; and we desire that they, as well as our own subjects, should enjoy that prosperity and that social advancement which can only be secured by internal peace and good government.[1]

These are just, generous and noble assurances proceeding from the highest authority of the British Government. They are assurances which greatly fortify the Native Princes and their States.

The rights and honour of Native Princes to be respected.

(2) Let us note that the rights, dignity and honour of Native Princes are not only to be respected but are to be respected as if they were Her Majesty's own. The assurance is thus as full and complete as the most ardent well-wisher of Native States could wish. It is a strong and sol-

emn assurance, which is the outcome of that exalted moral principle or precept of religion, whether Hindu or Christian, which bids us treat others as we would they should treat us. The rights, dignity and honour of Native Princes are thus secured in the strongest manner possible.

The rights claimed should be reasonable.

(3) In connection with this, however, one thing should be carefully remembered. The Native Princes should not claim any rights, dignity and honour, which are extravagant or unusual or incompatible with civilised society and civilised government. What they may claim, and what Her Majesty has graciously and solemnly promised to respect, are reasonable rights, dignity and honour.

Examples of rights not reasonably exercised.

(4) For instance, it would not be reasonable for any Native Prince to claim the right of forcibly taking into his *zenana* any woman he likes. It would not be reasonable for him to claim the right of arbitrarily putting any person into prison. It would not be reasonable for him to claim the right of making the British Resident sit on the floor without a chair, while he (the prince) himself sits high on the *gaddi*. It would not be reasonable for him to claim any rights which are contrary to the treaties and engagements by which he is bound. The few examples just given will serve to show what is meant and what is not meant by the paragraph of the Queen's Proclamation under advertence. The warning which they suggest may not be quite unnecessary because it is not impossible that a prince, in a moment of haste, might presume too much on this part of the Proclamation and get into serious trouble.

The British Government is

(5) From the words, "We shall respect the rights, etc., of Native Princes as our own", it

superior to that of the Native Princes.

will not be inferred that Her Majesty places the Princes on a footing of equality with herself. From the very nature of things, equality does not and cannot exist. The British Government is decidedly superior to the Native Princes in many essential respects, and especially in respect to power and influence. This is a fact which daily stares us in the face and no Native Prince can ignore it. What the words of the Queen's Proclamation mean is, that the rights, dignity and honour of Native Princes whatever they are, and as they are, will be respected and will be respected as much as if they were Her Majesty's own.

The rulers to promote internal peace and government.

(6) In the paragraph of the Proclamation under notice, Her Majesty declares the important truth that prosperity and social advancement can be secured only by internal peace and good government. In desiring, therefore, that the Native Princes should enjoy prosperity and social advancement, Her Majesty clearly desires that these princes should promote internal peace and government. It is, of course, the duty of every prince to promote peace and good government; and the aforesaid declaration of Her Majesty makes this duty all the more imperative.

The British Government will maintain all treaties with the Native Princes.

(7) Another paragraph of the Queen's Proclamation declares that all treaties and engagements made with the Native Princes will be scrupulously maintained, and further declares that Her Majesty looks for a like observance on the part of the princes. Though possessing irresistible power, the British Government thus distinctly declares that it is bound by the treaties and engagements with the Native Princes. In other words, the British Government

will scrupulously do all that the treaties and engagements promise and scrupulously abstain from doing all that they forbid. The declaration is the very foundation of the continued existence and security of the Native Prince.

Who in return should do the same thing.

(8) On the other hand, the Native Princes are expected to observe the treaties and engagements in the most scrupulous manner. This is obviously most right and proper. The Princes should therefore make themselves thoroughly, minutely and accurately acquainted with the treaties and engagements, carefully note everything which requires to be done or requires not to be done, and scrupulously act accordingly. The princes should be more careful not to give reason, or even the appearance of reason, to the British Government to say, "You have not observed the treaties and engagements, you cannot therefore expect us to observe them."

Peaceful industry and works of public utility to be promoted.

(9) The Queen's Proclamation concludes with the expression of a noble resolve which deserves to be taken to heart by every ruler, small or great. That resolve is expressed in the following memorable words:

> It is our earnest desire to stimulate the peaceful industry of India, to promote works of public utility and improvement, and to administer its government for the benefit of all our subjects resident therein. In their prosperity will be our strength, in their contentment our security, and in their gratitude our best reward.[2]

Govern for the benefit of all.

(10) The more, then, the Native Princes follow this noble example of a sovereign much greater than any one of them and much greater even than all of them put together, the more they will be in accord with, and the more will

they be esteemed by, the Imperial Government which, as already stated, holds sway over all India, with irresistible power, and which effectually protects each of them against another's aggression and protects all against foreign aggression. Each Native Prince should similarly resolve to govern for the benefit of all his subjects and not for the selfish pleasure and enjoyment of himself, and a narrow circle of friends and dependants. Let each Native Prince proudly say that in the prosperity of his subjects will be his strength, in their contentment his security, and in their gratitude his best reward.

Importance of those principles.

(11) We have thus derived some large and invaluable principles from Her Majesty's Proclamation in its bearing on the Native States—principles which restrain and control the action of the irresistible power of the British Government, principles without which that irresistible power would be an unmitigated curse to India. Let us now proceed to notice other principles which regulate the relations between the British Government and the Native States.

The duty of the British Government to protect the Native State against the violence of another.

(12) It is to be remembered that the British Government has undertaken the duty of protecting each Native State against the aggression or violence of another. This duty gives the British Government the right to see that each Native State does not provoke the aggression or violence of another. It is thus that the British Government has the right to prevent a Native State's aggression or violence against another Native State, and also the right to prevent such action on the part of a Native State as would provoke the aggression or violence of another Native State. In this respect the British Govern-

ment acts the part of a grand and powerful political magistrate over the Native States. Such a magistrate must necessarily have the right to restrain transgression by Native States.

Correspondence between two States.

(13) Hence it is that the British Government tells every Native State not to carry on direct correspondence with any other Native State. All correspondence between one Native State and another must pass through the offices of the British Government.

The Native State to refer disputes to the British Government.

(14) Hence it is that the British Government tells every Native State to refer to British officers every dispute or difference between it and any other Native State. The British Government takes means to bring about a just and peaceful settlement, which must be submitted to by the Native States concerned. The British Government has the right to enforce its settlement thus effected.

The Native State not to provoke aggression from foreign powers.

(15) Again, it should be remembered that the British Government has undertaken the duty of protecting each Native State against aggression or violence from foreign powers such as Russia, France, Germany, the United States of America, etc., etc. This duty gives the British Government the right to see that each Native State carefully abstains from provoking aggression or violence from such foreign powers.

The rights of the British Government.

(16) It is thus that the British Government has the right to prevent such action on the part of a Native State as would provoke a foreign power. Hence it is that the British Government tells every Native State not to carry on direct correspondence with any foreign power. Hence it is that the British Government has the right to compel any Native State to make any immediate reparation for any injury it may have caused to

any foreign power, as for instance, by unjustly imprisoning a subject of the foreign power, by unjustly depriving him of life or property, by plundering any foreign vessel wrecked on the coast of the Native State, and so forth.

The Native Prince not to provoke his subjects by misgovernment.

(17) Again, be it remembered that the British Government has undertaken, wherever treaties regarding a subsidiary force exist, to protect the Native Prince against the violence of his own subjects. This duty gives the British Government the right to see that the Native Prince does not provoke by gross misgovernment his own subjects to violence.

Good government depends on the personal character of the ruler.

(18) This point is clearly put in the following words of a high officer of the British Government. He says:

> The obligation* to protect the Prince from the dangers of internal anarchy or insurrection, from whatever cause it may arise, appears to involve the corresponding privilege of interfering to arrest the progress of proceedings tending to produce it; and the necessity of such interference is the greater and more frequent because, all the States of India being (with some few partial exceptions) purely monarchical, the good government of the country must ever depend upon the personal character and qualifications of the Prince.[3]

Lord Northbrook on misrule.

(19) The same view was put forth very recently and very strongly in the case of Baroda itself. It was done by His Excellency the Viceroy Lord Northbrook in his *kharita* to His Highness Malhar Rao Gaekwar, dated 25th July, 1874. The Viceroy emphatically said:

> My friend, I cannot consent to employ British troops to protect anyone in a course of wrong-

* British India Press edition: objection.

> doing. Misrule on the part of a government which is upheld by the British power is misrule, in the responsibility for which the British Government becomes, in a measure, involved. It becomes, therefore, not only the right but the positive duty of the British Government to see that the administration of a State in such a condition is reformed, and that the gross abuses are removed.
>
> If these obligations be not fulfilled, if gross misgovernment be permitted, if substantial justice be not done to the subjects of the Baroda State, if life and property be not protected, or if the general welfare of the country and people be persistently neglected, the British Government will assuredly intervene in the manner which, in its judgment, may be best calculated to remove these evils and to secure good government. Such timely intervention, indeed, to prevent misgovernment culminating in the ruin of the State is no less an act of friendship to the *Gaekwar* himself than a duty to his subjects.[4]

The British will interfere to prevent misrule.

(20) It follows that when the British Government is bound to protect a Native Prince against the violence of his own subjects, that government has the right to intervene to prevent such gross misrule by the prince as might provoke the violence of his own subjects.

The rights of interference with a Native State.

(21) Again, the British Government derives rights of interference with a Native State from the specific provisions (where such exist) of the existing treaties and engagements. The nature and extent of the interference under reference must be determined by the express terms of those documents. It may here be useful to take a brief and collective view of the interference which the British Government may exercise with a Native State as shown above:

(*a*) It may interfere in the relations of the Native State with other Native States.

(*b*) It may interfere in the relations of the Native States with foreign powers.

(*c*) It may interfere in the internal administration of the Native State to prevent or correct such gross misrule as would provoke popular rising.

(*d*) It may interfere in the internal administration of the Native State, in the manner and to the extent specially provided in the treaties and engagements with the Native State.

It is useless to resist interference.

(22) All this should be clearly understood and remembered and recognised. It would not be desirable, nor would it be of any use, to resist or even to deprecate such interference on the part of the British Government.

18

INTERNAL ADMINISTRATION OF NATIVE STATES

12th, 19th and 26th October 1881

When the British Government may interfere.

The last time we met here, we concluded with a brief and collective view of the interference which the British Government may exercise with a Native State, namely, under the following heads:

(*a*) In the relations of the Native State with other Native States;

(*b*) In the relations of the Native State with Foreign Powers;

(*c*) In the internal administration of the Native State to prevent or correct such gross misrule as might provoke popular rising requiring for its suppression the use of the British subsidiary force;

(*d*) In the internal administration of the Native State, in the manner and to the extent specially provided in the treaties and engagements with the Native State.

Such interference necessary.

(2) We must recognise such interference in certain contingencies as necessary and unavoidable. I go further and say that such interference may be recognised as highly beneficial.

Let the Native State avoid giving occasion for interference.

(3) Of course, the British Government should not and would not exercise any such interference unless there was occasion calling for the same. It follows that if the Native State conducts its affairs with due care and wisdom, it may mostly, perhaps altogether avoid giving occasion for the interference of the British Government.

How the Native State may avoid giving occasion.

(4) Such being the case, it becomes worthwhile to see more in detail how the Native State may avoid giving occasion for the active interference of the British Government under each of the four heads aforesaid:

(a) Relations with other Native States.

(*a*) The Native State should carefully attend to the following points in connection with the head (*a*):

(i) Correspondence how to be carried on.

(*i*) Do not correspond directly with any Native State. All such correspondence should be addressed to the British Resident or through him. This is already an established practice, which should be strictly adhered to. The spirit of the rule just stated requires abstention from allowing any servant or subordinate of one State or Chief to correspond with a servant or subordinate of another State or Chief in behalf of their respective States or Chiefs. Even oral messages should be abstained from.

(ii) Meeting any Chief personally.

(*ii*) Do not personally meet any Chief unless with the knowledge of the British Resident. Meeting any Chief with the knowledge of the British Resident, do not hold any conversation with that Chief such as may be disrespectful or offensive to the British Government.

(iii) Treat the Chief with honour.

(*iii*) Always treat the Chief with the courtesy and marks of honour due to him. He should have no reason to complain to British authorities in this respect.

(iv) Give the Chief his recognised titles.

(*iv*) In every communication which may have to be addressed regarding any Chief, or his important officers, or their action, give them their full recognised titles, and use courteous language. Abstain from imputing to them any bad motives. Abstain from violently criticising their action. In short, abstain from everything offensive or disrespectful.

(v) Giving police assistance.

(*v*) Render hearty police assistance to every Native State in the detection and apprehension of its offenders and in the tracing out of its stolen property, and also in surrendering the offenders and the stolen property.

(vi) Treat all the subjects alike.

(*vi*) In matters of civil or criminal justice, and also in those of general trade, treat the subjects of every Native State quite like your own subjects. I mean that no unfavourable distinction should be made in regard to them.

(vii) Avoid boundary disputes.

(*vii*) Avoid boundary disputes to the utmost extent possible by the necessary precautions. If, however, any occur, earnestly prevent breaches of the peace of every sort, and refer the dispute to the proper British authorities for their investigation and decision. When a boundary dispute has been demarcated by permanent pillars, see that these pillars are scrupulously preserved.

(viii) Render help to the Chief whenever necessary.

(*viii*) When a Chief happens to possess *wanta* or other private landed property in these territories, render him cordial assistance in the recovery of his rents, in the settlement of his dispute with his tenants, etc.

When a Chief happens to have *giras* allowance from our treasury, see that it is punctually paid to him.

In the construction of roads and bridges affecting the interests of both the territories, render due co-operation.

In short, respect in your turn, the rights, honour and dignity of every Chief as your own.

By steadily acting on these principles, we shall avoid giving occasion to the British Government to interfere with us under the head marked (*a*) above. I may here state that these principles almost equally apply to the relations of this State with its neighbouring British districts and British officers.

(b) Relations with foreign powers.

(*b*) Proceeding to the next head marked (*b*), I invite attention to the following points in connection therewith:

(i) Avoid unpleasant collisions with Europeans.

(*i*) It is to be remembered that in consequence of the facilities afforded by steam communication, the subjects of various European and American States travel abroad very much and may be, more or less, and now and then, met with in the territories of the Native State—I mean the subjects of England, France, Germany, Austria, Italy, Russia, the American Union, etc., etc., etc. For the purpose of brevity, I will call all of them "Europeans", which I may do as they all belong to the European race. It is to be also remembered that whatever the European may be, the government to which he belongs exercises a certain degree of protection over him. It will not allow him to be subjected to any gross violence or injustice anywhere, much less in a Native State. It follows that we must be very careful as regards any European in our territories. To state the matter briefly and generally, we must, to the utmost extent possible, avoid unpleasant collisions with Europeans. This is the main key of the policy to be pursued. I will, however, state some details.

(ii) Let the European have a

(*ii*) If a European stranger appears here and seeks an interview with the Maharaja, His proper introduction.

Highness should see him only if he has brought a proper introduction. He can always bring an introductory note from the British Resident. If the European stranger has brought no proper introduction, His Highness had better refer him to the Residency. If any European gentleman comes here properly introduced, show him all due courtesy and consideration.

(iii) When they commit errors, give warning.

(*iii*) European strangers are prone to commit errors or give offence in Native States from ignorance of Native habits and feelings. Be indulgent to them in this respect. For instance, a European may enter a native temple which he ought not to enter. He may shoot a peacock where such proceeding is highly offensive. He may be found fishing at some *ghat* held sacred by the Native community, and so forth. In such cases, no attempt should be made to punish him. Give him a gentle warning, and this will generally suffice, if not, move the British Resident.

(iv) Interdict searching their baggage.

(*iv*) Europeans have a great aversion to their baggage being searched for contraband and dutiable articles. They have a great aversion also to being detained by Customs officers. Therefore, as much as possible, interdict such searches and detentions in ordinary cases. Where merchants and goods for trade are concerned, they must, of course, submit to the ordinary rules.

(v) Avoid contracts with them.

(*v*) As much as may be fairly possible, avoid entering into any contracts with Europeans for supplies in the service, execution of works, etc., and where some few contracts are unavoidably entered into, perform your part of them with the most scrupulous exactitude.

(vi) No pecuniary dealings with them.

(*vi*) Have little or no pecuniary dealings with Europeans, such as lending or borrowing. This, however, does not apply to our purchasing

British Government securities or keeping a current account with such a bank as that of Bombay.

(vii) Their safety while travelling.

(*vii*) Take precautions that European travellers are not robbed in these territories.

(viii) No European to suffer personal ill-treatment.

(*viii*) See that no European suffers any personal ill-treatment in these territories at the hands of the people. If, unfortunately, a European happens to have suffered such, promptly and fully punish the offenders. I avail myself of this opportunity to make known one important and well-recognised principle, namely, that when a European has suffered an injury at the hands of our people the like of which he might suffer in his own country and, indeed, in any country however civilised, we become relieved of responsibility on that account, provided we trace out the authors of the injury and subject them to just punishment, and to reparation so far as may be possible in the circumstances of the case. By doing this, we shall have done as much as the sufferer's own government would have done in similar circumstances, and no more could be reasonably expected of us. But if, on the other hand, we fail to trace out the offenders and subject them to just punishment and reparation, and especially if this failure is due to imperfect arrangements for the security of life and property, or to negligence or indifference or anything worse in a particular case, then we shall be held, more or less, and sometimes fully, responsible for the injury caused by our people.

(ix) Offences by British European officers to be referred to the Resident.

(*ix*) In cases of minor offences by British European officers, such as beating or otherwise ill-treating our people, forcibly taking supplies from them, behaving disrespectfully to our authorities, etc., etc., represent the matter correctly and calmly to the British Resident, who will readily bring about a departmental disposal of the matter. The European officer concerned will probably be transferred, or degraded, or otherwise made to suffer for his misbehaviour.

(x) Giving redress.

(*x*) If any European seeks any kind of redress in these territories, whether criminal, civil, or political, promptly attend to his complaint and grant such redress as he may be justly entitled to.

(xi) Giving help to the shipwrecked crew.

(*xi*) If any ship be wrecked on any of our coasts, render every possible assistance, in order to save the passengers, crew and cargo. Shipwrecks, however, will be very few, now that we are providing the requisite lighthouses.

(xii) No European to reside or settle.

(*xii*) Do not permit any European to reside or settle in these territories and do not employ him in the public or Palace service, unless after duly consulting the British Resident and obtaining through that authority the sanction of the Government of India. I include in the public service a pleader in courts or *cutcherries*.

(xiii) European vagrants.

(*xiii*) European vagrants should be promptly sent out of these territories by moving the British Resident to take the necessary action.

(xiv) Emissaries from hostile European countries.

(*xiv*) It is within the range of possibility that, in certain circumstances or contingencies, secret emissaries from European countries, hostilely or adversely disposed towards the British Government, may come here to incite disaffection towards that Government. Be very much on your guard against such emissaries. Do not fail to inform the British Resident of everything you come to know of them. The various suggestions I have thus made, though they may not be exhaustive, will probably suffice to indicate the character or spirit of the policy which the Maharaja should pursue in this respect.

(c) Internal Administration.

(*c*) We have now to notice the head marked (*c*) above. I will offer a few preliminary remarks and then offer a few detailed practical suggestions as to the policy to be pursued.

(i) The British Army to help the Native ruler in case of emergency.

(*i*) It is the right of the Maharaja to ask for, and it is the obligation of the British Government to give, the aid of British troops in putting down any great popular disturbance in His Highness' territories. This arrangement affords to the Native ruler a strength and security unknown in former times. The very fact that the arrangement exists, the very knowledge that the British army will readily step in and crush the insurgents with the certainty of fate, largely prevents insurrection occurring, and British intervention puts it down.

(ii) What the exact situation is.

(*ii*) This is so far all very good for the ruler of a Native State, personally as a ruler. But how does it affect the people ruled? The following imaginary conversation between the people of a Native State on the one side and the British Government on the other will show the situation:

> THE BRITISH GOVERNMENT:
>
> You, people of the Native State, take note that if you rise against your ruler, we shall instantly send our invincible army against you and crush you if necessary, we shall kill any number of you and capture and imprison any number. Therefore, never rise against your ruler.
>
> THE PEOPLE:
>
> We quite understand what you have just said, but we beg you to give us a patient hearing. Our old *mamul* was occasionally to rise against our ruler when he, instead of preserving and promoting our welfare, cruelly

oppressed us. When his oppression became unbearable, we rose against him and demanded redress. If he refused redress, we deposed him and chose another ruler who would govern us better. You now tell us that we must never rise against our ruler, and that if we do, you will shoot us down. How then, if our ruler, becoming all the more emboldened, increases his oppression and tyranny? Maladministration would then proceed to any extremity, and would you support it against its victims with your arms? Would it be right, would it be just, would it be acceptable to God, that you should lend your unconquerable arms to one individual oppressor to enable him to destroy the happiness and deepen the misery of hundreds of thousands of innocent fellowmen? Friends of mankind! Ardent advocates of human liberty and progress! Do you come from the distant north only to redouble our chains and to intensify our miseries?

THE BRITISH GOVERNMENT:

By no means. Be sure that, by our wishing to support your ruler against internal disturbances, we do not at all mean that he should be enabled to misgovern you.

THE PEOPLE:

Thank you. But suppose he misgoverns as a ruler is only too apt to do when freed from the consequences of popular resentment. What then?

THE BRITISH GOVERNMENT:

In that case you may complain to us. We will certainly look into the matter. If we are satisfied that gross misgovernment is practised, we shall remonstrate with your ruler and get him to do better.

THE PEOPLE:

Quite so. But suppose he does not listen to your remonstrations and persists in gross misgovernment. How then?

THE BRITISH GOVERNMENT:

We shall, in that case, depose him and provide a better ruler.

It would be impossible for the British Government to give other replies than those above indicated.

(iii) The ruler to govern well.

(*iii*) It necessarily follows, then, that the obligation of the British Government to assist the ruler of the Native State in putting down internal disorder and disturbances carries with it the right to prevent or remedy gross maladministration by that ruler. It thus becomes additionally important for the ruler to govern well and to keep the British Government satisfied that he is governing well. In connection with the subject under advertence—in order to obviate the necessity of interference by the British Government in the internal administration of the State with the view of preventing and remedying maladministration—the great point for the Native ruler is to abstain from giving cause for his people to rise against him or to complain of gross maladministration. He cannot be too careful in this respect.

(iv) Moderate taxation and efficient police and military forces.

(*iv*) Let him see that taxation is moderate; make life, person and property secure; maintain a good Police backed by an efficient though small Military force; and the result will be that the great body of his people will be fairly contented and will seldom rise against him.

Some special precautions.

(5) In addition to these general conditions for the maintenance of contentment and

peace, some special precautions may be here suggested.

(a) Religion. (*a*) Do not interfere with the religion of the people, or any section of the people, for religion concerns the strong feelings of large numbers.

(b) Taxation. (*b*) For the same reason, do not suddenly increase any tax.

(c) Custom. (*c*) For the same reason, do not suddenly change any long existing and popular custom.

(d) Privileges. (*d*) Do not suddenly deprive large numbers of people of any privileges or indulgence they have long enjoyed.

(e) Restrictions. (*e*) Do not suddenly impose any unusual restrictions on large numbers of people.

(f) Improvements. (*f*) Do not suddenly order any such extensive Municipal improvements as would entail the destruction of a great number of houses.

(g) Discontent. (*g*) Do not take any step which would suddenly spread discontent through the troops.

(h) Punishment. (*h*) Even in dealing with criminal offences in which large numbers are concerned—for instance, whole villages—do not attempt to bring everyone to punishment. It would often suffice to limit action to the leaders.

(i) Excitement among classes. (*i*) Such classes of people as the *Bhils*, *Waghirs*, *Girasias*, *Thakurs*, etc., are generally ignorant and impulsive and are known to be actuated by a common spirit. Do not give cause for a common excitement among any of these classes. In short, abstain to the utmost extent possible from all such action as is likely to cause great dissatisfaction in large numbers at the same time.

Disaffection to be rooted out. (6) While the Native State thus pursues a just, mild and considerate policy, it should present a firm front to unprincipled and factious promoters of popular disaffection. There still are persons of this sort at Baroda. During these six years of strong administration, they have found it necessary to be quiet. After His Highness the Maharaja assumes power at the end of the year, those persons may possibly try their old tricks. They should be closely watched. If any of them commit any mischief, they should be apprehended and brought to condign punishment in due course of law. The Maharaja's views and determination in this respect may be made sufficiently manifest in various little ways on the principle that "prevention is better than cure."

19

RIGHTS OF THE BRITISH GOVERNMENT

9th November 1881

The relations of the State with the British Government as determined by the treaties.

We have now to take a view of the relations of the State with the British Government, as determined by the existing treaties and engagements. In doing this, we shall confine ourselves to the principal points, leaving minor ones to be specially studied as occasion may call for.

The State to be loyal.

(2) The State is bound to be friendly and loyal to the British Government. This is too obvious to require any detailed explanation.

The British, in turn, to be friendly.

(3) The British Government should, in its turn, be friendly to the State, and should do nothing against the just rights and against the welfare of the State.

Extension of the above principle: friends and enemies of either to be friends and enemies of both.

(4) The friends and enemies of either Government shall be the friends and enemies of both. It follows that if the British Government is at war with any power, this State cannot be on friendly terms with that power but must take the side of the British Government. The principle applies also to individuals. If any individual, for instance, is acting against the British Government—takes

part in any political agitation or movement of any kind injurious to the British Government—the Baroda State should not, in the least, give its support or even sympathy to such individual. Similarly, if any individual acts against the Baroda State—tries, for instance, to create disturbances in these territories—the British Government will not give its support or sympathy to such individual. On the contrary, the British Government will actually put him down. Even if the said individual lives in British territory and therefore beyond the reach of the power of this State, and carries on his operations from a base in that territory, the British Government will lay hold of him and bring him to punishment and adopt other preventive measures.

Abstain from use of force.

(5) This State is bound to abstain from committing any act of hostility or aggression against any power whatever. In other words, it is bound to abstain from the use of force against any State in any shape. If any differences arise between this State and any other, such differences should be referred to the British Government, which will adjust the matter in a just manner in communication with His Highness' Government. The British Government should be looked to, to enforce settlements in such matters.

Boundary disputes etc., to be referred to the British Government.

(6) Accordingly, all boundary disputes—disputes about certain *giras* rights; indeed, all disputes generally between this State and any other—are brought to the notice of the British Government, who gives decisions with every desire to do impartial justice.

Peace is thus ensured.

(7) The treaty provisions under advertence, applying as they do to all Native States, have put an end to those internal wars and commotions

which used, formerly, to afflict all India to a deplorable degree. Peace and security have thus been insured to all States.

No European to be employed without the consent of the British.

(8) The State is bound not to entertain in its service any European or American without the consent of the British Government. The object of this provision of the treaty is to prevent complications with European or American powers.

The British to assist the State with British forces whenever necessary.

(9) The British Government is bound to assist this State with British forces on all important occasions calling for such assistance. British forces will accordingly be employed to protect the person of His Highness the Gaekwar, to repress and chastise rebels and exciters of disturbance in His Highness' territories, to duly correct such subjects or dependents of His Highness as may withhold the payment of the *Sarkar*'s just claims, and generally to maintain tranquillity within and to prevent aggression from without.

A just ruler will have the utmost British protection.

(10) I have, however, already explained under what necessary conditions the British Government will use its forces in the interests of the Native State. The British Government will not employ its arms to favour any injustice or oppression on the part of the Native State. This limitation should be well borne in mind. The rights accruing to the British Government, as already stated, from this obligation to render military assistance, should also be carefully carried in memory. Any oblivion in these important respects might create a false and perilous of sense of security. In short, the ruler who rules justly will have the utmost British protection.

But the State to have its own army.

(11) The treaty expressly provides that the British Subsidiary Force shall not be employed on trifling occasions. Hence it is that this State

should maintain [a] moderate and sufficiently efficient military force of its own, by means of which it may ordinarily preserve internal tranquillity without calling upon the British Government to move its battalions. It is only when an emergency occurs, with which our own police and our own military force are not likely to be able to cope, that we can depend upon the British Government for its military assistance. Such emergencies must be rare. They must be rare in proportion as our government is good, and as our police and military forces are efficient.

What should be its strength.

(12) The Baroda State is bound to maintain a contingent of 3,000 horse for the use of the British Government. This is a very onerous obligation, and has been the source of much trouble and much discussion. This matter will, it may be expected, be placed on a more satisfactory footing in the course of time.

How tributes due to Baroda are collected.

(13) By existing arrangements with the British Government, the British Government collects the tributes (*jamabandi* and *ghasdana*) due to the Baroda State from the Princes and Chiefs and *Thakurs* of Rewa Kantha, Mahi Kantha, Palanpur and Kathiawar, and pays over the amount to this State. And this State is bound to abstain from sending its military forces to those provinces for the collection of those dues. This arrangement, however, has not extinguished the sovereignty or the suzerainty of the Gaekwar over such of the said tribute-payers as were subject to the same at the time the said arrangement was made. The practical effect has been that the Gaekwar's rights in this respect are exercised for His Highness by the British Political Agents of the above mentioned provinces.

Extradition of criminals.

(14) The mutual extradition of criminals is generally provided for by treaty and has been recently placed on a sound footing.* Principles and rules have been agreed upon, which work very beneficially.

Opium and salt.

(15) Certain arrangements have also been made in these territories in relation to opium and salt.† The primary object has been to aid the British Government in protecting its large revenues from its monopolies of these articles. This object has been carried out with due attention to the interests of our own subjects. It is of the utmost importance to adhere to these arrangements and to work them faithfully and vigorously.

The British guarantee to particular persons.

(16) It is to be remembered that the British Government, in the early times of its relations, gave its guarantee for the rights and privileges of several individuals in these territories. These guarantees became a fertile source of trouble, expense and vexation to this State, and of difficulties to the British Government itself. Fully realising this fact, the policy of the British Government has been to get rid of such guarantees as opportunities presented themselves. Accordingly, only very few such guarantees now remain. The Baroda State should scrupulously respect these still remaining guarantees.

Guarantee to *Girasias*.

(17) There is another set of British guarantees which must be adverted to at this place,

* In 1877 Baroda and British India agreed to abide by the provisions and procedures of the 1873 Extradition Act on a strictly reciprocal basis.

† Under intense pressure from Calcutta, Baroda introduced a monopoly over the production and retail of opium in 1879, and outlawed the production of, and trade in, contraband salt in 1880.

namely, guarantees to certain *Girasias*. Further particulars regarding these will be explained to His Highness by Mr. Pestanji.* I will here only suggest that the Baroda State should scrupulously respect these guarantees also.

The advice of the British Government.

(18) By treaty, His Highness the Gaekwar is bound to listen to the advice of the British Government respecting the welfare of His Highness' country. This is an important provision which has to be kept in view.

The right of the British representative in 1828.

(19) It would also seem that the British representative had, in 1828, the right to obtain some idea of the finances of the State, and to be consulted before any new expenses of magnitude were incurred.

The choice of the Prime Minister.

(20) The choice of his Prime Minister by His Highness the Gaekwar used to be subject to the approbation of the British Government. But in Maharaja Khande Rao's time, this condition was withdrawn in the belief that the Gaekwar will himself exercise every care and judgment in so important a matter. The Gaekwar has thus the right to appoint his own minister without previously obtaining the concurrence of the British Government. The right is a valuable one, and ought by all means to be preserved.

The Resident may be consulted in a friendly manner.

(21) Without, however, impairing that right, the Maharaja would perhaps do well, in doubtful cases, to have a little private and friendly consultation with the British Resident, in order to make sure that that authority has no serious objection to the person proposed by His Highness for the office of the Prime Minister. This course is recommended by good policy, for the complex affairs of this State can hardly

* Pestanji Jehangir, Minister for Settlement and Alienation, and the Military.

be satisfactorily conducted by a Chief Minister neither deserving nor enjoying the respect of the Resident for capacity and integrity. A similar consultation may perhaps be not undesirable when the Chief Minister is to be asked to resign. Indeed, the best method of preserving the valuable right of His Highness under advertence seems to be to take every care that any ministerial changes His Highness contemplates are not unacceptable to the British Resident.

The Viceroy's communication of 1874.

(22) As bearing on the whole subject under treatment today, I do well to quote here from a *kharita*, dated 25th of July 1874, addressed by the Viceroy Lord Northbrook to His Highness Malhar Rao Gaekwar. The following extracts from that important communication deserve special attention:

> I deem it, therefore, necessary to remind you that, both by the terms of treaties and by constant usage, the British Government has the right to advise you in public concerns affecting the good of the country, and to require the settlement, according to equity and reason, of any measures shown to be improper or unjust, and that, by consequence, it is at liberty to take such steps as it may deem necessary for the just exercise of that right, and the fulfilment of the obligations to the ruler and people of Baroda which flow therefrom.
>
> Your Highness must be aware that, from the earliest period of its connection with the Baroda State, the British Government has repeatedly found it necessary to intervene in Baroda affairs. This intervention has not been limited to the case of the guarantees to which Your Highness has referred but has been exercised in a variety of other ways, as for example, by investing the Resident with power of control over the finances, by assuming for a

time the management of portions of the State, by the removal of evil advisers; in short, whenever intervention has been deemed by the British Government necessary in the interests of the ruler or his subjects.

This intervention, although amply justified by the language of treaties, rests also on other foundations. Your Highness has justly observed that "the British Government is undoubtedly the paramount power in India, and the existence and prosperity of the Native States depend upon its fostering favour and benign protection." This is especially true of the Baroda State, both because of its geographical position intermixed with British territory, and also because a subsidiary force of British troops is maintained for the defence of the State, the protection of the person of its ruler, and the enforcement of his legitimate authority.

My friend, I cannot consent to employ British troops to protect anyone in a course of wrongdoing. Misrule on the part of a government which is upheld by the British power is misrule, in the responsibility for which the British Government becomes in a measure involved. It becomes therefore, not only the right but the positive duty of the British Government to see that the administration of a State in such a condition is reformed and that gross abuses are removed.

It has never been the wish of the British Government to interfere in the details of the Baroda administration, nor is it my desire to do so now. The immediate responsibility for the government of the States rests, and must continue to rest, upon the Gaekwar for the time being. He has been acknowledged as the Sovereign of Baroda, and he is responsible for exercising his sovereign powers with proper regard to his duties and obligations alike to the

> British Government and to his subjects. If these obligations be not fulfilled, if gross misgovernment be permitted, if substantial justice be not done to the subjects of the Baroda State, if life and property be not protected, or if the general welfare of the country and people be persistently neglected, the British Government will assuredly intervene in the manner which, in its judgment, may be best calculated to remove these evils and to secure good government. Such timely intervention, indeed, to prevent misgovernment culminating in the ruin of the State is no less an act of friendship to the Gaekwar himself than a duty to his subjects.[1]

The Viceroy's *kharita* went on to say that, if the Gaekwar, to whom it was addressed, failed to attend to the advice given by the Viceroy and if, in consequence, the condition of the Baroda administration remained unreformed, that the Gaekwar would be deposed, and other arrangements would be made to secure a satisfactory administration.

The subsequent event.

(23) What followed is well known. That Gaekwar was deposed, and other arrangements were made to secure a satisfactory administration of the Baroda State. It devolves on that Gaekwar's successor to maintain such administration.

The sum and substance of the communication.

(24) The Viceroy's communication, from which I have largely quoted, deserves to be most attentively studied. The truth of it is that the British Government will not interfere in the Baroda administration so long as it is satisfactory. But if the administration becomes grossly bad, the British Government will interfere in any manner it may judge best for its reform.

From what the right of interference is derived.

(25) The right and duty of the British Government to thus exercise interference are, the Viceroy says, derived from the treaties, from

constant usage, from the nature and consequences of the subsidiary alliance, and from friendship to the Gaekwar, and the duty due to his subjects.

What is bad administration.

(26) The Viceroy has indicated what constitutes bad administration. It is bad administration of justice, insecurity of life and property, persistent neglect of the general welfare of the country and people, and so forth.

Removal of evil advisers.

(27) The Viceroy also indicates the various rights of interference on the part of the British Government. These I need not recapitulate. It is noteworthy that the removal of evil advisers from the Gaekwar is included in those rights.

How far the rights extend.

(28) Subsequent events—that is to say, those which followed the Viceroy's *kharita*—show that the rights of the British Government extend to the deposition of the Gaekwar himself and the substitution of another Gaekwar for the better government of the country. These rights of the British Government are extensive and are not precisely defined.

Govern well.

(29) The safest, the simplest, and the soundest way for the Maharaja to avoid or to minimise the interference of the British Government is to himself govern his country in the best manner possible.

20

ADVICE OF THE BRITISH GOVERNMENT

16th November 1881

Limits to the exercise of the rights.

We have taken a survey of the rights of the British Government to interfere in Baroda affairs. Let us now consider [the] natural and rational limits [that] apply to the actual exercise of those rights.

Advice to the Gaekwar.

(2) The most important of these rights is to advise His Highness the Gaekwar [on matters] touching the affairs of his State. The Gaekwar is bound to listen to the advice which the British Government may give him.

The advice of the Viceroy to be distinguished from that of subordinate British Authorities.

(3) It is necessary to draw a clear distinction between the advice of the British Government itself on the one hand, and the advice of authorities subordinate to that Government on the other. The advice of the British Government is the advice of the Viceroy in Council, whereas the other advice is that of local subordinate British authorities locally doing business. The treaty obligation to listen to advice applies to the former advice, and not to the latter. I am very far from saying that His Highness the *Gaekwar*

should not listen to the latter advice. The advice coming from local subordinate British authorities may often be very valuable and deserving of cordial acceptance by His Highness. But this advice is not that which the Gaekwar is bound by treaty to listen to. What His Highness is thus bound to listen to is the advice of the British Government itself as represented by the Viceroy and Governor-General-in-Council.

The legal difference between the two.

(4) It is manifest that the advice of the local subordinate British authorities cannot claim to be put on the same level as the advice of the supreme British authority in India. There is a great natural difference between the two sets of advice under comment, and the treaty makes a great legal difference between the two.

The Gaekwar not bound to accept the advice of every grade of British Authority but that of the Viceroy.

(5) By way of further explanation, I may observe that the Gaekwar would be acting contrary to the treaty if he should refuse to listen to the advice of the Viceroy, whereas His Highness could not be taxed with violation of treaty if he should, for any reason, decline to accept the advice which any Political Officer, or Collector, or any other subordinate local British authority might offer as emanating from himself. This is as it should be. If it were obligatory of the Gaekwar to accept the advice of every grade of British authority in the same way as the advice of the Viceroy in Council, His Highness' liberty of action would be reduced to little or nothing, inasmuch as he would be obliged to accept advice coming from a plurality of sources indefinite as to its quantity, doubtful perhaps in regard to its quality, and not unfrequently conflicting in its character and its aim.

The Gaekwar is bound to listen to the advice of the

(6) The distinction under advertence is of considerable practical importance, and deserves to be kept in view. By its being kept in view by

Government of India.

the Gaekwar, His Highness will be free from the irritation or discontent which must result from the mistaken belief that he is obliged to accept advice coming from various sources and on any subject. On the other hand, by its being kept in view by the British authorities who have to deal with His Highness, these authorities will be induced to be duly moderate and considerate in offering their advice, and to abstain from pressing their advice with the force which exclusively belongs to His Excellency the Viceroy in Council. The conclusion, then, is that the advice which the treaty binds His Highness the Gaekwar to listen to, is the advice of the Government of India.

How the advice may be conveyed.

(7) Such advice of the Government of India may be conveyed to the Gaekwar either directly by means of its own communications addressed to His Highness, or indirectly through the British Resident. In the latter case, the British Resident will doubtless inform His Highness that the advice he conveys is under the authority of the Government of India. Conveyed in either way, the advice of the Government of India will possess all the weight accorded by the treaty. When the advice is intended to carry such weight, the Government of India will, no doubt, in an express or implied manner inform His Highness that the advice is given under the treaty.

The advice should be for the good of the State.

(8) To proceed. The advice which may be given as aforesaid should, by the terms of the treaty and from natural reason, be for the good of the Baroda State; in other words, for the good of the Baroda ruler or of the Baroda people.

No advice opposed to the good of the State to be given.

(9) Such being the case, no advice will, it is obvious, be given under the treaty, such as is opposed to the good of the Baroda State,

opposed to the rights, honour and dignity of this State. For example, His Highness the Gaekwar will not be advised to cede any portion of his territories and thus to reduce his dominions. He will not be advised to surrender any part of his civil and criminal jurisdiction over his subjects. He will not be advised to lower himself from rank and position and fall to the level of chiefs inferior to himself, and so forth.

What is good advice.

(10) Any advice which the Government of India may give under the treaty will, of course, be the result of due inquiry and deliberation, and as such, the advice will be for the good of this State. At any rate, the Government of India will give it under the belief that it is for the good of this State.

Discussion allowed in doubtful cases.

(11) It is conceivable, however, that instances may occur, though rarely, in which the Government of India indeed believes that the advice is for the good of this State, whereas His Highness the Gaekwar differs from this belief. In such instances, it is permissible for the Gaekwar to explain his own views, and endeavour to satisfy the Government of India of their correctness. In short, in doubtful cases, respectful discussion is allowable within reasonable limits. It is a priceless blessing that the British Government is pre-eminently amenable to fair and temperate reasoning. After discussion, whatever advice the Government of India may judge fit to give should, as a rule, be readily accepted under the obligation of the treaty. I say as a rule, because there may possibly be cases in which the gravity of the question may require a reference to Her Majesty's Secretary of State.

There must be a necessity for giving advice.

(12) Again, there must be a clear necessity for the British Government giving advice under the treaty—a necessity arising from ignorance or unwillingness on the part of the Native State in regard to the good intended to be effected by that advice. When the Native State itself is doing its work with honesty and intelligence, the best course will be to let it go on. The Government of India will, doubtless, by far prefer spontaneous progress on the part of the Native State to progress under pressure from without.

The British Government to intervene for the benefit of the State.

(13) Whenever, however, the Native State takes a decidedly and materially wrong course, it is both the right and the duty of the British Government to intervene under the treaty for the benefit of the State. It is certainly for the advantage of all the parties concerned that maladministration should not be allowed to accumulate and reach dangerous proportions.

The Government of India not to place too high an ideal.

(14) In judging Native rule for the purposes of giving advice under the treaty, the Government of India will, it may be presumed, abstain from assuming too high an ideal. The standard must be that of an average well-governed Native State.

The degree of pressure used in regard to advice.

(15) It may also be presumed that the Government of India will abstain from pressing the Native State to copy British modes of administration too much. When the Native State is actuated with good intentions, it will generally be well to leave it to its own judgment how far to adopt or follow the British models. The degree of pressure to be used in regard to advice by the British Government under the treaty must, obviously, be regulated by the importance or urgency of the subject matter of the advice. Where the object is to ensure attention to the essential or

fundamental conditions of ordinary good government, the British Government will be justified in using much greater pressure [than] where, what I may call, the luxuries of good government are concerned.

Advice not to descend into details.

(16) It may also be reasonably expected that any advice which the British Government may give under the treaty will generally be limited to large objects to be effected or to large principles to be adopted, and that the advice will not descend into details calculated needlessly to hamper the action of the Native State.

The advice not to weaken authority.

(17). The manner in which the British Government will give advice under the treaty will, of course, be courteous, kind and friendly, as far as may be possible in the circumstances. At any rate, it should be as little harsh, and as little calculated to weaken the authority of the Native ruler, as may be possible.

When there is a conflict of interests, the British Government to lean to those of the people.

(18) There is one guiding principle which it may be well for His Highness the Maharaja to bear in his memory. It is a sort of key to the prevailing disposition and action of the British Government. Whenever it is possible to reconcile both, the British Government will be equally mindful of the interests of the Maharaja as a ruler, and of those of his people as his subjects. But when these two interests are materially in conflict, the British Government will generally lean to the interests of the people.

21

THE BRITISH RESIDENT

23rd November 1881

Relations between the Maharaja and the Resident.

It is of very great importance that the relations between His Highness the Maharaja and the British Resident should be friendly and pleasant. To effect this object, attention and effort will be needed on each side.

Recognised precedents to be strictly followed.

(2) The Maharaja should always be careful to show to the Resident every due or customary mark of respect. In these matters, His Highness should strictly follow recognised precedents. These precedents have, therefore, to be well remembered. They should be regularly recorded and occasionally consulted in order to aid His Highness' memory.

Visits, *pan supari*, etc.

(3) When the Resident pays a visit, His Highness customarily receives him at the head of the staircase. This should be strictly adhered to, and no change should be made. Again, His Highness gives him the right side. Again, *pan supari* is given on certain occasions. Again, *pan supari* is given according to a fixed form. All

these and many other particulars should be carried out uniformly according to settled usage.

The Resident in the *Dassera* procession.

(4) Another instance may be here adduced just to show what minute attention is required. The Resident accompanies His Highness in the grand *Dassera* procession. It is desirable to see that the elephant which the Resident rides on this occasion is of about the same height as that which His Highness rides; that the animal is made to walk fully abreast of His Highness' elephant, that the *howdah* decorations, etc., of the animal are according to custom. Usage has settled all or most of these points and no change should be made or attempted.

All the customary respect to be shown to the Resident.

(5) In short, the Resident should have every reason to feel assured that His Highness is, at all times, most anxious to show him all the respect due and customary. The Resident should not have the slightest reason to suspect that His Highness would wish to diminish those marks of respect, if any opportunity offered for doing so. An example may be useful to explain what is meant. Suppose that, on any occasion the Resident is, by custom, entitled to sit on the right side of His Highness but that, from ignorance or inadvertence, the Resident takes the left side. In such a case, His Highness should not take advantage of the mistake of the Resident, but he should at once offer to the Resident the right side.

Regret any error.

(6) If, in spite of every care and attention, any mark of respect due to the Resident happens to be omitted on any occasion, His Highness should take the earliest opportunity to express his regret for the accident.

The Resident's attitude towards the Maharaja.

(7) Such feelings and action on the part of His Highness may well be expected to be cordially and constantly reciprocated by the British

Resident. The British Resident should invariably accord to His Highness all the respect due to His Highness in conformity with custom, and in recognition of His Highness' position as the sovereign of the country. His Highness should have every reason to feel assured that the Resident is, at all times, most anxious to do His Highness all the honour to which His Highness is entitled. His Highness should not have the slightest reason to suspect that the Resident would wish to diminish any marks of respect if an opportunity offered for doing so. Briefly, then, each of the high personages concerned should fully and cordially give and take whatever is due. They should have no jealousies, no fears, no suspicions in this respect. Then the intercourse between them will be quite smooth and friendly.

No presents to the Resident.

(8) Do not attempt to make any presents to the Resident beyond the customary ones of flowers and fruit, and such trifles. British officers are strictly prohibited from receiving any presents of value, and they are generally too conscientious to secretly evade such prohibition. In short, do not ever even appear desirous of laying any British officer under obligation to you in any undue or underhand manner.

Apply to the Resident for any information.

(9) If any information or papers be wanted from the Residency, apply direct to the Resident himself. Never attempt to obtain any surreptitiously.

Communications to the Resident, verbal or written.

(10) Everything that may be spoken or written to the Resident, whether officially or otherwise, must be scrupulously correct in point of facts. Veracity of the highest order should mark the same. Any default in this respect would soon be fatal to confidence and esteem. Courtesy and

perfect good temper also should mark everything that may be spoken or written to the Resident. This applies both to matter and manner. Courtesy and good temper are necessary when a difference of opinion is to be expressed or discussed.

Judicious compromise, where there is difference of opinion

(11) Some difference of opinion will occasionally arise. But these should be reduced to the smallest possible number. In a large proportion of instances, inquiry, consultation and calm reflection, will dissipate the grounds of difference and bring about an agreement. In other instances, judicious compromises should be effected. In others again, where the interests involved are trifling or transitory, the one party may yield in deference to the other.

When official discussion is necessary.

(12) There will thus remain a few instances in which the interests at stake are important and the difference of views is considerable. Such instances will necessitate official discussion. In such instances the communication representing His Highness' views should be very carefully drawn up, so that, when they go up to the higher authorities of the British Government, they may produce the desired effect. Those communications should be, so far as possible, complete and comprehensive in themselves; in language and tone, they should be courteous and respectful; in facts and arguments, they should be perfectly correct and clear, and the principles therein appealed to should be those which are well recognised by the British Government.

Experienced administrative officers to draw up communications.

(13) I would avail myself of this opportunity to suggest that lawyers, howsoever able, are not the best fitted to draw [up] such communications, unless they are practised in political correspondence also. The style in which a lawyer

may address a judge and that in which a Maharaja should address the British Government are in some respects materially different. The lawyer's arguments may always be utilised, but the Maharaja's communications should be drawn up by experienced administrative officers. I may add that similar remarks are applicable to editors of newspapers, whether natives or Europeans.

The Resident to send the Maharaja's communications in their integrity to the higher authorities.

(14) In referring any difference of opinion to the higher authorities, it is only right and proper that the Resident should send up in their integrity the communications which convey the Maharaja's views and arguments. It would hardly be fair to send up only extracts or summaries, for the Maharaja should not be deprived of the satisfaction of feeling that he has been fully heard.

The Maharaja's rights to be properly defended.

(15) With every necessary care and caution, the referring of a difference of opinion to higher authorities may sometimes involve a certain amount of unpleasantness. But obviously, this should not deter the Maharaja from requesting or allowing such a reference where his rights, honour and dignity or the welfare of his subjects is concerned. These need always to be defended with firmness as well as with wisdom and moderation. To defend these properly is the imperative duty of the Maharaja. If they be not vigilantly and vigorously defended, they would gradually decline and might eventually disappear. The British Government cannot blame a Maharaja for thus defending interests which Her Majesty's great Proclamation of 1858 has declared to be as inviolable as if they were Her Majesty's own.

The double capacity of the British Resident.

(16) When the Maharaja's views and wishes in these respects commend themselves to the Resident's sense of justice, the Resident may be

fairly expected to give his full and cordial support to them in his communications to superior authorities. In this connection, it is to be remembered that the British Resident has practically a double capacity. He is the protector of British interests, but he is also the protector of the interests of the Native State. It might, perhaps, have been otherwise if the Native State had its own representative of its interests at the court of His Excellency the Viceroy. But such is not the case. As matters stand, the Resident has to represent the interests of the British Government to the Maharaja and has also to represent the interests of the Maharaja to the British Government. Such a situation requires that the British Resident should hold the balance even between the two sides, that he should exercise perfect impartiality. It follows that he should not shrink from the duty of justly protecting the interests of the Native State when occasion demands it. It has been my good fortune to see not a few British Residents conscientiously high-minded enough to perform this duty even at the risk of temporary displeasure on the part of their superiors. It is this high order of political morality, it is this elevated standard of public duty which constitutes one of the main sources of strength and durability to the British Empire.

The Resident's ideal of duty.

(17) The fact, really, is that a Native State practically sees little of the character and quality of the British Government, except through the British Resident. As the British Resident appears to it, so it supposes the British Government to be. All the just and general assurances of Her Majesty, all the beneficent and magnanimous avowals of the Viceroy have little practical value to the Native State except as given effect to by

the local British representative. The British Resident has, therefore, to represent fully and faithfully all the disinterestedness, the justice, the moderation, the generosity and the friendly spirit which are the attributes of the British Government itself. The Agent's ideal of duty should be quite as high as that of the Principal. The Resident should be relied upon also to protect the State against any aggressive tendencies on the part of neighbouring Political Agents and other British officers.

Maintain principles already established.

(18) The Maharaja should firmly maintain and cling to the various solutions of important or difficult questions which have been made during His Highness' minority. They are the results of very elaborate consideration on the part of the several authorities concerned. They have got rid of many sources of confusion and controversy. They have established or restored right principles. His Highness should therefore strictly enjoin his officers to keep those settlements in view and not to depart from them at all. If in any instances the Residency loses sight of them, His Highness' officers should invariably refer the Residency to them.

Consult the Resident freely.

(19) In all important matters, His Highness will, no doubt, have sound views submitted to him by his council. If, however, His Highness should still feel any great doubt or difficulty, His Highness may freely consult the Resident, who will give disinterested advice. Some matters may be so important that, even without feeling any doubt or difficulty, His Highness will do well to talk them over with the Resident in order to secure the benefit of that authority's concurrence and sympathy. On the other hand, too frequently troubling the Resident might

imply some deficiency of thinking and governing capacity in the Native State. Consultation with the Resident may well be made by His Highness' instructions. In special cases requiring such a course, His Highness may himself consult the Resident personally.

Let the Dewan offer his own views.

(20) Important matters should not, I submit, be settled offhand and orally between His Highness and the Resident, without giving an opportunity to His Highness' Dewan to supply information, to afford explanations, and to offer his own views in the interests of the State.

What is orally settled to be reduced to writing.

(21) If anything be orally settled, it should by no means be left in that state. Better reduce the thing to writing; otherwise, great vagueness and uncertainty and probably misapprehensions and unpleasantness might ensue. As a rule, no important matter should be considered settled until the settlement is inscribed on paper and communicated in this form.

The Resident to inform the Maharaja before sending any proposal to the British Government.

(22) There should be an understanding that, wherever possible, the Resident should not send up to the British Government any proposal affecting His Highness' interests without previously ascertaining His Highness' views. This is a right principle, and it would obviate the Resident committing himself, under imperfect information, to any proposal and feeling the embarrassments necessarily arising therefrom.

The Resident not to interfere in the Maharaja's exercise of patronage.

(23) So long as His Highness carefully selects men for appointments and promotions, the Resident may be expected to abstain from all interference in the exercise of patronage—interference—direct or indirect, official, demi-official; and private experience has shown beyond all doubt that, where the Native Government is good, such abstinence is extremely necessary for its efficiency.

Replies to the Resident to be promptly despatched.

(24) His Highness should see that replies are sent to the Resident's references as promptly as may be possible, though, of course, hasty replies are to be avoided where the matter is of importance in itself or as involving an important principle.

The Maharaja to correspond only through the Resident.

(25) It is a strict rule that His Highness cannot write on any matter of business to the higher authorities of the British Government, independently of the British Resident. Every business communication from His Highness must be either addressed to the Resident or addressed to the higher authorities through the Resident. The rule is so strict that I would advise His Highness to adhere to it even in regard to letters of ordinary courtesy or compliment.

Do not trust to the efficiency of *khatpat*.

(26) I would earnestly advise His Highness not to trust to the efficiency of *khatpat*. Persons are still to be found who may come and whisper that they have great personal influence with the Viceroy or the Governor, or with his councillors, and that they are willing to use that influence in His Highness' favour. They may even venture to pretend to similar influence over the authorities in England. Such persons are generally unprincipled and wish to obtain money under false pretences. They must not be countenanced. They must be firmly avoided as they are sure not only to take away money but to bring discredit on His Highness.

Payments to the Residency Treasury.

(27) The State has to make several payments to the Residency Treasury on various accounts. Such payments should be made whenever they become due, without any delay.

Help to be given to the Assistant Resident.

(28) On the part of the State, cordial assistance should be given to the Assistant Resident who is in charge of the Thuggee and Dacoity

Department. Properly worked, this department does much good in pursuing thugs and dacoits wherever they may go. At the same time, some vigilance may be desirable in view to prevent the detectives of the department oppressing innocent people, and to prevent the department itself unconsciously encroaching on the rights of the State.

The rights of the Resident and members of his staff to be duly respected.

(29) There are certain special rights and privileges enjoyed by the British Resident and also by the members of his staff and even by servants, so also by the British troops stationed here. The State and its officers should be careful not to interfere with those rights and privileges. In short, duly honour the British representative, cultivate friendly relations with him, and win his confidence and support by a steady straightforward policy based on the best principles of government.

22

CONCLUSION

1st December 1881

Concluding advice.

As we now are very near the epoch when Your Highness will assume the government of your country, I must bring these lectures to a close.* Had time allowed, I should have gone on for some months more. Yet what my esteemed colleagues and myself have so far communicated to Your Highness may suffice, I trust, to indicate the great principles which a good ruler has faithfully to adhere to, in order to make his subjects contented and prosperous and thereby himself acquire honour and distinction.

The position of a Maharaja.

(2) Your Highness has now a fair idea of the great responsibilities which are inseparable from great power. The position of a Maharaja in these days is not one of abundant ease and unlimited enjoyment, it is not one in which he is at liberty to spend what public money he likes and in what manner he pleases, it is not one in

* Sayaji Rao ascended to the throne on 28 December 1881.

which power can be exercised without salutary constitutional restraint, it is not one in which the will of His Highness is the law. In these days a fierce light beats on the throne. It is a light which exposes every defect to the public gaze. It is a light which has immensely increased the responsibilities of rulers.

His great responsibilities.

(3) The Maharaja is responsible in various directions in regard to all his actions. He is responsible to God, and to his own conscience. He is responsible to established principles. He is responsible to his people. He is responsible to the British Government. He is responsible to enlightened public opinion in general.

Adhere faithfully to good principles.

(4) The principles with which Your Highness has become acquainted will largely enable you to discharge these responsibilities satisfactorily; Your Highness will remember those principles, Your Highness will allow others to remind you of those principles. Knowing and remembering good principles is not, however, the most difficult part of the duty of a ruler. The most difficult and the most important part is to adhere constantly and faithfully to those principles. This involves great self-denial. It requires great firmness in resisting multifarious seductive influences.

High ideal of duty.

(5) Your Highness will have always to maintain a high ideal of duty. This requires that you should surround yourself with advisers who have such an ideal of duty.

Under God's blessing, may Your Highness' career be long, happy and honourable, and pre-eminently distinguished for justice, wisdom and benevolence.

23

HINTS ON PERSONAL CONDUCT

8th June 1881

They are self-evident.

By way of some variety, I purpose to offer a few minor hints bearing on personal conduct. They will be offered just as they occur, but may be easily arranged in some order at the end. The hints are for consideration and for such attention as they may be found to deserve. Several may possibly be unnecessary, because they are self-evident, or because they are already known. Yet they are offered with the rest, because it is not easy to distinguish the one from the other.

No correspondence with tradesmen.

(1) When things have to be ordered from merchants, shopkeepers, etc., etc., His Highness the Maharaja need not address letters to such persons under his own signature. All business, in short, with such persons should be conducted for His Highness by some of his officials, such as Mr. Raoji Vithal.*

Private correspondence to be limited.

(2) All sorts of individuals will constantly address His Highness private letters on various subjects. Great care and discrimination will

* Raoji Vitthal Punekar, *Subah* of the Baroda Division.

have to be used in sending replies. The needless growth of private correspondence should be prevented. Letters and notes from the Maharaja should be rather rare as a rule. It would not be good that lots of common people should go about saying that they correspond with His Highness and parading his letters and notes. Many things lose their value by becoming too common.

Record to be kept.

(3) Arrangements should be made for keeping copies of all letters or notes sent by the Maharaja. It will be useful in many ways. So communications received by His Highness should be kept regularly by some official. Very small matters sometimes become important, and hence the papers must be available.

Important communications to be previously seen.

(4) In many instances, some official will have to address communications as directed by His Highness. Great care must be taken in order that the official does not go beyond the directions of His Highness, or use language not intended or desired by His Highness. Communications addressed as directed by His Highness, of course, commit His Highness and hence the care required. As a rule, the drafts of such communications should be previously seen by His Highness and initialled with a view to prevent mistakes.

Use the best stationery.

(5) Letters and notes from His Highness should be on the most approved paper. The best ink, envelopes, etc., should be used. Everything should be neat so as to befit His Highness' exalted position.

His Highness' visits not to be too common.

(6) The personal visit of the Maharaja is in itself a great honour. Its value should not be diminished by making such visits too common. I refer to occasions of marriage and other ceremo-

nies in private families. What precedents exist, may, of course, be attended to. But care has to be used in going beyond those precedents.

Introduction of strangers by a responsible officer and not a menial.

(7) If any stranger desires to pay a visit to His Highness, he must not do so without somebody to introduce him. The general rule should be that he should be properly introduced to His Highness, otherwise, all sorts of objectionable people will obtain admittance, which would not befit His Highness' position and dignity. It might be even unsafe.

It would not suffice that anybody introduces the strangers to the Maharaja. For instance, *jasoods*, menial servants and such persons are not proper parties to introduce. The introducer must be a person of position and responsibility. He should be held responsible that he does not introduce improper persons to His Highness, such as bad or condemned characters, low persons who are not in the category of gentlemen, unscrupulous adventurers and so forth. The introducer is responsible to fairly satisfy himself of the respectability of the stranger before introducing him to the Maharaja. In this respect the Palace arrangements may well be like those at Government House, Bombay or Calcutta.

The Maharaja to have previous information.

(8) When a stranger is to be introduced to His Highness, His Highness should have some previous information regarding that stranger, so that His Highness may know how to receive and treat him, what to say to him, and so forth.

Promises not to be made hastily.

(9) Many persons will press His Highness with many solicitations. The Maharaja has to be careful not to commit himself to hasty opinions or hasty promises. Generally, it is desirable for the Maharaja to take time to consult and reflect before expressing any decided opinion, or mak-

ing any definite promise. Great caution has thus to be exercised by those who are in high positions and power.

24

MENIALS AND INTRIGUERS

22nd June 1881

Avoid familiarity with menials.

The Maharaja should avoid familiarity with menial servants. These must be kept at a respectful distance, and must be limited to their respective duties.

Official to check them.

(2) The menial servants must be placed under the control and supervision of some responsible official who should see that they behave properly; and such official should have some power over these servants, so as to be able to influence them by means of hope and fear.

They should not overhear.

(3) The menial servants should be prevented from overhearing the Maharaja's conversations and reporting them abroad. Unless vigilantly looked after, they are generally only too apt to sell news of this kind.

Nor be allowed to beg.

(4) They should be prevented from going about to see the *Sardars*, *Darakdars*, etc., and also the officers, *sowkars* and people generally, and begging for presents and gratuities on one pretence or another. The Maharaja's servants making money in this way would be quite

opposed to the dignity of the Maharaja, while it would put people to inconvenience.

Visitors to be independent of them.

(5) The arrangements in relation to visitors to the Maharaja must be so made, that they may be quite independent of the favour or disfavour of these menial servants.

Menials not to indulge in criticism.

(6) The menial servants must, on no account, be permitted to speak to the Maharaja, or in the presence of the Maharaja, about matters which are far above them. For instance, they must not indulge in political discussions or speak of the merits of ministers.

Nor to present petitions.

(7) They must not be allowed to introduce strangers to the Maharaja, or to present petitions to the Maharaja on behalf of any stranger or indeed on behalf of anyone.

To be polite.

(8) They must be enjoined to be polite to visitors and others.

Post-mortem examination when necessary.

(9) Whenever any sudden, violent, or suspected death of any servants—indeed of anyone—occurs in the Palace, the Maharaja should, by all means, direct a regular *post-mortem* examination with the view of ascertaining and recording the real cause of death. This is a very necessary precaution to avert serious scandals or suspicions.

Wages to be cash.

(10) As far as possible, fix the wages or remuneration of the Palace servants in cash. This is most convenient to all concerned. The allowance of *sidhas* (provisions in kind) is always liable to great abuse.

No arbitrary dismissal.

(11) Palace servants are generally in the position of private servants. Yet, it is desirable that they should feel confident of continued employment, so long as they behave well. In other words, as a rule, they should not be arbitrarily or capriciously dismissed; and they should be promoted according to their good behaviour and as opportunities occur.

Liberal salaries to personal servants.

(12) Such menial servants as have much to do personally with the Maharaja should have really liberal salaries and should be so treated as to feel great personal devotion to His Highness. In instances of any specially good behaviour, they may be occasionally rewarded so as to encourage them. The same remarks equally apply to servants personally in service with the Maharanis and the children.

Punishment to be proportionate.

(13) The minor faults of such servants should not be too rigidly noticed or punished. All menial servants have such faults more or less. We must only see that they do not go beyond minor faults.

The Maharaja not to take a personal part.

(14) If any of the Palace servants so misbehave as to call for punishment, even then the Maharaja had better not appear to take a very prominent or active personal part in their punishment. Let that punishment be by the Palace officers, or by the public Magistracy, as the case may be. The object is to avoid, as far as may be possible, His Highness becoming an object of personal hatred.

The hereditary principle of employment is desirable.

(15) Giving effect to the heredity principle in regard to Palace servants, as far as may be convenient, is rather a desirable thing within certain limits, as it is conducive to greater attachment on the part of the servants. If an old servant dies or becomes disabled from age, sickness, or other cause, better give some employment to his son or brother, and so on. But the hereditary principle is quite objectionable in the public service where special qualifications are required.

Avoid intriguers.

(16) All palaces are, more or less, infested by intriguers. The Maharaja has to exercise constant vigilance against falling into their snares.

As soon as the Maharaja is installed in power—and even before—these intriguers will try their tricks. Therefore, a few hints in this direction may be of use.

They are selfish and only flatter.

(17) Intriguers are generally persons who are very selfish in their motives and who are devoid of, or deficient in, good principles. They are excessively fond of secret representations. They make false or reckless statements. They grossly exaggerate matters. They give a false colouring to circumstances. They endeavour to make themselves agreeable by constant flattery and obsequiousness. By bearing these distinguishing qualities in mind, and by means of close observation, some intriguers may be found out. When the Maharaja is able to discover intriguers by such means, His Highness should refuse to give ear to them. They should be kept at great distance. In short, the less the Maharaja has to do with them, the better will it be for His Highness' interests.

Intriguers of past times to be kept aloof.

(18) Again, if any person is known to have been an intriguer in past times, he may be generally presumed to be an intriguer at present also, unless there is any clear reason to suppose that the person has undergone a complete reformation. As a general rule, therefore, the Maharaja should keep at a distance such persons as are known to have practised intrigues in past times.

Trust faithful advisers.

(19) Again, if the Maharaja is assured that such and such a person is an intriguer—assured by some of those whom the Maharaja recognises as his sincere well-wishers and faithful advisers—His Highness will do well to accept such assurance and keep the intriguer at a distance. At any rate, the Maharaja should specially scrutinise the man. Acting on the foregoing hints, the

Maharaja will be able to get rid of numbers of intriguers, though not of the whole lot.

The qualities of an intriguer and a well-wisher.

(20) On further consideration, it appears to me that what I have thus far stated is not sufficient. To make the matter still more clear, I proceed to give below, in juxtaposition, the qualities which mark an intriguer and those which mark a real well-wisher.

	INTRIGUER	REAL WELL-WISHER
Not a real well-wisher.	(*a*) An intriguer is not a real well-wisher but one who simulates a well-wisher.	(*a*) A real well-wisher is what he is.
Base.	(*b*) In other words, an intriguer is base metal only coated with gold.	(*b*) A real well-wisher is a solid mass of gold.
Bad antecedents.	(*c*) An intriguer is generally one whose antecedents show him to be an intriguer.	(*c*) A real well-wisher's antecedents show him to be a blameless man.
Known as such.	(*d*) An intriguer is generally known as such by good men.	(*d*) A real well-wisher is generally known as such by good men.
Discontented.	(*e*) An intriguer is generally a discontented man and thinks that he has been badly treated and kept down.	(*e*) A real well-wisher has no particular discontent and is satisfied with his lot, like any ordinary man.
Thinks too much of himself.	(*f*) An intriguer has generally a very high opinion of his own ability and skill.	(*f*) A real well-wisher estimates himself at his work.
Selfish.	(*g*) The principal actuating motive of an intriguer is selfishness.	(*g*) The principal actuating motive of a real well-wisher is not selfishness.

Hope of large benefit.	(*h*) An intriguer works with the object of obtaining some large benefit for himself—for instance, he wants high employment in the public service, etc.	(*h*) A real well-wisher aims at the good of the Maharaja and of the people.
No secret of his designs.	(*i*) An intriguer will generally make representations which directly or indirectly point to the desirableness of his being benefitted in the way he desires.	(*i*) A real well-wisher will not confine himself to topics in which his personal interest is involved but will speak more at large.
Attacks men.	(*j*) An intriguer will generally speak more against men than against measures.	(*j*) A real well-wisher will speak more against measures than against men.
Particularly those in his way.	(*k*) An intriguer will generally speak most against those men who stand in the way of his obtaining the benefit he desires.	(*k*) A real well-wisher will speak generally of all men.
Gives them no credit.	(*l*) An intriguer will generally give no credit whatever to those men but will condemn them in every way.	(*l*) A real well-wisher will give credit where due. He will be more discriminating.
Speaks vaguely.	(*m*) Against those men, the intriguer will speak in general and very vague terms. For example, he will say that those men are bad; that they are unfaithful; that they are doing mischief; that they are selfish; that they wish	(*m*) A real well-wisher will be more specific. If he finds fault, he will exactly say on what account.

	to get the favour of the British Government at the expense of the Native State, and so forth.	
Draws adverse inferences.	(*n*) An intriguer will draw adverse inferences from any facts indiscriminately. For instance, if the revenues have increased, he will say that the people suffer from increased exactions. If the revenues have diminished, he will say that the State has suffered loss owing to mismanagement. If the expenditure has increased, he will say that it is the effect of extravagance and carelessness. If the expenditure has diminished, he will say that it is the effect of stinginess and of unfair reductions.	(*n*) A real well-wisher will give more impartial opinions. He will distinguish between legitimate and illegitimate causes of variation.
Misrepresents facts.	(*o*) An intriguer has little or no scruples. He will, for his own selfish ends, misrepresent or distort facts and circumstances so as to tell against those who are opposed to his own interests.	(*o*) A real well-wisher will scrupulously state facts as they are.
Even tells lies.	(*p*) An intriguer will even tell downright falsehoods to serve his	(*p*) A real well-wisher will never tell falsehoods. He will be

	own purpose, where the falsehood is not easily discoverable. For instance, he will impute all sorts of bad motives or intentions to his opponents.	perfectly truthful. Though he may criticise measures, he will generally give credit for good motives and good intentions.
Calls errors acts of mischief.	(*q*) An intriguer will be most eager to lay hold of mere errors or slips, such as the best of men must, more or less, commit, and will construe such errors into deliberate acts of mischief on the part of his opponents.	(*q*) A real well-wisher will act more generously. He will recognise the fact that the best men are not infallible. He will recognise the great difference between mere error and a deliberate act.
Works secretly.	(*r*) An intriguer is generally fond of darkness. He would actually prefer to make his visits during night. He always wishes to meet you secretly. He is full of mysterious whispers, hints and predictions. He makes it appear that what he discloses to you is only a very small part of what he knows of the misdoings of his opponents. He would frequently request you not to divulge what he says to you and would thus prevent you from obtaining the means of testing the truth of his allegations.	(*r*) A real well-wisher behaves differently from all this.

Promotes bad feelings.	(s) An intriguer, when he has not much to say on public grounds, is extremely fond of trying to bring about bad feelings between you and his opponents on private or trivial grounds. For instance, he would say that such an officer looks upon you with contempt; that that officer, the other day, said so and so about you—and so forth. Ask the intriguer where the officer spoke so? The reply would be that the words were spoken at home by the officer to one of his friends. Query—Would that friend tell me all about it if I refer to him? Answer—Would he betray his friend? Question—How did you, then, come to know of it? Answer—A certain servant of that officer overheard the contemptuous words. Question—Would that servant say all about it to me if called before me? Answer—How would the servant betray his master? Question—Let me then ask you again, how did you come to know of it? Answer—As you	(s) A real well-wisher would not stoop to such proceedings. He would rather advise the Maharaja not to listen for a moment to such tales—nor to listen to what this man or that man said in private, even if true, for an officer's conduct is to be judged by his official acts.

press me I must reveal the truth. The servant of that officer and my servant are friends. The former gave the information to the latter. My servant told me all about it. Question—Would your servant repeat it to me? Answer—I am not sure, but he may, if assured of protection. Therefore, perhaps, the simple Maharaja actually sends for that servant of the intriguer and questions him, after assuring him of protection and holding out some prospects of reward. And the servant repeats what he had been tutored by the intriguer himself to say! The Maharaja, ignorant of the rules of evidence, considers the matter proved! The intriguer then submits a few general remarks. He says it was a fortunate thing that the matter was proved to His Highness in this instance. But in many instances, such matters cannot be proved. If so severely cross-examined by His Highness and put to proof it would be very hard, and it would be better hereafter not to give any information. The Maharaja is thus induced to say "Never mind, I am now satisfied. You may go on giving me information without any fear." Under some such assurance, dose after dose of poison is administered, until the officer concerned is ruined in His Highness' estimation.

He would do anything to please the Maharaja.	(t) Another characteristic of an intriguer is that he would do anything to please the Maharaja. He would never express any opinion different from His Highness'. On the contrary, anything His Highness says, however trivial, he would applaud in terms of admiration, except as regards matters relative to the opponents against whom his intrigues are directed. He would assiduously cultivate the friendship of the Maharaja's principal friends and relations by various means, as for instance, by lending money, making acceptable	(t) A real well-wisher would avoid flattery and adulation. He would frankly express his own opinion, whether it happens to coincide with yours or not. He would behave with self-respect. He would be polite to your principal friends and relations, but would not go out of his way to court their favour in the manner as the intriguer would do.

presents, promising to do all sorts of service for them when he gets into power, and so forth.

The Maharaja to study character.

(21) Your Highness will do well to study thoroughly the foregoing characteristics. I have given you the result of long and careful observations. The foregoing furnish to you pretty good means wherewith you may be largely able to judge for yourself to say that such a person is an intriguer and not a real well-wisher—to say that this is brass and not gold. Of course, you will have to apply the tests patiently and attentively. The motives, the aims, the allegations, and the deportment of the given individual will have to be very carefully observed with reference to the criteria I have categorically stated. The Maharaja has frequent occasions to do this, for he has frequent occasions to judge of men. The process may appear somewhat laborious first. But repeated exercise will make it easy till you are able to judge almost with the rapidity of natural instinct.

General allegations of fact of no practical value.

(22) What an intriguer may say may be regarded in another aspect. Whatever he says must consist of allegations of fact and of opinion. Now, opinions from such a source are entitled to little or no weight. If the Maharaja seeks opinions, he may go to the reliable, recognised and responsible source. Allegations of fact remain. These are either vague and general or clear and specific. Vague and general allegations of fact are of little or no practical use. They may be generally rejected. Thus there remain only clear and specific allegations of

facts. If these are of sufficient importance, and if they appear probable, or are supported by *prima facie* evidence, the Maharaja may take some notice of them.

An example.

(23) To make this further clear, let us take an example. Suppose an intriguer says to the Maharaja, "Mr. A. is a very bad judge. He takes bribes. In such a case, the other day, he took a bribe of 1,000 rupees from such a person." Here, the first sentence merely expresses an opinion entitled to little or no weight. The second sentence contains a vague and general allegation of fact of little or no practical use. It is only the third sentence which contains a clear and specific allegation of fact. If the person alleging is prepared to give evidence or to point to evidence, then the Maharaja may direct his minister to make such enquiry as may be desirable and to report the particulars of the enquiry and the result thereof.

Only specific allegations of fact to be considered.

(24) The example I have above given is an extremely simple one, intended simply to make my meaning clear. But allegations of the kind are, generally, long and complex. They should all be sifted carefully with reference to the foregoing suggestions; and we should find out what the several clear and specific and important allegations of fact are, which alone have to be considered. In the course of my experience, I have found many an intriguer unable to stand such a sifting process.

Beware of unscrupulous persons.

(25) The Maharaja must know and constantly apply this sifting process. Otherwise, he will be apt to be carried away by long and wordy statements—to be deceived by designing and unscrupulous persons.

25

ANGER

29th June 1881

The Maharaja's temper daily exposed to trial.

The best of us are, at times, liable to anger. And a Maharaja's position is such that his temper and patience will be daily exposed to trial. Again, the Maharaja being the highest personage in the State, there are few persons who can exercise a check on him in this respect. Lastly, it is to be remembered that any harm or mischief arising from anger would be much greater in the instance of the Maharaja than in that of a private individual.

Take things coolly.

(2) These circumstances show how the Maharaja has need to be specially careful against the evils of anger. His Highness should, therefore, use his best endeavours to avoid anger altogether. Repeated efforts will establish the habit of taking things calmly and coolly.

Anger is temporary madness.

(3) When, however, in spite of every effort to the contrary, the Maharaja finds that anger has taken possession of him, then His Highness will do well to remember the following considerations. Anger is an excitement of the mind

which is, in many respects, like temporary madness. In that state of excitement, the mind takes one particular direction in a violent manner and is blind to those facts and reasons which require to be taken into account in order to form a sound judgment. In short, during anger, the most necessary and the most valuable faculty of judgment is in a state of paralysis.

When angry, refrain from acting or speaking.

(4) In such a state of mind, the safest course to pursue is to altogether refrain from acting or even speaking in regard to the matter which has excited that state of mind. Better altogether drop the matter for the time and turn the mind to something else—going to sleep will be a capital thing, for it has such an excellent pacifying effect, or His Highness may take a long ride or drive, or His Highness may devote himself to reading some interesting book.

Draw the mind away and avoid unpleasantness.

(5) I would strongly recommend that the mind be thus drawn away from the subject matter of the mental disturbance. If possible, better not return to that subject matter for a week or ten days. By following this somewhat simple advice, the Maharaja will save himself from many wrong acts and offensive expressions, which, if indulged in, might involve him in political embarrassment, or might entail upon him the loss of friends and well-wishers, or might inflict serious discouragement upon his faithful servants and dependants.

How to Get Another's Opinion

Avoid expressing your own.

(1) If the Maharaja desires to invite any person's opinion, the Maharaja had better refrain from expressing his own opinion at the outset. His Highness' own opinion had better not be indi-

cated or implied. Even should the person spoken to ask for His Highness' opinion, better avoid expressing it, if possible.

Two reasons:
(a) The other person may not express a different opinion.

(2) There are two main reasons for this suggestion: (*a*) If His Highness' opinion be expressed at the outset, the person addressed might hesitate to express a contrary or different opinion. At least he might feel a certain degree of restraint. But the object is to get the person's opinion as freely expressed as possible.

(b) The Maharaja's opinion may be incorrect.

(*b*) Again, any opinion prematurely formed by the Maharaja—formed before knowing the opinions of other persons'might be incorrect; and it is not desirable that His Highness should needlessly run the risk of expressing crude and incorrect opinions which would have to be given up upon due deliberation and consultation.

26

FIRMNESS

20th July 1881

A Maharaja must be firm.

Firmness is a virtue which is desirable in all persons and exceedingly desirable in those whom Providence has made rulers. If a Maharaja is wanting in firmness, it becomes very difficult to carry on public business. He has one opinion at one time and a different opinion at another. He has one purpose at one time and a different purpose at another. He orders one thing now and orders a different thing shortly afterwards.

Careful reasoning makes one firm.

(2) Genuine firmness is the result of careful study of facts, careful reasoning, and correct conclusions. It is the consciousness of having carefully studied the facts, of having carefully reasoned and of having correctly judged—it is the consciousness of having properly performed these processes that makes the mind firm. A Maharaja who has himself performed these processes will be quite right to feel and manifest firmness.

Do not be unsteady.

(3) It would, however, be impossible for the Maharaja to himself perform these pro-

cesses in the thousand instances in which he has to act. Is he then to be fickle in all those instances? No. If he were to be unsteady in all those instances, the conduct of public business would suffer very much.

Trust responsible counsellors.

(4) In those instances, then, the Maharaja should trust his trustworthy and responsible counsellors who have themselves performed the processes above mentioned. He should generally, in such instances, accept the opinions and advice given by such counsellors and show firmness of mind in acting upon such opinions and advice. What I have just mentioned is a very important principle which the Maharaja should thoroughly understand. If he does not understand and act upon that principle, he will be constantly placed in painfully embarrassing positions in daily life. Remember, it is only in a few—very few—instances that he can himself collect facts, reason on them, and form a correct judgment. In the great majority of instances in which he cannot perform these processes, what is he to do? Is he to be fickle? Then, the public business will materially suffer. Is he to form an arbitrary conclusion and stick to it? Then the public business will suffer still more. It is a bad dilemma.

Firm rulers know how to select their men.

(5) History shows many examples of public affairs suffering in the manner just stated because of the ruler concerned not understanding and acting on the principle under advertence. It will be found that those rulers who have been remarkable for the virtue of firmness have eminently known the principle—how to select worthy and faithful counsellors, to accept the carefully formed opinion and advice of such counsellors, and to exercise the virtue of firmness as founded thereon.

Obstinacy.

(6) From what I have already stated, it must be evident that firmness is a virtue when it is exercised in relation to right conclusions only. It is then a very valuable virtue in rulers. But the moment it comes to be exercised in relation to wrong conclusions, the quality ceases to be a virtue. It becomes a mischievous vice. It becomes simply obstinacy.

Difference between firmness and obstinacy.

(7) The vital difference between the virtue of firmness and the vice of obstinacy arises from the conclusions in the first place being right and the conclusion in the second case being wrong. Every ruler has, therefore, need to make sure that he is firm and that he is not obstinate by making sure that his conclusion is right and that it is not wrong. A firm Maharaja will do much good. An obstinate Maharaja will do much harm.

Obstinacy not to be mistaken for firmness.

(8) This difference between the virtue of firmness and the vice of obstinacy must be constantly remembered, lest obstinacy be mistaken for firmness. The virtue and the vice have much in common, and therefore a weak-minded ruler is only too apt to mistake the latter for the former. But a strong-minded ruler, with the advantage of education and with the further advantage of previous warning, will remember the essential difference between the virtue and the vice and make sure that he has the virtue and not the vice.

A wise ruler should change his view if wrong.

(9) It follows that a wise ruler is open to conviction, that is to say, he is open to argument and ready to change his view when it is shown to be wrong. On the other hand, an unwise ruler is obstinate—is not open to conviction—is not accessible to argument and will stick to the wrong conclusion.

Consult freely.

(10) It further follows that a wise ruler, in his anxiety to make sure that his conclusion is right, will, in matters of importance, freely consult his trustworthy and responsible counsellors and compare their conclusions with his own. On the other hand, an unwise ruler will think it beneath his dignity to consult such counsellors and will constantly run the risk of wrong conclusion and of all the mischief which must arise from the same.

Verify conclusions.

(11) One man, however able and experienced, cannot be sure of himself forming right conclusions in public affairs without consulting others. He may err in his fact; he may err in his reasoning; he may err from disregard of local conditions and circumstances. A dozen wrong conclusions may be found in any one case while there can be but one right conclusion. Hence it is necessary for every ruler who is anxious to save his people from the evil of wrong conclusions to verify his conclusion in every matter of importance by the means suggested above.

Success will arise by cooperation.

(12) Your Highness knows that I have dealt with the public affairs of important Native States for many years. I may venture to say that I have not been consciously wanting in care and diligence in dealing with important interests. Yet my experience has convinced me that I should make many serious errors of fact or of judgment if I did not freely avail myself of the assistance of others. I am credited with some success in the management of the public affairs of the Native States concerned. Let me tell Your Highness that one great secret of that success is that I have tried to be guided by the principles and considerations above set forth. But my own is a very humble example. Your

Highness may refer to persons immeasurably higher and Your Highness will still find what I have said is true.

Hypocrisy.

(13) To stick to a wrong conclusion is really most culpable. Men are sometimes tempted to do so by the desire to appear firm. But it is no real firmness. It is spurious firmness. It is simple obstinacy. The public very soon discover this and blame the man concerned for obstinacy and hypocrisy.

Discuss conclusions quietly.

(14) The wisest course for a ruler is to take every possible precaution against wrong conclusions before acting on the same. Let those conclusions be made known, tested, discussed, and thoroughly settled in council. All this may be done very quietly and without the public knowing anything about it. The public judge by the results. If the results show that the ruler avoids wrong conclusions only, then the public praise him as a good ruler and will not care by what means the ruler does so. To sum up. By all possible means make sure of your conclusion being right, and then act firmly in respect to it. Firmness thus exercised is a great virtue in a ruler.

A ruler to be firm but kind:

(15) Before concluding this part of the subject, I have to offer just a few further remarks.

(a) by patiently explaining to the party.

(*a*) Firmness, standing by itself, is one of the sterner virtues. Its harshness needs to be softened in practice. A ruler should be firm, yet kind and considerate. Each case, as it occurs, must suggest how this object can be accomplished. It is a matter of habit and the habit may be acquired by care and attention. Generally, the harshness which is an element of firmness may be mitigated by patiently explaining matters to the party who considers himself aggrieved by your firmness. Let him see that your refusal to comply with his wishes is, by no means, due to your want of kindness, but due to the claims of justice, to the principles of government, to the force of precedents, or to some such other cause, which makes it your duty to act in the particular manner and which leaves you little or no option. If you yourself have not sufficient time to offer such explanations, you may easily direct the departmental head to do so.

(b) By obliging the party in some other legitimate manner.

(*b*) Another way in which the harshness of firmness may be mitigated is to try and oblige to some extent the party concerned in some other and legitimate manner. One example will suffice to make this clear. A certain public servant has become old and useless, and is, therefore, dispensed with. He comes and bitterly complains. I would not cause him to be rudely pushed out. I would hear him. Then I would explain to him how necessary it has become in these days that the administration should be efficient; how the administration would become inefficient if superannuated servants do not retire; that all of us must sooner or later become old and useless and give place to others; and so forth. And if the person concerned deserves the favour, I would offer to employ his son somewhere according to his merits. The great thing is to be firm yet sympathetic and obliging.

27

ADVICE FROM OTHERS

[27th July, 1881?]

Judge charitably of persons and acts.

The Maharaja's position is a very exalted one. His Highness will have to deal with many persons. He will have repeatedly to judge of persons and of their acts. His Highness will, therefore, do well to cultivate the important habit of judging charitably. Men's acts and motives present various aspects. The Maharaja will do well, as a rule, to prefer that aspect which is most favourable to the person concerned. In other words, if an act or motive is open to several interpretations, the Maharaja will do well to prefer that interpretation which is most in favour of the man concerned. In other words, again, place the most favourable constructions on men's acts and motives.

Because men may be presumed to prefer good to bad acts.

(2) The reason of this advice is that, except where the man concerned is known to be a bad man, men may be presumed to prefer good acts to bad acts and to prefer good motives to bad motives. This is a reasonable presumption aris-

ing from the natural state of things. It is a presumption dictated by justice and generosity, which ought always to characterise the highest personage in the country—I mean the Maharaja.

The Maharaja is then universally respected.

(3) Such presumption accords also with good policy. When the Maharaja judges in a charitable spirit as indicated above, men regard him all the more with respect and affection. They are positively grateful for the justice and generosity exercised towards them. Good men are pleased that the Maharaja avoids treating their acts and motives with injustice, and they become all the more anxious that their acts and motives should be good and that they should thereby stand well in the estimation of so just and generous a master. If it should so happen that a bad man has been the object of the Maharaja's charitable view, even then the bad man feels ashamed and often changes his attitude and conduct for the better.

(4) To make the matter further clear, I will here give some practical examples:

Examples:
(a) The absence of a person from the *Darbar*.

(*a*) Suppose that an important officer or *Sardar* who had been invited to attend the *Darbar* is found absent. The omission to attend the *Darbar* may possibly be attributable to indifference, or to carelessness, or disrespect, or to sickness or accident or other unavoidable innocent cause. The principle I wish to impress on Your Highness ought to induce you to attribute the omission to some one of the unavoidable innocent causes rather than to some of those causes which imply blame on the part of the absentee officer or *Sardar*.

(b) The advice of a minister.

(*b*) Again, a good minister advises the Maharaja to yield some point to the British Resident. The advice may be attributable to good or bad motives. The Maharaja should attribute it to good motives rather than to bad motives.

(c) The advice of the Resident.

(*c*) Again, the Resident advises the Maharaja to undertake as little of judicial work as possible. The Maharaja should not attribute the advice to a desire on the part of the Resident to weaken the Maharaja, but should attribute it to his desire to save the Maharaja needless trouble and needless responsibilities.

(d) That of a philosopher.

(*d*) Again, a political philosopher advises the Maharaja to make the machinery of his government, to the utmost extent, self-acting, self-regulating, and self-correcting. The Maharaja should attribute such advice to the best intentions towards himself and towards his people, and should not attribute it to a desire to make the Maharaja as powerless as possible.

(e) Of a friend.

(*e*) Again, a friend and councillor says to the Maharaja, "Such and such a person is an unprincipled and intriguing character. I would advise you to avoid that person." The Maharaja should attribute the advice to good intentions and not to, say, selfish interest.

Smaller example:

(5) Let us take now some smaller examples:

(a) Theft of a jewel.

(*a*) A jewel is stolen from the Palace. The Dewan institutes an active inquiry which involves the examination of even some personal attendants of the Maharaja. Perhaps the Dewan makes some of the servants concerned responsible for the value of the jewel, as a corrective of their carelessness and as a warning for the future. Such action should be presumed to be the result of the Dewan's wish to protect Palace jewellery from loss, and it should not be presumed to be the result of any bad motives.

(b) Misbehaviour of a *Mankari*.

(*b*) Again, a *Mankari* misbehaves in a State procession, draws his sword, and causes a disturbance. The Dewan takes due notice of it and does something by way of punishing the *Mankari* for such misbehaviour. The action should be attributed to good intentions and not to bad intentions. Many more similar examples might be given, such as occur daily in life, but it would be needless. The great thing is, as I have already said, that the Maharaja should cultivate the habit of interpreting men's acts and motives charitably, unless the man concerned is known to be a bad man.

Attribute an act to error rather than to mischief.

(6) The principle I am explaining generally requires also that, when an act is attributable to error or misapprehension on the one hand or to deliberate mischievous intentions on the other, the Maharaja should prefer to assume the former rather than the latter. Such a habit of judging charitably is, as I have said above, a matter of justice and generosity and of good policy also. I may here add that it will be the means of conciliating people and of avoiding the needless making of enemies. It will make the Maharaja's career smooth and agreeable. It will save the Maharaja's mind from constant irritation or painful suspicion and secure it a calm composure and an elevated dignity, such as constitute one of the greatest ornaments of the throne. I feel quite sure that the cultivation of the habit I am speaking of, and its non-cultivation, will make a great difference in the happiness of the Maharaja.

It is a safeguard against intriguers.

(7) A Maharaja who has succeeded in acquiring the excellent habit I am speaking of will possess a great safeguard against intriguers. It must be remembered that an intriguer generally almost invariably puts the worst possible interpretation on the acts and motives of his enemies. But the Maharaja who has acquired the excellent habit I am speaking of will reject such

uncharitable interpretations and prefer those which are charitable. Even if charitable interpretations do not readily suggest themselves, the good Maharaja will actually seek for such. He will actually try to conceive such.

Seek explanation from person affected.

(8) The principle of charitable interpretations I have been speaking of will generally operate admirably when the Maharaja has to judge in a rough and ready manner and to pass on to other matters. There may arise, however, important occasions for the Maharaja to determine, with some degree of certainty, which of the available interpretations is really applicable to a given case, especially when circumstances suggest an unfavourable interpretation. In such circumstances, it is a good rule not to come to an unfavourable conclusion until after giving the person affected a fair opportunity to afford any explanations in his power. The principle is, "Do not condemn a man behind his back. Do not condemn him without hearing him."

Hear complaints of both parties.

(9) By way of illustration, suppose the Palace officer represents to the Maharaja that a certain expenditure, which he (the officer) had incurred under the orders of His Highness, is refused to be passed by the Auditor. The Palace officer may represent the matter in such a manner as to be quite disagreeable to His Highness and as to induce His Highness to be displeased with the Auditor. But I say, do not be at once displeased with the Auditor without hearing what explanation the Auditor has to give. Let the Auditor be, in due course, called upon to explain why he declined to pass such expenditure. In nine cases out of ten, the Auditor will give quite a satisfactory explanation. If, however, the explanation is not satisfactory, then, and then alone, blame him.

Arrive at right conclusions.

(10) The course thus recommended will enable the Maharaja to avoid errors and to arrive at right conclusions. It will enable him to do justice to his servants, public or private. It will inspire the servants themselves with confidence. Otherwise, they would feel that they are at the mercy of whims, caprices, and misrepresentations. All good servants should be made to feel that they would, on no account, incur the Maharaja's displeasure without real good cause.

Summary.

(11) To recapitulate briefly:

(*i*) When an act or motive is liable to several interpretations, the Maharaja should prefer that interpretation which is most favourable to the person affected.

(*ii*) If circumstances suggest that an unfavourable interpretation is the more probable one, the Maharaja should call for explanation from the person affected and then judge.

28

COMPROMISING SPIRIT

14th September 1881

Firmness to be controlled by prudence.

I have already explained what genuine firmness is, as distinguished from spurious firmness; and how useful the virtue is in rulers. But human affairs are such that it is not always possible or desirable to exercise firmness to its fullest extent—to exercise inflexible firmness. In rulers more especially, the exercise of one good quality has often to be controlled by other good qualities. Firmness has, for instance, to be controlled by prudence and circumspection.

Exercise a judicious spirit of compromise.

(2) Suppose A and B have much to do with each other in life. If, in any matter, A is determined to be so firm as to yield nothing to B, and B is determined to be so firm as to yield nothing to A, how can they get on at all? Difficulties and unpleasantness will ensue, and a deadlock may be the result, or A and B will have to part; or some other serious mischief may be the consequence. It follows that firmness has sometimes to be judiciously relaxed with reference to the circumstances of each case as it presents itself.

When the firmness of one person encounters the firmness of another, some concession may have to be made for the sake of conciliation, peace and co-operation. In other words, some judicious compromise should be effected. The wisdom of a wise ruler is shown in exercising a judicious spirit of compromise. There are many instances of rulers gaining much by the spirit of compromise. On the other hand, there are also many instances of rulers losing much from want of this sprit.

Statesmanship is a series of compromises.

(3) It is quite certain that there is nothing disgraceful or derogatory in exercising a judicious spirit of compromise. In private life, every sensible man often exercises this spirit. In public life, the greatest men often exercise the same spirit. So much is this the case that statesmanship is almost a series of compromises. No statesman expects to have his own way in all matters and at all times. All this must be well remembered lest a ruler should feel a false sense of humiliation and refuse all compromise, and thereby draw down serious difficulties or danger on himself. A ruler has often to give and take.

Avoid extremes.

(4) How far concessions should be made in any matter for the sake of effecting a compromise is a question for judgment in each case. It will depend on the strength of conviction, on the value of the principle at stake, on the force of the circumstances demanding concession, and so forth. Concession much beyond the necessities of the case may be weakness; and refusing concessions up to the necessities of the case, and thereby incurring serious difficulties or dangers, may be unwisdom. The right mark must be hit. The loss arising from a pro-

posed concession should be carefully weighed against the gain arising from the same; and if the scale incline to the latter, the concession may be made.

The stronger party to recognise the claims of reason.

(5) It may perhaps be briefly but usefully stated here that, other things being equal, where concessions between governments are concerned, the weaker party may have to concede more than the stronger. But the disparity, in this respect, is diminished in proportion as the stronger party recognises the claims of reason, justice and liberality as superior to the advantages conferred by mere might.

Importance of the compromising spirit.

(6) Without a judicious compromising spirit, individuals would make families unhappy, statesmen would make nations unhappy, and kings and rulers would make the world unhappy. The foregoing considerations need to be fully kept in view, and they should be allowed to modify to the necessary degree the exercise of the quality of firmness.

29

SUBSCRIPTIONS

[21st September 1881*?]

Numerous applications.

His Highness the Maharaja is sure to receive numerous applications for subscriptions and contributions to various objects and institutions. One applicant will ask for a number of copies being taken of a book which he is about to publish. Another will solicit aid for building a temple, or a *ghat*, or a *dharmshala*. A third will solicit a donation for horse races. His Highness' liberality will be invoked in favour of schools, hospitals, theatrical performances, horse shows, fine arts, new industries, and diverse other purposes.

Judge each on its merits.

(2) It is obvious that all such applications cannot be complied with. Due discrimination will have to be exercised by the Maharaja. Each case will have to be judged on its own merits, but

* Philip Melvill wrote to the Foreign Department in Calcutta on September 27, 1881 forwarding copies he had received that day of the lectures on 'Subscriptions' and 'Relations with British Government'. Since the latter lecture is dated September 21, 1881, this is likely the date of the former lecture as well.

the following considerations may afford some useful guidance.

Subscription to benefit the people of Baroda.

(3) It is to be remembered that the money concerned is part of the taxes paid by the people of Baroda, and therefore cannot be arbitrarily or capriciously given away. Grants of such money may be made mainly for objects which directly or indirectly benefit the people of Baroda.

Prefer local contributions.

(4) Contributions destined to be spent within the limits of Baroda territories are generally to be preferred to those which are to be spent outside those territories.

And those to the poor and to relieve pain.

(5) Those which benefit the poor are to be preferred to those which benefit the rich. Those which relieve pain are to be preferred to those which afford pleasure.

Amount to be moderate.

(6) The amount of contribution should be moderate so as to necessitate and induce others also to contribute. In other words, our contribution should not be so large as to induce others to say "From Baroda alone much of the required funds have come. We need not therefore give anything ourselves."

The object to be useful.

(7) Anything given should be in reference to the usefulness of the object, and not prompted by a mere spirit of vanity or rivalry, or by the pressure of importunity on the part of the applicant.

Discourage periodical subscriptions.

(8) It is better to give donations once for all or at sufficient intervals, than to commit the State to continuous monthly subscriptions from which it would be difficult to withdraw when necessary or desirable, owing to altered circumstances.

Examples.

(9) I may here adduce a few instances in elucidation of the foregoing principles:

(a) Racing.

(*a*) Baroda should not contribute to horse racing at Bangalore or Bombay—in short, any place outside Baroda. Even at Baroda any expenditure in this direction must be moderate and occasional as our people do not take much interest in racing.

(b) Fine arts.

(*b*) Baroda should not contribute to fine arts in Europe or America, but it should not be indifferent to the fine arts of India.

(c) Works of utility.

(*c*) Better to contribute for the construction of a bathing *ghat* on some river in Baroda territories, than for one on the Godavari, or the Krishna, or the Cauvery.

30

MAHARAJA'S ABSENCE

28th September 1881

The Maharaja should spend as much time as possible in his State.

It is desirable that, except for occasional travelling or on the ground of ill-health, the Maharaja should not needlessly leave his territories and spend his time outside. Some persons may recommend to His Highness to go to Matheran or some other locality outside and spend the summer there. Other persons may similarly recommend to His Highness to go somewhere else and spend the winter there. The cold weather with its festivities may in its turn tempt His Highness to leave his territories. But the subjects of Native States do not at all like their Maharaja's absence in these ways. They wish to see their Maharaja living in their midst and spending his share of the revenues in the country itself. They wish to see His Highness constantly among them, looking after their welfare. It is natural for them to dislike their ruler leaving country and people in search of personal pleasure.

The several restrictions while travelling.

(2) Moreover, a Native Prince attended with a large retinue is not generally welcome at places of resort by the European community.

Disturbance to sanitation and to public convenience is apprehended, and hence restrictions come to be imposed, by no means agreeable to the Native Prince. There are the other restrictions about carrying arms and ammunition. Disagreeable questions arise about the prince and his followers paying tolls and other municipal taxes. Difficult or delicate questions arise as to the relations of the prince and followers with the British police, magistracy and courts. Suits are apt to be preferred even when supplies and carriage have been fairly paid for.

The extra expense without any benefit to the State.

(3) Considering all this and also considering that the residence of the Maharaja outside his territories leads to great extra expense without the least benefit to His Highness' subjects, it seems clear that His Highness should not needlessly absent himself often from his country.

31

FAME

[12th October, 1881?]

No shortcut to fame. It is the reward of patience.

The Maharaja should not be in a hurry to become famous. Fame, as a good and benevolent ruler, is indeed a legitimate and laudable object of a ruler's ambition. Nothing is more gratifying in this world to noble natures than being recognised as the benefactors of communities. But such fame requires time to achieve. It is the reward of long years of the purest intentions, of the highest disinterestedness, of patient and careful study, and of sustained and arduous exertions for the public good. There is no shortcut to such fame. The ruler who sufficiently realises these facts will avoid an unnatural and feverish activity which would inconsiderately meddle with many resettled things—meddle merely for the sake of notoriety. He will pursue an even course steadily and smoothly.

No hungering after applause.

(2) That ruler would soon make himself miserable who hungers after applause every day and at every step. The world has too much business of its own to spare time to applaud its rul-

ers so often. Nor would the world be acting wisely to make its applause so cheap as to be given on trivial occasions.

Accounts of hired flatterers end in failure.

(3) A ruler who would not wait, but is impatient to get fame, sometimes employs puffing in the newspapers. Hired flatterers write long accounts of the most trifling acts of the ruler and invite the public to admire his bottomless wisdom and benevolence in every movement of his. But such attempts to force fame soon end, as they ought to end, in signal failure. A discerning public does not require a long time to discover the false or exaggerated claim urged by mercenary advocates.

Deserve fame.

(4) The best advice, therefore, to young rulers is—do good steadily, constantly and unostentatiously. Thus deserve fame, and leave it to come when it will; come it will in the end.

32

PERSONAL PLEADINGS BY VAKILS

19th October 1881

Should *vakils* plead before the Maharaja?

The Maharaja may occasionally have to enter into the merits of cases with a view to satisfy himself that justice has been done. This is all right and proper. But the question arises whether His Highness is to allow *vakils*, *mukhtiars*, lawyers, etc., to appear before him personally and to plead the cause of their clients.

No.

(2) It is not desirable that His Highness should allow such a proceeding. Even the Governor-General and the Governor do not allow it. The reasons are cogent. In the first place, the Maharaja could not at all spare time to hear professional pleaders. In the next place, it would hardly suit the dignity of His Highness' exalted position. Again, it would subject His Highness to grave difficulties and embarrassments. It will, therefore, be desirable to let it be known, on the first occasion which may present itself, that His Highness will not allow personal pleadings before him. This position will have to be maintained with great firmness.

Judge from the record of the case.

(3) The principle should be that His Highness judges for himself from the record of the case, which must include the pleadings on both sides. The parties have already had opportunities to set forth their respective facts and arguments, and they cannot bring in fresh matter at the last stage.

Parties to be heard in special cases.

(4) As a general rule, neither *vakils* nor even the parties themselves should have the right to be heard by the Maharaja. If in any special case it pleases His Highness to do so, His Highness may send for the parties and give them a hearing. This appears to be the safest, most convenient, and most dignified position.

33

DEPUTATIONS

16th November 1881

Every deputation not to be received by the Maharaja.

The Maharaja has to be very careful in receiving deputations personally. If His Highness be known to be disposed to receive, deputations would endlessly demand interviews with him—deputations from sections of his own subjects, deputations from neighbouring cities and towns, deputations from Bombay and Poona, and deputations from even more distant communities. They would present long addresses and make long speeches. They would even enter into troublesome discussions and expect His Highness to make definite replies. They would embarrass His Highness with matters civil, religious, political, aesthetical, and what not. And whatever His Highness says to them or even does not say to them would be publicly criticised with unsparing severity.

Ordinary deputations to be referred to the ministers.

(2) As a general rule, therefore, let the ordinary deputations be referred to the ministers of His Highness. If, for instance, a deputation has to make a representation on a revenue matter,

let it go to the head of the Revenue Department. If a deputation has to make a representation on an educational matter, let it go to the head of the Education Department. And so on. The head of the department concerned will receive the deputations, fully hear them, and do whatever may be necessary or desirable. In important matters the deputation might go to the Dewan or Chief Minister. This appears to be the best and the most convenient course where the deputation has to do with matters of business.

In important cases consult the Dewan.

(3) His Highness may consent to receive the deputation personally only when the matter, or occasion, or the deputation itself, is very important. Such cases must be rare and may be distinguished from the others by some consultation with the Dewan.

The Dewan to be previously informed of its nature.

(4) Even in such rare cases, the Dewan should be previously informed of the nature and object of the deputation. The Dewan should see the address or representation to be preferred by the deputation in order that he may be enabled to prepare His Highness for the same.

The reply to be cautiously framed, and its preparation to be entrusted to responsible ministers.

(5) His Highness' replies to deputations must be carefully and cautiously framed. When the reply can be clear and specific, let it, by all means, be so. But it often happens that a clear and specific reply cannot be immediately given by His Highness. The matter requires to be maturely considered hereafter. If so, His Highness' reply should not commit His Highness to any opinion or action prematurely or incautiously. The reply should raise no hopes—much less make any promises such as it might be difficult or embarrassing to fulfil hereafter. In short, such replies require much judgment and tact. It is not any person who merely knows to

write the language correctly that can properly prepare such replies. His Highness will do well to entrust the preparation of such replies to his responsible ministers. Even European sovereigns follow this course.

34

TAKING COUNSEL

1st December 1881

The object is to arrive at right conclusions.

Some weeks ago when we met here, I dwelt at some length on the importance, and indeed the necessity, of the Maharaja's taking counsel in all matters of public importance, the great object in view being to reach right conclusions for the purposes of good government.

Whose counsel should the Maharaja take.

(2) The question arises, whose counsel is the Maharaja to take? Surely not the counsel of anybody or of everybody. Scores of people are ready to undertake the honour of giving advice to the Maharaja in any and in every matter. And the most ignorant men are the most forward in this respect, because they are seldom troubled with doubts and difficulties.

Select the counsellors with care.

(3) The Maharaja has to exercise care and judgment in the choice of his counsellors. This is one of the greatest and imperative duties of His Highness. This is one of the most essential conditions of his success as a ruler.

The necessary qualifications.

(4) The Maharaja should exercise care and judgment to choose advisers possessing mainly the following qualifications:

(a) A real knowledge.

(*a*) Knowledge of the theory or of the principles or of the science of the business to be done.

(b) Practical experience.

(*b*) Practical experience which shows how that knowledge is to be applied and which supplies details.

(c) Love of truth.

(*c*) Love of truth, justice and disinterestedness as supplying the best motives.

Grasp these qualifications firmly.

(5) Let the Maharaja firmly grasp these qualifications, and choose advisers possessing these qualifications, and he will thereby prove to the world that he himself possesses ability and judgment. There is no doubt that the Maharaja's reputation and success as a ruler depend, in no small measure, upon the right choice of his advisers.

Don't seek advice from others

(6) It follows that the Maharaja need not seek advice from persons who do not possess the qualifications summarised above. Any advice coming from such persons would be of little value. On the contrary, it might be positively mischievous. If, therefore, any such persons volunteer their advice to His Highness, as they are often too apt to do, His Highness will do well not to pay much attention to the same. Indeed, it would be waste of time and attention even to listen much to such advice; and any serious consultations held by the Maharaja with such persons might only lower His Highness in the estimation of the enlightened public, and might have the further effect of shaking the confidence of His Highness' real well-wishers in His Highness' judgment, for these well-wishers would say—or at least think "The Maharaja does not seem to be able to distinguish between competent and incompetent advisers. Hence it is a mere chance whose advice will prevail."

Do not overrule wise advice.

(7) I have dwelt at some length on this topic because there are instances—indeed there are too many instances in Native States—in which the soundest and the wisest advice has been overruled by the advice of an intriguing *karkoon*, and even by that of a mere *jasood*, or of a narrow-minded priest, or of a clever musician. It is thus that some Native States have been misgoverned and others have been ruined.

Avoid incompetent advisers.

(8) By digesting and remembering the hints given above, the Maharaja will be able to relieve himself from the distractions of a crowd of incompetent advisers who abound in native courts (palaces) and who seek every possible opportunity to offer and even to press their advice. The Maharaja getting clear of incompetent advisers is a grand condition to begin with. Before, then, the Maharaja seeks or accepts any particular person's advice in any matter, let His Highness ask himself these questions: Does the person possess some theoretical and practical knowledge of that matter, and is he known to be a lover of truth, justice and disinterestedness? If the questions can be answered in the affirmative, the person in question is a competent adviser. If the questions cannot be answered in the affirmative, then the person in question is not a competent adviser.

How if advisers differ.

(9) Let us suppose now that the Maharaja has successfully learnt how to choose competent advisers. If these competent advisers all agree and give the same advice to the Maharaja, well and good. But the question arises, what is the Maharaja to do if these competent advisers disagree and give conflicting advice? The Maharaja may, at any time, be placed in this position, and it is very desirable that His Highness should know how to proceed.

Then judge carefully.

(10) When differing or conflicting advice is given by competent advisers, it will manifestly devolve on the Maharaja himself to carefully judge which advice should be selected as the best for adoption. This is a great function of the Maharaja and must be performed with intelligence as well as with care.

Prefer the advice of a responsible officer.

(11) I offer the following hints which may be of considerable use to His Highness in performing this great and necessary function. The choice of the best advice must be made on a combined view of several considerations, the chief of which I proceed to submit. Give decided preference to the advice which is given by the responsible officer over the advice which is given by an irresponsible individual. The latter, however able and conscientious, is not generally in the position in which the former is for judging correctly. A full sense of responsibility—a full sense of the loss of reputation, etc., which might be entailed in consequence of having given unsound advice to the Maharaja—forms a great security for sound advice, a security which must be wanting or must be imperfect in the instance of an irresponsible individual.

His advice to be in writing.

(12) In order to obtain the full benefit of this security, the Maharaja may, on important occasions, well ask that the advice given him may be committed to writing in the shape of a memo giving the reasons for that advice and bearing date and signature. It is a matter of experience that many a person who gives evidence without much thought and in an offhand manner in oral communication feels a far greater and clearer sense of responsibility when called upon to record that advice. Whatever he records will be

more deliberate, more clear and more precise than what he merely speaks.

Prefer the advice of an expert.

(13) Again, when the subject of the advice is one of general principles, prefer the advice of that person who is best versed in those principles. Similarly, when the subject of the advice is one of practical experience, prefer the advice of that person who most possesses such experience.

And that of the majority.

(14) Again, subject to the other considerations, that advice which the majority of competent and responsible advisers give should be preferred to that which the minority may give.

A few important considerations.

(15) Again, subject to the other considerations, prefer that advice which least disturbs the existing state of things. Again, subject to the other considerations, prefer that advice which least opposes the sentiments and wishes of the people. Again, similarly prefer that advice which is most in conformity with the course followed by a good neighbouring Government, especially by the British Government. Again, similarly prefer that advice which the Government of India is more likely to approve of in the interests of this State. The foregoing are important guiding considerations, all or some of which will enable the Maharaja to decide which advice he should consider the best for his adoption.

Weigh the considerations for and against.

(16) The most perplexing case will be that in which all the foregoing considerations do not tell the same way, but some tell in favour of and some against a given measure. In such a case, the considerations for and against must be carefully weighed, and the Maharaja's decision should be according to the balance struck. How the considerations for and against should be weighed, and how the balance should be struck,

it would be difficult to say exactly. It is a matter of habit and practice.

The advisers to discuss in the Maharaja's presence.

(17) It will often better enable the Maharaja to decide correctly if his competent and responsible advisers be made to discuss their differences freely in His Highness' presence. His Highness himself may take some part in the discussion and put questions in reference to the grounds of preference set forth above. Such a discussion may result in all reconciling their differences and reaching a common conclusion.

In the absence of a common conclusion, postpone the matter.

(18) If, however, a common conclusion is not arrived at, and if the Maharaja finds that he cannot, with confidence, *strike a clear balance* of consideration as above suggested, then the safest course may be, if possible, to postpone the matter altogether for future consideration and decision. At some future time, the way becomes more clear.

Or trust to the Chief Minister.

(19) If, however, the postponement of the matter be not possible and circumstances require some immediate decision, then the safest course for His Highness will probably be to trust to his responsible Chief Minister's advice above that of all others.

35

WORK

7th December 1881

Moderation of work necessary.

A Maharaja ought not to overburden himself with work. He ought not to undertake so much work that his health would suffer thereby, that his recreations would be cut off or reduced, and that the work itself could not be done with that knowledge and deliberation which are necessary for its proper performance.

The Maharaja has to work all his life.

(2) It is to be remembered that the Maharaja has to work all his life. It is not as if he should work very hard for a few years and then retire from business. This circumstance, all the more, imposes moderation of work.

Work about four hours.

(3) Roughly speaking, the Maharaja should have work for not more than four or five hours *per diem*. This will leave time for health, for recreation, for study, for family and social duties and pleasures. Whenever there is special extra business, His Highness may especially devote extra time to the same.

Do not do everything yourself.

(4) A great number of details His Highness may well devolve on his ministers. In respect to these, instead of His Highness passing orders in each individual case, His Highness may well give some general orders which will apply to whole groups of cases. This course will save time and labour. The principle should be that His Highness should not burden himself with such work as he can get others to do equally well. His Highness' position is like that of an engineer. The engineer need not himself turn every wheel in the engine. On the contrary, the more skilful the engineer, the more successful is he in arranging that the engine shall do the greatest amount of work so as to leave him abundant time to supervise the whole and to devise important improvements.

36

HOW TO AVOID WORRY

[Undated]

Necessity of protecting against worry.

For the preservation of the Maharaja's physical and intellectual health, it is very necessary that His Highness should protect himself against the terrible worry to which he would certainly be constantly exposed if he were not to take the requisite precautions.

How worry may arise.

(2) Numberless individuals are apt to pester His Highness with pressing solicitations for favours of various sorts. These may be mainly particularised as follows:

(*a*) Solicitation for appointments, promotions, increase of pay, and transfers from one place to another.

(*b*) Solicitation for granting of *nemnuks*, for their increase, or restoration of *nemnuks*, resumed or reduced.

(*c*) Solicitation for granting of *warshasans*, for their increase, or restoration of *warshasans*, resumed or reduced.

(*d*) Solicitation for presents of jewellery, *poshaks*, money for marriages.

(*e*) Solicitation for *sidhas*.

(*f*) Solicitation for loan of carriages, horses, *sowars*, etc.

(*g*) Solicitation for loans of money, advance payment of *nemnuks*, etc.

(*h*) Solicitation to set aside, alter or reopen decisions already given.

(*i*) Solicitation for religious and charitable grants or contributions. And so forth.

General principles to avoid worry.

(3) A great proportion of the worry thus arising may be avoided by remembering and pleading a few general principles. These may be briefly stated here:

(a) Non-interference with the heads of departments.

(*a*) In those cases in which His Highness has given power to the heads of departments to act, His Highness may, as a rule, refuse to interfere. This is only right and proper.

(b) Applicant to be asked to apply through the proper channel.

(*b*) In many cases, His Highness may, as a rule, tell the applicant that he should apply through the head of the department concerned.

(c) Inability to increase expenditure.

(*c*) In some cases, His Highness may say that he is unable, as a rule, to increase the existing limits of expenditure, as it is most important that the expenditure should be kept below the income as at present.

(d) Past *dakhalas* to be applied.

(*d*) In numerous cases, the limits of past *dakhalas* may be applied.

(e) The impropriety of reopening a matter once decided.

(*e*) In others, the principle may be enforced that, when a matter has once been fairly considered and decided, it cannot be allowed to be reopened unless upon fresh and cogent ground.

37

JUDGMENT

[Undated]

Cultivate habit of judgment.

Men who are in a high position and exercise great power—especially rulers—need to cultivate, constantly, the habit of judgment. It is the habit of weighing reasons on the one side and on the other, and striking the balance. It is a most necessary and useful habit, and may be acquired by making an earnest effort.

Let reason be your guide.

(2) Whenever anything has to be preferred out of several things, let not the preference be arbitrarily or capriciously made. The preference should be made for some good reason. This principle applies to small as well as to great matters. In short, on every occasion, let reason assert its sway. Any ruler who constantly walks under the guidance of reason will walk a safe path.

Ask for reasons.

(3) If anyone recommend anything to the ruler, let the ruler ask for the reasons for the recommendation. By doing everything according to reason, the ruler is greatly strengthened, because all reasonable men take his side. He

commands the sympathy and support of his subjects and of the general public.

Greater success is achieved by better judgment.

(4) In fact, it is the capacity of judgment which makes the greatest difference between one man and another. Given any two men in similar circumstances, that man will generally achieve the greater success who has the better judgment.

The quality of judgment to be patiently cultivated by daily reading.

(5) But the judgment is not an intuitive quality. It requires to be patiently and constantly cultivated. Its right exercise also requires the possession of a large stock of sound general principles. It is further desirable to study how men of acknowledged eminence judge in difficult or intricate matters. A part of daily reading may, therefore, be very advantageously directed to this end.

38

PROPOSALS

[Undated]

Exhaustive consideration of any proposal.

Whenever anything is proposed for his consideration, His Highness will do well to consider how that thing will affect:

(*a*) himself,
(*b*) his own subjects,
(*c*) the subjects of other States,
(*d*) the British Government,
(*e*) the general public, and
(*f*) all cases of the same sort occurring hereafter.

It is in this manner that the consideration should be exhaustively gone through in matters of importance.

The cardinal principle: Do to others as we should wish to be done by.

(2) One other important test of a measure is to consider how we should like it if others adopted such a measure. This has reference to the cardinal principle of doing to others as we should wish to be done by. What I mean is that the bearing of a given measure on the several

interests concerned should be fully examined, and it should be examined in regard to the immediate present and in regard to the future.

Disposition to alter proposals not desirable.

(3) Some Maharajas are very fond of wishing to make some alteration or other in any proposal placed before them, to make the alteration merely for the sake of making one—such a disposition needs to be guarded against. It is a disposition likely to impede the progress of business.

Every alteration not proof of superior wisdom.

(4) The disposition has its origin generally in petty vanity. The owner of the disposition supposes that he displays the superiority of his wisdom by making some alteration in the proposal before him. But this is, of course, a mistake. Any and every alteration cannot be a proof of superior wisdom. It is only when an alteration is supported by valid reason that it implies superiority. On the other hand, when an alteration is made without valid reason, and when it is made merely to lead other people to inferior or superior wisdom, it is the result of positive weakness. People soon discover the weakness. They distinguish the pretence from the reality.

Alter when necessary.

(5) The Maharaja may, to any extent, scrutinise the proposal before him. He may discuss it. He may suggest objections and obtain explanations. He may alter the proposal when he feels satisfied that there are good reasons for an alteration. But what is to be strongly deprecated is insisting upon alterations merely for the paltry motive of asserting superiority or power.

Do not be guided by flatterers.

(6) Such a motive is not chimerical, for I have seen it existing and operating; and I have seen it fostered and stimulated by flatterers, from whom few palaces are altogether free.

Trust the officers for details.

(7) That Maharaja greatly facilitates business who has the strength of mind firmly to say, "I concur", when he is satisfied in the main, and when he may trust his officers in regard to details. This is the only way to prevent a block of business and to realise sufficient leisure for His Highness to deal with the more important questions worthy of his attention.

39

MEANS FOR SUCCESS

[Undated]

Get a clear conception of the end in view.

To do anything well and successfully, the first necessary condition is to get a clear conception of the end to be accomplished. What is the specific end to be accomplished and what is not? These questions should be put and unequivocally answered.

Consider the best means.

(2) This being done, the next consideration should be directed to the choice of the means. There may be a variety of means to accomplish the end in view. Which of these means is the best? Determine this as carefully as possible.

The possible difficulties.

(3) Having selected the best means, consider and forecast all the possible difficulties and accidents which might occur to disturb or defeat the object in view, and adopt or be prepared with the necessary measures to prevent or counteract such difficulties and accidents.

Other considerations for attaining success.

(4) Then proceed with the undertaking with due regard to time, place, and circumstances. If such a course is pursued, success will be maxi-

mised; that is to say, success will be attained in the majority of cases.

Give full attention to the course.

(5) Simple and almost obvious as is the course above suggested, many persons neglect it or adopt it more or less imperfectly. It is the degree of attention given to the course above indicated which mainly makes the difference between one man and another in regard to their success in their careers. The person who pays full attention to the course is seldom taken by surprise. He simply goes through a carefully prearranged programme. On the other hand, the person who acts otherwise proceeds loosely, and is exposed to confusion and discomfiture at several stages of the given undertaking.

The remarks specially applicable to rulers.

(6) The remarks I have offered apply to all persons in general, but they apply especially to rulers who have continually to act, and who have often to act in important matters.

TREATMENT OF HIGH OFFICERS

Treat officers with confidence.

Assuming that high officers have been carefully selected for their capacity and probity, the Maharaja should treat them with confidence. It would be unjust and impolite to suspect them of a disposition to misrepresent matters to His Highness, or to misguide His Highness in disposing of the same. A Maharaja who has not learnt how to repose confidence in others will be able to accomplish but little in his career, because he will not secure cordial co-operation.

Preserve their self-respect.

(2) The self-respect of the high officers should be preserved and strengthened by His Highness treating them with courtesy and consideration.

To err is human.

(3) Men perfect in every human quality are not to be found in this world. Some imperfections may always be found in the most gifted.

His Highness should make generous allowance for this manifest truth. Take the man as a whole—

> Be to his faults a little blind,
> Be to his virtues very kind.*

Allow free discussions.

(4) Let every high officer be permitted to freely discuss matters and especially to express differences of opinion.

Do not speak ill of him behind his back.

(5) As a rule, abstain from speaking unfavourably of the high officer behind his back. Every unfavourable remark would be noted and printed abroad, and people would soon cease to feel that respect for him without which he could hardly fulfil his duties properly.

Nor allow him to be abused.

(6) For similar reasons, do not permit common persons, who frequent Native courts, to abuse high officers of the State in a light and reckless manner.

Do not admit petitions against them.

(7) Also, do not admit petitions which speak of high officers in needlessly disrespectful terms.

Make remarks privately.

(8) If there is occasion for His Highness to say anything unpleasant to a high officer, better say it to him privately than while others are present.

The ruler and the officers form one compact body.

(9) In short, let the country see that the Maharaja and his high officers form a coherent and compact body with all the strength which arises from identity of motives, sentiments and actions.

The high officers not to be overworked.

(10) I have advised that the Maharaja should not overwork himself. His Highness should also see that his high officers are not overworked. Let them have time for health, study and some recreation. They will do all the better service for being thus taken care of.

---

* Adapted from "An English Padlock" in *The Poems of Matthew Prior, Vol.* II, Chiswick: C. Whittingham, 1822, pp. 159–62.

40

GOOD FAITH

[Undated]

Good faith necessary in public affairs.

Good faith is absolutely necessary in the conduct of public affairs. It is even more necessary in the conduct of public than of private affairs. It may be generally affirmed that every virtue is even more necessary to a Government than to an individual, because the effects of governmental action are immensely more extensive.

Promises should be fulfilled.

(2) Good faith particularly requires that promises made should be made with the sincere desire to fulfil them, and promises made should be faithfully fulfilled.

The consequence of breach of promise.

(3) I am sorry to say that this principle has not been sufficiently attended to in many Native States. What is the consequence? The promises of Native States are not sufficiently believed in, not even the most deliberate and solemn promises.

Illustration: the public lending money to government.

(4) How this matter stands in Native States and in British India may be realised and measured by means of one illustration. Suppose a Native State announces a loan to the public—that is to say, the Native State desires to borrow

money from the public. Suppose the British India Government similarly announces a loan. It is certain that the public will rush to the British Government with funds, but not so to the Native State. The Native State may offer even a higher rate of interest; yet the public will generally prefer to lend money to the British Government at lower interest. Why this great difference? Because the public feel that the British Government will faithfully perform its promises, whereas they do not feel so to the same degree as regards the Native State.

Promises not to be recklessly made.

(5) Public ease, security and confidence, and public progress and prosperity require that the Maharaja should scrupulously fulfil the promises he may make to individuals or to the community. But this again requires that promises should not be recklessly made. Before any promise is made, let there be full enquiry and full deliberation.

41

REWARDS

[Undated]

Extravagance and parsimony.

The Maharaja should not be extravagant and indiscriminate in giving rewards, but he ought neither to be parsimonious nor too discriminating. He should be just and liberal. To be so is a public duty because it promotes public good.

Rewards stimulate useful service.

(2) Rewards are pecuniary or honorary, or both combined. Their object is to confer pleasure and to stimulate useful service. It follows that he who bestows rewards should take care that this fundamental object is fulfilled—that the reward proposed in a given case is adequate enough to confer pleasure and discriminating enough to stimulate useful service.

No special rewards for ordinary service.

(3) The ordinary pay which a servant draws is his remuneration for ordinary service, therefore no special reward need be granted. Indeed, it might even prove mischievous to grant special rewards for ordinary service. The question of reward should be entertained only if service beyond that ordinarily expected has been rendered.

No rewards for little or no service.

(4) *A fortiori* it follows that no rewards should be granted where there has been little or no service of any kind rendered. I mention this because there are not wanting in Baroda persons who expect special and liberal rewards because they have incurred large debts, because they belong to old families, and so forth.

A small difference may be sacrificed to obtain the reputation of liberality.

(5) In matters of pecuniary reward, whether the Maharaja gets the reputation of liberality or parsimony turns in a proportion of cases on comparatively small differences. A policeman does some extraordinary good service. Give him a reward of 75 rupees, it is deemed stingy. Give him 100 rupees, it is liberal, the difference being only 25 rupees. Take another example. A worthy officer retires from the public service. Give him a gratuity of 9 months' pay, it may be stingy. Give him a gratuity of 12 months pay, it is liberal, the difference being only three months' pay. Again, a *poshak* is to be presented. If it be of the value of 200 rupees, it looks stingy. If it be of the value of 300 rupees, it looks liberal. In such cases, the comparatively small difference may be sacrificed in order that His Highness may acquire the reputation of liberality.

Expressions of approbation.

(6) Similar remarks apply to rewards in the shape of expressions of approbation and praise. These should be adequate and even generous.

The recipient to be proud of the reward.

(7) One good test of the adequacy and liberality of a reward, in any case, is that the recipient of the reward should not be ashamed to show it to others. On the contrary, he should be able to show it with pride and gratification. It is only then that it operates as a stimulant and fulfils the object of reward.

Judicious exercise of the power.

(8) A Maharaja who judiciously exercises the power of rewarding immensely increases his influence for good.

42

POWER OF PARDON

[Undated]

The prerogative of mercy not to be arbitrarily exercised.

His Highness has the power of pardoning. This power is generally known as the prerogative of mercy. But it is to be remembered that no power whatever should be arbitrarily exercised.

A few principles.

(2) What, then, are the principles which should govern the exercise of His Highness' clemency?

(a) Only a convicted criminal can be pardoned.

(*a*) His Highness cannot grant a pardon until after the person concerned has been tried and convicted. In other words, it is only a convicted criminal that His Highness can pardon. In other words, again, His Highness cannot say, "Do not try this person, for I have pardoned him." Nor can His Highness say while the trial is going on, "Stop the trial of this person, for I have pardoned him."

(b) There must be some reason for clemency.

(*b*) What I have just stated is one important principle. Another is that His Highness cannot arbitrarily pardon any criminal he pleases. In short, there must be apparently some good reason for clemency. For instance, that the court concerned has manifestly misjudged the evidence and wrongly convicted the prisoner; or that, since the termination of the trial, some new evidence has come to light showing the innocence of the prisoner or making his guilt doubtful.

(c) Consult the judges.

(*c*) In practice, it is desirable, though not imperative, to consult the judges before His Highness grants pardon. They will be able to assist with their opinion as to whether the prisoner deserves pardon or not in the given circumstances. The opinion of the judges is entitled to much weight, though it is not binding upon His Highness.

The same principle to be applied to mitigating and commuting punishments.

(3) His Highness has also the power of mitigating or commuting punishments awarded. The exercise of this power, too, is governed by considerations similar to those above stated. I will only add that this power may be exercised where the sentences passed are harsh or oversevere in reference to the youth, or the sex, or the rank of the prisoner, or other circumstance denoting extraordinary sensibility.

The practice of pardoning convicts on occasions of rejoicing not desirable yet care to be exercised.

(4) On occasions of extraordinary public rejoicing, a certain limited number of convicts are sometimes pardoned and liberated. As this is a questionable practice, it must not be frequently adopted. It is not very clear why, when the Maharaja has reason to rejoice, he, the great guardian of the security of life, person and property, should to any extent weaken that security by letting loose on society a number of proved delinquents. If such a thing is to be done, it must be done on very rare and extraordinary occasions; and even then, great and intelligent care should be taken to select such convicts for pardon as are most likely to abstain

from offending after release. For instance, convicts may be selected whose offences have not been very heinous or have been the results of misfortune, and who have suffered at least one-half of the punishments awarded to them.

Refer to old precedents.

(5) In this respect, the principles which have guided us during these six years may be referred to with advantage as precedents. They will be found recorded.

43

RESPECT FOR OTHERS' FEELINGS

[Undated]

Respect others' feelings.

Every ruler—every person who has to deal much with men—should always be careful to respect the feelings of others. Nothing needlessly harsh or offensive or unpleasant should be said or done in matters, whether great or small. This is a most useful and honourable habit which is well worth the trouble it requires to acquire it. Observation and study are required for its acquisition.

How we should feel if others did that to us.

(2) One easy way of prejudging what might be harsh or offensive or unpleasant is to imagine how we should feel if others said or did that to ourselves. Many do not act on this principle well, but so many do not act on this principle in practice.

Watch those who respect others.

(3) Another help towards acquiring the habit in question is to watch the thoughts, words and deeds of men who are distinguished for having successfully acquired that habit.

44

NEWSPAPER OPINIONS

[Undated]

They are not always correct.

Because any opinion appears in print in the newspapers, it does not follow that it is correct. The real value of the opinion expressed depends upon the respectability of the newspaper and of the writer concerned. Not unfrequently we find this by no means very high. Persons of very imperfect knowledge or judgment sometimes take to writing in the newspapers. Sometimes, persons of very inferior probity do the same. Sometimes, persons supposing themselves to be injured or slighted write in the journals in the disguise of disinterested observers or critics. And persons are not altogether wanting who sell their opinions—that is to say, publish opinions to order according to money paid.

Do not attach much weight.

(2) In these circumstances, we have to be very careful as to what weight should be attached to newspaper opinions and criticism.

Papers honestly conducted not to be disregarded.

(3) Newspapers honestly conducted and representing public opinion, or expressing the ideas of honest and intelligent thinkers, should

not be disregarded. On the contrary, they should be read and considered as material aids to good government.

45

PRIVATE STUDY

[Undated]

Do not neglect private study.

The Maharaja's studies will not, I trust, be discontinued after assuming power. It is most important that they should be continued on some fixed plan. A large portion of His Highness' time and attention will, of course, have to be devoted to official business. Yet time should be found for private study—say about three hours every day.

The object of study.

(2) The objects to be aimed at in this direction are: (*a*) His Highness should increase his knowledge of the English language, (*b*) of useful truths.

Speak and write the English language.

(3) The English language being foreign to us and otherwise difficult, we have to exercise ourselves constantly in it. If not, we not only do not improve, but we go back. We must read a great deal of good English every day. We must also speak and write the language every day to some extent. The main object of knowing the English language is to acquire a knowledge of useful

truths. Therefore our reading should be made the means of also augmenting our stock of truths.

Plan of study.

(4) All these things being clear, my esteemed friend Mr. Elliot will, no doubt, suggest to His Highness a somewhat detailed plan of studies:

(a) Perusal of newspapers.

(*a*) The plan will, doubtless, include the regular perusal of some well-conducted newspapers. His Highness should follow the current history of the world generally and of India and England in particular. I mean that large facts should not be missed.

(b) Speeches of statesmen.

(*b*) The speeches of great statesmen like Mr. Gladstone* may be read with advantage when they relate to matters of wider than local importance.

(c) Parliamentary debates.

(*c*) The debates in Parliament, when they relate to such matters, will also repay perusal.

(d) Histories of Native States.

(*d*) Almost everything which relates to the Native States of India should be read and noted. The Viceroy's speeches on such matters must not escape notice.

(e) Blue Books.

(*e*) Parliamentary Blue Books relating to Indian affairs may be regularly got out and useful portions read.

(f) Administration Reports.

(*f*) The *Annual Administration Report* of the Bombay Government should be a book familiar to His Highness.

Vast readings bring large ideas.

(5) Much of this sort of reading will have a great bearing on His Highness' public duties, and will strengthen His Highness' powers to perform those duties. The reading should be such as to bring His Highness' mind into contact with large ideas and elevated sentiments and to

* William Gladstone, the famous nineteenth century statesman and four-time Prime Minister of Great Britain.

counteract the cramping influences of the ordinary company which is to be had in the Palace. The great danger to which Native Princes are exposed is that they are liable to limit themselves to such company whereby their ideas get dwarfed or contracted. They confine themselves to a narrow and fossilised world which shuts out the higher lights of a progressive age. The best antidote to this is that they should make themselves conversant with the thoughts of the most enlightened of mankind.

Read biographies and good novels.

(6) His Highness' reading may occasionally embrace some biographies and novels calculated to inspire high ideal of human excellence.

Maintain a high ideal of life.

(7) To maintain a high ideal of life and duty in an exalted station and in the exercise of great power requires considerable moral force, and this moral force stands in need of constant renovation in some way like that suggested.

46

CONCLUDING ADVICE

[Undated]

These hints will be useful in practical administration.

I have thus brought the minor hints to a close. These hints also will be found to be more or less useful to the Maharaja in practical administration. What I have communicated under both the major and the minor heads will, I hope, serve like a small compass which, though small, shows the broad line to be followed in navigation.

Theoretical knowledge to be supplemented by practical experience.

(2) Theoretical knowledge alone, however, is not sufficient in the government of human beings. To such knowledge must be constantly added the benefit of actual practical experience. I am anxious that His Highness should not be led to undervalue practical experience and thereby to underestimate the desirableness of consulting practical men in important matters as they arise. Let me here give an illustration which will impress the material difference between theory and practice. His Highness knows well how to write with his right hand. So far as the theory of writing is concerned, the left hand is quite equal to the right hand. And yet,

let His Highness try to write with his left hand and he will see that he can do it very imperfectly or perhaps not at all. Why? The theory is all right with respect to both hands, but the right hand has had the benefit of practice, which the left hand has not had. Mark the immense difference thus observable as arising from want of practice, and let it restrain overconfidence resulting from theoretical knowledge alone.

The importance attached to the principles.

(3) The principles I have expounded and the hints I have imparted deserve to be borne in mind. They are those which guide enlightened rulers. They are those which conduct them to the heights of happiness, honour, and fame. They are those which alone will secure the continuance of existing independence to Native Princes.

Extension of principles of British Government to Native States.

(4) I shall conclude by quoting, in support of this position, the following valuable observation made by Her Majesty's Government so lately as in 1879:

> It is in the gradual and judicious extension in the Native States of the general principles of government which are applied in British territory that their rulers will find the surest guarantee of their administrative independence and the best safeguard against intervention on the part of the paramount power.[1]

APPENDIX I

A Draft Constitution for Native States[1]

When a Native State, at any particular time, suffers so much from gross maladministration as to demand the interference of the British Government, such State ought not to be annexed. The remedy of annexation would be much like cutting the throat as a remedy for cough. Annexation would be equally unjust and impolitic.

Nor ought the State to be placed under the management of European officers, like a British province. Such a course would not only be unpopular in a high degree, but would render future withdrawal from it very difficult, if not impossible. The course would only lead to annexation in effect, though not in name.

What action then should the British Government take, consistently with practice, humanity and good policy, and so as to place its motives beyond possible misconstruction?

If I may venture to submit a reply to this momentous question, I would say that the British Government should prescribe a body of fundamental principles for the guidance of the Native State—in short, a constitution or plan of Government, which the prince should be bound to conform to on pain of his being set aside in favour of his next heir. And, prescribing such a body of fundamental principles, the British Government should charge its Political Agent with the duty of seeing that those principles are steadily carried out as far as possible.

In the following pages I have essayed to indicate those principles, adding under each a few remarks which may not, perhaps, be altogether superfluous.

I am far from flattering myself that all the requisite principles are exhaustively stated, or that each principle is enumerated with fullness and precision. On the contrary, I am conscious of many shortcomings. Though deriving assistance from notes I made some years since, I have been writing this under extreme pressure for time—indeed, I have been encroaching on the usual hours of rest during night, being anxious to place my humble views with as little delay as possible before those who have kindly shown a disposition to invite and consider them. While this circumstance will entitle me to some indulgence, I do not for a moment pretend to imply that I should have been, with more leisure at my disposal, able to submit quite a perfect plan. All I profess to do is to put forth a sketch—a mere outline, just suggestive of something far better of the same description. It will then be for British Statesmen and British lawyers to do a work which is beyond my own powers to accomplish, but which I am only able, as said already, just to indicate.

It will be observed that not a few of the fundamental principles are drawn from the British or American constitutions. They are principles of universal applicability, being principles founded in reason and practical experience.

The main objects aimed at in framing the following draft are:

1st. To substitute for arbitrary will, the laws gradually framed after due deliberation, and apart from the sinister interests operating or liable to operate in individual cases.

2nd. To establish some machinery for making laws.

3rd. To ensure the observance of laws.

4th. To define Prerogative.

5th. To protect the Public Revenues.

6th. To preserve the rights and liberties of the people by laying down certain general principles which are to serve as the foundation of future progress.

7th. To establish a proper administration of justice, the very foundation of public happiness and prosperity.

8th, and lastly, to ensure stability to the whole Political fabric.

It will be found that the interests of the Sovereign are duly secured, and that his power to do good is left untouched.

It will also be found that the influence of the British Resident is allowed due scope without giving it undue preponderance.

All legitimate interests will thus act together, so as to ensure results most conducive to their advancement *as a whole*, without giving undue ascendency to any particular set of interests.

With some such plan or scheme of Government, things will probably go on smoothly and harmoniously. There will be a common standard to refer to, instead of having, in every particular case as it arises, to fight for the general principle at the risk, and indeed the certainty, of reiterated unpleasantness. Declare and establish the fundamental principles *once for all*, and many practical difficulties will disappear.

I contend that mere general advice tendered by Viceroys and Governors, however, eloquent or earnest, will have but little practical effect in Native States. The *Darbar* over, the princes return to their respective States little wiser than before. They may understand that the Viceroy wants them to *govern well*. But what is *good Government?* This, for practical good, must be defined, and about this there ought to be clear understanding on both sides. In point of fact, there is no common understanding at present. Many a prince thinks he is governing well, and this, of course, according to his own very limited lights, while he may not in reality be governing well at all.

Even in Europe, where the progress of events has favoured the growth of freedom, no State is considered safe without a regular constitution laying down the essential and fundamental principles which are to be followed in the Government of the country. And can it be at all reasonably expected that Asiatic Despotisms will fulfil the sacred duties of Government to their subjects, without the salutary restraint of an established constitution? Only one answer is possible.

Some of the principles stated in the following draft might seem commonplaces to the eye of an Englishman accustomed for centuries to regular and constitutional Government. But the Constitutional History of England itself shows what length of time, what reiterated struggles, what amount of precious blood were required to establish these principles, and of what immense practical value they have proved themselves to be in the character of safeguards to the rights and liberties of the subject. I feel sanguine that almost every line of the proposed draft will check a mighty host of abuses.

As stated at the outset, it can be made the highest interest of the prince to adhere to and carry out the principles laid down for his guidance.

A body of such principles will be of great use to the British Resident himself, as he can, from time to time, refer to them as the standard prescribed by authority.

Those principles will, I am sure, bear good fruit even in Native States to whom they are not directly prescribed. Other princes will easily perceive that to the extent they spontaneously conform to those principles, they will render unpleasant interference from the Paramount Power unnecessary. This will be an immense gain. The good that will thus be done will reach millions of people in a quiet yet most effective manner.

An earnest and warm well-wisher as I am of the Native States, my strong belief is that their future existence and prosperity will depend upon their conforming themselves to the principles embodied in the following draft. I am convinced that if unqualified personal and arbitrary rule continue in Native States, they must inevitably collapse one after another, the event being only a question of time. This is a consummation which the British Government is too high-minded to desire, and hence the British Government may well be expected to avail itself of proper and favourable opportunities to bring about the establishment of some settled plan of Government in Native States *in the best interest of these States themselves*. I think that the desire of the British Government to see the Native States perpetuated cannot be better proved and better manifested than in the way I have ventured to suggest.

As I am extremely pressed for time, I must bring these preliminary remarks to a close by making one more observation. I do not mean to say that it would be possible for the generality of Native States to effect *at one stroke* complete conformity of administration with the principles of the following draft. What I advocate is the laying down of a standard. With such a standard in view the Native States will approach it as fast as they can according to the circumstances of each. Political Agents of capacity, temper, judgment, and tact will be able to assist such approaches in a quiet and yet effective manner.

APPENDIX I

Charter or Constitution

1. *The Maharaja as Sovereign is the highest authority in his dominions.*

   This requires no explanation.

2. *The happiness of the people, as the foundation of the strength, durability, and happiness of the ruling dynasty, shall be the paramount object of the Government of the country.*

   This may seem trite. Nevertheless, the full recognition of this important principle is of the highest use in Native States, where sovereigns are sometimes apt to forget if not controvert it. Hence, it is thus prominently laid down and in a manner to imply that the best interests of the dynasty depend upon its faithful observance.

3. *The Government of the country shall be carried on according to laws and customs, whether at present in force or established hereafter.*

   The object of this is obviously to do away with arbitrary Government altogether, and to induce the Government to conform its action to laws deliberately enacted and to customs established, in reference to public good alone.

4. *A* Darbar *for making laws shall be organised, composed of men of wisdom, virtue, property, and patriotism, and such* Darbar *shall assist in the framing of useful laws from time to time and under rules to be hereafter laid down.*

   As the Government is to be carried on according to law, something like a properly constituted machinery for making laws becomes at once a necessity. I reserve the details as to the construction of this *Darbar*, only remarking at present that, without much difficulty, a body may be constituted which, though far from perfect, may be practically competent to frame useful laws.

   The Prime Minister will, of course, have to preside in this *Darbar*.

   The *Darbar* will be only a consultative body, and nothing framed by it can pass into law unless assented to by the Sovereign on the recommendation of the Dewan or Prime Minster after consultation with British Resident. Thus no bad law can issue unless the Sovereign, the Dewan, the British Resident, and the *Darbar* all fail in their duty, a combination not likely to happen.

5. *The laws in force at any time shall not be altered, modified, suspended, abolished, or in any way interfered with, except by other regularly enacted laws duly promulgated.*

The object aimed at is the most important one of putting it out of the power of the Sovereign or the executive Government to interfere summarily or arbitrarily with the laws, by means of special orders, proclamations, etc., merely to suit a temporary or sinister purpose at the dictation of caprice, passion, or interest.

This provision is absolutely necessary to ensure Government according to law.

The student of the political history of even England knows how important this provision is. I have framed this provision in reference to the following clause in the Bill of Rights or Declaration, delivered by English Lords and Commons to the Prince and Princess of Orange, 13th February 1688, namely, "that the pretended power of suspending of laws or the execution of laws by regal authority without consent of Parliament is illegal."

If such provision is required in England itself it is *á fortiori** required in Oriental States, where there is a perpetual impatience of restraint and constant tendency to arbitrary rule.

The effect of this provision will be that no laws will suffer alteration etc., unless by means of laws. In short, a character of fixity will be imparted to all existing laws, and a guarantee established that they shall not be altered, or in any manner interfered with, except for a really good and approved purpose.

6. *No law shall be passed except after the draft of it, together with a brief and clear statement of its objects and reasons, shall have been published in the Official Gazette for at least ____ months.*

This is, of course, intended to prevent hasty or rash legislation, and to afford opportunity for the expression of public opinion.

This provision might be thought more properly to appertain to the rules and regulations which will have to be framed for the working of the *Darbar* for making laws. Still it forms so important a guarantee in behalf of public interest, that too much attention cannot be drawn to it thus inserting it prominently.

---

* A Latin phrase meaning "with greater reason".

7. *When however, public inquiry would not admit of this course, a law may be passed at once by the Sovereign under the advice of his Dewan, who will have duly consulted the British Resident. But such law shall not be valid for more than ____ months from the date of its promulgation, unless re-enacted in due course.*

Occasions, through rare, may be easily conceived, in which such a power as that given by this provision will be needed. The law thus passed is either good or bad. If good, it will be certainly re-enacted; if bad, it will of itself cease to be law after a short period, if not rescinded earlier. The period allowed may suffice for considering necessary amendments.

8. *No proposed law shall be submitted to the Sovereign by the Dewan for final approval, unless after due consultation with the British Resident.*

The object of this is to secure the advantage of the wisdom and experience of the British Resident in the important work of legislation. It will be a great advantage. The Resident represents the friendly interest of the British Government, and may well give his advice in such matters. His objections to unsound legislation will generally carry weight with the responsible Prime Minister of the prince. The effect, whether positive or negative, will prove very beneficial. I mean, it will lead to good or prevent evil.

9. *The Sovereign shall act through his responsible Minister the Dewan, selected by himself with the approval, and not removable without the concurrence, of the British Government. And it shall be understood that in public affairs this is the only legal and valid mode in which the Sovereign gives expression to his will.*

This embodies a most valued principle of the British Constitution. It is intended to prevent the direct action of the Crown without anyone being responsible for such action. It will prevent the vast amount of confusion and consequent irresponsibility usually arising in Native States from anyone issuing orders in the name of the Sovereign. It will fix responsibility on the Dewan, and will cut off the scope for many abuses which occur in Native States.

The Dewan's office is the most important in Native States. On him much of the character of the administration depends. He ought, therefore, to be a properly qualified man in every respect. The approval of the British Government will secure this. This provision will prevent unworthy men getting hold of the helm. It will cut off many dangerous intrigues for power. If the Sovereign makes a really good nomination, the British Government will, of course, approve of it. The provision will, therefore, be a standing inducement on the part of the Sovereign to make a right choice of his Dewan.

Similarly, the Dewan ought not be removable without the concurrence of the British Government. His very position exposes him to the storms of faction. In the conscientious discharge of duty, he will, not unfrequently have to incur considerable though perhaps temporary, odium. Unless his tenure of office is secured by rendering it necessary to obtain the concurrence of the British Government for his removal, there will be constant changes of Dewans; there will be perpetual court intrigues; there will be no steady attention to business; there will be every inducement for a servile subserviency on the part of the highest officer of the State. In such an important matter as a change of the first Minister, the Sovereign will always do well to consult the British Government, which can judge calmly and apart from local prejudices and passions.

The latter part of the provision under explanation implies that orders issued by the Sovereign, otherwise than through his responsible minister, are illegal and invalid.

10. *The Dewan shall be personally responsible if he refuses to take part in any act which he considers unadvisable or improper, without referring to the British Government for advice and instruction.*

Without such a provision the Dewan cannot be held responsible in the manner contemplated, for he might plead that he was compelled to carry out the order of the Sovereign, though unadvisable or improper.*

11. *The Dewan shall have free access to the British Resident, and may take his advice on all measures of importance.*

As so much responsibility will be devolved on the Dewan he will gladly avail himself of such a provision. The wisest Maharajah and the wisest Dewan might look for benefit from the advice of the British Resident. The more they are sincerely anxious for a good administration the more readily will they seek to consult with the Resident.

12. *If any unlawful act is done, the agent instrumental in the doing of such act shall himself be fully responsible to the laws, and cannot plead as an excuse obedience to the orders of the Sovereign.*

---

* *Footnote in the original text*: In this provision I have adopted the words of a rule laid down by an eminent Political officer of the British Government.

This is also a valuable principle of the British Constitution. It is absolutely necessary in the interests of the people, and also in the interests of the Sovereign personally. It is intended to deter any agent of the Sovereign from undertaking to carry out any unlawful order. It is also intended to give complete effect to the provision that the Sovereign shall act through his responsible Minster, the Dewan.

13. *The Sovereign will not administer justice personally, as he has delegated this power to the constituted judiciary.*

This, too, embodies an important principle of the British Constitution.

It would be obviously impossible for ordinary Sovereigns personally to administer justice. In Native States there is a perpetual desire, induced in the Sovereign by interested persons, to undertake personally a work which requires special qualifications, which a Sovereign is not expected to possess. The more a Sovereign yields to this desire, the more likely it is that justice would be perverted or sold. Even Frederick the Great of Prussia failed in such a work, and Frederick the Great is not a common character among the native princes.

14. *The Sovereign shall not constitute any special court to administer special justice in any particular case, but may direct any already existing court to be strengthened by temporarily transferring to it any judge or judges of other constituted courts.*

This is designed to prevent a court being arbitrarily and specially constituted to secure a given result in any particular case. As such, the provision forms an important safeguard. It has its analogy in the English Bill of Rights.

15. *The Sovereign shall in no case reverse the acquittal or enhance the sentence pronounced by a competent court of justice.*

This is also absolutely necessary to protect the subject against the effects of anger, or malice, or vindictiveness, or at least ignorance, on the part of courtiers about the Sovereign.

The provision is also, I believe, comfortable to the British Constitution.

16. *The Sovereign may, under the advice of his responsible minister, mitigate any sentence, if proper grounds exist, by reducing it, or commuting it for any other. And the Sovereign may, under similar advice, grant free pardons after trial, conviction, and sentence, in cases wherein error is patent or serious doubt has arisen about the correctness of the conviction.*

These provisions again are derived from the British Constitution. The Sovereign ought to be able to exercise clemency, a highly popular virtue, within proper bounds. Even should he ever err in the exercise of those prerogatives, no great mischief is likely to occur. The Dewan will, of course, be responsible to prevent error as far as possible.

These provisions are designedly so worded as to cut off the power which is sometimes exercised by the Sovereign, of pardoning criminal convicts on joyful occasions, such as the coronation, the birth of an heir, recovery from serious illness, and so on. Such pardons cannot but produce a baneful effect on the community. It is impossible to see why an occasion of personal joy on the part of the Sovereign should bring about a suspension of just penal laws in particular instances.

According to these provisions the Sovereign cannot grant a pardon in anticipation of a trial and conviction so as to enable any accused person to plead the pardon as a bar to trial, etc.

This provision, however, is not intended to interfere with the power of granting pardons to approvers for securing evidence. A special law will, of course, regulate the granting of such pardons.

17. *Every grant of pardon or mitigation of sentence, carried out under the foregoing provisions, shall be immediately notified in the Official Gazette, together with a brief and clear statement of the reasons which dictated it.*

The object here is to enable public opinion to operate as a check against the abuse of the power of remitting or mitigating a judicial sentence.

18. *No sentence of death shall be carried out unless after confirmation by the Sovereign under the advice of the responsible Dewan, who will consult the British Resident whenever he (the Dewan) finds difficulty in arriving at a definite conclusion himself.*

Life is so sacred, and a deprivation of it constitutes such an irrevocable and irremediable punishment, that too much caution cannot be brought to bear in this direction. As the provision is framed, no one will forfeit his life unless the highest judicial tribunal, the Dewan and Sovereign, and in many cases the British Resident, all err together, which is an improbable contingency.

As the Dewan is fully responsible, he will readily and often avail himself of the latter part of the provision. In very clear cases he may not do so, but act on his own responsibility.

19. *The Sovereign shall have a Civil List, fixed* under the advice of the British Government, for the support and maintenance of his personal dignity and of his household; and all payments made on this account out of the public Treasury shall be faithfully shown in the Administration Report of the State which shall be framed and published by the Dewan every year.*

This is intended to put an end to the unbounded license enjoyed in most Native States in the use of public funds. A fixed Civil List is manifestly one of the most essential requisites and characteristics of a well-ordered Government. The provision will bring about a useful separation between the private expenses of the Sovereign, and the public expenditure of the country. It will induce economy on the part of the Sovereign; it will facilitate the appropriation of the surplus revenue of the county for purposes of public utility. Where every rupee of the public revenue is looked upon as the private property of the Sovereign, extravagance must very often prevail, and useful outlays on public works must generally be grudged.

The latter part of the provision is necessary in view to give effect to the former. Expenses appertaining to the Civil List have a strong tendency to lurk under other heads, and this ought, by all means, to be prevented.

The opportunity has been taken to make the publication of the Annual Administration Report obligatory, as it will bring the whole administration under wholesome public criticism. An administration which has to be exposed to public view can seldom go far wrong.

20. *The public revenues shall not be answerable for private debts incurred by the Sovereign or any member of the Royal Family.*

Without such a provision as this, the fixity of the Civil List would be utterly a sham. This is too evident to require explanation.

21. *No suit shall lie in any court against the Sovereign or any member of the Royal Family on account of private debts incurred by them.*

This is necessary to exempt the Sovereign and members* of his family from the indignity of being put into court for their private debts; and

---

* *Footnote in the original text*: It is not meant that it should be fixed and unalterable for all time. It may be fixed from time to time, so as to enable the prince to duly share in the prosperity of his country as he is entitled to do.

* *Footnote in the original text*: What members, will have to be defined with some care.

the effect will obviously be to deter money-lenders from lending money to such persons. There is nothing, however, to prevent them from discharging their debts as matters of honour and moral obligation. Indeed, it is to be hoped that no Royal Family will be so depraved as to repudiate a just debt, in consequence of the legal irresponsibility conferred by this provision. Moneylenders, however, will be quite aware of this legal irresponsibility and take the risk with their eyes fully open.

The provision under remark has, I believe, its analogy in several European Constitutions.

22. *The Sovereign shall not make any permanent alienation of the land or other public revenues to any extent in favour of any private individual or any corporation unless under the sanction of a specific law regularly enacted and promulgated in due course.*

This provision appears very necessary for the very preservation of the revenues. It will restrain undue liberality and ill-judged favouritism, so much prevalent in native courts. It will protect the Sovereign against constant importunities and intrigues, and thus make his position easy and comfortable.

Where, however, a grant is justified by the circumstances of any case, a law may without difficulty be passed, specially authorizing the Dewan to make a permanent alienation in a given case. Those who must be parties to the passing of the law may be expected to exercise due care and caution in regard to the public revenue while yielding to just claims.

The most important effect of this provision will be that grants by the Sovereign, such as are hereby interdicted, would, if ever made, be illegal and invalid and, as such, revocable by that Sovereign himself at a subsequent period, or by his successors; thus permanent evil will be prevented.

23. *No public demand shall be remitted or suspended in part or whole, except on principles of public utility and general applicability.*

The design of this is to prevent venality, favouritism, and inequality. The principle is very often violated in Native States in reference to personal or private influences.

24. *The public revenues, or any surplus arising therefrom, shall not be applied to any but public purposes and the good of the country.*

This provision is not rendered unnecessary by the fixation of the Civil List. The object is to prevent undue grants of the public revenue to purposes other than the good of the country. It is desirable, for instance, to deter grants, excessive grants, to foreign institutions, merely in compliance with a morbid desire for the reputation of liberality. The people who pay the taxes have an undoubted right to demand that their taxes be not appropriated for purposes which do not benefit them.

It is not intended to prohibit reasonable contributions to foreign institutions. In determining the Civil List, a fair margin should be allowed for such contributions, and then such contributions will be made personally by the Sovereign out of his Civil List. Such an arrangement will effectually check prodigality, detrimental to the interests of the State.

25. *A reserve, equal to half a year's revenue, shall be ordinarily maintained in the public treasury, so as to be readily available in periods of unexpected financial difficulties, such as those which are consequent on the failure of rains, etc. if the reserve be so availed of, the amount shall be replaced as soon as possible.*

Native States cannot afford to incur public debts; they must never become insolvent; hence this precaution, which will ensure safety and ease. The reserve may be held invested in British Government securities, so as to obtain some interest for the State. The securities can, of course, be sold whenever cash is required.

26. *The rights and liberties which are now enjoyed by the people under existing laws and customs shall continue unabridged to the utmost extent possible.*

This provision is necessarily vague, it is intended to preserve unreduced whatever rights and liberties have heretofore been conceded. It will prevent backsliding.

27. *Nothing shall be done affecting or likely to affect, the rights and liberties of the people except by means of regularly enacted laws duly promulgated.*

The object in view here is to prevent the executive taking upon itself to issue proclamations, notification, or circular orders, calculated to interfere with the rights and liberties of the people. This provision, though difficult of being fully carried out, will act as a check.

A previous provision says that the laws in force at any time shall not be altered, etc., except by other regularly enacted laws. But it is to be remembered that the laws in force at any time may not have occupied all the ground which laws might occupy. There may thus be spare or unoccupied ground. What is here aimed at is to prevent the executive summarily occupying this spare ground, and to compel regular legislation where the occupation of this ground, or any part of it, may be desired.

But it is not intended by this provision to prevent the executive issuing notifications, etc. in conformity with existing laws and customs.

28. *The taxation of the country might not be altered or interfered with, except by regularly enacted laws duly promulgated.*

This is, strictly speaking, included in some of the previous provisions. Still, this matter is so extremely important that, rather than leave it to be inferred, express and prominent mention of it ought to be made in some shape like this.

The effect of this provision will be that no new taxes can be imposed, or old ones increased, or even reduced, without a new law, fully discussed in the *Darbar*. Great and effectual security will thus be, in a great measure, established against maladministration in a matter deeply affecting the property and welfare of the people.

29. *No loans shall be incurred by or for the State, except by regularly enacted law.*

This provision is intended to fortify and give complete effect to the immediately preceding one. A little reflection will make this obvious.

30. *No man's property or services shall be taken or demanded for public exigencies without fair and adequate compensation.*

This is a provision peculiarly fruitful of good in Native States.

I remember seeing a provision very like this, if not perhaps in these very words, in either the Constitution of the United States of America, or that of some of the States comprised in the Union.

31. *All subjects shall have a right to hold public meetings peaceably, to discuss public matters freely, and to petition the Government for redress of grievances; and the writers and subscribers of such petition shall not be punishable for anything true, or in good faith believed to be true, that they may express in the petition.*

This provision is the same in substance as that included in the English Declaration of Rights. In this celebrated document it is stated "that it is the right of the subjects to petition the king, and all commitments and prosecution for such petitioning are illegal." The same is found embodied in the constitution of the United States of America, wherein it is provided that "Congress shall make no law... abridging the freedom of speech, or of the press, or the right of the people peaceably to assemble, and to petition the Government for a redress of grievance." But it is needless to cite authority in support of a right which no civilized Government can think of refusing to a people whose welfare it really has at heart.

32. *No person shall be taken, or imprisoned, or deprived of his estate, or exiled or condemned or deprived of life, liberty, or property, unless by due process of law.*

This provision is of vital importance to ensure good government, and to exclude arbitrary proceedings so rife in most Native States. I have framed this by almost adopting the words of Kent,—*vide page 623, vol. I.*, of his *Commentaries on American Law.*[2]

33. *The right of deliverance from all unlawful imprisonment shall be ensured to the subject by such means as he may avail himself of freely, easily, cheaply, and expeditiously.*

I mean, of course, that something analogous in effect to the English writ of *Habeas Corpus* shall be enacted for the protection of the subject against the infraction of the right which the English secured at Runnymede.

34. *Excessive bail shall not be required, nor excessive fines imposed, nor cruel and unusual punishments inflicted.*

There is a certain degree of vagueness in the words "excessive", "cruel", and "unusual". Still the sense intended is plain enough.

This provision is taken from the English Declaration of Rights, and I have adopted the very words used in the Constitution of the American Union—vide Kent, vol. I., page 675.[3]

It might be objected to this provision,—why have it, while the laws will lay down the limits of bail, fines, and punishments? The answer is not difficult. We are laying down fundamental principles for the Government of a Native State where there are scarcely regular laws. The fundamental principle embodied in this provision is to guide the framing of penal laws.

35. *The right of the people to be secure in their persons, houses, papers, and effects against unreasonable searches and seizures shall not be violated; and no warrant shall issue but upon probable cause, supported by oath or affirmation, and particularly describing the place to be searched, and the persons or things to be seized.*

This, again, is taken from the Constitution of the United States—vide Kent, vol. I., page 675.[4]

The most arbitrary and sometimes intolerably vexatious searches are too often made in Native States. This broad provision will be a standing remembrancer both to the legislature and the executive.

36. *No person in the county shall, at any time, or in any wise, be molested, punished, or called in question for any differences in opinion in matters of religion, who does not disturb, or is not likely to disturb the civil peace of the country.*

This grand principle of religious toleration is expressed very nearly in the words used in the charters of some of the States comprising the great American Union—*vide Kent, vol. I., page 658.*[5]

37. *The public press shall be as free in the country as in British India.*

This requires scarcely any explanation. One of the most potent checks on any Government will thus be permitted to act with full force. Public opinion, expressed in British India in a manner legally permissible, will thus find circulation in the territory of the Native State.

38. *The right of the people to have the best qualified persons appointed to perform public duties shall be at all times fully and faithfully respected.*

As a general rule, in Native States any man is thought fit to perform any function, including that of a judge. This provision is intended to keep constantly and prominently before the eye of the prince the importance of selecting duly qualified persons for public appointments.

39. *As a general rule, no public servant shall be removable "quamdiu bene se gesserint".* This particularly applies to Judicial Officers.*

This principle is, I believe in full force in British India. Judicial officers are specially protected by this principle in the British and American Constitutions.

This provision is not, of course, intended to operate in cases where the public servant is incapacitated by sickness or superannuation, nor in cases where he has been engaged on special contact for a specified term of years.

40. *No judge of the superior courts shall be appointed or removed except by the Sovereign under the advice of the responsible minister, the Dewan, who will have duly consulted the British Resident.*

---

* A Latin phrase meaning "as long as he behaves himself properly".

It is of supreme importance to secure the uprightness and independence of good judges, and hence this provision. In the generality of Native States, good judges stand in need of special protection, as they often incur the enmity of the rich and influential in honest endeavours to protect the poor and uninfluential masses.

41. *Every judge shall solemnly bind himself to administer justice according to the laws and customs of the country and in conformity with the provisions herein laid down.*

This hardly requires explanation or remark.

42. *No judge shall, privately or publicly, directly or indirectly hold any office, pension or allowance, or receive any remuneration, present, or gratuity from the Sovereign in addition to his proper salary as judge.*

This is an obviously useful and necessary restriction to secure the proper independence of the judge, and is recognized as such in European systems. This restraining provision is very essential in Native States, where the practice of making special presents, etc. very largely prevails.

43. *The judges of the several courts shall have ascertained salaries not subject to reduction at any time during their continuance in office. Nor shall the salary of a newly appointed judge be made lower than the usual rate in view to raise it by degrees to that rate.*

This safeguard of judicial independence, originally found in the British Constitution, and improved by that of the American Union, is absolutely required in Native States.

The latter part, however, is my own. It is designed to prevent the evasion of the former part. The effect of the whole as it stands, is that the full appointed salary shall be given to the judge when first appointed, and that it shall not be diminished during his incumbency.

This leaves it open to the State to raise the salary as a general measure whenever necessary. It likewise leaves it open to the State to reduce the salary at the time of appointment if the object is a permanent reduction. Thus, the influences adverse to judicial independence are minimized, while just liberty of action is reserved to the State.

44. *Every law, proclamation, order, or custom which may be opposed to the provisions herein laid down shall be null and void, so far as it is opposed.*

Without this special provision, this collection of fundamental principles would be useless. This provision will have both a prospective and retrospective effect.

45. *The provisions herein laid down shall not be altered, modified, or set aside wholly or partially unless under the advice or with a concurrence of the Viceroy and Governor-General of India in Council.*

In the first place, it would never do to make these provisions so fixed and rigid as absolutely to shut out all future improvement according to times and circumstances and as the result of valuable experience to be gained hereafter. Hence this provision properly leaves the door open for future improvement.

In the next place, it would be equally undesirable to render alterations, etc. so easy as to lead to constant tampering with the fundamental rules which it is our aim to lay down.

Framed as this provision is, there is every reasonable guarantee against hasty or unwise meddling. If any alteration be really required, it will clearly set forth with all the advantages of local knowledge and information; and then it will be impartially judged by a central authority inaccessible to local passions and prejudices, and able to take large views. Besides, there is generally a great lawyer in the Viceroy's Council, who is sure to give valuable advice in matters relating to constitutional law.

46. *The provisions herein laid down shall be fully promulgated in the languages of the country, through the Official Gazette of the State.*

I attach much importance to such publicity. Let every man in the country know and be familiar with the fundamental principles which guide the Government under which he lives. Let him know what his rights and liberties are and how they are secured. In every case of their infringement, let him by all means be in a position to quote the particular fundamental principle which has been infringed.

APPENDIX II

A Scheme of Special Education[1]

It is obvious that the only satisfactory and effective security for the preservation and promotion of good government in these territories hereafter is the proper education of His Highness the young Gaekwar in his duties as a ruler. I refer to his special education in reference to his special works, as distinguished from the general education which has been going on.

2. The object and scope of this special education in the duties of rulership require to be clearly realized, and hence I will offer a few observations on this topic.
3. If any ruler stands in need of such special education, it is the native prince in the position of His Highness the Gaekwar. Most rulers of civilized countries have their duties more or less defined in some way or another. Such rulers have some constitutional rules and traditions for their observance or guidance. They are restrained from incurring errors or perils, by some sort of checks. But, in the instance of the native prince, it is *personal* rule, it is a rule which largely, I may say excessively, takes its character and complexion from the personal intelligence of the prince. And it is to be remembered that the prince in his own territories is the depository of supreme power. The native prince, therefore, pre-eminently needs to be specially instructed in his duties and responsibilities. Otherwise, in nine cases out of ten, he is likely to

go wrong notwithstanding his mere general education, excellent as it may have been in its own way.

4. Those duties and responsibilities are, in most respects, of the highest order. They must be clearly distinguished from those of mere ministerial officers or agents. It is not that we want to make the Maharaja a clever *karkoon*, or a skillful accountant, or a judge or even a Dewan. *Karkoons*, accountants, judges and Dewans, he can engage the services of, from time to time, as circumstances require. What we really want to make of the Maharaja is a good ruler, one who will direct and control the whole machinery of Government under the guidance of sound principles.
5. To make the matter more clear, I should say that the education of the Maharaja as a ruler must differ from that of a ministerial agent just as the education of an engineer differs from that of a mason or carpenter; as the education of a commanding officer differs from that of a sepoy or *sowar*; as the education of a captain of a ship differs from that of the crew.
6. It is of the most vital importance that the Maharaja should be taught those large and enlightened principles which constitute the safeguards of public welfare and of his own stability. Those principles will enable him to appreciate and to preserve those reforms which will have been already effected. They will enable him to make further progress in the same direction. They will enable him to perceive when the State machinery is going wrong and to perceive what corrective should be applied. They will enable him, every day and every hour, to judge what is politically right and what is politically wrong. They will enable him to possess a standard to which, those who discuss public measures with him from time to time, may appeal with force and effect.
7. The Maharaja, being thus early impressed with the necessary fundamental principles of government, will be prepared to appreciate and accept numerous other principles which follow as necessary deductions from the primary sources.
8. By way of illustration, I will now mention some of those fundamental principles which are in view.
9. First and foremost, the Maharaja should be taught that he is made for the people, and not that the people are made for him.

10. That the position of a ruler is materially different from that of the owner of a private landed estate.
11. That a ruler is justified in being at the head of the State, and of its resources, only because he is to promote the greatest happiness of his people.
12. That everything should be regarded as secondary to the welfare of the people.
13. That in order to promote the greatest happiness of the people, security of life, person and property should be thoroughly established.
14. That for this purpose, a necessary military force, a police, and a judiciary must be always maintained in a state of efficiency.
15. That for the same purpose, there should be some definite laws regarding life, person, and property, and that these laws should be enforced with impartiality.
16. That the arbitrary and capricious will of the Maharaja should never be substituted for those laws. The Maharaja should be the foremost person to respect the laws. He should never himself arbitrarily order a subject to be put to death, to be imprisoned, or to be deprived of his property. Such things should be left to be dealt with by the constituted magistrates and judges under the appointed laws.
17. That the Maharaja should not arbitrarily order a person to be exempted from the operation of the laws. For instance, the Maharaja should not arbitrarily order the release of a person imprisoned lawfully by the magistrates and judges. His Highness should not arbitrarily remit the punishment or liabilities of a person, as declared by the magistrates and judges.
18. That the Maharaja should never incur the guilt of receiving bribes under the name of *nazarana* or any other in connection with the administration of justice. Nor should he permit any corruption is any quarter. The nearest relations and the closest friends of the Maharaja should be made to feel that they would be sternly dealt with in case they venture to misbehave.
19. That as bearing on the happiness of the people which is the primary object of government, sanitary, medical, and educational institutions should be kept up in a state of efficiency.

20. That trade and industry should be carefully fostered, and their natural development should be freely allowed by the removal of fiscal and other impediments.
21. That useful and reproductive public works should be undertaken as may be found necessary from time to time.
22. That the Maharaja should not think of levying the largest possible revenue from the people, but that he should levy no more than what may be found necessary to maintain good government.
23. That no new tax should be imposed on the people when the revenues, already levied, suffice to meet the necessary expenditure.
24. That the less the revenue collected, the more will be left with the people, and the happier they will be.
25. That what revenues are collected should be levied in the least oppressive manner. The Maharaja may be taught the leading characteristics or criteria of good taxes and of bad taxes.
26. That the Maharaja has a right to a fair proportion of the public revenues for his own expenses and for the maintenance of his dignity and State, but that the palace expenditure should not be left indefinite. Fair limits should be fixed and carefully observed.
27. That all prodigality in palace expenditure is wrong, such as giving excessive allowances or gifts to persons who do not, in any way, contribute to the happiness of the people; also spending extravagantly on objects which have no bearing on public welfare.
28. That the Maharaja should not think of abstracting monies from the public revenues and of hoarding them up in the palace.
29. That he should not lay out much more on the purchase of jewelry. The existing stock is more than sufficient.
30. That His Highness should not alienate any land or revenue. He must not reduce his Raj and resources by such alienations.
31. That he should carefully abstain from making even money grants in perpetuity. Such grants may be made, if necessary, for one or two or at most three lives.
32. That he should avail himself of legitimate opportunities to retrench such expenditure as does not, in any way, contribute to the public welfare. While he is bound to do so, he should of course be most careful not to increase such expenditure himself.
33. That the palace and personal expenditure of His Highness should be kept quite distinct from the general expenditure of the State,

that the past practice of transferring items of palace and personal expenditure to the public treasury is highly objectionable and should cease.

34. That His Highness should be careful to encourage real merit in the exercise of his generosity and in the dispensation of rewards, pecuniary or otherwise; that some useful industry, knowledge or skill should be encouraged and not mere idleness, flattery, and buffoonery.

35. That His Highness should avoid incurring debt, as a paramount obligation.

36. That he should scrupulously keep up the reserve which we have invested in British securities for him. If, in a pressing emergency, any portion of this reserve be drawn upon, it must be replaced at the next earliest opportunity so as to restore and keep up the reserve.

37. That he should keep up full and efficient administrative establishments; that curtailing these would be misjudged economy. Officers who are charged with high duties and responsibilities should be adequately and liberally remunerated so as to insure the best ability and the highest probity.

38. That His Highness should not make appointments and promotions according to his own arbitrary will and pleasure, but according to the best principles which apply to the subject. Merit should be the chief guide. All classes of subjects, Mahrattas, Gujaratis, Mahomedans, Parsis, etc., should be selected from in a spirit of impartiality.

39. That His Highness should no longer for a moment suppose, as most of preceding Gaekwars did, that any man is fit for any post. Every post requires its own special qualifications, and these must be most carefully secured if good government is to be maintained. This principle has to be impressed on His Highness in the strongest manner, because it lies at the very foundation of successful administration, and also because I know that, as this moment, some of the most illiterate and ignorant persons here cherish the wish and expectation of succeeding to the most important offices in the State when the Maharaja will have attained his age, and assumed the reins of government.

40. That His Highness should not absorb and exercise all the patronage himself; that he should leave appointments to the responsible heads of departments; and that, even in the instance of the higher appointments, His Highness should consult his Ministry and accept their reasonable recommendations.
41. That His Highness should do everything to promote security in the tenure of office. There should be no arbitrary dismissals. Every honest and well behaved public servant should have abundant reason to feel that he is safe in office.
42. That His Highness should guard against the too common system of having favorites, and of indulging in favoritism. The evils of such a system must be made apparent to him. The benefits of having good and worthy companions should also be dwelt upon.
43. That His Highness should be in his life and daily conduct a bright moral example to his subjects.
44. That His Highness should strongly put down *khatpat*, intrigue, backbiting, etc. Many useful hints have to be given to him in this direction.
45. That he should be firmly set his face against all persons who pretend to exert private influence with the high officers of the British Government, whether at Baroda, or at Bombay, or at Calcutta, or in England. His Highness should spend no money in this direction. Any resort to such persons would bring great disgrace on the State.
46. That His Highness should abstain from needlessly burdening himself with the detailed business of administration. Such business must be left to be transacted by his responsible ministers. His Highness should reserve to himself the great and worthy work of controlling and directing the administration as a whole.
47. That he should hold full consultation and discussion with the heads of departments, and where the matter admits of it, also consult the intelligent independent members of society, before adopting or sanctioning any measure of importance. He should, as a rule, refrain from taking any important action against the unanimous or nearly unanimous advice of his responsible ministers.
48. That, in matters of public importance, he should be guided mainly by the advice of his responsible ministers, and by no means by the advice of irresponsible hangers-on of the Palace.

49. That His Highness should carefully note and watch certain *results*, whereby to judge whether or not the administration is getting on successfully. For instance—Is there always sufficient money in the public treasury for carrying on the administration for the next six months? Are all public salaries paid regularly and punctually? Is the total expenditure kept well below the total ordinary income of the State? Is justice dispensed with impartiality? Are crimes kept down within normal limits? Does the administration maintain a high standard of purity? Are the people in general happy and contented? Is the British Government satisfied with the character of the administration? and so on. His Highness will have to be taught the necessary criteria, whereby to judge of the successful working of each principle department of the State.

50. That His Highness should not revive the *izara* or farming system of land revenue, a system most prejudicial to the *ryots*.

51. That His Highness, as a rule, should respect and preserve whatever reforms and improvements have been introduced during his minority.

52. That His Highness should firmly observe the rule that whatever has been once carefully considered and decided should not be re-opened merely on account of the importunity of interested parties or other inadequate cause.

53. That His Highness, should not revive the past system of important matters being transacted orally and without proper recordation.

54. That he should, on no account, disturb the resumption of *doomala* villages carried out by Maharaja Khande Rao, a measure which the administration during minority has strenuously upheld.

55. That he should always inquire into precedents, look into past records, and consult previously recorded opinions before passing orders in any matter of importance.

56. That in matters of privileges and indulgences and exemptions, etc., he should generally plead precedent in order to resist solicitations for their increase or extension. He should seldom depart from precedent, for one departure would only lead to another.

57. That he should not take up and decide individual cases of complaint independently of the constituted authorities. If he receives

any petitions, they should be referred to the constituted authorities for attention and due disposal or report.

58. That he should not further augment religious and charitable expenditure or assignments as they are already very large.
59. That he should always respect enlightened and disinterested public opinion and criticism.
60. That he should not vindictively pursue any individual who may have written against him in the public prints.
61. That he should treat all he may come in contact with, with courtesy and consideration, and be careful never to lose control over his temper.
62. That he may occasionally make a tour through the principle parts of his territories, but care should be taken that the number of followers is limited as much as possible, and that the *ryots* are not troubled or oppressed on account of the tour.
63. That he should set his face against gratuitous labour and gratuitous supplies from his subjects. All labour and all supplies should be fairly paid for.
64. That he should carefully note the principle errors of the ways of preceding Gaekwars and carefully avoid them.
65. That he should, as a rule, avoid employing his relations in offices of trust and responsibility.
66. That he should treat the *Sardar* and *Darakdar* classes with kindness and consideration, but on certain fixed principles.
67. That he should be deeply impressed with a sense of the invaluable benefits which India has derived from British domination. He should be enabled to realize adequately the enormous calamities which would overwhelm India if that domination were withdrawn.
68. That he should be specially impressed with the fact that the Baroda State itself is deeply indebted to the British Government.
69. His Highness should be taught the outlines of the British constitution.
70. His Highness should know something of the constitution of the British Indian Government.
71. He should study the treaties between the British Government and the Baroda State, and have a clear perception of his rights and obligations under those treaties.

72. Many useful hints may be given to His Highness as to his maintaining smooth relations with the British representative [at] his court, and availing himself of the benefit of his friendly advice.
73. His Highness should be impressed with the great importance of his continuing to publish an annual Administration Report. It will be an effective guarantee of continued good government.
74. I have given the foregoing items almost at random without special attention to logical order or sequence. But they are by no means exhaustively enumerated. Many other equally important items may suggest themselves, but what I have mentioned is sufficient to make my meaning clear.
75. The continuance and promotion of good government in Baroda will essentially depend on the special education of the Maharaja on the lines above indicated. It is with primary principles of that sort that the Maharaja has to be strongly impressed. Every principle will produce great good or avert great evils. A Maharaja imbued with such principles alone will be able to keep up and promote good government; and without such principles he will not be able to do it, whatever his knowledge of mere details of departmental work.
76. The work of thoroughly inculcating and impressing a body of such principles will, I think, require about a year's time. Every principle has to be clearly expressed, explained, repeated, illustrated, and imprinted on His Highness' mind. His Highness may have a series of notes given [to] him, and he will have to be interrogated in regard to each principle, so as to make sure of his thorough comprehension and recognition of the same. After his learning the primary principles so necessary to form a good ruler, he may enter into the details of the work of each department in succession.
77. The principles, will, I think, be most effectually communicated and impressed by someone, who has had opportunities practically to feel and appreciate their great political value.

APPENDIX III

Correspondence Between the Dewan and the Agent to the Governor-General [1]

27th July 1881

My dear Sir,

I was glad to learn the other day that you had seen my lectures to the Maharajah. I may inform you that, besides these regular lectures, I give His Highness a paper under the head of "Minor Hints". Under this head, I am enabled to place before H.H. a lot of miscellaneous & personal matters which may be of no insignificant practical value to a young ruler. As samples of this subsidiary paper, I beg to send herewith in a separate cover two papers which may be perused and returned at your perfect leisure and convenience.
Yours very sincerely,

T. Madava Row

P.S. It is not that my papers are simply read to H.H. I enter into explanations, illustrations, and so on so as to impress in detail what is noted in substance in these papers.

27th July 1881

My dear Sir,

I have read with much pleasure the two papers of "minor hints" which you have sent me this morning. The idea is excellent. I should like to be able to see all your lectures & papers as *c.c.* immediately after they are delivered, if possible, for they are very interesting.

I return the papers.

Yours very sincerely,

P.S. Melvill

4th August 1881

My dear Sir,

I beg to send herewith in a separate cover my paper on the subject of "The Palace" with which I was occupied with His Highness yesterday. I feel much encouraged by the favourable opinion you have generally expressed regarding these papers. I am taking some pains in the preparation of these papers in the hope & belief that they will have a beneficial influence on the future of the Baroda State.

Yours very sincerely,

T. Madava Row

APPENDIX IV

Extracts from the Report on the Administration of the Baroda State for 1878–79[1]

[...]

82. The petitioners also plainly object to the new police which has been established by the present Administration. The country needed this measure more than anything else. No doubt, the new police is expensive; but without it, the State could not discharge its fundamental duty of protecting life and property. Life and property used to be, in large portions of our territories, in a fearful state of insecurity. Fields and highways, and even villages, were infested with impunity by organized gangs of inveterate and merciless marauders, both homebred and foreign. Depredations in broad daylight and attended with serious wounding and loss of innocent life were of painfully frequent occurrence. Happily, this intolerable state of things has ceased, and this result is owing chiefly to the instrumentality of the new police.
83. The petitioners object to the new police chiefly because, according to their own judgment, instead of organizing the new police, the Administration should have increased the *karkhanas* of the *Sardars* and increased the allowances of the *Sardars*. I can only say that it is not possible to agree with the petitioners in this opinion, which does not seem to spring from higher motives than

those of self-interest. This divergence of opinion needs to be unreservedly recorded here. I certainly think that if the Administration had done what the petitioners say it should have done, it would have perpetrated an inexcusable blunder.

84. The petitioners take occasion to assert with surprising confidence that, in their opinion, the new police "scarcely performs its duties with half the success which used to attend our arms." But the petitioners are hardly competent to form a correct opinion on this point.

[...]

98. The petitioners express, in the course of their petition under remark, a feeling that they are not treated with confidence by the Administration, and they exemplify this general allegation by allusion to the fact that none of them was utilized in the repression of crimes of violence in the Karri Division.

99. I do not think that the status of the petitioners in this respect has really undergone any material alteration injurious to their interests. But, in any circumstances, it seems manifest that public confidence is a thing which should be won, and not exacted. The Administration is willing to give confidence, but there is the correlative duty on the other side to deserve confidence. It has to be deserved on the part of the petitioners by the acquisition of knowledge, by the exercise of judgement, by the constant exhibition of disinterested motives, and by sincere devotion to public welfare. This is a long and laborious process.

100. With reference to the special illustration adduced by the petitioners, I must offer some detailed observations. The Administration would be only too happy to avail itself of the services of any of the petitioners in putting down an outbreak of crimes of violence, if only they were prepared to render such services as the occasion and circumstances would require. Having conferred with some of the petitioners on the subject, I fear they are not so prepared. They are hardly prepared to proceed with a light equipage and with a small staff: they are rather addicted to what are analogous to processions of State. They are hardly prepared to move about in a moderately expensive manner; on

the contrary, they desire to spend a great deal on entertainments, on *nautches*, in making presents, and generally on pomp and show. They are hardly prepared to move about in a manner unoppressive* to the rural population: it is to be feared that their demands for impressed carriage, for forage and provisions, etc., etc., would be excessive and often intolerable. They are not prepared to act under the orders and restraints of the local magistrates whom they superciliously regard as very much their inferiors in rank and dignity. Obviously, the Administration cannot let loose a number of *Sardars* with bodies of armed followers to roam aimlessly over the realm without any guidance and control from the local magistrates responsible for the peace of the country. Apart from all this matter, the *Sardars* have yet to acquire the knowledge essentially necessary for acting rightly and within proper bounds even in suppressing crimes of violence. It is essential to know, for instance, in what circumstances they could order their men to fire or to use any deadly weapons, and in what circumstances they would not be justified in so ordering.

101. And there are other difficulties also. A *Sardar*, if employed on the work of suppressing crimes, would have frequent occasion to give his evidence in criminal trials. But the *Sardars* think it a great loss of *abru* to attend and give evidence.

102. Again, when persons are killed, an inquest must, of course, be held to ascertain that there has been no needless loss of life. It would devolve on the *Sardar* to testify to the precise circumstances in which his action caused death. But the *Sardars* are extremely averse to such proceedings. Their petition itself shows how unwilling they are to attend judicial investigations and how unwilling they are that even their followers and dependents should attend such investigations. They desire for themselves and for all their relations, retainers, servants, and *karkoons*, exemption from the jurisdiction of the ordinary tribunals.

---

* Per the original: inoppressive.

103. Again, a *Sardar*, employed in the responsible work of suppressing crime, might really misconduct himself, or might be liable to a *prima facie* charge of misconduct. The matter must be investigated by the local Magistracy. The *Sardar* would, in such a case, have to be placed in the position of a defendant. The *Sardar* who imagines it derogatory to appear even as a witness would probably refuse to appear as a defendant before the local Magistracy. In this refusal he might be backed by his ignorant armed followers and dependents. It would then entail the necessity of sending another military force to reduce the recalcitrant *Sardar* to obedience.

104. The result would be that the *Sardar* would have to be punished, first, for his original misconduct; and, secondly, for his resistance to lawful authority. However measured and mild the punishment, his fellow *Sardars* would consider it extremely hard and humiliating, and would afford their abundant and active sympathy to their compeer in trouble.

105. It is because I have carefully anticipated these and other difficulties and embarrassments, that I have not been eager to employ any of the *Sardars* in the work of suppressing crime in the Karri Division. I regret to be compelled by duty to express my conviction that the employment of the *Sardars* generally in such work at present would be a remedy far worse than the disease. Every consideration of duty and good policy induced me to decidedly prefer to intrust the work to our regular police. The regular police has done the work.

106. Among the motives which actuate me to abstain at present from employing the *Sardars* in such work is certainly included one of kindly feelings to the *Sardars* themselves. Such employment of them without the necessary preliminary training would only end in their dismissal one after another, a consummation which I devoutly deprecate.

[...]

APPENDIX V

Circular of 23 October, 1875[1]

1. All heads of departments and other officers who have the power of appointing and promoting, and of fixing, suspending, degrading and dismissing any public servants should themselves be guided by the under-mentioned principles, and see that officers subordinate to them are guided by the same.
2. It should be remembered that these powers furnish the means of rewarding on the one hand, and of punishing on the other. Upon the manner in which these powers are exercised will largely depend [on] the character, efficiency and reputation of the administration.

Appointments & Promotions

3. Official aptitude—the possession of the qualifications required for the satisfactory performance of the duties of the particular office concerned—should be the chief ground of selection.
4. Persons already employed in the department itself should have preference over those employed in other Departments.
5. Persons employed in other departments of the State should have preference over persons not in employment.
6. Persons thrown out of employment for no fault of their own, but in consequence of recent State measures should be re-employed to the utmost extent possible. Lists of such persons should be

obtained from the *Huzur*, and such persons should be otherwise sought out.

7. Persons who are natives of the country should have preference over strangers.
8. Promotions should be so made as to benefit the largest number of servants possible.
9. When it becomes absolutely necessary to import strangers they should be employed under sanction of the *Huzur* and, generally, on a year's probation.
10. Minors and superannuated men should not be employed on any account.
11. Men who were dismissed for misconduct indicating moral turpitude, should not be appointed.
12. Too many of one class of individuals, likely to form pernicious cliques, should not be appointed in the same department. There should be a judicious mixture or variety. Though there ought to be a preponderance of Mahrattas and Gujaratis, there ought to be a due proportion of Parsis, Mahomedans etc.
13. Too many relations of one and the same person should not be employed in the same department. Indeed, such relations should not be employed unless there be a clear and unavoidable necessity.
14. No head of department should employ or promote his own relative without sanction of the *Huzur*.
15. A similar rule applies to the employment of any relative of the head of any other department.

Fining, Suspending, Degrading & Dismissing

16. These punitive powers should be firmly exercised whenever necessary, but with all due deliberation and with due consideration. Nothing should be done in impatience, haste or anger. There should not be even the appearance of such.
17. Before any punishment is inflicted, the party concerned should have every fair opportunity to afford any explanations in his power, and such explanation should be fully and fairly considered.

18. Repeated fines should be avoided.
19. Fines should be generally very moderate in amount, the object being to mark displeasure, and not to starve the servant and his family.
20. No person should be suspended unless there is a *prima facie* case fairly made out.
21. A suspended servant should not be kept in suspense needlessly. The requisite investigation should be speedily completed, and a definite conclusion arrived at.
22. Similar principles apply to degrading and dismissing.
23. As a person, once properly dismissed, will not be re-employed anywhere in the public service, the utmost care, not falling much short of judicial exactitude, should be used to ascertain the sufficiency of the grounds for dismissal.
24. To enable higher authorities to judge of the punitive action taken, the grounds of such action together with the defence of the party punished should be fully but briefly and clearly recorded at the time itself. And such record should be sent up to higher authority whenever required.
25. The party punished should be furnished, without any delay, with an endorsement showing the grounds of his punishment, if he applies for the same.

    Note: This need not be [done] in the instance of fines, a Register shall be kept in the department concerned.

General Remarks

26. The capital objects to be aimed at are,
    i. The most qualified persons should be secured.
    ii. Good conduct should be stimulated by the prospect of secure tenure of office and of probable promotion.
    iii. Bad conduct should be discouraged by the prospect of punishment and permanent exclusion from the service.

T. Madava Row
Dewan

A NOTE ON PREVIOUS EDITIONS

The original, handwritten memos (or lecture manuscripts) that constitute the first part of *Hints on the Art and Science of Government* have been traced to the Mythic Society in Bengaluru (henceforth referred to as the *Mythic* Mss.)[1]. The *Mythic* Mss. contains the memos on fundamental principles of public administration, the original, handwritten memos on personal conduct remain untraceable. Page marks indicate that the *Mythic* Mss. was previously housed in the library of Madhava Rao's eldest son, T. Ananda Rao, who served as Dewan of Mysore from 1909 to 1912.

Copies of two memos ('Subscriptions' and the first part of 'Relations with British Government'), which Philip Melvill sent to Calcutta for the Viceroy to peruse, are located at the National Archives of India in New Delhi (henceforth referred to as the *NAI* Mss.).[2]

Little is known about prior publications of Rao's lectures. We do not know when they were printed or how many copies were printed. Three editions remain in circulation. All were printed with the misleading title *Minor Hints* (which was actually Rao's informal title for the lectures on personal conduct only).

One edition was printed by the Bombay-based Times of India Press (henceforth the *Times* edition).[3] The only copy still in circulation is a microfilm version held by the Center for Research Libraries in Chicago (which is itself a copy of a now untraceable microfilm scanned in 1982 by the Library of Congress Office in New Delhi). The *Times* edition is the closest match to the *Mythic* Mss. and *NAI* Mss. Like them, the *Times* edition subtitles every lecture as a 'memo'. It also numbers the paragraphs in the same way. It differs in one respect: it employs distinctive running heads (a heading printed along the top of each page) that highlight the key theme of the associated section. This indicates editorial intervention, though by whom remains a mystery.

At least two distinct editions of *Minor Hints* were printed at the Bombay-based British India Press. One edition eventually made its way via Arvind Desai, an antiquarian bookseller in Ahmedabad, to the University of California (henceforth the *Desai* edition).[4] This is the only physical copy in circulation today. The text of the *Desai* edition is identical to the *Mythic* Mss. and *NAI* Mss. as well as the printed *Times* edition. However, the presentation differs in a number of respects. The *Desai* edition adds paragraph summaries throughout the text, numbers the memos, and includes an index. It even re-numbers some of the paragraphs within the memos. For example, the original memo entitled 'Relations with British Government' consists of a sequentially numbered list of points from (1) to (29). The *Desai* edition retains the text but reduces the numbering to (14) points, because it converts some of the paragraphs into sub-paragraphs marked by small case letters (a) to (g). All this indicates significant editorial intervention, though by whom once again remains a mystery.

A second edition from the British India Press only survives on microfilm. It too is held by the Center for Research Libraries in Chicago.[5] This microfilm is of a copy that once belonged to Chandrojirao Angre, a prominent landlord in Gwalior and later key figure in the Hindu Mahasabha, who was interested in the topic of personal conduct, even writing about it himself (henceforth the *Angre* edition).[6] The presentation of the *Angre* edition differs from the *Desai* edition in two respects. It features a "Short Summary of Contents of the Minor Hints by Raja Sir T. Madhavrao"—in effect a very detailed table of contents—which is entirely missing from the *Desai* edition. The heading of this curious section suggests that *Angre* edition was not overseen by Madhava Rao's associates or descendants, since it spells his name in a way that was used by the Marathi press, but which was not how he spelt his name in his letters or publications (where he used Madava Row or Madhava Rao). The *Angre* edition also differs from the *Desai* edition in placing the index after the table of contents rather than at the end of the book.

All three editions described above—*Times*, *Desai*, and *Angre*—are undated, making it difficult to ascertain their relationship and sequencing. The variances detailed above suggest that they were products of different minds. We have a little more to go on when it comes to dating the *Desai* edition. There are noticeable similarities in presentation between the *Desai* edition and two related compendiums—*Notes of Lectures* by Pestanji Jehangir, who lectured Sayaji Rao on the Settlement and Military Departments, and *Lectures Delivered to H.H. The Maharaja Gaekwar*, which brought together the lectures delivered by Kazi Shahabuddin on revenue administration, Anna Bhivrao Tahmane on accounts, and Cursetji Thanawalla and Janardhan Gadgil on law respectively.[7] All three texts were printed at different presses but they format the text in identical fashion. In particular, all three have emblazoned on the title page in identical type the phrase "For Private Circulation". This leads to the conclusion that one of these texts served as the template for the others. So which came first?

Lectures Delivered to H.H. The Maharaja Gaekwar by Shahabuddin et al appears to have been printed after 1888.[8] If so, it was preceded by Jehangir's *Notes of Lectures*, which was printed in Ahmedabad in 1884 (a second edition followed in 1890).[9] Thus, arises the question: was the book that has come down to us as *Minor Hints* printed before 1884? Rao never alluded to the existence of *Minor Hints*. Nor is there any mention of the text in the press or the catalogs of the India Office. It is highly unlikely that Rao would have permitted the lecture notes to be printed without correcting the title as well as obvious spelling and typographical errors. All this suggests that the *Desai* edition was printed posthumously—in other words, after 1891. Bear in mind, however, that because the surviving microfilm copy of the *Times* edition lacks a title page, we do not know exactly how it relates to the *Desai* edition. It is very possible that the more spartan *Times* edition came first, being printed only as a souvenir, and that Jehangir's more polished *Notes on Lectures* promoted the Gaekwad's aides to use it as a template for the *Desai* edition as well as *Lectures Delivered* by Shahabuddin et al, with the *Angre* edition being a still later venture. This is only a conjecture, however.

There may be other editions (or additional copies of the editions noted above) still held privately in India that could shed light on the puzzles noted above. We know from Philip Sergeant's *The Ruler of*

Baroda and Edith Tottenham's *Highness of Hindostan* that Sayaji Rao's guests examined a copy of *Minor Hints* in 1928 and 1934 respectively.[10] The copy seen by Sergeant included the phrase "For Private Circulation", making it very likely that it was a British India Press edition. The Gaekwad's descendants may still retain this copy. There appears to be a third British India Press edition, held by Madhava Rao's great-great granddaughter, Urmila Rau Lal (henceforth the *Rau* edition). This edition was apparently printed in 1905.[11] It is not open to inspection at present.

An abridged Hindi-language edition of *Minor Hints*, entitled *Rajya Prabandh Shiksha* (or *Instruction on Public Administration*), appeared in 1913. This translation, by the renowned Hindi scholar and critic Ramachandra Shukla, was commissioned by the Kashi Nagari Pracharini Sabha (Society for the Promotion of the Nagari Script and Language), the celebrated Benares institution that translated a number of important texts into Hindi. The text was based on a copy of *Minor Hints* gifted to the Sabha by Uday Singh, the Raja of Bhinga. Unfortunately, this *Kashi* edition is no longer in circulation. However, the translation was republished by the Sabha in 1928 with The Indian Press in Allahabad.[12] The only physical copy of this *Allahabad* edition still in circulation can be found at the University of Wisconsin-Madison. It is possible that additional copies still exist in India (Osmania University in Hyderabad appears to have once had a copy, which can now be found online).

A modern reprint of *Minor Hints* was published in 1985 by the Ahmedabad-based Sahitya Mudranalaya Press (henceforth the *Mudranalaya* edition).[13] Commissioned by the Education Department of the Government of Gujarat, this was a reproduction of the *Desai* edition, to which was appended a foreword by K. P. Yajnik. Copies of the *Mudranalaya* edition are held by the Library of Congress in Washington, DC and Parliament Library in New Delhi. There will be additional copies archived in Gujarat.

A Summary of the Manuscripts and Printed Editions

Mythic Mss.: the original handwritten memos or lectures on fundamental principles of public administration, held by the Mythic Society in Bengaluru.

A NOTE ON PREVIOUS EDITIONS

NAI Mss.: copies of two memos ('Subscriptions' and the first part of 'Relations with British Government'), held by the National Archive of India in New Delhi.

Times: undated, printed at the Times of India Press, held on microfilm by the Center for Research Libraries in Chicago.

Desai: undated, printed at the British India Press, once owned by Arvind Desai, now held by the University of California, Santa Barbara.

Angre: undated, printed at the British India Press, once owned by Chandrojirao Angre, held on microfilm by the Center for Research Libraries.

Rau: apparently dated 1905, printed at the British India Press, held by Urmila Rau Lal, copy presently not available for inspection.

Kashi: published 1913 by the Kashi Nagari Pracharini Sabha, abridged and translated into Hindi by Ramchandra Shukla, no longer in circulation.

Allahabad: published 1928 by The Indian Press, reprint of the 1913 *Kashi* edition, held by the University of Wisconsin-Madison.

Mudranalaya: published 1985 by Sahitya Mudranalaya Press, a reproduction of the *Desai* edition, held by the Library of Congress in Washington, DC and Parliament Library in New Delhi.

NOTES

PREFACE

1. These important works include Robin Jeffrey, *The Decline of Nair Dominance: Society and Politics in Travancore, 1847–1908*, New Delhi: Manohar, 2014; *Manu Bhagavan, Sovereign Spheres: Princes, Education and Empire in Colonial India*, New Delhi, Oxford University Press, 2003; Caroline Keen, *Princely India and the British: Political Development and the Operation of Empire*, London: I.B. Tauris, 2012; Ian Copland, *The British Raj and the Indian Princes*, New Delhi: Orient Longman, 1982; Barbara N. Ramusack, *The Indian Princes and their States*, New York: Cambridge University Press, 2003; Manu Pillai, *The Ivory Throne: Chronicles of the House of Travancore*, New Delhi: HarperCollins, 2016; Ajit K. Neogy, *The Paramount Power and the Princely States of India, 1858–1881*, K. P. Bagchi & Co., 1979; Waltraud Ernst and Biswamoy Pati, eds., *India's Princely States: People, Princes and Colonialism*, London: Routledge, 2007.
2. S.V. Puntambekar, "Raja Sir T Madhava Rao's Prince or the Law of Dependent Monarchies", *Indian Journal of Political Science*, Vol. 5, No. 4, 1944, pp. 293–305. Also see C.S. Srinivasachari, "The Political Ideas and Ideals of Rajah Sir T Madhava Rao", *Indian Journal of Political Science*, Vol. 5, No. 4, 1944, 407–08.
3. M. Rama Jois, *Raja Dharma with Lessons on Raja Neeti*, New Delhi: Universal Law Publishing Co., 2014. xvii, xxiii–xxiv.

INTRODUCTION: THE PROGRESSIVE MAHARAJA

1. Madava Row, *Testimonials of Sir T. Madava Row*, Bombay: Times of India Steam Press, 1875, pp. 5–6.
2. Madava Row, *Three Addresses*, Madras: Higginbotham & Co., 1884, p. 17.
3. [Vishakham Tirunal], "A Native Statesman", *Calcutta Review*, Vol. 55, No. 110, 1872, p. 230.
4. John Bruce Norton, "Address on the Twelfth Anniversary of Patcheappah's Institution 1855" in *The Educational Speeches of the Hon'ble John Bruce Norton*, Madras: C. D'Cruiz, 1870, p. 31.

5. V. Nagam Aiya, *The Travancore State Manual*, Trivandrum: Travancore Government Press, 1906, p. 588.
6. "Progress of the Young Princes of Travancore, in their Education Under Madava Row", Madras Proceedings, 24 February, 1854, Nos. 17–19, p. 763 (British Library, IOR/P/321/8).
7. "Progress of the Young Princes of Travancore", p. 730.
8. "A Native Statesman", p. 237.
9. Row, *Testimonials*, pp. 12–13.
10. [Vishakham Tirunal], "A Political Sketch of Travancore", *Madras Athenaeum*, 25 October, 1856.
11. [Tirunal], "A Native Statesman", pp. 244–45.
12. Norton, "Address on the Twelfth Anniversary", p. 31.
13. Robin Jeffrey, *Politics, Women and Well-Being: How Kerala Became 'a Model'*, London: Palgrave, 2016, p. 163.
14. Robin Jeffrey, *The Decline of Nair Dominance: Society and Politics in Travancore, 1847–1908*, New Delhi: Manohar, 2014, pp. 89–90, 98–100.
15. [Tirunal], "A Native Statesman", pp. 250–51.
16. Row, *Testimonials*, pp. 23–32.
17. "An Instance of the Indirect Effects of Our Rule", *The Friend of India*, 15 January, 1863, p. 59; "Travancore", *The Friend of India*, 30 August, 1866, p. 1018.
18. *The Pioneer*, 6 July, 1870.
19. Manu Pillai, *The Ivory Throne: Chronicles of the House of Travancore*, New Delhi: HarperCollins, 2016, Ch. 9.
20. Henry D. Daly, *Report on the Political Administration of the Territories Comprised Within Central India Agency 1871–72*, Calcutta: Foreign Department Press, 1873, p. 2; Henry D. Daly, *Report on the Political Administration of the Territories Comprised within the Central India Agency for the Year 1868–69*, Calcutta: Foreign Department Press, 1870, p. 11.
21. "Appointment of Sir Madava Rao as Minister of Baroda", India Proceedings, Foreign Department, Political, August 1875, No. 78, p. 95 (British Library, IOR/P/776).
22. "Presentation of A Farewell Address to Sir T. Madava Row", *The Times of India*, 7 May, 1875, p. 3.
23. Behramji M. Malabari, *Gujarat and the Gujaratis: Pictures of Men and Manners Taken from Life*, London: W.H. Allen & Co., 1882, p. 70; *Report on the Administration of the Baroda State for 1875–76*, Calcutta: Foreign Department Press, 1877, p. 3.
24. Malabari, *Gujarat and the Gujaratis*, p. 53.
25. *Report on the Administration of the Baroda State for 1880–81*, Calcutta: Foreign Department Press, 1882, p. 155.
26. Malabari, *Gujarat and the Gujaratis*, pp. 49–50.
27. "Present Administration of the Baroda State", India Proceedings, Foreign Department, March, 1876, No 569, p. 523 (British Library, IOR/P/1031); *Report on the Administration of the Baroda State for 1876–77*, Calcutta: Foreign Department Press, 1878, p. 22.

28. *Report on the Administration of the Baroda State for 1879–80*, Calcutta: Foreign Department Press, 1881, p. 53.
29. *The Times of India*, 1 December, 1875, p. 2
30. Malabari, *Gujarat and the Gujaratis*, pp. 78–79.
31. *The Groans of Baroda or An Appeal on Behalf of Distressed Humanity*, Baroda, 1881, pp. 7–8 (British Library, Tr. 506(n)). Also see *Amrita Bazar Patrika*, 30 June, 1881. The title was a play on *The Groans of the Britons*, a famous mid-fifth century document, wherein Britons appealed to the Roman Empire for aid against invaders.
32. "Col. Biddulph's Note on Baroda Affairs", Foreign Department, Confidential-B, Internal Branch, Section-A, 1895, pp. 11–12 (British Library, IOR/R/1/1/1040).
33. William Waterfield to Alfred Lyall, 12 June, 1881 in "Baroda Affairs", Political and Secret Memoranda, Section D, 1881 (British Library, IOR/L/PS/18/D77).
34. Robert Bourke to Frederick Temple, 14 January, 1888 in *Papers of the 1st Marquess of Dufferin, Correspondence in India Vol. I* (British Library, IOR Neg 4367/2–4368/1).
35. "The Death of Sir Madhava Rao", *The Pioneer*, 7 April,1891.
36. "Raja Sir T. Madhav Rao K.C.S.I.", *Quarterly Journal of the Poona Sarvajanik Sabha*, Vol. 14, No. 1, 1891, pp. 1, 35. Originally published anonymously, the essay was later included in *The Select Writings of M. G. Ranade on Indian States*, ed., Vasudeo Waman Thakur, Indore: Datta Printing Works, 1942.
37. The number, extent, and wealth of the Native States varied over time. For instance compare C.U.A [Charles U. Aitchison], *The Native States of India: An Attempt to Elucidate a Few of the Principles which Underlie their Relations with the British Government*", Simla: Government Central Branch Press, 1875, p. 1; George Robinson, *The Native States of India: A Paper Read Before the Leeds Philosophical and Literary Society*, London: Kegan Paul, Trench & Co., 1886, p. 4; William Lee-Warner, *The Protected Princes of India*, London: Macmillan and Co., 1894, v.
38. *Report on the Administration of the Baroda State for 1875–76*, Calcutta: Foreign Department Press, 1876, pp. 19-20.
39. Robinson, *The Native States of India*, p. 23.
40. Robinson, *The Native States of India*, p. 28.
41 Observations (Speech of Samuel Liang), 24 May 1867, *Hansard*, London: Her Majesty's Stationery Office, Vol. 187, Col. 1054.
42. Observations (Speech of Viscount Cranborne), 24 May 1867, *Hansard*, London: Her Majesty's Stationery Office, Vol. 187, Col. 1074.
43. *Baroda Enquiry Commission Report, 1874*, pp. 4-8 in *Papers of Sir Lewis Pelly* (British Library, Mss. Eur F126/78).
44. John Malcolm, *The Government of India*, London: John Murray, 1833, Appendix D, p. 154. More generally see, Michael Herbert Fisher, *Indirect Rule in India: Residents and the Residency System, 1764–1858*, Delhi, Oxford University Press, 1998.
45. Robinson, *The Native States of India*, p. 7.
46. Observations (Speech of Viscount Cranborne), 24 May 1867, Col. 1074.
47. Robinson, *The Native States of India*, p. 24.
48. George R. Gleig, *The Life of Major-General Sir Thomas Munro*, London: Samuel Bentley, 1831, Vol. 2, p. 350.

49. Question (Speech of Viscount Cranborne), 22 February 1867, *Hansard*, London: Her Majesty's Stationery Office, Vol. 185, Col. 831, 839.
50. John Malcolm, *A Memoir of Central India*, London: Kingsbury, Parbury & Allen, 1824, Vol. II, pp. 457–462.
51. Daly, *Report on the Political Administration of the Central India Agency 1871–72*, p. 3.
52. Question (Speech of Viscount Cranborne), 22 February 1867, Col. 841.
53. Observations (Speech of Stafford Northcote) 24 May 1867, *Hansard*, London: Her Majesty's Stationery Office, Vol. 187, Col.1068.
54. *Ibid*.
55. Anand A. Yang, "An Institutional Shelter, The Court of Wards in Late Nineteenth-Century Bihar", Modern Asian Studies, Vol.13, No. 2, 1979, pp. 260-61.
56. [Takhtsinhji] Bhavsinhji, *Forty Years of the Rajkumar College, 1870–1910: An Account of the Origin and Progress of the Rajkumar College*, London: Hazel, Watson & Viney, 1911, p. 5.
57. Chester Macnaghten, "Rajkumar Colleges", *Calcutta Review*, Vol. 68, No. 136, 1879, p. 270.
58. Bhavsinhji, *Forty Years of the Rajkumar College*, p. 6.
59. Bhavsinhji, *Forty Years of the Rajkumar College*, p. 7.
60. Lewis Bowring, *Eastern Experiences*, London: Henry S. King & Co., 1871, 210–12.
61. Francis Napier to Thomas Baring, 16 May, 1872, p. 2 in *Papers of the Earl of Northbrook* (British Library, Mss. Eur C144/13).
62. *Baroda Enquiry Commission Report, 1874*, p. 6.
63. "Report by the Viceroy, Lord Northbrook, Giving his View on the Conduct of Affairs in Baroda", 9 April, 1875, p. 3 in *Papers of Sir Lewis Pelly* (British Library, Mss. Eur F126/93); Robert Phayre to Charles Gonne, 17 November, 1874 in *Correspondence Relating to the Appointment of a Commission to Investigate Certain Charges Against the Gaekwar*, London: Her Majesty's Stationery Office, 1875, p. 6.
64. *Baroda Enquiry Commission Report*, p. 8.
65. *Report of The Commission Appointed to Inquire into The Administration of The Baroda State*, London: Her Majesty's Stationery Office, 1875, p. 10
66. *Baroda Enquiry Commission Report*, pp. 9–10.
67. *Report of The Commission*, p. 69–70.
68. *Report of The Commission*, p. 79–80.
69. *Report of The Commission*, pp. 349–51.
70. *Report of The Commission*, p. 353.
71. Thomas Baring to Madava Row, 11 May, 1875, p. 92 in *Papers of the Earl of Northbrook* (British Library, Mss. Eur C144/17).
72. Robert Bulwer-Lytton to Robert Cecil, 11 May, 1876, pp. 149–50 in *Papers of 1st Earl of Lytton* (British Library, Mss. Eur E218/18).
73. Robert Cecil to Robert Bulwer-Lytton, 28 July, 1876, p. 148 in *Papers of 3rd Marquess of Salisbury* (British Library, IOR Neg 11688/2).
74. Robert Bulwer-Lytton to Robert Cecil, 8 February, 1878, p. 101 in *Papers of 1st Earl of Lytton* (British Library, Mss. Eur E218/20).

75. Robert Bulwer-Lytton to James Gordon, 8 September, 1879, p. 727–28 in *Papers of 1st Earl of Lytton* (British Library, Mss. Eur E218/21).
76. Governor-General-in-Council to the Secretary of State for India, 22 May, 1879 in India Proceedings, Foreign Department, Secret, July, 1879, No. 311, pp. 380–81 (British Library, IOR/P/1389).
77. Robert Bulwer-Lytton to James Gordon, 21 June, 1878, p. 425 in *Papers of 1st Earl of Lytton* (British Library, Mss. Eur E218/20).
78. Robert Bulwer-Lytton to Alfred Lyall, pp. 27–28 in *Papers of Sir Alfred Lyall* (British Library, Mss. Eur F132/22).
79. "Transfer of Administrative Power to the Gaekwar of Baroda", Foreign Department, Political-A, Nos. 51–63, KW No. 1, July 1881 (National Archives of India).
80. "Transfer of Administrative Powers to Gaekwar", India Proceedings, Foreign Department, July, 1881, No. 60, pp. 103–05 (British Library, IOR/P/1742).
81. William Waterfield to Alfred Lyall, 2 July, 1881, in "Baroda Affairs", p. 4.
82. "Conduct of Business in Baroda State After Accession of Gaekwar to Power", India Proceedings, Foreign Department, April, 1882, No. 225, pp. 192–94 (British Library, IOR/P/1917).
83. *Ibid*.
84. Waterfield to Lyall, 2 July, 1881, in "Baroda Affairs", 4.
85. Waterfield to Lyall, 2 July, 1881, in "Baroda Affairs", p. 6; *Charu Varta*, 1 August, 1881 in *Report on Native Papers Week Ending 13th August 1881*, 1881, No. 33, p. 2 (British Library, IOR/L/R/5/7).
86. "A Draft Constitution for Baroda", *Amrita Bazar Patrika*, 21 July, 1881, p. 3. Also see *Amrita Bazar Patrika*, 11 August, 1881, p. 6; *The Tribune*, 27 August, 1881, pp. 6–7.
87. *The Pioneer*, 8 July, 1881, 1.
88. Waterfield to Lyall, 2 July, 1881, in "Baroda Affairs", p. 6.
89. Alfred C. Lyall, "Memorandum", 20 September, 1881 in "Conduct of Business", No. 222, p. 185.
90. Lyall, "Memorandum", p. 186.
91. Waterfield to Lyall, 12 June, 1881, in "Baroda Affairs", p. 3
92. "Baroda. Education of Young Gaekwar. Raja's School", India Proceedings, Foreign Department, January 1876, No. 112, p. 82 (British Library, IOR/P/1031).
93. "Baroda. Education of Young Gaekwar. Raja's School", p. 82.
94. "Baroda. Education of Young Gaekwar. Raja's School", p. 82.
95. Henry Butler to Thomas Baring, 17 September, 1875 in *Papers of the Earl of Northbrook* (British Library, Mss. Eur. C144/23).
96. Richard Meade to Thomas Baring, 8 November, 1875, p. 413 in *Papers of the Earl of Northbrook* (British Library, Mss. Eur. C144/17).
97. "Baroda. Education of Young Gaekwar. Raja's School", p. 81.
98. Madhava Rao to Frederick Elliot, 15 December, 1875 in "Education of H.H. The Maharaja Saheb", Huzur Political Office, Section No. 74, Daftar No. 54, File No. 1, 1876–1881 (Baroda Records Room).

99. Khasherao Jadhav, *Wake Up Princes*, Bombay: Karnatak Press, 1921, pp. 112–13. More generally see Ramachandra Pant Amatiya, "The Ajnapatra or Royal Edict", trans. S. V. Puntambekar, *Journal of Indian History*, Vol. 8, No. 1, 1929, p. 97.
100. Madhava Rao to Frederick Elliot, 22 August, 1876 in "Education of H.H. The Maharaja Saheb".
101. *The Times of India*, 18 January, 1882, p. 4.
102. Philip Melvill to Madhava Rao, 19 April, 1876 in "Education of H.H. The Maharaja Saheb: Establishment of H.H. The Maharaja Saheb", Huzur Political Office, Section No. 74, Daftar No. 54, File No 5, 1879–1881 (Baroda Records Room).
103. *Ibid*.
104. Madhava Rao to Frederick Elliot, 25 August, 1879 in "Education of H.H. The Maharaja Saheb".
105. Madhava Rao to Frederick Elliot, 24 November, 1876 in "Education of H.H. The Maharaja Saheb".
106. "Suggestions to His Highness the Gaikwar of Baroda Regarding the Future Constitution", *The Quarterly Journal of the Poona Sarvajanik Sabha*, Vol. 4, No. 3, 1882, p. 29.
107. Madhava Rao to Philip Melvill, 19 August, 1880 in "Education of H.H. The Maharaja Saheb".
108. Stanley Rice, *Life of Sayaji Rao III*, London: Humphrey Milford, Vol. 1, 1931, p. 35.
109. "Memorandum by Sir Madhava Rao, 27th September 1880", India Proceedings, Foreign Department, No. 53, July, 1881 (British Library, IOR/P/1742).
110. "Transfer of Administrative Powers to Gaekwar", p. 98.
111. "Transfer of Administrative Powers to Gaekwar", p. 99.
112. Madhava Rao to William Waterfield, 3 May, 1881 in "Report on the Education of H.H. the Maharaja Saheb Submitted by the Tutor and Governor", Huzur Political Office, Section No. 74, Daftar No. 54, File No. 6, p. 40 (Baroda Records Room).
113. Frederick Elliot to Philip Melvill, 3 January, 1882 in "Report on the Education of H.H.", p. 48.
114. Madhava Rao to Philip Melvill, 27 July, 1881 in "Section 5: Baroda Durbar: The Gaekwar and His Ministers" in Baroda Residency Files, Daftar No. 112, Serial No. 560, Vol. 667, pp. 369–71 (Baroda Records Room).
115. Philip Melvill to Madhava Rao, 27 July, 1881 in Baroda Residency Files, Daftar No. 112, Serial No. 560, Vol. 667, p. 373 (Baroda Records Room).
116. Madhava Rao to Philip Melvill, 4 August, 1881 in "Report on the Education of H.H.", p. 34.
117. "Sir Madhava Rao's Lectures to the Young Gaekwar of Baroda on the Administration of State", Foreign Department, Political B, File No. 59–61, January, 1882 (National Archives of India).
118. Elliot to Melvill, "Report on the Education", pp. 46–47.
119. Amatiya, "The Ajnapatra", p. 95.
120. Amatiya, "The Ajnapatra", p. 96.

121. On liberalism in British India, see Christopher A. Bayly, *Recovering Liberties: Indian Thought in the Age of Liberalism and Empire*, New York: Cambridge University Press, 2012, especially Chap. 2–3.
122. *The Ordinances of Manu*, trans. Edward W. Hopkins, London: Trubner & Co., 1884, p. 153.
123. Amatiya, "The Ajnapatra", p. 98.
124. Ramachandra Pant Amatiya, "The Ajnapatra or Royal Edict-II", trans. S. V. Puntambekar, *Journal of Indian History*, Vol. 8, No. 2, 1929, p. 208.
125. Amatiya, "The Ajnapatra-II", p. 219.
126. For instance, see Manu S. Pillai, *False Allies: India's Princes in the Age of Ravi Varma*, New Delhi: Juggernaut, 2021, Ch. 4, which describes some of the advice as "infantilizing".
127. Contrast with Niccolò Machiavelli, *The Prince*, London: J.M. Dent, 1908, Chapter XIV.
128. Machiavelli, *The Prince*, Chapter VI, p. 45.
129. Compare with Machiavelli, *The Prince*, Chapter XVIII.
130. Observing how "bad faith" caused the "destruction of commerce" in medieval Europe, Montesquieu writes that "it turned out that great acts of authority were so clumsy that experience itself has made it known that only goodness of government brings prosperity. One has begun to be cured of Machiavellianism, and one will continue to be cured of it. There must be more moderation in councils" (*The Spirit of the Laws*, eds. Anne M. Cohler, Basia C. Miller and Harold S. Stone, New York: Cambridge University Press, 1989, IV:20, p. 389).
131. *Report on The Political Administration of Baroda State for 1875–76*, p. 39.
132. Elliot to Melvill, 3 January, 1882 in "Report on the Education of H.H.", p. 49. Also see V. K. Chavda, "A Note on Minor Hints", *Proceedings of the Indian History Congress*, Vol. 26, Part II,. 1964, p. 226.
133. *Report on the Administration of the Baroda State for 1880–81*, pp. 75–77.
134. "Installation of the Gaekwar of Baroda", India Proceedings, Foreign Department, April, 1882, No. 299, p. 279 (British Library, IOR/P/1917).
135. *Madras Mail*, 11 February, 1882, p. 2.
136. *The Pioneer*, 4 March, 1882, p. 1
137. "Col. Biddulph's Note on Baroda Affairs", p. 13.
138. "Removal of British Troops from Baroda", Foreign Department, Internal-A, Nos. 65–81, June 1885, KW, p. 15. (British Library, IOR/R/1/1/699).
139. "Col. Biddulph's Note on Baroda Affairs", pp. 20–24. See Machiavelli, *The Prince*, Chapter XXVI. The translation was by Govind Sardesai, *Rajadharma* (Baroda: Baroda Vatasal Press, 1890, pp. 2–4).
140. Sayaji Rao Gaekwad to Harry Carnegy, 28 May, 1902 in "Objectionable Attitude of the Gaekwar of Baroda in Connection with his Proposal to Undertake a Sea Voyage", Foreign Department, Secret-I, No. 33, Enclosure No. 3 (British Library, IOR/R/1/1/284).

141. "Unsatisfactory Attitude Adopted by His Highness the Gaekwar of Baroda Relative to the Inception and Growth of Sedition in his State and in his Opposition to the Policy of the Government of India", Foreign Department, Secret-I, Nos. 37–55, February, 1912, p. 11 (British Library, IOR/R/1/1/466).
142. "Unsatisfactory Attitude Adopted by His Highness", p. 27.
143. "Sedition in Baroda and Gaekwar at Durbar", Political and Secret Department, Internal, Secret, 1911–1916 (British Library, IOR/L/PS/10/264/1).
144. Foreign Department, Secret - Internal, Nos. 1 -12, August 1913 (British Library, IOR/R/1/1/511); "Baroda Affairs", Political and Secret Department, 1917–1929 (British Library, IOR/L/PS/10/264); "Report on Baroda Affairs", Foreign and Political Department, Secret - Internal, Nos. 14–16, July 1916 (IOI/R/1/1/56).
145. "Baroda Affairs", Political and Secret Department, Secret, Internal, 1920, No. 2, (British Library, IOR/L/PS/10/264).
146. File 1294/1912 Pt 2: Baroda Affairs, Political and Secret Department, 1917–1929 (British Library, IOR/L/PS/10/264/2).
147. See, for example, "His Highness Shrimant Sayaji Rao Gaekwad of Baroda", *New Indian Antiquary*, Vol. 1, No. 12, Mar, 1939, p. i–ii; Clayton Sedgwick Cooper, *The Modernizing of the Orient*, New York: McBride, Nast & Co, 1914, Ch. IX; Lalbhai Dholakeya, "Sayaji Rao Gaekwar: The Maker of Modern Baroda", *Feudatory and Zemindari India*, Vol. 9, No. 5, 1930, 235. For a broader overview see David Hardiman, "Baroda: The Structure of a Progressive State" in Robin Jeffrey, ed., *People, Princes, and Paramount Power*, New Delhi: Oxford University Press, 1978; Manu Bhagavan, "Demystifying the 'Ideal Progressive': Resistance through Mimicked Modernity in Princely Baroda, 1900–1913", *Modern Asian Studies*, Vol 35, No. 2, May 2001, 385–409.
148. "Education of Sampatrao and Other Boys", Huzur Political Office, Section No. 74, Daftar No. 54, Years 1881–1885, File No 9. (Baroda Records Room).
149. Foreign and Political Department, 1925, File No. 28 (24)-P(Secret) (British Library, IOR/R/1/1/1482); Foreign and Political Department, R Branch, 1928, File 109(11)-R(C) 1928 , Nos. 1–4 (British Library, IOR/R/1/1/4676); Foreign Department, Confidential - B, Internal Branch, Section-A, No. 147, 1894 (British Library, IOR/1/1/1037); Foreign Department, File S I, January, 1912, Nos. 24–28 (British Library, IOR/R/1/1/463).
150. "Purchase of Property in England by HH the Gaekwar of Baroda", (British Library, IOR/L/PS/11/193); "Proposed Purchase by His Highness the Gaekwar of Baroda", (British Library, IOR/R/1/1/283).
151. "Private Investments of the Gaekwar of Baroda for the Benefit of his Family. Sale of the State Heirlooms and Jewelry by His Highness", Foreign Department, Secret-I, No. 4, December 1905, p. 4. (British Library, IOR/R/1/1/326).
152. "(1) Trial of Mr. V. S. Bapat on Charges of Corruption and Extortion. (2) Reversion to British Service of Mr. F.A.H. Elliot", Foreign Department, Secret-I, Nos. 64–69, November 1895, KW No. 3, p. 14 (British Library, IOR/R/1/1/162).
153. "Visit of H. H. the Gaekwar of Baroda to the Poona Sarvajanik Sabha, an Extremist

Society at Poona", Foreign Department, Confidential-B, Internal Branch, Section-A, Nos. 7–8, 1910, p. 10 (British Library, IOR/R/1/1/1079).

154. "Visit of H. H. the Gaekwar of Baroda to the Poona Sarvajanik Sabha", pp. 31–32.
155. "Memo. on the Gaekwar of Baroda and the Officials of the State", Foreign Department, Confidential-A, Internal Branch, Section-A, No. 22, 1907, p. 6 (British Library, IOR/R/1/1/1000).
156. "Correspondence Regarding the Debts of Jai Sing Rao, a Son of the Gaekwar of Baroda and his Doings in America", Foreign and Political Department, Secret, Internal, No. 32, August 1916 (British Library, IOR/R/1/1/1900).
157. "Affairs of the Baroda State", Foreign Department, Confidential-B, Internal Branch, Section-A, No. 8, 1907, p. 13 (British Library, IOR/R/1/1/1069); "Papers regarding Prince Shivajirao", Huzur Political Office-Confidential Files, Daftar No. 28, File No. 414, 1917–1918 (Baroda Records Room).
158. "Arrangements Made for the Education of Maharaj Kumar Pratap Singh of Baroda" (British Library, IOR/R/1/1/923).
159. "Baroda: Affairs of Maharaj Kumar Dhairyashil Rao", Political (Internal) Department Collection, 1938–1940, No. 16 (British Library, IOR/L/PS/13/1016); "Removal of Maharaj Kumar Dhairyashil Rao", Foreign and Political Department, 1923, File No. 1453-P-Secret (British Library, IOR/R/1/1/1428).
160. Philip W. Sergeant, *The Ruler of Baroda*, London: John Murray, 1928, p. 256.
161. V. K. Chavda, *Sayaji Rao Gaekwad*, New Delhi: National Book Trust, 1972, p. 28; St. Nihal Singh, "H. H. The Maharaja Gaekwar's Administrative Record", *Modern Review*, Vol. 21, No. 3, 1917, p. 310.
162. "Lectures Given to Prince Pratap Singh by R.B. Khaserao B. Jadhav in 1924", Huzur Political Office, Confidential Files, Daftar No. 27, File No. 399, 1924 (Baroda Records Room). Also see Sayaji Rao Gaekwad, "The Education of Princes", *East and West*, Vol 1, No. 3, Jan, 1902.
163. S. C. Srinivasa Charier, *Political Opinions of Raja Sir T. Madava Row*, Madras: Ripon Press, 1890, p. 10.
164. Charier, *Political Opinions*, pp. 92–95.
165. Dadabhai Naoroji, "Poverty of India" in Chunilal Lallubhai Parekh, ed., *Essays, Speeches, Addresses and Writings of the Hon'ble Dadabhai Naoroji*, Bombay: Caxton Press, 1887, pp. 160–291.
166. Charier, *Political Opinions*, pp. 11, 24.
167. Charier, *Political Opinions*, pp. 11, 45.
168. Charier, *Political Opinions*, p. 3.
169. Charier, *Political Opinions*, pp. 26–27, 116.
170. *The Indian Nation Builders Part II*, Madras: Ganesh & Co., 1915, pp. 354–55.
171. "An Indian Statesman on the Congress", *The Tribune*, 26 January, 1889.
172. The Indian Nation Builders Part II, pp. 356.
173. Charier, *Political Opinions*, pp. 12–13.
174. Charier, *Political Opinions*, p. 26.
175. Charier, *Political Opinions*, p. 69.

176. "Madava Row's Successor", *Madras Mail*, October 11, 1871.
177. Rao, *Three Addresses*, p. 33.
178. Charier, *Political Opinions*, p. 49.
179. *The Times of India*, 3 March, 1890, p. 5
180. Charier, *Political Opinions*, pp. 78–79, 87–88.
181. Rangaswami Parthasarathy, *A Hundred Years of the Hindu*, Madras: Kasturi and Sons, 1978, p. 57.
182. The line was adapted from Virgil's *Georgics* (see *Georgics of Vergil*, trans., J. B. Greenough, Boston: Ginn & Co, 1900, Book III:95). The original reads:

    Hunc quoque, ubi aut morbo gravis aut iam segnior annis
    deficit, abde domo nec turpi ignosce senectae.

183. *The Indian Nation Builders Part II*, pp. 356–57.
184. "Sir Madhava Rao", *The Pioneer*, 19 May, 1890, p. 7.
185. Charier, *Political Opinions*, pp. 40, 117.
186. *The Times*, 14 April, 1890, p. 5
187. "Death of Sir T. Madhava Rao", *The Tribune*, 22 April, 1891.

GLOSSARY

This Glossary draws upon the following dictionaries: *A Glossary of Vernacular Judicial and Revenue Terms, and Other Useful Words Occurring in Official Documents*, Calcutta, Superintendent of Government Printing, 1874; Charles Philip Brown, *The Zillah Dictionary*, Madras, Christian Knowledge Society's Press, 1852; T. Craven, *The Royal Dictionary*, Lucknow: Methodist Publishing House, 1900; John Borthwick Gilchrist, *Hindoostanee Philology, Vol. 1*, Edinburg: Walker and Greig, 1810; Ramdhun Sen, *A Dictionary in Persîan and English*, Calcutta: Baptist Mission Press, 1841; *The British Indian Monitor, Vol. 2*, Edinburgh: Walker and Greig, 1808; W. Yates, *Introduction to the Hindustani Language*, Calcutta: Baptist Mission Press, 1843; Henry Yule and Arthur Coke Burnell, *Hobson-Jobson: Being a Glossary of Anglo-Indian Colloquial Words and Phrases*, London: John Murray, 1886.

CHAPTER 3: THE MILITARY FORCE

1. *Report on the Administration of the Baroda State for 1878–79*, Calcutta: Foreign Department Press, 1880, pp. 100–102.
2. François de Salignac de la Mothe-Fénelon, *The Adventures of Telemachus, The Son of Ulysses*, trans. John Hawkesworth, New York: Leavitt, Trow & Co., 1847, pp. 389–92, 400.

CHAPTER 5: DUTIES OF KINGS

1. Emmerich de Vattel, *The Law of Nations: Or Principles of the Law of Nature, Applied to the Conduct and Affairs of Nations and Sovereigns*, Philadelphia: T. & J. W. Johnson, 1844, pp. 12–13.

2. Vattel, *The Law of Nations*, p. 14.
3. Vattel, *The Law of Nations*, p. 16.
4. Vattel, *The Law of Nations*, p. 16.
5. *The Institutes of Manu*, trans. William Jones, Madras: J. Higginbotham, 1863, p. 159.
6. *The Institutes of Manu*, p. 151.
7. *The Institutes of Manu*, p. 263.
8. *Oude: Papers Relating to*. Presented to Both Houses of Parliament by Command of Her Majesty, London: Harrison and Sons, 1856, pp. 165–66.
9. *Oude: Papers Relating to*, pp. 13–14. The original text reads:

   It is not, therefore, to be wondered at that the unexpected ascension of so young a prince to the throne, with the habits described by Captain Shakespear strong upon him, surrounded by low menials who had assisted him in his dissipation, and with only that degree of education which native princes receive, should have led His Majesty to consider himself as having arrived at the height of earthy felicity and, wondering what bonds and laws were to curb the will of a King, to indulge in acts of favouritism to his attendants, without regard to the injury inflicted on his subjects.

10. *Oude: Papers Relating to*, p. 159.
11. *Oude: Papers Relating to*, p. 165.
12. *Oude: Papers Relating to*, p. 61.
13. *Baroda Enquiry Commission Report*, 1874, p. 9 (British Library, Mss. Eur F126/78).
14. *Report on the Administration of the Baroda State for 1878–79*, p. 11.

CHAPTER 8: PUBLIC WORKS DEPARTMENT

1. Edmund Burke, "Speech on Nabob of Arcot's Debts, 28 February 1785" in P. J. Marshall and William B. Todd, eds., *The Writings and Speeches of Edmund Burke, Vol. 5*, India: Madras and Bengal, 1774–1785, Oxford: Oxford University Press, 2014, p. 522.

CHAPTER 16: RELATIONS WITH BRITISH GOVERNMENT

1. Proclamation by the Queen in Council to the Princes, Chiefs and People of India, 1 November 1858, p. 1 (British Library, IOR/L/PS/18/D154).

CHAPTER 17: RELATIONS WITH BRITISH GOVERNMENT

1. Proclamation by the Queen, p. 1.
2. Proclamation by the Queen, p. 2.
3. Neil B. Edmonstone to Thomas H. Villiers, 25 February, 1832 in *Minutes of Evidence Taken Before the Select Committee on the Affairs of the East India Company, Vol. 6*, London: House of Commons, 1832, p. 102.
4. Governor-General of India to His Highness the Gaekwar of Baroda, July 25, 1874

in *Report of the Commission Appointed to Inquire into the Administration of the Baroda State*, London: Her Majesty's Stationery Office, 1875, pp. 355–356.

CHAPTER 19: RIGHTS OF THE BRITISH GOVERNMENT

1. Governor-General of India to His Highness the Gaekwar of Baroda, pp. 355–356.

CHAPTER 46: CONCLUDING ADVICE

1. Secretary of State for India to the Governor-General-in-Council, August 7, 1879 in *Political and Secret Dispatches to India*, Vol. 5, p. 810 (British Library, IOR/L/PS/7/324).

APPENDIX I

1. [Sir T. Madava Row], "Memorandum", printed as Appendix A to "Minute by the Honorable Mr. Tucker" in *Report of the Commission Appointed to Enquire Into the Administration of the Baroda State*, London: Her Majesty's Stationery Office, 1875, 65–79. Henry Pendock St. George Tucker was Pusine Judge of the Bombay High Court and member of the Bombay Legislative Council. Heavily abridged versions of this memorandum were published posthumously as "The Constitution of Native States: An Important Memorandum of the Late Rajah Sir T. Madhava Rao", *Indian Review*, Vol. 7, No. 11, 1906, pp. 422–431; and T. Madhava Row, "Administration of Indian States", *Feudatory and Zemindari India*, Vol. 6, No. 5, 1927, pp. 829–832.
2. James Kent, *Commentaries on American Law*, Boston: Little, Brown and Co, 10th edition, 1860, Vol. 1, p. 623. The text cited reads: "It may be received as a self-evident proposition, universally understood and acknowledged throughout this country, that no person can be taken or imprisoned, or disseised of his freehold, or liberties, or estate, or exiled or condemned, or deprived of life, liberty, or property, unless by the law of the land, or the judgment of his peers".
3. Kent, *Commentaries on American Law*, pp. 623, 675.
4. Kent, *Commentaries on American Law*, p. 675.
5. Kent, *Commentaries on American Law*, pp. 657–661.

APPENDIX II

1. "Memorandum by Sir Madhava Rao, 27th September 1880", India Proceedings, Foreign Department, No. 53, July, 1881 (British Library, IOR/P/1742). An abridged version of this memorandum was posthumously published as "The Education of the Ruling Princes: A Note by the Late Raja Sir T. Madhava Rao", *Feudatory and Zemindari India*, Vol. 1, No. 2, September, 1921, p. 100.

APPENDIX III

1. Baroda Durbar: The Gaekwar and His Ministers: Section 5(o), Baroda Residency Files, Daftar No. 112, Serial No. 560, Volume 667, 1876–1886.

APPENDIX IV

1. *Report on the Administration of the Baroda State for 1878–79*, Calcutta: Foreign Department Press, 1880, pp. 52–53, 55–57. In January 1879, some sixty *Sardars* sent the Government of India a petition protesting Madhava Rao's reforms including his establishment of a modern police force, which they saw as intruding on their ancestral right to preserve law and order. Rao initially rebutted the petition via a confidential memorandum submitted to Philip Melvill in June 1879. He subsequently published extracts from this memorandum in the *Report on the Administration of the Baroda State for 1878–79*.

APPENDIX V

1. This circular is incorporated in the *Mythic* Mss. (*Report on Administration of Baroda*, 1881 (Mythic Society, 350.00054RAB)).

A NOTE ON PREVIOUS EDITIONS

1. *Report on Administration of Baroda*, 1881 (Mythic Society, 350.00054RAB).
2. Philip S. Melvill to Charles Grant, September 27, 1881, Foreign Department, Political B, File No. 59–61, January, 1882 (National Archives of India).
3. [Anonymous], *Minor Hints*, Bombay: Times of India Press, [undated]. (Center for Research Libraries, 82/61053).
4. *Minor Hints: Lectures Delivered to H.H. The Maharaja Gaekwar, Sayaji Rao III by Raja Sir T. Madhava Rao, K.C.S.I*, Bombay: British India Press, [undated] (University of California, Southern Regional Library Facility, JC248.M34).
5. *Lectures Delivered to H. H. The Maharaja Gaekwar, Sayaji Rao III G.C.S.I by Raja Sir T. Madhava Rao, K.C.S.I: Minor Hints*, Bombay: British India Press, [undated] (Center for Research Libraries, 83/61194).
6. Chandrojirao S. Angre, *Letters to My Son*, trans. V. K. Datar, Gwalior: C.S. Angre, 1926. Also see Sayaji Rao Gaekwad to Chandrojirao S. Angre, December 4, 1926 in *Selected Letters of His Highness the Maharaja Sayaji Rao Gaekwar, Vol. 4*, Baroda: Baroda Press, 1936, pp. 1292–93.
7. Pestanji Jahangir, *Notes of Lectures Delivered to His Highness Maharaja Sayajirao Gaekwar of Baroda on the Subject of the Settlement and Military Department of the Baroda State*, Ahmedabad: United Printing, 1884; [Kazi Shahabuddin, Anna Bhivrao Tahmane, Cursetji Rustomji Thanawalla, and Janardhan Gadgil], *Lectures Delivered to H.H. The Maharaja Gaekwar, Sayaji Rao III*, Bombay: Karnatak Press, [undated].
8. The catalogue to Sampat Rao Gaekwad's personal library contains an entry entitled "Notes on Revenue Accounts, and Law and Justice, published by the order of H. H. the Maharajah Gaekwad" that is dated 1888. This appears an early version of the lecture notes that Shahabuddin, Tahmane, Thanawalla and Gadgil subsequently printed at the Karnatak Press (see *The Classified Catalogue of English Books in the Shri Sayaji Library of Shrimant Sampatrao K. Gaikwad*, Bombay: Gujarati Press, 1891, p. 63).

9. Jehangir's *Notes of Lectures* appears in *The Classified Catalogue of English Books in the Shri Sayaji Library of Shrimant Sampatrao K. Gaikwad*, p. 60, and in *The Catalogue of the Library of the India Office*, Vol. 1 (Supplement), London: Eyre and Spottiswoode, 1895, p. 63. None of the texts discussed here appear in *An Index Catalogue of the Books in the Laxmi-Vilasa Palace Library of H.H. Maharaja Sayajirao Gaikwad of Baroda*, Bombay: The Times Press, 1910.
10. Philip W. Sergeant, *The Ruler of Baroda*, London: John Murray, 1928, pp. 46–48; Edith L. Tottenham, *Highnesses of Hindostan*, London: Grayson & Grayson, 1934, pp. 233–34.
11. See the citation in Urmila Rau Lal, *Diwan Sir Thanjavur Madhava Row: Statesman, Administrator Extraordinaire*, Mumbai: Bharatiya Vidya Bhavan, 2015, p. 160.
12. Ramchandra Shukla, *Rajya Prabandh Shiksha*, Allahabad: The Indian Press, 1928, p. 6.
13. Sir T. Madava Row, *Minor Hints: Lectures Delivered to the Maharaja Gaekwar Sayaji Rao III*, Ahmedabad: Sahitya Mudranalaya, 1985.